evolutionary interpretations
of WORLD POLITICS

Evolutionary Interpretations

of WORLD POLITICS

Edited by William R. Thompson

ROUTLEDGE

New York and London

Published in 2001 by
Routledge
29 West 35th Street
New York, NY 10001

Published in Great Britain in 2001 by
Routledge
11 New Fetter Lane
London EC4P 4EE

Routledge is an imprint of the Taylor & Francis Group

Printed in the United States of America on acid-free paper
Design and typography: Jack Donner

10   9   8   7   6   5   4   3   2   1

Library of Congress Cataloging-in-Publication Data

Evolutionary interpretations of world politics / William R. Thompson, editor.
    p.   cm.
Rev. versions of papers originally presented at conference held Dec. 1998, Indiana University,
    Bloomington, Ind.
Includes bibliographical references and index.
ISBN 0–415–93058–8 — ISBN 0–415–93059–6 (pbk.)
    1. World politics—Congresses. 2. International relations—Philosophy—Congresses.
    3. International cooperation—Congresses. 4. Power (Social sciences)—Congresses.
    5. Political psychology—Congresses. I. Thompson, William R.

D32 .E98 2001
327.1—dc21   00–066485

Contents

Acknowledgments

Earlier versions of the papers presented in this volume were first presented at a December 1998 conference on evolutionary approaches to international relations theory held at Indiana University in Bloomington under the auspices of the IU Center for the Study of International Relations. We are grateful to the Center for its 1998 support. But it should also be noted that this conference followed two earlier ones held in Seattle in the mid-1990s under the leadership of George Modelski. The attempt to construct evolutionary IR paradigms thus has a lineage within which this volume is only the most recent manifestation. The lineage should also underscore the work-in-progress nature of this undertaking. As in other evolutionary processes, there is a great deal of experimental trial and error in constructing new IR frameworks and theories. Hopefully, we will get it right some day and when we do, that product, too, will also need to continue to evolve. Along the way, it should be recognized that a number of other people participated in the 1998 conference but for various reasons were unable to participate in this volume: Emmanuel Adler, Fulvio Attina, Lars-Erik Cederman, Tanisha Fazal, Robert Jervis, Miles Kahler, Scott Sagan, and John Vasquez. We have all benefited from their contributions to the 1998 conference. We are equally grateful to Eric Nelson and Routledge for making possible the wider circulation of our arguments, for it will not be possible to judge whether this particular effort is successful until or unless other IR scholars choose to join our search for evolutionary interpretations of world politics. Hopefully, the publication of this edited volume will encourage precisely that outcome.

Evolving Toward an Evolutionary Perspective

William R. Thompson

Students of international relations (IR) are familiar with realist, liberal, marxist, and, more recently, constructivist paradigms. Each has a set of assumptions that reflects a singular perspective on how international relations work. A perspective that is less familiar—in large part, because it is only now emerging—is the evolutionary paradigm. There is no one evolutionary paradigm, just as other IR paradigms also possess multiple variations. But the core assumptions go well beyond the most minimal meaning, and perhaps most common employment, of evolution, that is an emphasis on change. The most critical assumptions involve variation and selection. The principal unit of analysis, whether it be states, regime types, economic innovations, ideologies, strategies, or policies, exists in different formats. For instance, at a given point in time, there may be variation in the types of states (city-states, empires, nation-states) or the types of ideologies (fascism, communism, liberal democracy, socialism) that exist. At a subsequent point in time, some of the state types and ideologies will have disappeared. Nation-states, by and large, have been selected over city-states. Liberal democracy has been selected over fascism and communism. The question is then why one approach is selected and others abandoned or ignored. The general answer is found in the interaction between changing environments and actors. As environments and actors change, so too do the probabilities that some approaches will survive and flourish while others wither and may even disappear.

An emphasis on variation and selection goes beyond the minimalist emphasis on mere change. Most evolutionary paradigms in IR, however, stop short of emulating a maximal approach, which could be described as emulating biology's emphasis on genetic combinations, success in sexual reproduction, and blind and slow reactions to external change. Ironically, evolutionary biology initially borrowed some of its conceptualization from the social sciences. But it is not necessary to treat human actors as if they were plants or simple organisms incapable of modifying their environments. Human actors do react to external and internal changes in their environments. They are also capable of anticipating and bringing about environmental change. While there is no need to exalt humans above other species, their behavior can certainly be more complex. Paradigmatic treatments need to reflect this additional degree of complexity.

But is there a need for still another set of paradigms in the study of international relations? Different people will respond differently to this question. Evolutionary interpretations offer a number of advantages over alternative frameworks. Most obviously, evolutionary arguments cannot evade the need to examine historical change. It may well be that analysts drawn to questions involving long-term, historical change are most likely to be drawn to this type of analysis. But, evolutionary analyses offer considerable flexibility in foci on units of analysis and problematiques. One can focus on states, groups, firms, ideas, or individuals, or all of the above—as long as one anticipates evolutionary processes at multiple levels. One can study processes related to war, inequality, technological change, and identity formation and, conceivably, all at the same time. The point is that the evolutionary paradigm does not privilege a type of actor or a type of problem as the core foci. The other IR paradigms do. Moreover, evolutionary approaches allow the analyst to mix attractive elements from various paradigmatic approaches without betraying the coherence of the analysis. Thus, an evolutionary approach to world politics and political economy is highly flexible.

Other advantages of an evolutionary approach include the analysis of increasing complexity, interdependencies, and coevolving subsystems. World politics and international political economy are not just about diplomatic exchanges and war. Nor is it solely about the exchange of trade and interstate financial flows. It does not focus exclusively on technological change in industries or military practices. Rather, students of world politics and international political economy attempt to deal with all of these topics (and others) simultaneously. If one allows for variable influence patterns over time, changes in one subsystem influence changes in others. Processes and structures are not givens in these interactions, they emerge and, in some cases, eventually disappear. Evolutionary interpretations facilitate the analysis of the life cycles of various topics ranging from norms to hegemonic dominance.

Another advantage of an evolutionary approach is its modesty in forecasting the future. Some level of prediction is feasible for the relatively near-term. Long-range forecasts are made more dubious by contingencies, chance, and increasing complexity. The emphasis is placed on explanation and not on a linear and often mechanistic extrapolation of past values into the future.

Nevertheless, the ultimate advantage of an evolutionary interpretation is whether it leads to better theories than we currently possess. That is a process still very much in its infancy. We are still struggling with alternative visions of how an evolutionary paradigm might or should appear, and in so doing, we have directed little energy to developing competitive theories based on evolutionary assumptions. This edited volume does not resolve this problem but it does break new ground in bringing together a number of focused debates about different dimensions of evolutionary theorizing in international relations. Specific theories are also advanced. Beginning with the most general questions, successive chapters move toward increasingly specific applications to conflict/cooperation and the international political economy.

Before plunging into the details of evolutionary arguments, however, it makes sense first to spend a bit more time introducing the vocabulary of the evolutionary world politics paradigm. Paradigms are a bit like soups: The key terminology performs the role of the broth. Within the broth swim chunks of meat or vegetables, that is, the theories associated with the paradigm. At this point in time, though, we have more broth than paradigmatic meat and vegetables. Nevertheless, wouldn't it help to know something about the soup's ingredients before tasting it?

SOME TERMINOLOGY FOR
AN EVOLUTIONARY WORLD POLITICS PARADIGM

When major changes take place in world politics, they are apt to be interpreted differently by various observers. One reason for this propensity toward conflicting interpretations is that interpretation proceeds within the parameters of more or less explicit perspectives or paradigms. Paradigms are basic frameworks for analysis. They alert us to what we should look for and give us some clues about how processes are related. For instance, the demise of the Soviet Union is unlikely to be viewed in the same way by realists, liberals, or marxists. A realist might regard it as a temporary respite from U.S.-Soviet tensions, with a revived Russia or China likely to resume where the Soviet Union left off. A liberal might see the collapse of the Soviet bloc as dramatic evidence of the triumph of liberal ideas. A marxist might interpret the demise of the Soviet Union as a major impediment in moving toward a world governed by socialist instead of capitalist principles.

The problem is that they might all be at least partially right. Each set of paradigmatic blinders has its liabilities, just as each possesses inherent advantages and insights. Realists handle conflict with ease but are less comfortable with cooperation. Their view of world politics is rather static because the important features do not change. States remain the critical actors; conflict, competition, and rivalry are and will always be the predominant modes of interstate interaction. Liberals are the opposite. They are comfortable with cooperation and less so with conflict. Their bias is toward progressive change leading to a fundamentally altered world politics in which states and conflict become less important. One difficulty is determining how to view reality in the interim as one moves away from the old system toward the new one. Marxists have been good at stressing the existence of inequalities but think that the direction of progressive evolution is clear, inevitable, and much different from the liberal version. Consequently, they are uncomfortable with the possibility that the progression may be moving along a different trajectory.

These very brief observations imply that there may well be room for still another paradigm—preferably one that does not force analysts to choose among unit foci, assumptions about trends in conflict and cooperation, or the progressiveness of movements toward a better future. An evolutionary paradigm that focuses on the ubiquity of change, at all conceivable levels of analysis and does not prejudge the normative desirability of the changes should hold obvious attractions. Moreover, the evolutionary paradigm enables analysts to take what they want from one or more of the other perspectives without also being forced to assume their individual liabilities.

What are the important components of an evolutionary paradigm for world politics? First, there is a very strong emphasis on *change*. Change is not viewed as something extraordinary. Rather, it is the norm. This perspective reverses prevailing tendencies to theorize about equilibrium states. From an evolutionary perspective, equilibrium is never quite attained. We may be moving away from or toward equilibrium, but such a state is never attained. Things are always in motion and rarely at rest. The expression "after the dust settles" is appropriate. A commotion raises dust and we are cautioned to wait for the dust to settle before evaluating what has taken place. From an evolutionary perspective, the dust never settles. Dust in motion is the norm.

Flux as a norm does not imply that change is a constant. Constants make explanation extremely awkward, if not impossible. But changes can be minor or major in significance. Change can come about gradually or abruptly. Its scope, or the degree to which it is diffused throughout the system, can be extensive or negligible. The basic point is that different types of changes, or, alternatively, changes in different circumstances, are likely to lead to different outcomes. To the extent that *evolution* is about patterned change, the questions raised concern how changes come about and what difference, if any, they make.

For many people, evolution and change are completely interchangeable terms. If that is all that is involved here, we would be talking about a vocabulary for analyzing world politics, as opposed to a new paradigm for its analysis. The crux of an evolutionary paradigm's interpretation of how evolution occurs looks something like the following diagram:

(fitness)   (diffusion, imitation, and reinforcement)

Environmental Change —> innovation —> variation —> selection ——————> evolution

The classical source of change in evolutionary models is *environmental*. In classical Darwinian models, environmental impacts alter subjects in an involuntary fashion. The subjects have no say in the process. Species either adapt and reproduce successfully or they die. If their food source is high to reach, some giraffes with longer necks may be more successful at survival than giraffes with shorter necks. Over time, the longer-necked giraffes survive and the shorter-necked giraffes become less common. Whether this story explains how giraffes developed long necks is an awkward example to apply to social science situations involving human decision-makers and populations. People can do things giraffes cannot do. They can make artificial long necks to reach otherwise inaccessible places. They can develop new food sources that grow in accessible areas to replace the vegetation that has been overconsumed. Perhaps like the giraffes, humans can also be held responsible for changes in their environment, namely, overconsumption of accessible food sources. Whatever the case, the bottom line is that humans can remake their environment as opposed to being mere passive reactors to the changes that affect it. However, this does not make human populations immune to environmental change. It just means that the weight given to it as a causal agent or source of causality should be less in social science situations than in biology or geology. The impact of environmental change is much more likely to be mediated by human manipulation (in either direction).

Environmental change can generate variation without human intervention. For instance, climate change appears to have altered the likelihood of early urbanization in the Middle East. Warmer climates melted glaciers leading to increased water levels in rivers and oceans. The location of coastlines, swamps, and deserts all changed as a consequence, which, then created new challenges and opportunities for people in Mesopotamia and Egypt six thousand years ago. Therefore, in the evolutionary figure presented earlier, we might have an arrow connecting environmental change directly to variation. Nevertheless, one working hypothesis is that the environmental changes with which we are most likely to be interested are mediated by human innovations. These mediations have some potential for overcoming the substantial *inertia* that comes to be associated with the customary way people do things.

Innovations are like mutations in biology except that they do not necessarily occur randomly or blindly. They represent new ways of doing things. They may be adaptations encouraged by environmental change. They may have been introduced in advance of environmental change and their potential only belatedly realized. Or, they may have been introduced in order to bring about environmental change. In biology, animal are conventionally viewed as being acted upon by the environment; human animals, however, are capable of anticipating and creating environmental changes—as opposed to simply adapting to radical changes for survival purposes should such changes occur. An evolutionary paradigm cannot duck the agent-structure question. Structure and structural change influence the agents but the agents are capable of making structural changes.

Once innovations are introduced to a field of routine ways of doing things and characterized by substantial propensities toward inertia, *variation* exists. Variation simply means that the inventory of available strategies encompasses multiple ways of performance. Given variation, the critical questions then become, which strategies emerge as the predominant method of function? Which strategies are chosen and become successful in that they have been selected over the alternatives available? *Selection* mechanisms or processes for determining successful strategies are thus rather central to this perspective.

The concept of *fitness* is not identical to the message implicit in the "survival of the fittest" phrase. Fitness is about suitability in specific contexts. Actors are fit to the extent that they possess attributes that facilitate the successful adoption of innovations. Strategies are fit to the extent that they correspond to the problems that they are supposed to address, and they generate successful outcomes when applied.

But how do actors choose strategies? From an evolutionary perspective, the rational assessment of costs and benefits associated with alternative approaches is one possibility but not the most likely choice. *Trial and error* searches more likely involve actors groping experimentally (and with changing versus fixed *preferences*) for paths to survival and success, perhaps without full awareness of what they are doing when they are doing it. The consequences of their experimental searches are unlikely to have been fully anticipated and unintended consequences, in general, are often as important as the ones that were intended. Accordingly, short-term futures may be predictable but the future becomes increasingly less certain because of the complexities associated with getting there.

The *level of analysis* that needs to be privileged according to an evolutionary paradigm is variable. Other paradigms in international relations are fixed on individuals, ideas, states, international institutions, or systems. Yet all are capable of evolving and, therefore, all are suitable foci for analytical emphasis. To complicate matters further, it is also possible to view evolution as ongoing in nested circumstances. *Nesting* refers to the probability of simultaneous (but not necessarily identical) evolution ongoing at multiple levels of analysis. The question is whether it is feasible analytically to ignore other evolutionary developments while choosing to focus only on one level at a time. Alternatively, the interactive *coevolution* of different subsystems of action affords a different take on how things work. How do long-term changes in, for example, international politics influence long-term changes in international economics and vice versa?

Undoubtedly a premium is placed on *history* and historical processes because the most interesting evolution at whatever level tends to be characterized by *long-term* processes. If *path dependency* makes a difference to understanding how something has evolved into its present form, it is necessary to trace its transformation over time and often back to its beginning points. Which trajectories or paths evolution takes (that is, which innovations are selected) is presumably sensitive to initial conditions and alternatives. *Learning* is another important historical process. Learning occurs to the extent that actors adjust their strategies based on perceptions about the success or failure of earlier prevailing strategies.

Note that the above terms delineated in italicized type do not tell us in what circumstances inertia will be overcome, how actors learn, when nesting or coevolution cannot be ignored, or how the specifics of fitness or selection operate. These signify tasks for theory construction. Paradigms offer only broad frameworks that alert us to look for some dimensions of reality and to ignore others. Paradigms provide us with general assumptions about what is most important. The evolutionary paradigm suggests that the basic process at work is the occasional tendency for inertia to be overcome by innovation within a context of internal and external environmental change. But only some innovations are selected. This leads to the fundamental question of why some innovations are selected and others are rejected, ignored, or defeated. Theories developed within this general paradigm are then expected to carry the explicit burden of explaining the more specific processes of innovation, selection, and diffusion.

CENTRAL QUESTIONS

One would not expect a consensus on how to most definitively conceptualize about political evolution. *Evolutionary Interpretations of World Politics*, the first explicit and focused discussion of evolutionary approaches to IR, is no exception to this generalization. The authors of the various chapters do not agree on how best to proceed, either in terms of constructing a new paradigm or how to situate comprehensively their own interests within such a paradigm. In the lead chapter, George Modelski rejects approaches that he describes as "extra light" (historical-descriptive analyses employing the term evolution in the title alone), "light" (analyses employing some evolutionary concepts outside of an explicit evolutionary theoretical framework), or "heavy" (analyses that conceptualize everything as being susceptible to the same explanatory framework). The first two approaches may yield substantive information but stop short of advancing an explicit understanding of evolutionary processes. The "heavy" approach has yet to emerge. Instead, Modelski promotes a "strong" variant (an explanatory theory of a particular problem utilizing evolutionary concepts and tracing processes of change). He provides as example his own previous work on evolutionary world politics (EWP) that focuses on competing strategies for global problem management. The evolution of these particular processes are characterized by a sequence of phases and an alteration in the leadership structure that is the principal carrier of innovation.

Vincent Falger views Modelski's approach as a "top-down" explanation. He focuses on institutions and strategies at the global level. Falger prefers a "bottom-up" emphasis on biological evolution. Put another way, the EWP perspective is all macro, with no micro. The sort of micro Falger has in mind is illustrated in discussions of in-group/out-group formation, gender biases, and generational change. The bottom line remains that macro processes must be explained ultimately by micro factors even though micro factors cannot account for all the variation in macro phenomena. To omit evolutionary psychology from the equation is to stop short of a comprehensive explanation. Yet evolutionary psychology needs EWP.

Somehow, we need to find a way to merge bottom-up and top-down perspectives on evolutionary change.

While Modelski and Falger are committed to different versions of evolutionary approaches, David Rapkin raises fundamental problems that characterize both top-down and bottom-up interpretations. Four questions are emphasized. What are the units that evolve? Do actors respond to the environment or can they also sometimes influence the environment? How does the environment serve as a selection mechanism? Must evolutionary change be directed? Rapkin does not have comprehensive answers for his questions, but he does offer some suggestions on how to answer the questions he poses. His solution divides paradigmatic questions into core and non-core components. Within the core, it should be assumed that different elements or populations are capable of evolving and serving as units of analysis. Environmental selection operates on variations in knowledge and is both Darwinian (environments influence actors) and Lamarckian (actors influence their own environment). All other inquiries should be regarded as auxiliary to an evolutionary paradigm's core.

BRIDGES TO OTHER PERSPECTIVES

The first three papers on paradigms address the most general questions. A second set of three chapters continue a similar line of investigation but with a somewhat less exclusively evolutionary point of view. While the first set of chapters focuses on evolutionary questions per se, the second set builds explicit bridges to alternative frameworks. One chapter looks at existing IR theory and asks about current evolutionary realist and liberal arguments. A second examines the implications of the question of state convergence. If all actors must adopt to environmental changes or perish, should we expect all states to eventually assume the same form? The answer is no. Darwinian arguments must be qualified by strong doses of organizational and learning theory. Finally, a third chapter rejects existing IR theory as satisfactory in dealing with changes in ideas and norms and demands a new and more explicitly evolutionary approach.

Jennifer Sterling-Folker suggests that IR theory already has considerable experience with evolutionary theorizing. In contrast to the assumption that rational choice predominates IR theoretical assumptions, Sterling-Folker contends that both realist and liberals accept the idea of evolutionary adaptation as a central premise but disagree over how adaptation comes about. Realists stress competitive survival in an anarchic environment that cannot be altered substantially. Liberals stress the role of technological change and consequent institutional adaptations that do alter anarchic contexts. If realists emphasize structural continuity and the persistence of successful coping strategies, then liberals emphasize structural discontinuities and the need for innovative strategies. Seen from this light, some of the debates within IR theory might be ameliorated if the evolutionary element is made more explicit, rather than left largely implicit as it is now. Reality probably lies somewhere in between what realists and liberals choose to emphasize. An explicitly evolutionary perspective might offer a more balanced point of view.

Hendrik Spruyt counsels caution in adopting an evolutionary perspective. He is particularly concerned that social scientists will adopt biology's emphasis on unintentional natural selection and, as well, the mistaken notion that there is only one fit solution to be selected. He employs as example the likelihood that all states will converge into a single form. But this is only likely to be the case if we omit the possibilities for actor intent, learning, and anticipation of environmental change. If actors are permitted to choose different niches (or institutional strategies), convergence in state form is not particularly likely. Spruyt's argument is not so much antagonistic to evolutionary theorizing as it is suggestive of the need to be careful of how we construct evolutionary paradigms for IR problems. If we appropriate the wrong insights from other disciplines already committed to evolutionary perspectives, we may end up with analytical structures that do more harm than good.

Stewart Patrick disagrees with the idea that realist and neoliberal perspectives are up to the task of dealing with the role of identities, norms, and values in international relations. For realists, rules and institutions constitute only a thin veneer for the all-important distribution of power. The possibilities of innovation and novelty are ignored. Norms are only complied with if it happens to be expedient. Yet while neoliberals concede a greater independent role for ideas and institutions, they fail to allow ideas and institutions to change actor identities and goals. Even constructivists are taken to task for overemphasizing the prevailing distribution of ideas and norms without accounting for how that distribution changes over time. The solution for Patrick involves an analysis of normative evolution through a cycle of conception to their eventual disappearance. Change encourages the search for new ideas. With the help of entrepreneurs, some take hold, out compete their rivals, and become embedded and legitimized via socialization and institutionalization. Eventually, the old winners are challenged by change and new ideas. They may or may not give way. Existing IR theory is not designed to handle this conceptualization of normative life cycles. Therefore, a new and explicit emphasis on normative evolution is not only desirable, it is the only way—or so it is contended—to deal with the phenomena in question.

APPLICATIONS TO CONFLICT AND COOPERATION

The next set of three papers focuses on one type of conflict and cooperation— intergroup rivalry relationships. Why do rivalries form? Why do they terminate? These processes are argued to be central to understanding conflict and cooperation in IR and yet we have few answers to how the processes work. All three authors argue that these problems can be best addressed in evolutionary modes even though they may not agree exactly on how best to construct an evolutionary interpretation. Still, the underlying common denominator is how actors choose strategies to cope with changes in their environment and/or how they proceed to change their security environments in which they are attempting to survive and remain competitive.

Paul Hensel takes issue with one argument that claims that interstate rivalries are predetermined by structural conditions. Rather, he believes they evolve as a consequence of domestic parties and groups choosing to emphasize antagonistic relations with an external adversary. Territory, already in dispute, that experiences an abrupt upward adjustment in its perceived value is especially helpful in encouraging these changes in emphasis. A history of previous conflict is also facilitative. Hence, interstate rivalries emerge not strictly as international phenomena but rather as a function of coevolutionary change in domestic politics as well as changes in the interactions of two international antagonists. This point of view is illustrated by an examination of the emergence of the Bolivian-Paraguayan rivalry.

The chapters written by William Thompson and Karen Rasler are not entirely independent; that is, they both focus on the same, new theory of rivalry deescalation and termination. Thompson applies the theory to an interstate rivalry (the Sino-Soviet dispute) while Rasler applies the theory to what so far has been an intrastate rivalry (the Israeli-Palestinian conflict). The theory, laid out in more detail in the Thompson chapter than in the Rasler contribution, focuses on the interaction of shocks, expectational change, policy entrepreneurship, reciprocity, and reinforcement. Both papers use the opportunity to explore the fit of the theory to their cases. However, the linkage to evolutionary arguments is made by focusing on strategic adaption to changing environments. The question is not whether some actors adapt their strategies but how they do so. By examining changes in strategies, an explicit link is made between Thompson and Rasler's approach and Modelski's paradigmatic arguments made in chapter 2. Yet whereas Modelski's emphasizes the most restrictive level of world politics—how world powers rise, fall, and create order for short periods of time—both Thompson and Rasler extend the scope of the evolutionary interpretation to more "mundane" actors in international relations. They both also find that their new deescalation theory not only has considerable powers of synthesizing a variety of older interpretations of conflict resolution, the theory also seems to have considerable explanatory utility in the cases they examine.

APPLICATIONS TO INTERNATIONAL POLITICAL ECONOMY

The last set of papers stresses topics pertaining to various aspects of international political economy (IPE). In IPE, evolutionary arguments tend to emphasize the role of innovations in altering the range of variation and how actors choose to respond to the variation (and the changes therein) from which they must select their coping strategies. One chapter focuses on the reciprocal relationship between major changes in economic frameworks and social movement behavior. The economic changes make some types of social movement behavior more probable and, in turn, the social conflict facilitates the shifts in economic structure. The second chapter also looks at the succession of industrial paradigms but asks whether a new one centered on the soft- and hardware of computer architecture is emerging. If a new paradigm is indeed emerging, which firms and states are most likely to adapt to it, and why? The third chapter in this trio shifts the focus away from radical technological change and its implications in order to stress the acceleration of capital movements and its implications for global political economy. While the emphasis is placed on financial flows as opposed to industrial production, the argument is still about how political-economic actors create and respond to changes in economic practices and political regulation strategies.

Craig Murphy argues that industrial change and social conflict coevolve. Major technological innovations usher in new economic eras centered on the new ways of doing things. Each era goes through a cycle of building, thriving, and clashing. In the building phase, the emergence of new leading industries is facilitated by significant investment that, in turn, is encouraged by relative social calm. The thriving phase is one of peak prosperity as the new industries maximize their profit potential. Things begin to unravel in the clashing phase. Prosperity is reduced as the marginal returns of one-time new industries declines. Firms seek ways to cut costs. At the same time, social movements organized against prevailing inequalities are likely to become more active. What happens next depends in part on new economic innovations and the outcomes of political conflict between social movements and defenders of the status quo. These outcomes depend in part on the success of sociopolitical innovations in resolving social conflict. To the extent that the conflict is resolved, a conducive environment for investing in a new wave of economic innovation will have been created.

Sangbae Kim and Jeffrey Hart argue that we have moved through several industrial paradigms in the past two centuries, with Fordism and Toyotism dominating in the twentieth century. The next paradigm is called "wintelism," and reflects the success of Microsoft (Windows) and Intel in defining how most personal computers operate. If industrial paradigms represent a solution to technical problems that becomes increasingly diffused throughout the economy in time, what drives the process of firm adaptation to the new practices? Which countries are best suited for adapting new practices? The latter question is addressed primarily in terms of types of national governance structures while insulation from competition is stressed in regard to the firm-level adaption question. The general point, though, remains that each successive industrial paradigm favors certain patterns of government-corporate interaction. The nature of wintelism, it is argued, favors decentralized governance structures that engage in regulatory practices in coordination with or through horizontal corporate linkages. While new paradigms pressure firms and nations to adjust, one may still anticipate considerable variation in how actors choose to adjust or, for that matter, whether actors are able to adjust successfully.

Finally, Brian Pollins moves the discussion beyond the national level by looking at evolution in the global political economy. Pollins addresses two questions. The first is descriptive but not as straightforward as it seems. Is the expansion of global finance after 1973 comparable to the explosion in capital movements in the 1870 to 1914 era? His answer, based on empirical documentation, is that the rate of growth in the current era is as high, if not higher, than the earlier period of rapid expansion. The second question concerns whether political liberalization or one of its effects was a cause of the expansion? Here Pollins finds that the processes of the post-1973 era do not merely duplicate those of the earlier expansive era. Both periods were characterized by the absence or reduction of barriers to capital movement (that is, liberalization). Yet the first period was subject to the Gold Standard and its control of risks pertaining to exchange-rate fluctuations. The current expansion began only after the demise of Bretton Woods exchange-rate controls. Pollins argues that the relation to these seemingly contradictory factors is similar to the way private finance developed new methods of dealing with exchange-rate fluctuations after 1973. Public risk management was privatized in order to take advantage of the freer environment for capital movement. The bottom line to this story seems to be that IPE explanations cannot focus exclusively on the interaction of state and international regulatory regimes. The national and international regimes are important but so too is private finance. Innovation is not a monopoly of any one of the three and they coevolve to the extent that they adapt to changes in the other spheres of action.

BACK TO THE LARGER TASK AHEAD

Do these chapters resolve the problems associated with constructing a new paradigm? Of course not—they only continue the task begun by the rather few existing publications explicitly interested in this subject.[1] Indeed, we have a long way to go in creating a paradigm that is either competitive with, or complementary to, the older paradigms of IR. Why that is the case is an interesting question in its own right. After all, there are evolutionary subfields in such disciplines as archaeology, anthropology, psychology, economics, sociology, and ecology. Political science and IR have remained unusually resistant to similar developments. The reason for this, advanced by Kahler (1999), is that a strong interest in history is a prerequisite to being prepared to invest some time and energy grappling with evolutionary questions. No doubt, there is considerable validity in this contention, and it is equally true that an interest in history has not always figured prominently in contemporary analyses of politics and political economy. The only remedy is to construct powerful theories of politics and political economy in which history plays an important role.

One reason why historical questions or approaches are not more highly valued is, of course, the prevailing fixation on relatively short-term questions; the second reason is the increasing commitment to assumptions about rational choice in politics and political economy. This is not the place to take on this issue directly—even though many, if not all, of the chapters in this volume do address the question at least indirectly. Suffice it to say for the present that perhaps the greatest obstacle to the full-fledged development of an evolutionary paradigm for world politics and political economy is the paucity of explicit works that suggest how to accomplish an understanding of pertinent evolutionary processes. Overcoming this obstacle will take time. Hopefully, the chapters assembled in this volume will encourage others to make their trial-and-error contributions. For, in the final analysis, an evolutionary paradigm is unlikely to emerge abruptly and in full shape. Rather, it will evolve slowly in fits and starts and only gradually fill out into a full shape as we continue to struggle with the analytical problems created by real-world changes. Once the paradigm does begin to resemble something more mature, one only hopes that it will continue to evolve.

NOTE

1. The most explicit, published discussions of an evolutionary paradigm for world politics and political economy are found in Modelski and Poznanski (1996), Modelski (1996), and Kahler (1999). Readers interested in additional work would do well to begin with the special issue of *International Studies Quarterly* edited by Modelski and Poznanski that includes articles by Farkas (1996), Florini (1996), Hodgson (1996b), and Gilpin (1996). George Modelski maintains an extended bibliography on evolutionary theoretical material on his web page (for an address, see Modelski, this volume). Additional studies in international relations from an evolutionary perspective include Spruyt (1994) and Cederman (2001). Agent-based modeling is another research niche with strong evolutionary payoff for international relations (see Axelrod 1984, 1997; Ridley 1996; Cederman 1997). Punctuated equilibrium models have attracted IR attention (see Somit and Peterson 1989 and Diehl and Goertz 2000). Useful introductions to evolutionary epistemology include Brewer and Collins (1981), Plotkin (1982), and Bowler (1989). Also very suggestive is related work going on in other social sciences such as economics (Nelson and Winter 1982; Leydesdorff and Van Den Beeselaar 1994; Vroman 1995; Hodgson 1996a) and anthropology/archaeology (Durham 1991; Teltsler, 1995; O'Brien 1996; and Maschner 1996). Evolutionary game theory is another source of ideas (see especially Young 1998).

REFERENCES

Axelrod, Robert. 1984. *The evolution of cooperation.* New York: Basic Books.

———. 1997. *The complexity of cooperation: Agent-based models of competition and collaboration.* Princeton, N.J.: Princeton University Press.

Bowler, Peter J. 1989. *Evolution: The history of an idea.* Rev. ed. Berkeley: University of California Press.

Brewer, Marilynn B. and Barry E. Collins. 1981. *Scientific inquiry and the social sciences.* San Francisco: Jossey-Bass.

Cederman, Lars-Erik. 1997. *Emergent actors in world politics: How states and nations develop and dissolve.* Princeton, N.J.: Princeton University Press.

———. 2001. Back to Kant: Reinventing the Democratic Peace as a Macrohistorical Learning Process. *American Political Science Review.*

Diehl, Paul and Gary Goertz. 2000. *War and peace in international rivalry.* Ann Arbor: University of Michigan Press.

Durham, William H. 1991. *Coevolution: Genes, culture and human diversity.* Stanford, Calif.: Stanford University Press.

Farkas, Andrew. 1996. Evolutionary Models in Foreign Policy. *International Studies Quarterly* 40: 343–61.

Florini, Ann. 1996. The Evolution of International Norms. *International Studies Quarterly* 40: 363–89.

Gilpin, Robert. 1996. Economic Evolution of National Systems. *International Studies Quarterly* 40: 411–31.

Hodgson, Geoffrey M. 1996a. *Economics and evolution: Bringing life back into economics.* Ann Arbor: University of Michigan Press.

———. (1996b. An Evolutionary Theory of Long-Term Economic Growth. *International Studies Quarterly* 40: 391–410.

Kahler, Miles. 1999. Evolution, Choice and Change. In David A. Lake and Robert Powell, eds. *Strategic choice and international relations.* Princeton, N.J.: Princeton University Press.

Leydesdorff, Loet and Peter Van Den Besselaar, eds. 1994. *Evolutionary economics and chaos theory.* New York: St. Martin's Press.

Maschner, Herbert D. G. 1996. *Darwinian archaeologies.* New York: Plenum Press.

Modelski, George. 1996. Evolutionary Paradigm for Global Politics. *International Studies Quarterly* 40: 321–42.

———, and Kazimierz Poznanski. 1996. Evolutionary Paradigms in the Social Sciences. *International Studies Quarterly* 40: 315–19.

Nelson, Richard and S. G. Winter. 1982. *An evolutionary theory of economic change.* Cambridge, Mass.: Harvard University Press.

O'Brien, Michael J., ed. 1996. *Evolutionary archaeology: Theory and application.* Salt Lake City: University of Utah Press.

Plotkin, H. C., ed. 1982. *Learning, development and culture: Essays on evolutionary epistomology.* New York: John Wiley.

Ridley, Matt. 1996. *The origins of virtue: Human instincts and the evolution of cooperation.* New York: Penguin.

Somit, Albert and Steven A. Peterson, ed. 1989. *The Dynamics of evolution: The punctuated equilibrium debate in the natural and social sciences.* Ithaca, N.Y.: Cornell University Press.

Spruyt, Hendrik. 1994. *The sovereign state and its competitors.* Princeton, N.J.: Princeton University Press.

Teltser, Patrice A., ed. 1995. *Evolutionary archaeology: Methodological issues.* Tucson: University of Arizona Press.

Vromen, Jack J. 1995. *Economic evolution.* London and New York: Routledge.

Young, H. Peyton. 1998. *Individual strategy and social structure: An evolutionary theory of institutions.* Princeton, N.J.: Princeton University Press.

part I
Central Paradigmatic Questions About Interpretation

chapter 1

Evolutionary World Politics

Problems of Scope and Method

George Modelski

CHARACTERISTICS OF AN EVOLUTIONARY APPROACH TO WORLD POLITICS

Evolutionary approaches share the premise that world politics is subject to evolutionary processes, that all world politics is, in some respect, evolutionary. This is a powerful assertion because it importantly claims that this field of inquiry is subject to regularities that makes it amenable to modes of thought, theories, and procedures current in other branches of knowledge. Of course, however, it is also basically a conjecture inviting refutation, one whose full verification remains to be pursued and might never be fully attained to everyone's complete satisfaction.

The assertion is also powerful because it runs counter to the traditional understanding of international relations (IR) as the study of the operation of the nation-state system—the Westphalian system said to have been founded in 1648 and one that in its essential characteristics still claims to exist today, and will in the discernible future. The Westphalian system is commonly described as primitive, anarchic, and based on self-help. An evolutionary approach highlights not the static operations of such a system but rather the fact that the structure of world political arrangements is subject to pivotal processes of change whose nature needs to be better understood. The question being, not why global politics might or might not be thought to be primitive today, but whether and why it is less primitive today than it was, for instance, one thousand years ago; indeed, why it was less primitive in the year 2000 than in 1900. In other words, an evolutionary approach problematizes the nation-state system; for this reason, the evolutionary approach is not an "international politics" but more accurately a "world-politics" approach.

In the end, though, the insights yielded by an evolutionary approach are what will make or break it. If it helps to illuminate the "big picture" of how the world works and changes, then it will endure and enter the domain of conventional wisdom. In any event, it cannot be expected to solve all the problems that might be asked of students of the IR field, rather, it can only offer careful answers to some key questions.

In that spirit, let us put forward four characteristics, or criteria, that seem to be necessary concomitants of an evolutionary approach in this "big picture" area.

First, an evolutionary, world-politics program is a human species approach; that is, it inquires how the human species as a whole organizes and reorganizes itself. In that sense it is a "big picture" approach, or, in our parlance, a *systemic* approach, whose specific subject of inquiry is the global political system. Global politics promotes the evolution of new forms of political organization: alliances and institutions; or, it provides us with a basis for understanding war and peace, forms of leadership, and organizations of several kinds. Nations or national societies do not evolve, but rather policies, strategies, and institutions that cope with global problems confronting the human species do.

Second, an essential dimension of an evolutionary approach is *time*. That is, an evolutionary mode of thinking is particularly adept at illuminating change, and in particular long-term change that is necessarily a process of time. In other words, an evolutionary mode is suitable for capturing phenomena—long-term processes linked to institutional changes, stages of historical development, and periods of history—that are customarily thought to lie within the province of historians. Evolutionary concepts help to organize historical data in a form suitable for social scientists, and they help produce theoretically sound explanations of structural change.

Third, evolutionary theories employ evolutionary concepts. There is, of course, no single theory that commands universal acceptance. But there is some considerable agreement that progress in evolutionary thinking has had much to do with identifying the *mechanisms* of change. Important insights have come less from recognizing evolution as basically a self-evident process, and more from the explanations of how such self-actualizing paradigm shifts in fact occurred. A preeminent example of this is the Darwinian concept of natural selection as a mechanism that accounts for the origin of species. In the social sciences, we deal mainly with social-selection mechanisms, such as markets or party and electoral systems, without being aware of their evolutionary characteristics. That is why selection mechanisms have a central place in every evolutionary theory, together with those of cooperation, mutation/innovation, and reinforcement—all components of social-learning processes.

Fourth, an evolutionary theory of world politics will clarify, and reconstruct, the relation of global political evolution to *other evolutionary processes*. In the first instance, structural changes in world politics might be explained, as the working of political mechanisms, as when a global war is considered the result of competing foreign policies striving for leadership. In the second instance, however, the political factors must be seen as related to evolutionary developments in the global economy, the rise of democracy, and the tide of world opinion. We are all familiar with the interrelationship of global economics and politics, at least as recently and thoroughly explored in a number of works of international political economy (IPE); we are beginning to substantiate our insights about the relationship of democracy to war, hunger, and free markets, but we have yet to explore more fully the role of world opinion and the processes that mold world culture.

Conceived in this way, Evolutionary World Politics (EWP) is not a speculative enterprise, or a philosophical tendency; it is, rather, a social science—theoretical perspective, and a distinct research program. No one claims it to be a set of established truths, and the propositions derived from it need to be checked by empirical evidence, which is often a difficult task. Still, it remains more a set of important questions than a set of complete answers. EWP involves premises that may never be fully explored and it remains a work-in progress.

BIOLOGY AND WORLD POLITICS

In popular thought, an evolutionary approach is often seen as purely biological, that is, demonstrating the influence of biology, for example, on world politics. Indeed, human biological evolution is another evolutionary process whose influence we might wish to trace, if our question calls for it. When considering global political changes such as the rise of a new world power or the emergence of global institutions, in the spirit of Durkheim, the initial explanation will be, in terms of "social facts" (that is political) and other social evolutionary processes. There is no need, however, to argue that these social facts are totally isolated from biological processes that shape human evolution.

That is, there is no need, at this point, to enter the well-known nurture-nature controversy, so as to maintain, along lines laid out influentially by anthropologist Leslie A. White (ca. 1960) that human nature, biologically defined, is virtually constant, and can therefore be eliminated from explanations of human behavior in favor of culture. More acceptable is Theodore Dobzhansky's (1962: 18,73–74) position that human evolution is the "interaction of biology and culture." More generally, human evolution might be seen as the product of biological (genetic) endowment, cultural inheritance, and social institutions and organization.

To illustrate his argument about the importance of the genetic basis of human evolution, Dobzhansky (1962: 284–85) cites, among others, two studies by biologist F. S. Hulse, illustrating how the relative importance of "British stock" had changed in the past three to four centuries. In 1600, wrote Hulse, there were three million people of "British stock" in the world. By 1960, there were 150 million, a fifty-fold increase that occurred during a time when the world population increased only six-fold. This means that the relative importance of people of British background rose significantly in that time.

Hulse's data need to be rechecked,[1] but the general thrust of his argument is interesting and has face value. The question is, How might his conclusion be interpreted? Ignoring problems of definition and method, it could be argued that this more than proportionate increase of people of "British stock" in the world population is attributable to the special characteristics of the genetic endowment of British people. Assuming that advances in the mapping of the human genome continues, it might be possible to assert that "British" combinations of genes might be specifically identified, traced back to 1600, and/or shown to be absent in other populations. But even then the following question would arise: Why did the genes take off in 1600 and not five hundred, or one thousand years earlier (or later)?

Alternatively, it could be argued that the strong rise in British stock is due to the active participation of the British in global political and social evolution since 1600 (consult Figure 1-1 below). Britain's position of global leadership over two cycles, as well as her facilitation of America's rise to power, explains a great deal. In other words, it is the quality of British institutions that is crucial here, and makes the best case for the increase in the number of people of British descent in the world population (and where world politics shapes biology). This alternative argument supports our initial intuition about "social facts" but the other one, the genetic, is not inherently incompatible with it.

Two other channels of biological influence might be mentioned at this point. The first is human nature (Falger 1994), and the potential for changing it. Has human nature remained unchanged in the past five thousand years of civilization? And if so, what might have been the effect on the architecture of social institutions? Sociobiologists, and more recently evolutionary psychologists, have pointed to certain behavioral patterns (such as aggression, or coalition behavior) that human beings share with higher animals, and in particular the primates. They have also argued strongly that all human beings share these traits, thus underscoring a certain psychological unity for the human species. But must we assume that these traits have remained unchanged all this time? Or should we rather conceive of social institutions as basic tools for channeling and controlling behavioral tendencies that are too close to the substratum of our biological origin? And might not innovative global political institutions be one instance of the application of such tools?

The other channel from biological processes is via the demographic and systemic phenomenon of generational change. Human populations replace themselves every thirty years or so by a process of biological reproduction. That is, the crews that man social institutions change ever so slowly, but in a regular, predictable, and unavoidable process. There are reasons to think that this turnover of generations has much to do with the timing of social evolutionary processes, and the four-phase structure of the long cycle of global politics in particular (Modelski 1998). This particular link between biology and society remains to be fully investigated.

In sum, this research program, inspired as it is by evolutionary biology, offers no obstacles either in principle or in practice to inquiries suggested by either past or future work in the life sciences. The only relevant question is: How does such work shed new light on structural change in world politics?

BASICS OF EVOLUTIONARY WORLD POLITICS

Evolutionary World Politics (EWP) is the application of evolutionary theory to understanding the social organization of the human species in its political dimensions, and with an emphasis on structural change.[2] It is situated in the general field of social evolution (the emergence and transformation of social systems). Social evolution needs to be distinguished, in the first place, from cosmological, biological , and cultural evolution, the first being the concern of the physical sciences, the next, of the life sciences, and the last, of cultural studies. A principal criterion differentiating these four domains is the rate or speed of the relevant evolutionary process. The cosmological process operates on a scale of billions of years; the biological in terms of millions or hundred-million years, the social, in hundred-thousand years, and the cultural in millennia.

Social evolution lies in the domain of the social sciences. That is, social change, proceeding at a rate faster than biological evolution, might be understood as an evolutionary process. Among the social sciences engaged in inquiries into such processes is evolutionary economics, which includes such names as Thornstein Veblen, Joseph Schumpeter, Friedrich von Hayek, Richard Nelson, and Sidney Winter; in anthropology we have Gordon Childe; and more recently in evolutionary psychology, as well as evolutionary epistemology, we have Donald Campbell and Karl Popper. Each social scientific inquiry makes forays into areas other approaches might leave unexplored. For example, an evolutionary economist illuminates problems of competition, innovation, and technological change; an anthropologist traces stages of historical process; an evolutionary psychologist points to humanity's heritage of hunting and gathering, and the epistemologist portrays scientific progress as steered by repeated trials and error-elimination procedures. An exemplary and fully up-to-date exposition of an "evolutionary realist methodology" for the natural and social sciences is Jane Azedevo's *Mapping Reality* (1997).

In each of these cases the use of evolutionary theory is now largely analogical, and so it is in EWP. The analogy proceeds from the consideration that there is a basic similarity between the evolution of life on earth and the origin of the species, on the one hand, and the rise of social organizations, social institutions, and in our case, of political institutions, on the other. We observe that social interaction generates a variety of social organizations and institutions: marriage, slavery, states, markets, international law, and diplomacy. Institutions regulate behavior and organizations develop and pursue policies and strategies. World politics might thus be seen as a population of strategies, some of which persist, and others that fail. Politics has also evolved distinct selection mechanisms for the elimination of some policies and the selection and reinforcement of others.

If we take the electoral process as a basic paradigm of politics, we can then recognize the following analogical relationship:

Natural selection : evolution of life = election mechanism : evolution of politics

In other words, natural selection, a basic Darwinian mechanism accounting for the origin of species, that now serves as the theoretical basis of biology, stands to origin of life as, for example, electoral processes (a social selection mechanism) stand to the evolution of politics. Analogy calls for the establishment of a clear relationship of similarity and proportion, and needs to be distinguished from metaphor, which is a more literary device.

We might, at this point, draw a distinction however fluid, between human behavior, and social institutions and organization. Institutions and organizations are forms of social behavior that are routinized (or rule-bound), sanctioned, and involving multiple interactions over time. They need to be distinguished from behavior pure and simple, that of course might be biologically determined, as there might be genes for a disease, for blindness, or obesity. Social institutions and organization (marriage rules, medicine) will then be seen, among others, as ways of dealing with such problems.

The analogy between natural selection (that is, selection by forces of nature, such as climate, natural environment, or predators) and mechanisms of social selection such as elections is a close one. More generally, in the social sciences, including political science, a number of other key concepts have analogs in evolutionary theory. The analog of mutation is, of course, innovation, and structural change is a story of coping with social and technical innovations. Cooperation is another evolutionary mechanism that is basic to explaining change. The rise of new traits—the story of Darwinian evolution—is directly equivalent to the rise of new institutions and organizations. More generally, social and political evolution might be seen as a form of learning that produces new forms of behavior *in time* that runs directly parallel to biological evolution giving rise to new structures of organism (*in space*). Social learning that produces new institutions is not just a metaphor; it is the evolutionary process operating on the social system (in a fashion first explored by social psychologists; see Modelski 1987, chapter 5). Learning is the form that adaptation—a central concept of evolutionary biology—assumes in the social world.

An analogy points to the fact of similarity, and is basically a form of inductive reasoning from one case to another. It highlights the existence of probable connections, and as such is a fruitful source of hypotheses. By itself an analogy is no proof, but if it does suggest verifiable hypotheses then its scientific value is unmistakable. But at the end of the day, any analogy rests upon generalizations that establish fundamental connections between the two sets of phenomena that are being compared. In the case of evolutionary theory, they rest upon some such proposition that all forms of change in the universe exhibit an evolutionary logic. In our case, this amounts to asserting that biological adaptation and social learning exhibit the same underlying principles of change: that evolution occurs whenever evolutionary potential is in place.

VARIETIES OF EVOLUTIONARY PERSPECTIVES
ON WORLD POLITICS

That idea that world politics might be approached through evolutionary theory, however powerful, is hardly a new one, and has been around about as long as has Darwinian evolutionary theory.[3] Furthermore, elements of evolutionary analysis might also be found in the main contemporary orientations to international relations (IR). In particular, the realists' central concept of "struggle for power" has long carried overtones of evolutionists' "struggle for survival," and the neo-Realists' stress on the competitive aspects of the international system has used allusions to selection to account for the success of some states and the failure of others. The liberals, on the other hand, have made the case for institutional change and emphasized its capacity for transforming the international system. Realist approaches might generally be described as materialist because they stress both military and economic power, but they lack a theory of institutional evolution; liberal-institutionalist approaches are broadly idealist in that they deal with cognitive and evaluative dimensions such as opinions, values, interests, and solidarities. Both are needed components of an evolutionary approach to world politics as outlined here, and both can be , and have been, accommodated within it.[4]

As an alternative view on evolutionary perspectives in IR let us propose, for the purpose of highlighting certain essential features, a classification of literature in that field. In a somewhat light-hearted manner, let us label such studies, solely in respect to their "evolutionary content," as one of the following four "flavors": extralight, light, strong, or heavy.

We might call *extra light* approaches those that carry the term "evolution" in their title but otherwise pay little or no heed to the concept, and treat their subjects in a descriptive-historical manner. Two examples of such a treatment might be Amos Yoder's text on *The Evolution of the United Nations System* (1993), or Gilbert R. Winham's *The Evolution of International Trade Agreements* (1992). A third is Lawrence Freedman's substantial *The Evolution of Nuclear Strategy* (1981).

In each case, the subject under discussion is a global institutional system, or a problem of global strategy, and the inclusion of the term "evolution" in the title is meant to indicate that the treatment will have an extended historical component, and that the dimension of time is therefore accorded an important place. But there is no evolutionary analysis in the body of these works and no use of evolutionary concepts, and evolution does not appear in the index. Freedman (1981: xv, 399) did indeed express concern that the major unresolved task of nuclear strategy was to "address the future of nuclear arsenals in a world of political change" that is in a world subject to evolution. It is also instructive to note the remarks in his "Introduction," wherein his own use of the term "evolution" in the title is somewhat misleading because it suggested "progress along a learning curve," when, in fact, his study found that expectation to be false. Perhaps the interval of system time (1945 to 1980) that he covered was not long enough to allow him to observe world politics undergoing a learning process.

Let us call *light* those approaches that treat global institutional change and time seriously, and actually employ evolutionary concepts in their analysis in an explanatory fashion. We might use as an example Immanuel Wallerstein's (1996) program of world-system research.[5] Wallerstein believes that "social scientists study . . . the evolution of historical systems" and that the modern world-system is one such system, characterized by the three phases of inception, normal functioning, and demise (or transition to a new historical system), as well as by a division of labor, and a mixture of cyclical and secular trends, hence by some regularities. But he says little if anything about transitions from one historical system to another. Christopher Chase-Dunn and Thomas Hall (1997: 55) recognize three types of world-systems in world history: kin-based, tributary-based, and capitalist (as well as socialist in the future), and propose a program for the study of the transformations of these systems.

World-systems theories accept as basic framework an account of stages of historical development of which the capitalist stage (with its own logic) is at the center of analysis, and that is a basically evolutionary (and materialist) framework. But besides positing historical evolution their employment of evolutionary concepts, or their concern with evolutionary mechanisms is at most implicit, and there is no effort to maintain contact with contemporary evolutionary thought in this area.[6]

We now come to what we should like to call the *strong* version of evolutionary theory. By strong we mean an explanatory theory in answer to a key problem of EWP, employing concepts and tracing evolutionary mechanisms through the workings of global politics, and, foremost, by incorporating a strong principle that is testable, and falsifiable, one that has been exposed to testing and found nonrefutable, and also one that illuminates some significant portion of our problems, both of understanding past world politics, and of offering guidelines for thinking about the future.

Let us take as an example of a strong principle, the statement that "social evolution is proportional to time" and that, consequently, global political evolution is likewise. A general principle of this kind has recently been gaining currency in studies of human evolution serving as the basis for estimating the rate of hominid development, relying on studies of what has come to be known as the "molecular clock" and that is now also extended to genetic and linguistic studies (Lumley 1998: 26; Modelski 1996: 337–38).

A representation of the claim that global politcal structures evolve in theoretically controllable fashion, and in a manner proportional to time is the "Matrix of Evolutionary World Politics" (Figure 1-1) that is a product of this research program. The Matrix is a schematic mapping of three-nested, and self-similar, four-phase evolutionary processes (Modelski 1996, 1999) at three levels of political organization: the institutional, the organizational, and the agency level.[7]

Figure 1.1 Matrix of Evolutionary World Politics Modern Era (III)
(world organization)

Agenda-Setting (global problems) Periods	Coalition-Building	Macrodecision (major warfare/ global war)	Execution After 1500: WORLD POWER next challenger
A. EURASIAN TRANSITION	(preconditions)		
930 information	960 Song founded	990 war with Liao	1020 LC1 Northern Song
1060 integration	1090 reform parties	1120 war with Chin	1160 LC2 Southern Song
1190 world empire?	1220 Mongol confederacy	1250 Mongols conquer China	1280 LC3 Genoa Mongol Empire
1300 trade	1320 shipping links	1350 Genoa, Mongols routed	1380 LC4 Venice Timur
B. ATLANTIC EUROPE	(global nucleus)		
1430 discovery	1460 Burgundy-Hapsburg connection	1494 wars of Italy and Indian Ocean	1516 LC5 **PORTUGAL** Spain
1540 integration	1560 Calvinist International	1580 Dutch-Spanish wars	1609 LC6 **DUTCH REPUBLIC** France
1640 political framework	1660 Anglo-Dutch alliance	1688 wars of Grand Alliance	1714 LC7 **BRITAIN I** France
1740 industrial revolution	1760 trading community (global organization)	1792 Revolutionary/ Napoleonic wars	1815 LC8 **BRITAIN II** Germany
C. ATLANTIC-PACIFIC			
1850 knowledge revolution	1878 Anglo-American special relationship	1914 World Wars I & II	1945 LC9 **USA**
1973 integration	2000 democratic transition	2026	2050 LC10
2080 political framework	2110	2140	2170 LC11
2200	2230	2260	2300... ....LC12

LC long cycle of global politics (numbered)

1. At the institutional level, the Matrix represents the best part of the Modern era of world system evolution of the past five millennia, one that analytically can be described as one of collective (species-wide, or world) organization (Modelski 2000: 33–37). The main features of the Modern Era (III) are the emergence of a global political system (a process that can be described as political globalization), and leading it, the rise of nation-states.

2. At the organizational level, the Matrix schematizes the evolution of global politics, as moving (so far) through three distinct periods of organizational change; within each a distinctive form emerges to define that period, and initially also shapes the issues of the next one. The first period (Eurasian Transition) was (politically) defined by the Mongol bid for world empire. The second period (Atlantic Europe) was one of emerging nation-states exercising global leadership and constructing the nucleus of the world system, within which Westphalian sovereignty was protected by a European balance. The third period (Atlantic-Pacific) is projected as one of global political organization that might be expected to take firm shape in the third cycle (LC11). The elaboration of this prognostic is a main theoretical task of the EWP program.

3. At the agency level, the Matrix shows, in successive rows, the agents or innovators that, in competition with others, drive global political evolution. That is the long cycle of global politics: the learning process at the micro-level of global politics, by which, over the past five hundred years, one nation-state had acquired global leadership; the long cycle also explains successive changes in the structure of the system. The four columns represent the four phases of the learning process, each the length of a generational period of approximately twenty-five to thirty years. The world powers and their challengers are the agency that has linked the micro- and macro-levels of world organization.[8]

Upon close inspection the Matrix might thus be seen to present not only a theory as to how and by what mechanism the system of global politics has regularly evolved over the past millenium, but also how the evolution occurred over phases of roughly equal length. Each mechanism consists of a set of three learning processes composed of four phases that optimize one evolutionary mechanism (variation, cooperation, selection, and reinforcement). While open to falsification, the Matrix does briefly record some data that offer at least preliminary evidence that the experience of global politics does match the prediction illustrated. Of course, other studies, including those of sea power, the global economy, and the practice of global leadership, have put more meat on the bare bones of the theoretical structure. The Matrix makes a strong statement about the past, not only offering in effect "a brief history of global politics," but also by posing it in a way that is grounded in the institutional evolution of the human species (see Modelski 2000). Finally, it also illustrates a theoretical framework for thinking about the next century and a sharply defined glimpse of the predicted future (as elaborated in Modelski and Thompson 1999).

The EWP Matrix represents a process that is "endogenous" to the global political system But that is not intended to suggest that developments exogenous to world politics are irrelevant to this analysis. Students of world politics need to keep track of evolutionary developments in the global economy (following in particular the fortunes of the lead economy, and of the world's leading sectors), of democratization that is an evolutionary process of distinguished lineage, and a great future, and in the emergence of long-term world opinion. Indeed, a data-based study of the co-evolution of global economics and politics similarly confirms the strong principle and shows, over a time span corresponding to the Matrix , a surprisingly regular pattern of alternation of leading industrial or commercial sectors in the global economy matching changes in the global political structure (Modelski and Thompson 1996).

Finally, let us not forget the possibility of a *heavy* approach to these problems. The heavy approach might be defined as one that constitutes a seamless fabric of description and explanation that meshes with other similar enterprises in the other social sciences, and with evolutionary theories of the more general kind, that is, sociological, biological, and cosmological. Unfortunately such an approach is not at hand, and we cannot offer an example of it. There is little harm, however, in at least aspiring to some theory of evolution that would in the terms outlined by David Deutsch (1997: 28–29) for instance, constitute, side by side with quantum physics, epistemology, and the theory of computation, one of the four main strands of explanation of the first "Theory of Everything."

The most eloquent recent statement of the case for the unity of knowledge has been E. O. Wilson's recent book, *Consilence*. His argument (1998: 292–93) for a "consilient" world view, primarily asserts that "culture, and hence the unique qualities of the human species will make complete sense only when linked in causal explanation to the natural sciences. Biology in particular is the most proximate and hence relevant of the scientific disciplines." Some might wish that the social (and political) sciences had been assigned a more active role in the Wilsonian world view, but the importance of that great future enterprise of "synthesis" is unarguable. The vision, perhaps unattainable, of "existence coherent enough to be understood in a single system of explanation, yet still largely unexplored" is too attractive to be ignored.

A PERSPECTIVE AND A RESEARCH PROGRAM

Let us recapitulate briefly the essentials of a strong approach to evolutionary world politics (for a fuller statement see Modelski 1996):

1. The global political system is a population of competing strategies or policies for the management of global problems; viewed as sets of instructions or programs these innovative strategies become the vehicles of evolution. That is to say that at

certain (specified) times, nation-states have served as carriers of global policies but nation-states as such are not the basic units of this analysis. This makes possible process analysis of changing event sequences.

2. Global politics forms a complex system that has a propensity to evolve, and does so in conditions and areas of high evolutionary potential. That makes evolutionary change in the first instance a property of regions, countries, and/or sectors (active zones) where evolutionary potential is palpable, where, for example, variety, openness, and mobility might be found in abundance. Change then diffuses at large.

3. Accounting for world political evolution at the agency, organizational, and institutional levels is a four-phased learning sequence (or algorithm) whose operators are variation, cooperation, selection, and reinforcement. This sequence explains structural innovations as the product of world-power-challenger interactions. The learning process at each level has a distinct period, which makes evolution proportional to time, but distinctly different in length. The long cycle (at the level of agency) is the best studied so far, but the pace and other characteristics of global organizational evolution offer the greatest theoretical challenge for the future.

4. Global politics coevolves, for example, with global economics, democratization, and movements of world opinion; it also nests within the macro-process of world system evolution.

It cannot be emphasized enough that the EWP research program is basically concerned with only one question: What explains structural change in world politics over the past millennium, in a way that also gives us a purchase on the future? Indeed, this an important "constitutional" or "constitutive" question that suffices to engage many scholars and promises to fuel substantive and methodological debates for years to come. To the extent that it yields useful answers, the whole will add up to a critical subfield, "evolutionary world politics," as a subfield of the more general field of international relations. But it most certainly neither answers all the questions that might be asked about world politics, or the hosts of policy questions that invariably engage world political observers, nor purports to represent an "integrated theory of politics."

So what does it do, and what can it accomplish? First, the question has the potential for the development of a productive social science theory because it exhibits all the necessary features of such a theory: causality (it answers the question: why and how does world politics evolve); parsimony (it does so efficiently, with relatively few variables); generality (it offers the "big picture" of world politics over one millennium); and testability (it can be, and has been, tested against a variety of empirical evidence). It is also linked to a wider theoretical universe.

Second, in its strong version, it closely meets the requirements of the evolutionary approach that we sketched out at the beginning of the chapter. Arguably, and more particularly, it can do three things well: First, it offers a theoretically viable "big picture" of world politics. That is, it gives the study of international relations a temporal dimension and a way to master what have so far appeared to be the intractable intricacies of world history. Among other things, it offers a framework for a course on the evolution of world politics that ought to be part of every IR program. Second, it supplies a way of looking at the future that is in effect a timetable of global development. That timetable will surely be tested by events yet to come, but it does offer at this time a reasonable framework for discussion. Third, it specifies the conditions of optimal change and of success for policies that respect the evolutionary mechanisms and the rhythms of world politics.

Over and beyond that however it must also be understood as a work-in-progress. The question of what explains structural change in world politics is a strong inquiry that must withstand further investigations than thus far performed. Let there be more debate.

NOTES

1. According to Colin McEvedy and Richard Jones (*Atlas of World Population History* 1978: 43,45,344) the population of England, Wales and Scotland in 1600 is estimated as about 5 million, and the world population rose by a factor of about seven between 1600 and 1975.
2. For an overview see The Evolutionary World Politics Home Page at http://faculty.washington.edu/modelski
3. For a review of the literature consult, among other things, "Bibliography" on the The Evolutionary World Politics home page, cited in note 3.
4. Emanuel Adler (1997) argues that "a dynamic theory of institutional selection is a natural complement of constructivism" because constructivist theory must be able to answer which interpretations and whose interpretations become social reality (such as, we might add, the definitions of global problems, or the formulations of world opinion). He errs, though, in describing the "long cycles evolutionary theory" as highlighting the selection of global political systems "only by material power." Fulvio Attina (1999: 49–84) on the other hand, places the evolutionary theory of world politics under the categories of equality and cooperation.
5. Stephen Sanderson (1991: 168) has argued that Wallerstein's is a "quintessentially evolutionary theory" because the modern world-system is his basic unit of analysis.
6. Another example might be George Liska's *The Ways of Power* (1990), that includes chapters on "Motor and Mechanism of Evolution" and "Evolutionary Progression Short of Progress."
7. This implies a more complex conception of the structure of world politics, comprising world political institutions that change over the long term of one or two millennia; organizations that function in the medium term of some half millennium; and agents or innovators that drive global politics in the short-term of a century or so.
8. In as much as each successive "long cycle" repeats the four-phase learning sequence, the process exhibits a rhythmic, or cyclical element. But each such long cycle also has new features and others that cumulate, which make the process evolutionary. That is why overall this is not a "cyclical" but an "evolutionary" theory of world politics.

REFERENCES

Adler, Emanuel. 1997. Seizing the Middle Ground: Constructivism in World Politics. *European Journal of Internatiaonal Relations* 3(3): 319–363.

Attina, Fulvio. 1999. *Il Sistema Politico Globale*, Roma-Bari: Editori Laterza.

Azevedo, Jane. 1997. *Mapping reality: An evolutionary realist methodology for the natural and social sciences.* Albany: State University of New York Press.

Chase-Dunn, Christopher and Thomas D. Hall. 1997. *Rise and demise: Comparing world systems.* Boulder, Colo.: Westview.

Deutsch, David. 1997. *The Fabric of Reality.* New York: Allen Lane: The Penguin Press.

Dobzhansky, Theoodore. 1962. *Mankind evolving: The evolution of the human species.* New Haven, Conn.: Yale University Press.

Falger, Vincent S. E. 1994. Biopolitics and the Study of International Relations: Implications, Results, and Perspectives. *Research in Biopolitics* 2: 115–34.

Freedman, Lawrence. 1981. *The Evolution of Nuclear Strategy.* New York: St. Martin's Press.

Liska, George. 1990. *The ways of power: Pattern and meaning in world politics.* Cambridge, Mass.: Blackwell.

Lumley, Henri de. 1998. *L'homme Premier; Prehistoire, Evolution, Culture.* Paris: Odile Jacob.

Modelski, George. 1987. *Long cycles in world politics.* London: Macmillan.

———. 1996. Evolutionary Paradigm for Global Politics. *International Studies Quarterly.* September, 321–42.

———. 1998. Generations, and Global Change. *Technological Forecasting and Social Change* 59: 39–45.

———. 1999. The Evolution of Global Politics: From Leadership to Organization. in V. Bornschier and C. Chase-Dunn, eds. The Future of Global Conflict. London: Sage.

———. 2000. World System Evolution in R. Denemark et al., eds. World System History. London: Routledge.

Modeleski, George and William R. Thompson. 1996. Leading Sectors and World Powers: The coevolution of global economics and politics. Columbia: University of South Carolina Press.

———. 1999. The Long and the Short of Global Politics in the 21st Century. *International Studies Review.* September, 109–140.

Sanderson, Stephen K. . 1991. The Evolution of Societies and World-Systems, pp.167–92 in C Chase-Dunn and T. Hall, *Core-periphery relations in precapitalist worlds.* Boulder, Colo.: Westview.

Wallerstein, Immanuel. 1996. The Modern World-System and Evolution. *Journal of World-Systems Research*, (1) 19.

Wilson, Edward O. 1998. *Consilience: The unity of knowledge.* New York: Vintage Books.

Winham, Gillart R. 1992. The evolution of international trade agreements. Toronto, Can.: University of Toronto Press.

Yoder, Amos. 1993. The evolution of the United Nations system. 2nd ed. Washington, D.C.: Taylor and Francis.

chapter 2

Evolutionary World Politics Enriched
The Biological Foundations
of International Relations

Vincent S. E. Falger

> Once one views international relations through the lens of sex and biology, it
> never again looks the same. (Fukuyama 1998: 33)

INTRODUCTION

"An evolutionary approach [of international politics] revives the importance of history," is one of the important and innovative conclusions George Modelski draws from his project called Evolutionary World Politics (EWP). It is truly innovative, because for the first time a systematic analysis of "international history," stretching back as far as 3500 B.C., has been made on the basis of an evolutionary theory of world politics. The demonstration of historical evidence of the four phases of evolution of modern world politics and the four steps in the evolution of global politics, leads to the well-known long cycle of global politics (see the previous chapter). Of course, this is not the first cyclical conception of (world) history, but it is the first modern one in which world politics is perceived as subject to (social) evolution.

In this chapter the central role of evolution and its related aspects in EWP is analyzed from a conceptually related, but for the rest, quite different background in biopolitics, or the biobehavioral perspective on human behavior, up to and including international relations and world politics. I hope to demonstrate that so far there is a difference between the social-evolutionary approach of George Modelski's EWP project and the biobehavioral or evolutionary approach of human behavior in other social sciences, such as psychology and anthropology. The question of whether this difference is of any importance depends on the view one holds of the general analysis of human behavior: If we see ourselves as actors in a grand structure that is the result of one or two hundred generations of interacting individuals and groups—the top-down perspective—we might not be very much interested in the still deeper structure of a bottom-up view, inherent to *biological* evolution. This deepest structure, formed by the evolutionary history of *Homo sapiens sapiens* during some ten thousand generations, manifests itself in the probability with which individual behavioral choices are made. Human nature, to use that classic phrase, is supposed to be relevant also for the study of international relations (IR).

Ideally, the two perspectives could reinforce each other and push the EWP project to the center of the modern biological-evolutionary analysis of human behavior. The prospects but also difficulties of such scientific holism will be discussed here, from biopolitics and evolutionary epistemological perspectives first. Then a number of issues in IR that lend themselves to a biobehavioral approach are presented, such as in-group/out-group formation, cooperation and conflict, territoriality, sex differences, generational sequences—human nature, for short. To conclude with, the risks of introducing biology in the social sciences as an explanatory foundation are discussed. Is determinism an unavoidable consequence of any evolutionary approach? Is it an inherently conservative, status quo–confirming way of analyzing social life, in the end inviting racists to abuse science for political purposes? Although this last question is more a matter of political ideology than of scientific relevance, it is a well-known cause of hesitation with social scientists not to engage in evolutionary approaches in the first place, and therefore deserves to be addressed.

Since this chapter is an invitation to find out whether the EWP project and biopolitics could be of mutual interest, it is sensible to point at the themes of EWP most relevant for biopolitics first.

EVOLUTIONARY WORLD POLITICS
AS SEEN FROM THE BIOBEHAVIORAL POINT OF VIEW

In a recent review article on biopolitics, Somit and Peterson (1998) argue that the study of genetic influences on political behavior is the most significant area of biopolitics. This is so because it reflects on the manner in which our species' evolutionary history has left *Homo sapiens* genetically endowed with certain social and behavioral tendencies.[1] It will be clear that this is the typical argument of bottom-up evolution, which starts with different individual organisms reproducing offspring. The essence of what happens in evolution could hardly be described in a more condensed fashion than as follows: "Sex provides variety by mixing genes from two parents, producing combinations of traits in their offspring that they do not show themselves. Natural selection, in the form of environmental pressures, then takes care of deciding whether these new features are worthwhile. New genetic combinations that give a better chance of survival, or reproduction, tend to come out on top."[2] Later on I will turn to some of the social and behavioral tendencies (which in principle are no less subject to selective pressures than are physical characteristics), but here we meet an important theme for comparison between top-down EWP and bottom-up biopolitics.

Modelski, who stresses evolution as the distinguishing feature of the EWP project, adheres to "social evolution" that is to be distinguished from biological or genetic evolution, even if the structures of both processes are the same. In this particular conception of social evolution there is no need for sociobiology: Evolutionary world politics does not posit "a primary causal influence from genetic endowment or biological make-up to human social behavior" (Modelski 1997a: 2), and "the question is not how much like biological systems are social systems," but instead "the question is: Given that the theoretical basis of biology is micro- and macro-evolution (in the sense that both change and directionality are essential components of evolutionary theory), what additional analogies might there be for the social sciences, if the social system of the human species, mutatis mutandis, is viewed as subject to evolutionary processes?" (Modelski 1996: 327). His conclusion is that there is no need to let the social sciences have an evolutionary theory that is identical in evolutionary biology (see also Modelski and Poznanski 1996: 316).

From a biopolitical perspective this is a regrettable separating statement that detracts from the parsimonious character that is supposed to be one of the main attractions of the biological-evolutionary theory. Although Modelski does not deny the possibility of a causal influence from biological make-up to human social behavior, it is considered to be irrelevant in the analysis of institutions and long-term historical developments. This may be a safe standpoint in modern social science, but it closes the mind to absolutely relevant developments in the biobehavioral sciences. So, where the EWP interests regard the (evolving) institutional structures in which human behavior of individuals express itself, biopolitics would propose to reverse the picture, and begin with human social behavior *tout court*. A *biological*-evolutionary approach of human behavior starts at the bottom. Human behavior itself is a product of evolution and contains many highly relevant clues that also work out in more institutionalized frameworks, from so-called "primitive" to modern international-political ones.

Of course, a Darwinian type of evolutionary paradigm for global politics would not deny the importance of the extended phenotypic character of culture and structures, but it would reintroduce emphasis on the individual (human) organism and its behavior as the unit of selection. Without human individuals there are no social structures left—leaving aside for the moment the possibilities of self-replicating machines.

From a biopolitical point of view the EWP project would be less vulnerable to two other very different points of critique, had it taken the bottom-up line. First, Modelski's evolutionary paradigm has an element of structural determinism in it in so far that it is completely sex-neutral. The question if there is any difference between male and female humans operating in politics, from domestic to international politics, is evolutionarily very relevant, but is not posed in the EWP project. This accentuates the traditional androcentric quality of most political science, and certainly of IR theory. What difference it makes to introduce a sex/gender dimension is to be demonstrated later on, but for now we can argue that just forgetting about it may indicate an insensitivity toward what evolution is about.

A second point of critique that flows from the absence of a bio-evolutionary behavioral foundation is the paradox of partial ahistoricity of the EWP project. It is an interesting paradox, because even if there are evidently no IR theorists with a wider range of interests in historical development than George Modelski—his work covers the period from the origin of the first cities and states to far into the next millennium (Modelski 1997b)—the human species is prehistorically apparently not worth mentioning before the neolithic agricultural revolution. A biopolitical scientist would request serious attention to possible reconstructions of human behavior models before the period of cumulative civilization because the behavioral tendencies involved in the group life to be associated with cities and proto-states have not disappeared suddenly, or became irrelevant, with the rise of "civilization." Indeed, an evolutionary approach of international politics does revive the importance of history, but that does not begin with the undeniably revolutionary innovation of cities and states. Isolating a particular type of political phenomena—in this case international or inter-group politics—from its prehistory for conceptual reasons is certainly acceptable in a developing research tradition as the one in EWP, but once it is possible, or indeed, desirable, to anchor this research in other fields of research, like evolutionary psychology and anthropology, it would be a waste not to do so. This would even draw the attention to not only the analogy with chimpanzee and bonobo behavior, but also to the homology of it (see next section on homology). In evolutionary biology anthropocentrism is not done—unless for conventional social science reasons—and in the end political science will gain from cross-species perspectives.

In short, the introduction of evolutionary theory in IR analysis is laudable, but in a biobehavioral view it is not complete, because the very *basis* is missing. In contrast to what the *auctor intellectualis* of the EWP project is arguing—— that the social sciences can do without an evolutionary theory other than his—a biopolitical approach would advise to pay very much attention explicitly to the original edition of it, in fact, to start with it. Because the conceptual framework of the EWP project is so familiar with the larger evolutionary perspective, it is worthwhile looking for other obstacles and possibilities.

EVOLUTIONARY EPISTEMOLOGY

An important matter of discussion in the search for links between the EWP project and biopolitics should be the concept of evolution as used in the project. Recognizing that nobody has the exclusive right to monopolize the word "evolution," it nevertheless goes without saying that the *biological* connotation of evolution is most prominent. Modelski himself rightly points at the increasing use of the word "evolution" as part of titles of books and articles that most of the time does not imply that the evolutionary dimension in such work has more significance than mere semantics.[3] In his own work "evolution" is taken very seriously, also from a biological point of view, but here in fact only as an *analogy*, a source of inspiration for hypotheses and theorizing. As such this is inspirational, but it also leads one to wonder how representative is Modelski's conception of evolution.

Analogy and homology are important and related concepts in biology. Homology is resemblance in structure and origin, and a homologous feature has the same evolutionary origin and basic form to one in a different organism, but may not have the same final form and function (compare for example the skeleton of a bat wing and a human arm). Analogy, according to the *Cambridge Encyclopaedia of Human Evolution*, is resemblance in function, but not in structure and origin. An analogous structure has a similar function to one in a different organism, but has completely different evolutionary developmental origin (for example, the wings of a bat and an insect). A biological approach of a phenomenon, as phrased by the ethologist Niko Tinbergen, implies a consciousness of the fact that the phenomena—an organism, but also behavior—independent of how they are caused, serve certain functions and have arisen evolvingly on a historical foundation to which the phenomena for the fulfillment of the function have adapted (Tinbergen 1963). The three resulting questions, causal, functional, and historical respectively, can be condensed into the goal of the modern adaptionist program: to recognize certain features of organisms as components of some special problem-solving machinery. "The subject matter of the adaptionist program is structural, physiological, behavioral, or psychological phenotypic features that have been shaped by selection to serve some function" (Symons 1992: 155). In evolutionary psychology this leads to the presumption that the human brain/mind has many functions, that it has been designed by selection to solve very different kinds of problems. Instead of supposing some sort of generalized "learning" or "capacity-for-culture" mechanism, human perceptions of, for example, sexual attractiveness are underpinned by many specialized mechanisms that operate according to their own distinctive rules and principles. In the end studies in evolutionary psychology and anthropology provide insight into the human environment of evolutionary adaptedness—at least, that is their generally acclaimed scientific aim (Symons 1992). It will be clear that from this perspective analogous argument is considerably less convincing than homologous argument. Analogies are not rejected altogether, however, but they apparently do need to be extra defended as legitimate constructions, as can be read about the analogy between genes and culture in Boyd and Richerson's *Culture and the Evolutionary Process*.

Another problem of evolutionary epistemology is the question of whether Modelski's four-phased learning process—the evolution of the world system, and of world politics—is an evolutionary *model* or an evolutionary *metaphor*. The answer, based on the analogous quality of the underlying conception of evolution, is that it is mainly of a metaphorical character. This is accentuated by the ease with which central concepts in EWP such as "selection," "variation," and "reinforcement" are attributed to Darwinian thought, but "cooperation" is presented as much contested in that domain (see Modelski 1997a: 2). Perhaps the image of Darwinian thinking here is quite old-fashioned, because in particular, the modern biological-evolutionary approach of animal and human behavior has extensively demonstrated how important is cooperation.

A last remark of epistemological relevance regards the use of "evolutionary learning." This concept plays a central role in the EWP paradigm, and its importance is summarized in the author's own words: "The evolution of the world system, and of world politics, is a learning process for the human race, and not just one learning process but an array of learning processes' (Modelski 1997a: 2). "Evolutionary learning," or *learning as evolution* is based on a not very well-known article by the Cambridge zoologist J. W. S. Pringle (1951), and the main thesis is that there is a parallel between the process of organic evolution and the process of learning. The basic argument refers to the unique kinematic nature of the process that results in a selection of variations.[4] Pringle's article deals with learning in animals and it is clear that in the EWP project the parallel, in the original article applied to individual animals, is upgraded to a macro-social analogue that gives the impression of being overstreched considerably—hence, again, a confirmation of the mainly metaphoric character of the use of evolutionary terminology. The theme of metaphoric use is also a point of discussion in evolutionary psychology itself. The difference between adaptiveness and adaptation may seem of semantic magnitude, but for John Tooby, one of the leading evolutionary psychologists, the study of adaptiveness "merely draws metaphorical inspiration from Darwin, whereas the study of adaptation *is* Darwinian" (paraphrased by Symons 1992: 150).[5]

So, keeping the EWP project to the perspective of modern evolutionary analysis of human behavior, on the one hand, we see a classical *social* evolutionist's idea of evolution, based on analogy, and on the other hand quite, strong indications of rejecting the factual evolutionary dimension: homology. Darwinian theory and selection are also used in an analogous way that lead to the conclusion that only those parts of the evolutionary paradigm that are helpful to construct a theory of politics are used. This theory is *called* evolutionary, but is not such in substance. Given the developments in modern social science, in particular the evolutionary approach, an evolutionary theory of behavior, (world) politics included, cannot do without starting bottom-up. However, this does not mean that the EWP project is not worth being paid attention by political scientists with an affinity for the fundamental quality of evolutionary approaches. On the contrary, it may ask "little" more than to be interested in the discovery of new knowledge. "The behavioral and social sciences borrowed the idea of hypothesis testing and quantitative methodology from the natural sciences, but unfortunately not the idea of conceptual integration" (Cosmides, Tooby, and Barkow 1992: 12). I think this fits the EWP project perfectly, but instead of stopping here, it could also be taken as a stimulus to jump from metaphor and analogy to an integrated theory of politics, based in evolutionary foundations. The following section presents some points of departure.[6]

EVOLUTIONARY PSYCHOLOGY: HUMAN NATURE AND CULTURE

Of the human social sciences, so far psychology has benefited most from the application of evolutionary theory. The expanding field of evolutionary psychology has gained a status of its own by many publications of theoretical and empirical significance (for example, Tooby and Cosmides 1990; Barkow, Cosmides, and Tooby 1992; Betzig 1997). The still small, but very active field converges advances in evolutionary biology, cognitive psychology, and palaeoanthropology in a fundamental new view of the human mind that cannot but affect other social sciences. The landmark publication *The Adapted Mind* argues convincingly that with the advent of the cognitive revolution human nature can be identified as a set of information-processing programs that operate below the surface of observed cultural variability. The origin of these cognitive programs dates back to the Pleistocene when our hunter-gatherer forebears had to solve their daily problems in an adaptive way (Barkow, Cosmides, and Tooby 1992).

The resulting view of the human mind is that of a collection of functionally specialized "computers." The logic behind evolutionary psychology is the same as the one physiologists have used to answer their questions of what is this or that organ "designed" for. The human mind was not designed for a single function, like the eyes or wings, but for many parallel ones: sensing, thinking, imaging, interpreting, communicating, and so forth. In particular John Tooby and Leda Cosmides argue that the concept of a universal human nature, based on a species-typical collection of complex psychological adaptations, is valid, even under recognition of the existence of substantial genetic variation that makes each human individual genetically and biochemically unique (Tooby and Cosmides 1990).

By distinguishing between an individual's innate psychology and his or her manifest psychology and behavior (corresponding with the genotype or inherited basis of a trait and the phenotype or the observable expression of such a trait), it is possible, according to Tooby and Cosmides, to observe variable manifest traits and behaviors between individuals and across cultures as the *product* of a common, underlying evolved innate psychology, operating under different circumstances.

> The mapping between the innate and the manifest operates according to principles of expression that are specified in innate psychological mechanisms or in innate developmental programs that shape psychological characteristics; these expressions can differ between individuals when different environmental inputs are operated on by the same procedures to produce different manifest outputs. This set of universal innate psychological mechanisms and developmental programs constitute human nature. Individual differences that arise from exposing the same human nature to different environmental inputs relate the study of individual differences to human nature in a straightforward way. (Tooby and Cosmides 1990: 23)

Although the authors would not for one moment deny the enormous genetic diversity of human individuals, they argue that the idea of different human natures is incorrect. They see genetically caused individual differences as almost entirely constrained variation "within an encompassing, universal, adaptively organized superstructure: human nature" (24). Central to their evolutionary perspective is adaptation, the most important concept of evolutionary biology, which gains its explanatory value by relating the organization of living phenomena to adaptive requirements. The main question for an evolutionary psychologist, then, is to determine which personality phenomena are adaptations and which are not. Of course, this calls for clear standards for recognizing adaptations, and this is how Tooby and Cosmides (24) deal with them, following the well-known "adaptionist program" of Hamilton, Williams, and Dawkins: "An adaptation is a characteristic of the phenotype developmentally manufactured according to instructions contained in its genetic specification or basis, whose genetic basis became established and organized in the population because the characteristic systematically interacted with stable features of the environment in a way that promoted the reproduction of the individual bearing the characteristic, or reproduction of the relatives of that individual."

To stress the distinctiveness of an *evolutionary* approach of adaptive functions, Tooby and Cosmides set them apart from nonbiological notions of function that may have their own usefulness, but lack the explanatory power of evolutionary adaptation. Standards such as happiness, success, goal-realization, and self-actualization may in many circumstances correspond with the promotion of the reproduction of the individual and/or his or her relatives, but it is the *biological* definition of function and adaptation "that track the forces that have shaped us" (24).

For the social sciences, like political science, a link between this individual-related evolutionary concept of human nature and macro-social phenomena needs to be demonstrable before we can answer the question of whether evolutionary psychology is somehow useful in IR theory. The requested link is provided by applying the same evolutionary logic to behavior between nonrelatives. On the basis of Hamilton's kin selection theory, Trivers, Axelrod, and Hamilton constructed the reciprocal altruism theory. This very important chapter of evolutionary theory applied to behavior can be condensed to the testable statement that if cooperation between two or more (whether or not related) individuals results in a reproductive benefit for each of the actors, "then individuals who engage in this kind of reciprocal helping behavior will out reproduce those who do not, causing this kind of helping design to spread" (Cosmides and Tooby 1992: 169). The social exchange theory, which the authors sometimes call "social contract theory," is in fact an iterated Prisoner's Dilemma between nonrelatives, dressed up with all kinds of restraints varying in time and place, but still the basis for natural selection to "solve" the adaptive problems posed by cooperation.

After a careful analysis of the existing literature and their own experimental work, including the cheater problem, Cosmides and Tooby conclude that the human mind includes procedures that are adaptations for reasoning about social exchange (that is, cooperation among (non-) relatives). They argue that it is social exchange and the underlying constellation of cognitive adaptations that support it, and the magnitude, variety, and complexity of these social exchanges, that differentiate humans strongly from all other animal species. "If one removed from our evolutionary history and hence from our minds the possibility of cooperation and reciprocity—of mutual contingent benefit-benefit interactions arrived at through mutual consent—then coercion and force would loom even larger as instruments of social influence, and positive relationships would be limited primarily to self-sacrificial interactions among kin. Such conditions do, in fact, typify the social life of most other animal species (Cosmides and Tooby 1992: 207). Thus, cooperation is just as important a part of the human evolutionary legacy as is competition (see also Alexander 1979).

However, an evolutionary psychologist does not use what is called the "standard social science methodology" (SSSM) of culture to answer the question of what psychological mechanism allows human beings to behave so differently from most animals. Evolutionary psychologist contest that the prevailing opinion enclosed in the SSSM is that " 'culture' builds all concepts as sophisticated and as content-specific as social exchange from scratch, using only content-free general-purpose mental processes" (207; see Tooby and Cosmides 1992 for an evolutionary vision on the classic nature-nurture problem, that is no problem for evolutionists). The consequence they draw is that within-location similarities and between-location differences in thought and behavior, traditionally and typically seen as cultural variation, are better understood as *transmitted* culture (processes whereby the thought and behavior of some individuals—usually from the preceding generation—is passed on to other individuals, thereby causing the present pattern) operating together with *evoked* culture (similarities triggered by local circumstances, but proceeded by our universal, evolved information-processing mechanisms that are context-dependent) Cosmides and Tooby 1992: 209–10).

Although the authors do not pretend to have already developed a complete "computational theory of social exchange," they nevertheless express confidence in the possibility to develop in detail a coherent analysis of individual and cultural variation within the context of a universal human nature. They realize that many crucial questions are still to be answered if we are to understand all social exchange in its intra- and cross-cultural diversity, but in their own brief summary Cosmides and Tooby clearly indicate the theoretical relevance of their evoked culture construct. An important additional advantage is the greater parsimony of the evoked culture model when cultural change, for example, under influence of dramatic new circumstances (from migrations to natural disasters to new technologies—and even developments in the international system), and its dynamics are to be explained. Transmission models can account for stable conditions, but even the spread of new cultural forms through transmissions is under the influence of dynamics that are powerfully structured by our content-sensitive evolved psychology. In a world beyond the hunter-gatherer social exchange patterns, it is always important to remember that "although our cognitive mechanisms evolved to promote adaptive decisions in the Pleistocene, they do not necessarily produce adaptive decisions under evolutionarily novel modern circumstances" (Cosmides and Tooby 1992: 219).

All this boils down to the rejection of two central tenets of the so-called SSSM, rejections that should be understood as quite strong indications of the existence of a universal human nature. First, there is no human mind containing a single "reasoning faculty" that is function-general and content-free. In different situations, then, different sets of functionally specialized procedures are activated exploiting "the recurrent properties of the corresponding domain in a way that would have produced an efficacious solution under Pleistocene conditions" (221). The metaphor for the human mind as a single-purpose computer is exchanged for an intricate network of functionally dedicated computers. The second tenet of SSSM rejected is the proposition "that all contentful features of the human mind are 'socially constructed' or environmentally derived." Cosmides and Tooby support the view that "the human mind imposes contentful structure on the social world, derived from specialized functional design in its evolved architecture" (221).

Jerome Barkow, one of the other authorities in evolutionary psychology, has among other things developed evolutionary foundations underlying social stratification, an apparently new dimension in social life. Indeed, he confirms the unlikelihood of institutionalized social hierarchies in the small-scale foraging band-level societies. The "invention" of social classes probably does not antedate ten thousand to twelve thousand years ago when domestication developed in the Near East. Social stratification, the institutionalized social hierarchy in a society, must therefore be relatively recent, not much more than 10 percent of the time of the existence of our species (supposing that it is about 200,000 years old). Social stratification is a group-level phenomenon, generated by the social interaction of individuals over time, but 10,000 years is certainly too short a period to have been directly selected. "The psychological traits that enable individuals to generate stratification, however, presumably are products of natural selection."[7] In this evolutionary perspective, the genesis of social class is seen as the result of three hominid psychological traits: (a) the pursuit of high social rank; (b) nepotism; and (c) the capacity for social change and formation of coalitions. The striving for higher relative standing usually takes the form of seeking control over surplus production or over the means of production. Members of ruling social classes collectively enjoy political power and control of economic resources at the expense of others. And to do so, they must engage in numerous political and economic exchanges (Barkow 1992: 632–35).

In politics, all else flows from this, up to and including world politics. In my view, there is no need to keep a biologically informed conception of politics at arm's length from the EWP project, even if its main argument would not change a iota by it. Integrating a biopolitical dimension in the project, or using it as the project's behavioral foundational theory, would add to parsimony and terminological coherence. To insist that there is no need to do that, implies ultimately the rejection of the only serious scientific-evolutionary approach that survived competing theories for nearly 150 years. However, accepting the biobehavioral theory as the basis is not a guarantee for success; very much still needs to be done. In the past more than one macro-evolutionary theory crashed under eclecticism and the fixation on proximate problems to be analyzed. In my self-chosen task to invite cooperation between EWP-minded people and those attracted to biopolitics, I will present shortly three issues that are suited for a biobehavioral approach: in-group/out-group formation; sex differences, and generational sequences. In the closing part of this section I point to the synthetic approach of Steve Sanderson as the already available synthesis to start the necessary work-in-progress immediately.

BIOPOLITICAL ISSUES

In-Group / Out-Group Formation and Coalition Building

In the "environment of evolutionary adaptation" (EEA), but not less today, the interpretation of reality by individuals is a complex activity of information processing in which belonging to a group helps to reduce that complexity. The differentiation between one's own group, the *in-group*, and all other groups is not accidentally positively biased toward the own group. In-groups, of whatever constitution, develop from an individual but shared need for self-definition and social reality. Such an interpersonal theory of group formation is not the only one; social identity-theory points at intergroup comparison in which the need for positive distinction in relation to other groups as an important element of individual self-categorization. Belonging to a group has far-reaching consequences for individuals' self images.

The basic in-group/out-group differentiation implies usually in-group favoritism and out-group homogenization, and both are bases for stereotyping, badging, and other forms of complexity-reducing psychology.[8] Group identity in general is more important than personal identity; emotions and ill-informed information about other groups all help to consolidate a relatively safe defense against all kinds of uncertainties. Since these forms of group formation are constantly repeating all the time and everywhere (accepting that individuals may sometimes behave otherwise), it is safe to consider the universality of these processes, the causal links between them, attitude formation and individual behavior as essential characteristics of human social behavior. These considerations have consequences for how to study individual behavior—for example, attitude formation *vis à via* multiethnic situations, which is the focus of Thienpont's study, but is of course no less relevant for international politics—and lead to the conclusion that it is essential to gain insight in the development of in-group/out-group processes.

This study cannot do without resorting to evolutionary biology, without rejecting classic social science–conflict theory (see van der Dennen 1995 for a review of the literature). The traditional approach is summarized best by serving the *proximate* causation, but it is the *ultimate* causal approach that adds the evolutionary dimension. Here we meet again the much longer time perspective and the functionalist approach. Applied to the in-group/out-group phenomenon, we can argue that social group life is adaptive in the light of competition for scarce goods and means. Groups are the necessary means with which individual survival and reproduction can be optimized. The strategies individuals employ are part of the "normal" evolutionary heritage of mankind in general; the individual will first see to his own interest, then to those of his close relatives (and pseudo-relatives like friends), and then to the interests of the larger group. Motives and intentions, however conscious or unconscious they may be, link individuals to groups. "The relevance of the group as a social system is that this form of life constitutes an important part of the selective environment of people. . . . The factor "social life" in interaction with other factors has been decisive for the course of human evolution, for the complex character of the contemporary way of social life, and so also for the way groups relate to each other" (Thienpont 1999: 34). Cognitive processes, such as thinking in stereotypes, can be considered stable strategies of evolution.[9]

Even without going deeper in the evolutionary ratio of social life in groups, it should be evident by now that not only is our behavior as individuals strongly predisposed toward being group members, but also that the original environment in which this type of behavior was functional, has changed quite dramatically. Our behavioral predispositions, however, did not disappear but expressed themselves in new contexts—sometimes without problems, though not with fewer negative consequences for those who did not behave according to the group mores, or the rules of out-group individuals. *This* is the ultimate, evolutionary basis for explaning of all forms of behavior for individuals who identify with certain groups by distinguishing themselves from other groups. Geographical and social boundaries have reinforced these predispositions, and any evolutionary theory of politics should take this into account, in fact start with it.

Although very elementary, I hope to have shown that the biobehavioral analysis of individual behavior is the starting point for answering that hardly ever put but highly relevant question: Why is Man a social species in the first place? The fact that in most social sciences this question is neither considered relevant outside social philosophy or even political science, nor can it be answered with a strictly social or cultural explanation, indicates the presence of a mental barrier between the real evolutionary approach and the rest. How inspirational and innovative evolutionary psychology, anthropology, biopolitics, and so forth, can be for those grown up with the SSSM, might also be concluded from the next section.

Is Politics a Male Preoccupation?

Anthropologist John Pfeiffer published in 1969 a well-known book, *The Emergence of Man*, which was renamed as *The Emergence of Humankind*, now in its fourth edition (1985). The greater perceptiveness for the role of women in the study of human behavior reflects not only some political correctness but also the consequences drawn from an evolutionary approach. Although socially deconstructed gender analyses drew increasing attention to differences in male and female reproductive strategies, it was empirical observation in primatology that led to hypotheses on analogy and homology (see de Waal 1982 and Betzig 1986). Ann Tickner was fully right in pointing to the androcentric character of Hans Morgenthau's six principles of realism (Tickner 1991). The implicit androcentric character of the EWP project is neutralized by referring to the structural quality of the empirical basis: Who plays politics is not supposed to influence the cyclical nature of world politics (Modelski, pers. comm.). Viewed from the top down this may be the case, but it leaves the question unanswered of why males so overwhelmingly dominate politics. Top-down this is not interesting, bottom-up it is the logical next question after answering why "Man" is a social species. Even if it does not change the essentials of EWP—which remains to be demonstrated—it does put an evolutionary foundation under the project that it does not, in and of itself, have.

If male domination in the spheres of politics is evident, from earliest historic records on and cross-culturally, then one answer why this is so is the evolutionary background of these differences in strategy. Generally, in terms of reproductive interests, females invest in raising their children (quality) and males in siring them (quantity). Of course this is a crude picture, but the essence is not only demonstrable in humans but also in many other primate species. In fact "politics" is a relatively successful behavioral repertoire for attaining or defending a comparatively better position in the competition for scarce resources, sexual partners included.

The male-male competition is the classic setting for politics, as Frans de Waal has described so vividly in his books, and the male-female relationship has only very recently (and only in some parts of the developed world) come under the influence of reproduction regulation technology fallen in the hands of women who have changed the evolutionary rationale for the first time in human evolution. Instead of pointing exclusively to the cultural quality of the male-female relationship, however, it is also worthwhile to wonder about Charles Darwin's "female choice" as the other selective force—and underestimated outside evolutionary biology. Even if the time span since the introduction of chemical contraceptives is evolutionarily absolutely insignificant—at most two generations of women in mostly Western countries have been able to limit the number of children they want—it did open up the much more substantive possibility of female competition in the traditional realms of politics and economics. It would certainly be premature to draw solid conclusions from less than half a century of emancipatory politics in the West, but so far it does not look like the traditionally male dominated occupational fields—certainly not the top positions—are taken over by women by more than a few percent. There is a quantitative, but not structural, change, in the Nordic countries, and much less so in other countries of Western Europe and the United States.

However, in one respect a change under influence of women has been recognized and attractively formulated as an evolutionarily inspired analysis of ultra contemporary and future politics, so far mainly of and in the West. Francis Fukuyama, known for his fundamental discussion of the future of history after the victory of economic and political liberalism over communism in *The End of History and the Last Man*, published under the challenging title "Women and the Evolution of World Politics" a digestion of primatology, evolutionary psychology, and increasing individualization and democratization of social life.[10] I consider the article to be a very welcome stimulus in IR theory in general, and for the EWP project in particular.

Starting with the increasingly shared idea among primatologists that male dominance and bonding in chimpanzees and humans are homologous features, and that males and females employ different social life strategies, Fukuyama draws the conclusion that in no area is sex-related difference clearer than with respect to violence and aggression. However, if we realize that the genetic basis for sex differences is first of all making a statistical assertion regarding the distribution of certain characteristics, then we avoid biological determinism. Different "male" and "female" bell-shaped distributions will overlap partially, as illustrated by the (so far) well-known exceptions of Margaret Thatcher and Golda Meir. Based on the strong statistical correlation between male enjoyment of camaraderie and experience of aggression, Fukuyama argues that "A truly matriarchal world would be less prone to conflict and more conciliatory than the one we inhabit now" (Fukuyama 1998: 33).[11]

The "feminization of world politics," which will be promoted by more participation of women—as leaders, officials, soldiers, and voters—not only articulates women's interests but can also shift the underlying male agenda. Empirical research has shown that in the United States women are consistently less in favor of military action than men, and it can be predicted "that increasing female participation will probably make the United States and other democracies less inclined to use power around the world as freely as they have in the past" (35). This leads to the "democratic peace" argument of which the essence is the correlation between the degree of consolidation of liberal democratic institutions and interdemocratic peace. Fukuyama calls this "one of the few nontrivial generalizations one can make about world politics," and although the reasons for this correlation is still a matter of discussion, he points to a factor that has not drawn much attention so far: Developed democracies also tend to be more feminized than authoritarian states (in terms of expansion of female franchise and participation in political decision making).[12] "It should therefore surprise no one that the historically unprecedented shift in the sexual basis of politics should lead to a change in international relations" (36).

Another fundamental biological factor will probably increasingly influence international politics: the decrease in family size in economically developed countries. This makes the few children a couple has extra costly for them emotionally, and where military actions are concerned, extra weary of body bags. The recently fought war in Kosovo resulted in zero casualties for NATO, a perfect illustration of the dilemma of democratic states and governments amidst the non-democratic, more war-prone countries. In the richer and democratic European nations, where the immigration ratio is much lower than the United States, the demographic composition within a few decennia will be such that a growing elderly population will not be prepared to sacrifice their youth to political-military causes. This will be expressed in the countries' foreign policies. Meanwhile, however, the difference between males and females remains, and this leads Fukuyama to a reconfirmation of his earlier views: "Liberal democracy and market economies work well because, unlike socialism, radical feminism, and other utopian schemes, they do not try to change human nature. Rather, they accept biologically grounded nature as given and seek to constrain it through institutions, laws, and norms" (40).

This is quite another type of evolutionary world politics than that of the EWP project. However, the tendencies of both do not differ very much, and I would like to assume that both types will integrate very well. Such a synthesis would be a genuine change of paradigm—ideally prepared for accommodating the new results from the life sciences that will certainly marginalize the social sciences that continue to believe that reality is postmodernly socially constructed. To end this section, the concept of "generation" in the EWP project is reviewed, again from a biological-evolutionary perspective.

Generation

In the EWP project generations play a central role. The generation is the "basic beat" in the cyclical theory of world politics and Modelski's conception of it is a good summary of the possibilities and limits of linking the biological and social evolutionary processes. "In evolutionary terms, the generational process is the closest link there is between biology and society, between biological and social evolution" (Modelski 1998a: 41). It is biological because it is the process of replacement/ succession of the older generation, reproduction for short. In the combination of heritable traits the adaptive quality of sexual reproduction is situated, because individuals with (slightly) different traits than those of each of the parent individuals may be better adapted to environmental conditions that may have possibly changed—or worse, their adaptation may just be the essence of natural selection. Thus, biological evolutionary theory without generations does not work.

Modelski adds that the generational cycle is also an important social and learning process in which one generation transmits, or fails to do so, its accumulated heritage to the next generation. However, the individuals of the new generation acquire their personalities in a learning process during the first twenty to thirty years, and the major events of the period will exert influence on that personality growth. So much so, that what distinguishes one "generation" from another is the more or less common historical experience leading to "common persona and character" (45). "Overall, the generational learning process might be viewed as supplying the raw material or the soil in which new institutional developments take root; it is the generator of variety in social evolution every 20–30 years or so" (ibid.).[13]

This is an intriguing conception that incorporates both a serious biological approach and a marginalization of it. From the top-down perspective this is enough, but from the bottom-up it gives the impression that the innovative quality of evolutionary thinking resides in *social* evolution.[14] It is precisely this SSSM thinking (learning and culture are sufficient to explain things cultural) that blocks the application of modern biobehavioral insights. The adaptionist program, that also starts with the individual, postulates evolutionary constraints that lead to recurring behavioral patterns (male dominance, sex roles, in-group/out-group differentiation, to name only these) that are of underestimated importance in standard social science. For example, even if Modelski's projection that democracy will have diffused in less than a century from now on to about 90 percent of the world's population (44), this will not have changed human nature itself, as it most probably has not been changed significantly since the start of sedentary civilization in the Fertile Cresent ten thousand years ago. It would be a serious misunderstanding to conclude that factors as constant as human nature for that reason do not help to explain long-term historic trends. On the contrary, they should form the basis of any behavioral theory without which the rest is constructed *in vacuo*. Modelski's accentuation of the generational learning process neglects, perhaps ignores, the thin line to biological evolution he himself has so correctly laid out. Although it is even possible to pose fundamental questions about "learning" and "culture," that would, however, ask too much of the social scientists who have been so trained in disregarding the relevance of biology in their disciplines.[15]

Now that I have indicated the difficulties that the EWP project faces in the eyes of a biopolitically interested colleague of IR theory, I should immediately add that these difficulties can absolutely be taken as very fruitful starting points for a matching operation. I would summarize my evaluation of the EWP project as motivated by SSSM with an open eye for "evolution," that the program stays at the safe side of the line between the "new biology," to use Fukuyama's phrase. Classic social science has, I think, much to do with the prejudice against using biology more than minimally in the social sciences. Although this is partly a hard-core ideological issue (for the opponents), and so difficult a matter for nuanced debate or reflection, I nevertheless will discuss some of the objections frequently raised.

IMAGINED AND REAL RISKS OF INTRODUCING BIOLOGY
IN THE SOCIAL SCIENCES

Both Modelski and Fukuyama, like many other social scientists who are receptive to evolutionary thinking, dissociate themselves from sociobiology. Fukuyama distinguishes between deterministic sociobiology on the one hand and the neo-Darwinism of evolutionary psychology and anthropology on the other. This is not the place to discuss the hard-boiled misconceptions of determinism ascribed to sociobiology, but suffice it to say that this is more the product of the reputation that political opponents successfully attached to sociobiology in the 1970s and 1980s (see Segerstrale 1998 for an interesting sociology-of-science account of this process). Indeed, sociobiology as a concept has become disreputable by this process of out-grouping, but it is also correct—and in the end much more important— that the basis of sociobiology (and ethology) survived under the new labels of evolutionary psychology and anthropology. Even if the leaders of evolutionary psychology do their best to dissociate themselves from sociobiology, they do so by incorporating not rejecting sociobiology. Indeed how could they do anything else?

Whether one calls it sociobiology or evolutionary psychology, the biological-evolutionary (biofunctionalist, adaptionist) approach is the essence, which is flourishing indeed, as discussed earlier. However, the objection of determinism should be faced and addressed. Determinism can be seen from two angles: One labels "determinist" as any theory that argues on the basis of genetic predispositions that make some behavioral outcomes more frequent and persistent than others, even if these outcomes are politically less desirable. The other is the "biology is destiny" idea, which, when applied to sex, race, or intelligence, leads to the conclusion that because this is "nature," it should not be changed. The first kind of determinism is "name-calling," that is, not based on serious knowledge of evolutionary biology. Name-calling exemplifies a type of political correctness that is counterproductive and which deserves to be disregarded by anyone who is seriously interested in fundamental behavioral theory.[16] If the EWP project were to try to connect with evolutionary psychology, it might be accused of being biologically deterministic, but this would be a self-defeating, uninformed critique.

The second type of determinism has a sadly well-documented history, of which certain justifications of ethnocentrism and white racism still are very active. Although no serious biobehavioral scientist will want to see himself as a white supremacist (or a black supremacist), it cannot be denied that there are shady areas that attract people with more or less hidden agendas. There is no guarantee against abuse of biological argumentation in political issues, but one safe line would be to avoid the natural fallacy that trespasses the logical line between what is and what ought to be.[17] It goes without saying that the number of people who demonstrably mobilize scientific arguments for racist purposes is very small in the scientific forum itself. It would be sincerely dishonest to disrepute a whole field on the basis of activities of these few; they themselves are constantly under fire within the scientific community. Although they do exist, a more serious problem is the interference of complete outsiders—up to and including intellectually disturbed extremists—selectively blowing conclusions out of context for political purposes. This is something to be aware of and deserves to be fought if they expound theories that extend beyond the limits of decency.[18] It would be absurd, however, to suppose that the biobehavioral project is *a priori* suspect; in fact all theories run the risk of a certain political (ab)usefulness.

To conclude this short exposition on using biology in the social sciences, I would like to state that any knowledge, or political ideology and religious belief as well, can be abused beyond the original aims. However, the substantial self-critical mass in the highly competitive scientific forum is the best guard against abuse, although it is no guarantee. To leave evolutionary biology out of the EWP project for fear of political damage would in the end be self-defeating. The SSSM will increasingly have to give way to a biological-evolutionary informed social science, is my expectation. It may take a couple of decennia, but evolutionary psychology shows the future (not to speak of the potential of biosciences and technology). Of course, the macro-social sciences will follow much later, but, as biopolitics demonstrates, there are already pockets of experience and experiments.[19] The EWP project would fit in very well.

INSTEAD OF CONCLUSIONS

As should be clear by now, it would be sensible to start with inserting a biobehavioral theory of politics, and connect this to the structural dimension of EWP. This requires giving up any prejudice against a meanwhile outdated notion of biological determinism as ascribed to sociobiology, but surrounding all biological approaches of human behavior, and accepting that the SSSM's basic assumption—to know that human social organization is relatively uninfluenced by human biology and evolutionary history—is not an adequate starting point. Steve Sanderson (1998: 18ff., here very much condensed) provides the ideal synthetic underground or basis for the EWP project:

1. Theories of social life must take into consideration the basic features of human nature that are the products of human evolution (among other things behavioral predispositions).
2. The resources that humans struggle for, which allow them to survive and prosper, are in short supply. This struggle is inevitable and unceasing, and humans give overwhelming priority to their own selfish interests and to those of their (close) kin.

Human beings' most important interests and concerns are reproductive, economic, and political. Political life is primarily a matter of using resources to promote reproductive success (without conscious recognition of these motives). The individual pursuit of interests—the core of social life, according to Sanderson—leads to both highly cooperative and highly conflictive social arrangements. Thereupon, people are unequally endowed to compete in the social struggle, and as a result social domination and subordination often appears as basic features of social life.

NOTES

1. A second and not less important reason is that this area is significant from a theoretical perspective because "it runs directly counter to the dominant disciplinary paradigm which sees behavior as stemming from nurture, not 'nature'" (Somit and Peterson 1998: 561–62). The biopolitical position is that the dichotomy is misleading.
2. *The Economist*, June 26, 1999: 110. See Colby (1996) and Fukuyama (1998) for further elaboration.
3. For example, "The Domestic Sources of Regional Regimes: The Evolution of Nuclear Ambiguity in the Middle East," by E. Solingen in *International Studies Quarterly* 1994 and a book edited by R. L. Rothstein, *The Evolution of Theory in International Relations* (Columbia: University of South Carolina Press, 1991).
4. Kinematics: branch of dynamics that deals with aspects of motion (as acceleration and velocity) apart from considerations of mass and force (Websters' *Third New International Dictionary*, 1986).
5. Here we see an important nuance in what is sometimes called Darwinian social science: Those coming from human sociobiology, human behavioral ecology and evolutionary biological anthropology are said to construct a psychologically agnostic science of human behavior based on the hypothesis that human beings are reproduction (or inclusive fitness) maximizers. The deep structure of human affairs, in Symons' representation, flows from reproduction only; hence "adaptedness. " Others add psychology, that is characteristically human (which equals species specific), to Darwinism, in casu the assumption that the brain/mind has many functions and in fact constitute "human nature. " Human nature as an adaptation is not teleological, but refers to something produced in the past by natural selection: the environment of evolutionary adaptation (EEA). See also the next section.
6. Necessarily, this must be treated in a condensed form, leaning on Barkow et al.'s (1992) important volume and Falger (1997).
7. In the discussion about whether natural selection is strictly individual or also group selectionist in character, Barkow follows the usual individual selectionist path, although he admits that a group selectionist might argue that stratification may have been directly selected (Barkow 1992: 636n).
8. Language, religion, skin color, ethnicity, social class, political ideology, and so forth, can all be sufficient to differentiate between "us' and "them. " This section benefited from Thienpont (1999), but of course there is a large quantity of relevant literature. From a biobehavioral point of view, Reynolds et al. (1987) and Shaw and Wong (1989) are particularly relevant.
9. To suppress false conclusions, this position has no normative implications. If something happens to be true or most likely true, no moral statement is implied. In biobehavioral studies the naturalistic fallacy should be kept at a safe distance.
10. In the early nineties, Fukuyama wrote typically about "Man, " not "humans. " The

book in all its erudition did not indicate that women were also subject to Fukuyama's Hegelian/Nietzchean fight for *thymos* or recognition. The book's view of Man is indeed a classic androcentric view of men in action.

11. Fukuyama (1998: 33) continues "Where the new biology parts company with feminism is the causal explanation it gives for this difference in sex roles. The ongoing revolution in the life sciences has almost totally escapted the notice of much of the social sciences and humanities. . . . "

12. Here we meet a problem: voting in democratic countries everywhere tends to decrease steadily. Only in countries that make it an obligation to show up at the polling station (that is still not equal to the obligation to take a vote), this pattern does not express itself. But should democracies force people to the ballot-box? A side-effect is that right extremism has developed into a considerable political factor, as Belgian elections have clearly shown. In European elections, those for the European parliament score worst in terms of turnout, even if the significance of "Europe" in daily life has increased enormously. Thus Fukuyama's thesis is a half-way house: with democracy itself firmly established, new fundamental problems arise.

13. In the EWP project the central focus is on these institutional developments, so it is not directed to individual development but to economic, political, social, and cultural processes. See Modelski (1998a) for his reaction to an example of the biobehavioral approach.

14. In his 1998b article, Modelski (1998b: 44) criticizes the work of two other social scientists working with "generation" for only being tentative in relation to "deeper levels of explanation, such as evolutionary theory. "

15. Under the heading of "The Twilight of Learning as a Social Science Explanation," Tooby and Cosmides (1992: 122–23) draw an interesting analogy and make a prediction that deserves to be quoted in full:

> Of course, as most cognitive scientists know (and all should), "learning"—like "culture," "rationality," and "intelligence"—is not an explanation for anything, but rather a phenomenon that itself requires explanation. In fact, the concept of learning has, for the social sciences, served the same function that the concept of "protoplasm" did for so long in biology. For decades, biologists could see that living things that did not form inside the nonliving (growth, the manufacture of complex chemicals, the assembly of useful structures, tissue differentiation, energy production, and so on). They had no idea what causal sequences brought these useful results about. They reified this unknown functionality, imagining it to be a real substance, and called it "protplasm," believing it to be the stuff of which life was made. It was a name given to a mystery, which was then used as an explanation for the functional results that remained in genuine need of explanation. Of course, the concept of protoplasm eventually disappeared when molecular biologists began to determine the actual causal sequences by which the functional business of life was transacted. Protoplasm turned out to be a heterogeneous collection of incredibly intricate functionally organized structures and processes—a set of evolved adaptations, in the form of microscopic molecular machinery such as mitochondria, choroplasts, the Krebs cycle, DNA transcription, RNA translation, and so on.
>
> Similarly, human minds perform a host of singularly useful things, by which they coordinate themselves with things in the world: They acquire skill in the local community's language; upon exposure to events they change behavior in impressively functional ways; they reconstruct in themselves knowledge derived from others; they adopt the practices of others around them; and so forth. Again, psychologists did not know what causal sequences brought these useful results about. They reified this unknown functionality, imagining it to be a unitary process, and called it "learning." "Learning" is a name given to the unknown agent imagined to cause a large and heterogeneous set of functional outcomes. This name was (and is) then used as an explanation for results that remained in genuine need of explanation. We expect that the concept of learning will

eventually disappear as cognitive psychologists and other researchers make progress in determining the actual causal sequences by which the functional business of the mind is transacted. Under closer inspection, "learning" is turning out to be a diverse set of processes caused by a series of incredibly intricate, functionally organized cognitive adaptations, implemented in neurobiological machinery. . . . The replacement of the concept of protoplasm with a real understanding of the vast, hidden, underlying worlds of molecular causality has transformed our understanding of the world in completely unexpected ways, and we can only anticipate that the same will happen when "learning" is replaced with knowledge."

If this view is taken to its utmost consequence, the conception of "social evolution" also has to be modernized. But since the adaptionist program has not moved that far yet, it would be improper to criticize the EWP project, in which social evolution is the very essence, beforehand.

16. George Modelski certainly falls into the category of seriously interested people.
17. See Falger (1995) for an example of the analysis of biological argumentation on a politically very sensitive issue.
18. Principal defenders of the First Amendment will argue that this is political correctness. As European, however, I cannot respect the "free speech route" to racism. Once or twice a year a discussion in the electronic mail list of the Human Behavior and Evolution Society are ruined by two or three extremists popping up from nowhere in the name of free speech. However, this problem is not confined to biobehavioral lists.
19. It is worth visiting the following websites: Association for Politics and the Life Sciences <www.lssu.edu/apls>, Human Behavior and Evolution Society, and European Sociobiological Society <http://jurix.rechten.rug.nl/rth/ess.ess.htm>.

REFERENCES

Alexander, R. D. 1979. *Darwinism and human affairs*. London: Pitman.
Barkow, J. H. 1992. Beneath New Culture Is Old Psychology: Gossip and Social Stratification. In J. H. Barkow, L. Cosmides, and J. Tooby, eds. *The adapted mind: Evolutionary psychology and the generation of culture*, 627–37. New York: Oxford University Press.
Barkow, J. H., L. Cosmides, and J. Tooby, eds. 1992. *The adapted mind: Evolutionary psychology and the generation of culture*. New York: Oxford University Press.
Betzig, L. L. 1986. *Despotism and differential reproduction: A darwinian view of history*. New York: Aldine De Gruyter.
Boyd, and Richerson. 1985. *Culture and the evolutionary process*. Chicago: University of Chicago Press.
———, ed. 1997. *Human nature: A critical reader*. New York: Oxford University Press.
Colby, C. 1996. Introduction to Evolutionary Biology. <Http: //fp.bio.utk.edu/darwin/default.html.>
Cosmides, L. and J. Tooby 1992. The Psychological Foundations of Culture. In J. H. Barkow, L. Cosmides, and J. Tooby, eds. *The adapted mind: Evolutionary psychology and the generation of culture*. New York: Oxford University Press.
de Waal, F. B. M. 1982. *Chimpanzee politics: Power and sex among apes*. London: Jonathan Cape.
Falger, V. S. E. 1995. Biology as a Scientific Argument in Political Debates: A European Illustration. *Social Science Information* 43: 321–32.
———. 1997. Human Nature in Modern IR. Part I: Theoretical Backgrounds. *Research in Biopolitics* 5: 155–75.
Fukuyama, F. 1998. Women and the Evolution of World Politics. *Foreign Affairs* 77: 24–40.

Futuyama, D. J. 1997. *Evolutionary biology.* Sunderland, Mass.: Sinauer.

Modelski, G. 1996. Evolutionary Paradigm for Global Politics. *International Studies Quarterly* 40: 321–42.

———. 1997a. What is Evolutionary Politics? The Evolutionary World Politics Home Page, <http://weber.u.washington.edu/~modelski/WCITI2.html>

———. 1997b. Cities of the Ancient World: An Inventory (–3500 to –1200). The Evolutionary World Politics Home Page <http://weber.u.washington.edu/~modelski/WCITI2.html.>

———. 1998a. Generations and Global Change. *Technological Forecasting and Social Change* 59: 39–45.

———. 1998b. Book Review of *The origin of war: The evolution of a male-coalitional reproductive strategy* by J. M. G. Van der Dennen. *Politics and the Life Sciences* 17: 88–90.

Modelski, G. and K. Poznanski 1996. Evolutionary Paradigms in the Social Sciences. *International Studies Quarterly* 40: 315–19.

Pfeiffer, Joh. 1985 [1969]. *The emergence of humankind,* 4th ed. New York: Harper and Row.

Pringle, J. W. S. 1951. On the Parallel Between Evolution and Learning. *Behavior* 3: 174–214.

Reynolds, V., V. S. E. Falger, and I. Vine, eds. 1987. *The sociobiology of ethnocentrism: Evolutionary dimensions of xenophobia, discrimination, racism and nationalism.* London: Croom Helm.

Sanderson, S. 1998. Synthetic Materialism: An Integrated Theory of Human Society. Paper presented at the annual meeting of the American Sociological Association, San Francisco, August 21–25.

Segerstrale, U. 1998. Truth and Consequences in the Sociobiology Debate and Beyond. *Research in Biopolitics* 6: 249–73.

Shaw, R. P. and Y. Wong 1989. *Genetic seeds of warfare: Evolution, nationalism and patriotism.* Boston, Mass.: Unwin Hyman.

Somit, A. and S. A. Peterson 1998. Review Article: Biopolitics after Three Decades—A Balance Sheet. *British Journal of Political Science* 28: 559–71.

Symons, D. 1992. On the Use and Misuse of Darwinism in the Study of Human Behavior. In J. H. Barkow, L. Cosmides, and J. Tooby, eds. *The adapted mind: Evolutionary psychology and the generation of culture.* New York: Oxford University Press.

Thienpont, K. 1999. *In-group/out-group Gedrag in Evolutiebiologisch Perspectief.* Brussels: CBGS Document.

Tickner, J. A. 1991. Hans Morgenthau's Principles of Political Realism: A Feminist Reformulation. In R. Grant and K. Newland, eds. *Gender and International Relations*, 27–40. Milton Keynes, U.K.: Open University Press.

Tinbergen, N. 1963. On Aims and Methods of Ethology. *Zeitschrift fur Tierpsychologie* 20: 410–33.

Tooby, J. and L. Cosmides 1990. On the Universality of Human Nature and the Uniqueness of the Individual: The Role of Genetics and Adaptation. *Journal of Personality* 58: 17–67.

Trivers, R. L. 1985. *Social evolution.* Menlo Park, Calif.: Benjamin/Cummings.

Van der Dennen, J. M. G. 1995. *The origin of war: The Evolution of a male-coalitional reproductive strategy.* Groningen, Nth.: Origin Press.

Williams, G. C. 1996. *Plan and purpose in nature.* London: Weidenfeld and Nicolson.

chapter 3

Obstacles to an Evolutionary Global Politics Research Program

David P. Rapkin

At first glance, the central concepts of evolutionary biological theory seem to provide quick purchase on many issues of global politics, especially those involving change. Over long historical time, increased complexity and differentiation have clearly been displayed by territorial states and other types of sociopolitical organizations, their characteristic strategies and practices, the multilateral institutions they have formed, as well as the larger global political economy that they comprise. Technological development, human imagination, and routine trial-and-error processes have thrown forth a stream of innovations (variation) as material for selection, and less "fit" organizational forms and practices—feudal principalities, large territorial empires, socialism—appear to have been "selected out." Questions of directionality, and especially progress, raise more correspondences of substance, method, and value.

Fuller consideration of how evolutionary theory might be applied to the subject matter of global politics, while not necessarily diminishing its promise, does reveal a series of linked problems and issues that must be sorted out if that promise is to be realized. These include (1) specification of the units, or populations of units, that are subject to evolutionary processes; (2) the relationship of these units to the larger environment within which they operate; (3) how this environment serves as a selection mechanism, and the relationship of this mechanism to other forms of adaptation, viz., social learning or "directed" adaptation, and; 4) questions of directionality, that is, is the evolution of global politics cumulative in the sense of leading to *more* (or less) of something, or, in stronger form, does it lead to something that we might agree is *better* in some normative sense than what preceded it? The purpose of this brief essay is to spell out these issues and why they are of critical importance if evolutionary theory is to provide the foundation of an alternative research program for understanding global politics.

UNITS/POPULATION

Just what is it that undergoes evolutionary processes? What kinds of units (or more properly, which populations of units) generate variations, are subject to selection pressures, adapt or fail to adapt, and demonstrate change that can be made more intelligible by an evolutionary perspective? What is the relationship between the evolution of different kinds of units, for example, states, nations, non-governmental organizations (NGOs), or firms? These are fundamental issues on which some measure of consensus will eventually be needed if disparate evolutionary approaches are to coalesce into a coherent research program. The most common approach focuses on *states*, viewing them as having evolved, first supplanting other, smaller-scale forms of political organization and since tending to become larger, ever more complex and functionally differentiated, and more widely diffused.[1] Though states are often referred to as an undifferentiated, generic category, we should also consider different types of *roles* that states play—leaders, followers and challengers, patrons and clients, colonizer and colonized, trading states, neutral states, and occupiers of other niches in the global political system—perhaps as a kind of analogue to different species.

From another perspective, it is not states so much as state *practices*, more specifically *strategies, policies,* or *behaviors* (for example, balancing, deterrence, or multilateralism), that are selected and that hence comprise the relevant population (Modelski 1996). An alternative evolutionary focus is on *ideas, norms,* or *values* that pertain either to states' internal organization or to their external relations (for example, sovereignty, self-determination, human rights, and democracy), and on the *cognitive processes* by which ideas are popularized, diffused, and implemented (see, Florini 1996).

An evolutionary framework can also be applied to the development of a number of *nonstate actors* relevant to global politics, including nations, ethnic and racial groups; intergovernmental organizations (IGOs) of different functions and scope; NGOs of various sorts; and, not least, firms, industries, and sectors of the economy, as well as entire national economies.[2] And we have not yet considered the evolution of either the *interstate political system*; or, more expansively, the *global political economy*, encompassing non state as well as state actors; or geographically or functionally defined subsystems of this larger global whole.

This quick, nonexhaustive survey suggests that the range of actors or units that may be examined fruitfully from an evolutionary standpoint is quite wide. Indeed, the available alternatives seem to parallel closely the more traditional methodological problem of choice among levels of analysis. So, it is reasonable to ask, what is the problem? Just as scholars ply their trade at one or another level of analysis with little or no concern for what is being done at other levels, why should not proponents of evolutionary approaches simply proceed with whatever they are doing without regard for the overall coherence of their combined efforts? It is certainly plausible that many or all of the populations (of states, strategies, norms, and so forth) change according to evolutionary logic(s). And, absent a clear-cut, compelling choice, say that provided by an exemplary research accomplishment, this kind of diversity is normal and healthy at the early stages in the development of a research program. It may in fact (as suggested by evolutionary epistemology) lead to the emergence of a clear best choice or to a solution that imposes some order on the array of different kinds of units involved, for example, a theory of how the various populations coevolve, or how evolutionary processes change as we move from micro- to macro-levels of social aggregation.[3]

There is no need to push prematurely for such a solution, but without one it will eventually become difficult for research findings to cumulate and thus for evolutionary approaches to gain wider acceptance. To understand why it will be necessary sooner or later to impose some order on the welter of units that are experiencing evolutionary change, we need to extend this discussion of units to include the environment within which those units exist.

UNITS AND ENVIRONMENT

If the first task is to specify those populations undergoing evolutionary change, the second is to develop a comprehensive framework for understanding the relationships among like and different types of (co)evolving units. This is particularly important because the various populations form the environment both for themselves (for example, one state's security environment is comprised primarily of other states) and for other populations (for example, states constitute an important element in the environment of firms). These circumstances are not so different from those obtained in natural selection, where an organism's environment includes members of the same species, as well as other species, insofar as that organism must compete with these others for scarce food supplies. Other species are also part of this environment in the sense that they themselves may be predators or prey.

Crucial differences arise when applying these ideas to the evolution of global politics. Here too there is a natural, or physical, environment—consisting of such things as territory, topographical features (mountain ranges or insularity, and the security they provide), resources and arable land, gravity—and this environment is exogenous to the social units that exist within it.[4] But the environment, more accurately, multiple environments, of global politics also contain various human-made elements, for instance, states, firms, norms, IGOs, and NGOs. This environment cannot be exogenous to these units in that it is not independent of, or logically or temporally prior, to them. Again, lack of exogeneity in this sense does not amount to a radical departure from the natural-selection model. There is, however, another, much more problematic way in which the environments of global politics are not exogenous to the units they contain: More powerful units are able to shape the environment so as to alter the constraints and opportunities it poses for themselves and for other units. For example, hegemonic states exercise structural (or meta-) power to set the agenda of global issues, impose ordering principles, promote certain norms and types of collective action, and, more generally, to determine the "rules of the game" for other states and for other types of social units.

Since the central explanatory insight of the theory of natural selection (as developed in connection to biological evolution) is that the environment induces adaptations, logical problems arise immediately when applying this theory to the evolution of global politics, wherein members of the populations that are supposed to be adapting are instead influencing their environment in ways that shape consequentially other members' prospects for adaptation. Moreover, we now have to contend with the fact that the evolutionary course of global politics is in significant part the result of purposive action rather than the kind of blind, mechanistic selection among random variations that is the defining feature of Darwinian evolution. These divergences lead directly to the next problem facing the nascent evolutionary research program: how to theorize the operation of selection mechanisms and adaptive processes.

SELECTION AND ADAPTATION

The Darwinian argument rests squarely on selection pressures placed on populations by their environment. Those randomly generated mutations that improve the fitness of the organism in question are rewarded, via selection, with enhanced prospects for reproduction. In this fashion, heredity ensures that the trait so selected will gradually become more prevalent over successive generations, at the expense of course of those lacking the trait. This form of adaptation to selection pressures exerted by the environment is *competitive* because it pits species and organisms against the other in a struggle for survival.

Some aspects of global politics, such as military or economic competition, can be usefully conceptualized in these terms, for example, the introduction of new military technologies induces states to adapt accordingly, either by deploying like weapons or by undertaking other military or diplomatic countermeasures. Possibly, too, new products or production processes may render old ways, and the firms and national economies that cling to them, obsolete. This analogy to Darwinian-style, competitive-selection environments holds for some purposes, but it breaks down when we consider the role played by learning, purposive behavior and, more generally, *directed adaptation* to environmental pressures. Selection and adaptation are fundamentally different processes if social actors are able to observe changes in their environment, consciously formulate and implement strategies to adapt to them, assess the effectiveness of their actions, and then adjust accordingly.[5] The motor force of evolution shifts from outside to inside the unit, from environmental selection operating on variation to intentional responses to environmental change. Or in Allen's (1988:109) formulation, "The fulcrum of evolution passes from 'genetics' to 'perception-judgment-behavior'."

Although Lamarckian-directed adaptation has been unequivocally falsified as a theory of biological evolution, it is apparent that some version of it must be included in an evolutionary research program for global politics. Here, *endogenous* selection takes place by a process of trial-and-error among technical, institutional, and ideational innovations, all of which are human-made and some of which are devised specifically to respond to environmental pressures. Most innovations are simply efforts to adapt with no intent to alter the environment. But, as pointed out in the previous section, other innovations, especially by more powerful actors, represent attempts to modify the environment in such ways as to shape the selection pressures faced by others. With a few exceptions, then, we are a considerable distance from the exogenous, competitive selection environment borrowed from the theory of biological evolution, as attractive as its parsimony and status as scientific exemplar might be. And since such a Darwinian mechanism can only partially account for the evolution of global politics, it must be supplemented with explicit consideration of learning and directed adaptation. But, as Kahler (1999: 193) points out, such an amalgam is inherently problematic: "Evolutionary models are capable of conceding many different readings of the existence of rational and foresighted behavior at the individual or institutional level; they cannot assign that behavior overwhelming explanatory weight, however, or the importance of the selection environment in creating unanticipated outcomes would recede sharply."

How then to reconcile the two kinds of selection and adaptation? When and under what circumstances is one operative and not the other? Or both? Can exogenous selection mechanisms be circumvented by means of endogenously generated innovations? Do different units within the same population, say strategies implemented by weak states and firms as contrasted with those of their stronger counterparts, face different selection mechanisms (mirroring the difference between price-takers and price-makers)? These questions are not insoluble, but neither are the answers self-evident. In light of the centrality of selection and adaptation in evolutionary theory, some answers will have to be forthcoming if assorted evolutionary approaches are to coalesce into an evolutionary global politics research program.

DIRECTIONALITY

If we consider evolutionary change as stemming from a long, ongoing sequence of selections and adaptations, we are left with the question of whether it should be required that any evolutionary theory of global politics specify the direction(s) in which this change is headed. Stated this way, it is not necessary for the evolutionary process to move closer to some idealized vision of order, justice, or any other desired end state, but rather simply that evolutionary change be cumulative. What then is expected to cumulate? One property that shows directionality is the stock of innovations available for selection, that is, the source of variation, which grows ever larger. As Deudney (1997: 309) puts it, "History has direction simply because there is a cumulative increase in scientific knowledge and technological capability." Indeed, this stock of *knowledge* (including technology and information) serves as the principal repository of variation that supplies other social evolutionary processes.

For example, another widely agreed upon, directional process that depends upon the stock of knowledge is the *complexity* of social and political organization: "Over the past 13,000 years the predominant trend in human society has been the replacement of smaller, less complex units by larger, more complex ones" (Diamond 1997: 281). The stock of *wealth* and the means of producing it likewise derive directly from the stock of scientific knowledge and technological know-how, as does the lethality of the *means of destruction*. Some other likely evolutionary processes that exhibit directionality and bear on global politics include functional differentiation, interconnectedness, institutional density, democratization, and observance of human rights.

These last two possibilities are contested concepts, in large part because they are fraught with normativity. As such, they raise the question of progress, or ". . . evolution in a direction that satisfies certain criteria of value" (Modelski 1996: 325). While directionality is essential to an evolutionary research program, the more controversial notion of progress arguably is not. Evolutionary researchers of course may privately attach whatever value they like to democratization, human rights, and associated normative concepts. The exigencies of building a research program, however, suggest that until the directionality of these phenomena is empirically sorted out questions of value should be set aside. Otherwise, the nascent research program may become a premature victim of avoidable normative controversy. Eventually, though, questions of progress, and thus also of value, will have to be addressed.

CONCLUSION

The fact that a large body of well-established evolutionary theory exists in the biological sciences and other fields both helps and hinders formation of an evolutionary global politics research program. It helps by providing a theoretical apparatus that can be borrowed from and adapted to the task at hand. But it also hinders by creating predispositions and expectations that cannot be met by applying this theoretical apparatus to the quite different realm of global politics, in particular, expectations concerning how units relate to their environment or how selection and adaptation take place. Thus, recognizing that there are large areas of divergence, Modelski and Poznanski (1996: 316) prudently delimit the relationship between biological and social evolution to one of analogy.

This essay has set forth a series of linked issues—mostly methodological, theoretical, and empirical, but some with normative implications—in order to explore where the broad analogy holds and where it does not. At those points where the analogy breaks down, I have tried to identify the kinds of questions that will need to be resolved in some fashion if an evolutionary research program is to emerge, win over a significant number of adherents, and challenge the currently prevailing research programs in the study of global politics.

What then might an evolutionary research program for the study of global politics look like? In his original exposition of the elements of a research program, Lakatos (1970) distinguishes between what he terms its *negative* and *positive heuristics*. The negative heuristic is a research program's "hard inner core," which consists of beliefs, primitive statements, and theoretical postulates that the program's practitioners designate, by methodological fiat, as immune from test and refutation. It is surrounded by a positive heuristic that forms a protective belt and that is subject to test, falsification, and adjustment. The negative heuristic is subject to challenge only if the overall research program fails to produce progressively more empirical content and intermittently is able to corroborate empirically some of this content. The essay concludes by sketching briefly and tentatively how the various ideas discussed earlier might be fit into the categories of negative and positive heuristics.

The negative heuristic, shielded from attempts at falsification, should contain basic propositions that:

1. change in global politics is fundamentally an evolutionary process;
2. the core of social evolution is the cumulated stock of knowledge, which serves as the source of variation for all social evolutionary processes;
3. the evolution of different populations relevant to global politics evolve interdependently, i.e., they coevolve, both with each other and with their environment;
4. selection and adaptation take place through both competitive, Darwinian mechanisms and Lamarckian directed learning.

Around this hard core is the positive heuristic, which consists of hypotheses concerning:

1. the evolution of various kinds of populations;
2. specification of how different units relate to the environments within which they exist;
3. how coevolution works;
4. how and when the two forms of selection/adaptation operate and the relationship between them;
5. how other evolutionary processes feed upon the variation (innovations) located in the stock of knowledge and information.

Various other substantively more specific hypotheses and models could also be part of this outer protective belt, subject to testing and flexible enough to accommodate adjustments in the face of anomalies and contrary evidence. I suggest this preliminary scheme as a kind of conjecture that hopefully will stimulate further thought and debate on the issues raised, and perhaps will help in some small, indirect way to organize future research on the evolution of global politics.

NOTES

1. Spruyt (1994), for example, examines how the state form of political organization (based on sovereignty and territorial exclusivity) was "selected" in the wake of European feudalism from among other non-territorial alternatives such as city-states and urban leagues. Kahler (1999:186–191) reviews the evolutionary literature on this question, i.e., the "fitness" of states, as well as that addressing their scale, which is to say, why the size of states increased (but not to the extent that they were superseded by empires) until the latter half of the twentieth century. In a slight variation on this state-as-unit emphasis, Gilpin (1996) argues that the basic unit of analysis in evolutionary models should be "national systems of political economy."

2. For examples of evolutionary models applied to firms, industries, and national economies see Nelson and Winter (1982); the selections in Dosi et al., eds. (1988), and Hodgson (1996).

3. For applications of the concept of coevolution, see Modelski (1996:339–40) and Modelski and Thompson (1996:136–41). Thompson (2000) presents a useful conceptual discussion.

4. I am overlooking here for the sake of brevity the growing capacity of humans to intervene in their natural environment. In Anderson's (1987:30) view, "*Homo sapiens* could be as accurately be called *Homo intervenor*, the tireless modifier of environments and manipulator of plant and animal life."

5. Hence, Anderson's (1987: Epilogue) notion of "participatory evolution."

REFERENCES

Allen, Peter M. 1988. "Evolution, Innovation and Economics," 95–119 in Giovanni Dosi, Christopher Freeman, Richard Nelson, Gerald Silverberg, and Luc Soete, eds. *Technical change and economic theory*. London: Pinter Publishers.

Anderson, Walter T. 1987. *To govern evolution: Further adventures of the political animal*. Boston: Harcourt Brace Jovanovich.

Deudney, Daniel (1997. "Geopolitics and Change," 91–123 in Michael W. Doyle and G. John Ikenberry, eds. *New thinking in international relations theory*. Boulder, Colo.: Westview Press.

Diamond, Jared (1997. *Guns, germs, and steel: The fates of human societies*. New York: W.W. Norton.

Dosi, Giovanni, Christopher Freeman, Richard Nelson, Gerald Silverberg, and Luc Soete, eds. 1988. *Technical change economic theory*. London: Pinter Publishers.

Florini, Ann. 1996. "The Evolution of International Norms." *International Studies Quarterly* 40, 3 (September): 363–89.

Gilpin, Robert. 1996. "Economic Evolution of National Systems." *International Studies Quarterly* 40, 3 (September): 411–31.

Hodgson, Geoffrey. 1996. "An Evolutionary Theory of Long-Term Economic Growth." *International Studies Quarterly* 40, 3 (September): 391–40.

Kahler, Miles. 1999. "Evolution, Choice, and International Change," 165–96 in David A. Lake and Robert Powell, eds. *Strategic choice and international relations*. Princeton, N.J.: Princeton University Press.

Lakatos, Imre. 1970. "Falsification and the Methodology of Scientific Research Programmes," 91–196 in Imre Lakatos and Alan Musgrave, eds. *Criticism and the growth of Knowledge.* New York: Cambridge University Press.

Modelski, George. 1996. "Evolutionary Paradigm for Global Politics." *International Studies Quarterly* 40, 3 (September): 321–42.

Modelski, George. and Kazimierz Poznanski. 1996. "Evolutionary Paradigms in the Social Sciences." *International Studies Quarterly* 40, 3 (September): 315–319.

Modelski, George. and William R. Thompson. 1996. *Leading sectors and world politics: The coevolution of global economics and politics.* Columbia: University of South Carolina Press.

Nelson, Richard R. and Sidney G. Winter. 1982. *An evolutionary theory of economic change.* Cambridge, Mass.: Harvard University Press.

Spruyt, Hendrik. 1994. *The sovereign state and its competitors.* Princeton, N.J.: Princeton University Press.

Thompson, William R. 2000. *The emergence of the global political economy.* London: Routledge.

part II

Bridges to
Other Perspectives

chapter 4

Evolutionary Tendencies
in Realist and Liberal IR Theory

Jennifer Sterling-Folker

INTRODUCTION

This chapter examines realist and liberal international relations (IR) theory from an evolutionary theoretical perspective.[1] It argues that evolutionary themes, concepts, and concerns inform each theory's assumptive frameworks and the research agendas pursued by its practitioners. There are several reasons why such an examination and conclusion are important. First, it could serve as a necessary corrective to the voguish tendency to lump realism and liberalism together merely as theories of rational choice. Ruggie is representative in this regard, arguing that the more popular variants of realism and liberalism—neorealism and neoliberal institutionalism—are "neo-utilitarian" theories that stipulate that "identities and interests of states are given, a priori and exogenously," and "both assume that states are rational actors maximizing their own expected utilities" (1998: 9).[2] The premise that realism, liberalism, and rationalism may simply be equated with one another is what has justified the development of an approach such as constructivism that is committed to sociological history instead. Realism has even been described as "a generic commitment to the assumption of rational state behavior" with little content variance to distinguish it from other IR theories (Legro and Moravscik 1999: 53).

These assertions, while popular, reflect considerable confusion over what it means to share a positivist epistemology versus agreement on theoretical substance (Smith 1996). As Jervis points out, rationalism and constructivism are styles of thought that "need to be filled with content in order to become theoretical statements, and much of their explanatory power must come from auxiliary assumptions about the identities of actors, their goals, and their beliefs" (1998: 975). He goes on to argue that because realism and liberalism provide the necessary auxiliary assumptions, "rationalism then should not be contrasted with liberalism or realism" because it "needs theories like these to do any explanatory work" (1998: 976; see also Little 1996, 83–84). Indeed the relationship among realism, liberalism, and rationalism threatens to obscure the substantive differences that continue to exist between these two theoretical paradigms. Realism and liberalism provide not only the necessary auxiliary assumptions in order for a rational-choice approach to work, they also provide *alternative* and *contrasting* auxiliary assumptions that produce very different explanations as a result. The fact that practitioners of either theory may adopt a common epistemology does not also make the substance of their auxiliary assumptions or the theoretical frameworks within which they operate similar.

In addition, the extent to which the substantive theoretical frameworks of either realism or liberalism rely upon or demand a rational choice assumption is questionable. It is just as common for evolutionary terms and concepts to be invoked when characterizing them. Realism is often described in evolutionary terms because of its reliance on a "survival of the fittest" imagery. Lebow (1994: 273) equates realism with Darwinism in his discussion of the post-Cold War order, because "like Darwin, Waltz assumes that the environment (international structure in the language of neorealism) rewards certain adaptations in structure and behavior and punishes others" (see also Lapid and Kratochwil 1996: 213–14; Thayer 2000). In a similar vein, Modelski and Poznanski (1996: 319) assert that "in its emphasis on competition and self-help, neorealism shows a close affinity for social Darwinism (though not Darwinism itself) which marked social thought at the turn of the twentieth century."[3] And at least one of the reasons why realism may be described in these terms is because the connection between rationalism and realism is by no means obvious. While Elman (1996: 43–44) points out that "the dominant reading of neorealism is that it employs a rationality assumption, not an evolutionary selection mechanism," Kahler (1998: 923) also notes that realism's "relationship with rationalist theorizing has been uneasy, in both its classical, power-maximizing form and its neorealist and structural variants" (see also Schweller 1999).

The same may be said for liberalism that, like realism, has also frequently been described in evolutionary terms. Hasenclever, Mayer, and Rittberger (1997: 367) note, for example, that although Keohane (1984: 64) explicitly dismisses "a Darwinian type of explanation," at the same time he relies heavily upon the idea of "the evolution of norms and rules" in *After Hegemony*. This is consistent with Zacher and Matthew's (1995: 110, 117) characterization of liberalism as an "evolutionary perspective" that involves the belief "that international relations are evolving (or probably will evolve) gradually and irregularly along lines that will promote greater human freedom." Modelski and Poznanski (1996: 319) note that "in its search for sources of harmony in world organization" liberalism stands "close to those strands of evolutionary thought that take cooperation to be a basic organizing principle or survival strategy." These characterizations suggest that the ahistorical, atomistic quality of rational choice theorizing cannot be so pervasive within these two paradigms as is commonly alleged. If, as Modelski (1996: 327–28) argues, "rational choice is the study of decisions" while an evolutionary approach is "the study of long-range social processes," then the ability to successfully recast realism and liberalism as theories of global institutional evolution should underscore why the differentiation of explanations for global phenomenon *merely* on the basis of epistemology can actually obscure more than it reveals.

A second reason why it is valuable to examine realist and liberal evolutionary tendencies is because an interest in evolutionary world politics demands the delineation of theoretical parameters. IR scholars interested in such a subject are certainly not required to utilize realism or liberalism, but the development of new evolutionary approaches to IR will, at the very least, have to contend with realism and liberalism as alternative explanations for the evolution of human social practices on a global scale. One of the purposes of this study is to delineate the types of issues that *any* evolutionary approach to IR and global social practices must address, thereby providing a conceptual basis upon which to differentiate among alternatives.

A final reason why a comparison of realist and liberal evolutionary tendencies is an important undertaking is because it provides new ways of looking at old things. The introduction of an approach or perspective such as evolutionary world politics into IR theorizing can have considerable value if it can recast ongoing questions into new, interesting, and provocative ways. One of the ways in which a new approach may be particularly productive is if it can also highlight what differentiates both epistemology from theoretical substance and particular theoretical frameworks from one another. An evolutionary perspective has all of these capacities. Beyond positing only that organisms will adapt to their environment, an evolutionary approach says nothing about the nature of the auxiliary assumptions necessary to make the approach work as explanation. A host of building-block assumptions still must be specified, including the nature of the organisms involved, the nature of the environment and the organism's relationship to it, and how selection of characteristics would work within the given environment.

By examining the assumptions made by realism and liberalism regarding each of these elements, it is possible to recast them as alternative theories of world political institutional evolution that remain fundamentally and irreconcilably at odds over why and how political institutional adaptation occurs in the first place. Both are concerned with similar types of organisms, namely human institutions and collective practices as they relate to the allocation of resources. Both are concerned with multiple types of political organisms, whether it be "an individual, a cabinet, a legislature, a political party, a regime, a nation-state, an international organization, or a revolutionary movement" (Rosenau 1981, 3). Both are concerned with the "politics of adaptation," defined by Rosenau (1981: 2) as "the need for every political organism to keep fluctuations in its essential structures within acceptable limits." Both provide what an evolutionary biologist would call "just so stories" for why world politics looks the way it does. That is, they both provide speculative histories and prehistorical hunches for how we got to where we are today with regards to global politics.[4] Both also draw upon these stories to make predictions about what the future of world politics will look like. But because their assumptive building blocks are substantively and fundamentally different, the stories each theory tells about the evolution of global political institutions and social practices are very different as well.

There are many advantages to be gained by examining realism and liberalism from an evolutionary perspective as a result. Not only does such a recasting once again highlight what is essential and hence different about each of these paradigms, but it also allows us to recast old debates and questions into new and sometimes startling reconfigurations. That such a recasting is appropriate is the primary subject of this chapter. In the sections that follow I compare realism and liberalism to the development of evolutionary theory in its biological context and to one another in light of their evolutionary tendencies. Not only do obvious parallels exist between theories of evolutionary biology and theories of IR in the utilization of common concepts, themes, and connecting logics, but the philosophical disagreements that informed the development of evolutionary biology are replicated as well. The issue that continues to divide many evolutionary biologists, paleontologists, and sociobiologists is the extent to which biological insights apply to human beings, or whether the ability to construct their own social realities make human beings too unique for such applications.

Realism and liberalism parallel alternative evolutionary biological perspectives on the subject. Realism concurs with Darwinism that human beings are primarily shaped by their environment so that the institutions they create and nurture are affected by a "selection-by-competition" logic. Liberalism, on the other hand, concurs with Lamarckian perspectives that human beings are primarily shapers of their environments and the institutions they create are determined by a "selection-by-learning" logic. These alternative logics produce very different accounts for the process of global institutional adaptation. Hereto, realists parallel Darwinian perspectives on evolutionary gradualism and continuity, while liberals parallel paleontologists who argue for periods of discontinuity and "punctuated equilibrium." The final section of the chapter applies their alternative logics to the European Union (EU) in order to illustrate how both realism and liberalism have theoretically viable accounts of that institution, yet remain at fundamental odds over what it represents. Such an example also underscores why viewing realism and liberalism through a prism informed by evolutionary concepts and concerns may promote new insights and perspectives in the study of global institutional phenonemon.

Caveats and Standards

Before turning to this comparison, several caveats regarding the scope of this discussion and an explication of the standards used to assess evolutionary tendencies are required. This examination is by no means meant to exhaust the subject of evolution in IR theorizing. In fact practitioners of world-system history have long argued for a historical, evolutionary perspective that does not subscribe to the assumptive frameworks of either realism or liberalism.[5] This chapter focuses only on the two dominant paradigms of the field and contains some initial, tentative thoughts about how they rely upon or utilize evolutionary concepts and logic. In so doing they evoke themes and debates that have occurred in other evolutionary theoretical contexts as well.

Furthermore this examination is not meant to be the final or even exhaustive word on what is evolutionary about realism and liberalism per se. For some evolutionary concepts I assert an equivalency that is open to challenge and debate. The same may be said for my characterization of the theories and their differences with regard to global institutional evolution. In particular the realist evolutionary perspective delineated here may appear to be relatively unique given the orthodox association of rational choice and realism within the field. Yet the discussion is consistently informed by both realist and liberal texts, and I have attempted to focus on those core elements of each theory that even practitioners and critics who are committed to a rationalist interpretation should find familiar. In addition, the theories are neutrally juxtaposed so that the tendencies of *each* as evolutionary theories (albeit alternative theories) can be fully appreciated.[6] Thus the discussion touches upon some of the major themes and questions that must be addressed in any attempt to develop or employ evolutionary theory in the field of IR. In that context, it is meant to serve as a starting point of differentiation even for those scholars inclined to reject both paradigms as adequate for evolutionary IR theorizing.

In undertaking to map out comparatively the evolutionary tendencies in realist and liberal theory, one is also immediately confronted with the question of to what they should be compared. To assert that they have evolutionary tendencies implies that there exists a single theory of evolution to which they may be neatly contrasted. Yet many disciplines utilize the concept of evolution and it has different implications and meanings in each context. Bowler (1984: 8) notes that the term evolution "means no more than the belief that the existing structure of the world we live in has been formed by a long series of natural changes," but that, "as soon as we begin to unpack this basic statement, we realize that there are many different ways in which these changes can be imagined to have taken place."

One way to proceed is to establish the conceptual criteria that must inform any theory of evolution regardless of discipline. Along these lines, Modelski (1996: 323) cites R. C. Lewontin, who argued for a hierarchy of principles, including "change, order, direction, progress and perfectibility," and "evolutionary theories are distinguished by how many of these are successively included as essential." A problem that immediately arises with this approach, however, is that these concepts are not value-free within the context of IR theorizing. Many IR scholars automatically equate "change" and "order" with liberal theory because, as Buzan, Jones, and Little (1993: 27) point out, continuity and change already had specific connotations within the field. As a result there would be a tendency within the field to preclude realism as theoretically adequate from the start, despite the fact that upon closer inspection realism does offer a deductively viable explanation for historical change in global political institutions.

There is, in addition, a danger that listed principles will be treated as if they constituted an ideal model to which an evolutionary theory must aspire, rather than merely as a list of those issues with which evolutionary theories have been most often concerned. Alternatively, Bowler argues that it may be more appropriate to differentiate theories according to the way in which they imagine the processes producing change to have worked. He cites Gould in listing three fundamental pairings—steady-state versus development, internal versus external control of evolution, and continuity versus discontinuity—for categorizing and differentiating evolutionary theories (1984: 9–13). Hereto, however, it is difficult to determine what these pairings mean outside the context to which they are most appropriate, that is, evolutionary biology.

In fact, it is no accident that when illustrating the content of each distinctive pairing Bowler consistently draws upon evolutionary biology. While other disciplines might utilize evolutionary concepts, the development of evolutionary theory occurred earliest in association with the ideas of Charles Darwin and has been most developed in the study of biology. Eldredge (1995: 1) argues, in fact, that, "Charles Robert Darwin was truly the founding father of evolutionary discourse, and all sides of the basic evolutionary disputes legitimately find their patrimony in his work." Given its pertinence to evolutionary theorizing in general and its influence on all other disciplines, evolutionary biology is my starting point for comparison as well. I am aware, however, that this will make some readers uncomfortable.

There is, for example, the argument that neo-Darwinism is a hegemonic discourse grounded in European scientific and enlightenment values. Hence it gives us no greater purchase on the "real" parameters of evolution, particularly of human institutions and social practices, than any other discourse one might call evolutionary. This charge deserves serious consideration, particularly if realist and liberal theories are replicating the parameters of this discourse, because it involves the degree to which we as scholars propagate "just so stories" that simply reify the discourses in which we have been trained. Yet my goal here is to examine the extent to which realists and liberals have been participating in what is considered the hegemonic discourse to begin with. The marginalization of other evolutionary discourses is not as relevant to these purposes, although it is a legitimate issue that might be considered in an alternative venue.

Another concern with utilizing evolutionary biology as the comparative standard is that the use of evolutionary biology appears to imply a recouching of IR theories in biological terms. Yet the dominant versions of realism and liberalism are currently systemic in focus, and so this would appear to preclude a severe reductionism that traced IR outcomes to processes of genetic reproduction and behavioral predispositions. My argument on this point is two-fold. First, as I will attempt to demonstrate throughout this discussion, practitioners of each paradigm continue to rely upon alternative assumptions about human nature and these remain fundamental, albeit implicit, to the internal logic of each paradigm's systemic variants. In other words, the bio-genetic component never disappeared from realist and liberal assumptive frameworks; it was simply submerged from view by its practitioners. The reasons for this submersion are numerous.

One of the more obvious is that policy-makers and the social scientists whom they sometimes rely upon for advice do not have a particularly good track record of borrowing bio-genetic insights appropriately. Eugenics, Social Darwinism, and their impact on German thought prior to WWII are frightening examples of social programs that drew upon concepts in evolutionary biology to justify abhorrent social practices. The normatively dangerous social implications derived from biological evolutionary theory have typically been the result of theoretical misuse by social scientists themselves.[7] This has tended to engender the opinion that it is better to steer clear of biology entirely than risk justifying disreputable social practices.

Even when social scientists have consciously avoided deriving policy implications, the explanatory difficulties of applying biogenetics to political and social behavior remains, as critics have been only too happy to remind sociobiologists.[8] The isolation of causal mechanisms (particularly the role of culture), the issue of causal reductionism and unit-level equivalence ("nations, races, and ethnic groups are not separate isolated gene pools" as Goldstein (1987: 36) has pointed out), and dubious inferences to particular international and global outcomes or behaviors (with war resulting from innate male aggressiveness being the most long standing example within the discipline of IR) have encouraged American social scientists to avoid biological discussions altogether. So too has the milieu in which the American social sciences developed, which has always subscribed to an "ideology of progress" that would make biological theorizing particularly unattractive (Hoffmann 1995: 219).[9] The result is that although all IR theoretical paradigms rely on assumptions about human nature, IR theorists do not often explicitly state the biological case for their arguments.[10]

The second point to make regarding the current preference for systemic theorizing is that this does not actually preclude the inclusion of biology and genetics as causal factors. In fact, it is the very emphasis on the systemic level-of-analysis that makes realism and liberalism so eminently comparable with theories of evolutionary biology. This is because theories of evolutionary biology are not simply about positing genetic predispositions but about the interaction between an environmental context and the genetic response of organisms within it. In this context systemic-level analysis firmly introduced the concept of environment into realist and liberal discussions, and in so doing it has allowed each to develop a more complex and complete picture of how and why human beings adapt their institutions and social practices as they do. It also simultaneously avoids the random selection of genetic bases for IR behavior and outcomes. This is particularly true for neorealism that Waltz proposed in part to avoid classical realism's tendency to trace IR outcomes to human predispositions.[11] And as debates within evolutionary biology illustrate, even if there is common agreement with the general idea that an environment encourages adaptation to it, there is still substantial room for disagreement over how to characterize an organism's relationship to its environment and hence how adaptation occurs. How this may be the case in the context of IR is the subject of the next section.

ENVIRONMENT AS THE IMPETUS FOR ADAPTIVE CHANGE

In much the same way that realism is often used in IR theory as a point of departure for discussion and disagreement, the theory of natural selection proposed by Charles Darwin in the *Origin of Species by Means of Natural Selection* (1859) became the springboard or touchstone for the development of almost all biological evolutionary theory thereafter. Yet it would be misleading to argue that the notion of evolution was Darwin's alone. The idea that the environment encouraged adaptation to it had a venerable scientific history long before Darwin, and his own theory was well-informed by existing ideas on the subject. It was also the general and preexisting acceptance of the idea of evolution within the scientific community that provided the atmosphere in which Darwin's ideas could be accepted by other scientists at the time (however controversial his ideas remained to the public). As Bowler (1984: 177) notes, naturalists were particularly receptive to Darwin's arguments, and "without the support of this group, Darwinism would have died an early death."

What made Darwin unique was not his proposition that the environment encouraged organisms to adapt to it, but his annunciation of how the process or mechanism of encouragement and adaptation actually worked. Thus it was quite possible for a scientist to accept the general idea of evolution but disagree with Darwin's particular explanation for how it worked to produce tremendous species variations. Before turning to the subject of natural selection and the mechanisms of evolution, then, it is important to highlight that evolutionary theory in its biological context involves the general acceptance of environmental adaptation, but that this is distinguishable from explanations for *how* adaptation occurs.

This distinction is important because it has direct parallels to theorizing in an IR context. Theorizing at the systemic level of analysis quite explicitly involves the assumption of an environmental context to which organisms must adaptively respond. The organism that has received the most attention in IR is the nation-state, although analysis (even realist analysis) has included or been extended to any political unit that operates transnationally or globally (such as international organizations, multinational corporations, interest groups, and so on). The current emphasis on systemic-level analysis in the field of IR reflects agreement across these two paradigms that there is an environment to which pertinent political organisms attempt to adapt. It also reflects agreement that it is essential to specify and examine the repercussions of that environment not only for the larger picture of global politics but also for the internal composition of political units within it. And as with evolutionary biological theory, both realism and liberalism can accept the idea of environmental adaptation without necessarily agreeing on the nature of the environment and how adaptation occurs.

Gourevitch's (1978: see also Almond 1989) "Second-Image Reversed" remains the definitive statement in this regard, as it outlines how structures within nation-states can be examined as consequences of alternatively specified global political environments. Depending on which characteristics the IR theorist emphasizes about the international system, it is possible to draw different conclusions about its consequences for state formation and domestic politics. With the English and Prussian domestic political orders as prime examples, Gourevitch (1978: 896) examines arguments that "the vulnerability of states to [anarchic] pressures is not uniform since some occupy a more exposed position than others. Hence, the pressure for certain organizational forms differs."[12] And because the notion "that international market forces affect politics and have done so for a long time seems incontrovertible," he (Gourevitch 1978: 884) also reviews arguments "which posit systematic relationships between such forces and certain configurations of regime type and coalition pattern."[13] His analysis amply illustrates that there already exists a rich and varied history of IR theorizing, including, but hardly limited to, realism and liberalism, which accepts the basic idea that human beings adapt their political institutions to a given environment or external context.

As with the acceptance of the idea of evolution in its biological context, many IR theorists are already persuaded that the environment is an important cause for institutional adaptive change in the units within it. And they can agree on this point without necessarily concurring with one another's characterization of the environment or how institutional adaptation actually occurs. In other words, the debates in IR theory today are usually not about whether the international system has an impact on the units within it. Rather they involve how to define the system, its pertinent characteristics, and the mechanisms of selective adaptation that are most relevant to change and stasis in global political practices and institutions. These differences also determine which types of organisms or political units are of most interest to the scholars of each paradigm.

In addition, because a "second-image reversed" perspective is not an argument about the selection mechanism of adaptation itself (that is, *how* adaptation occurs) but rather a general and relatively nondenominational observation that the international system has consequences for the internal characteristics of the units within it and for the ways in which they interact, *all* the major IR paradigms have some practitioners who subscribe to this perspective. Thus there are IR scholars of all theoretical stripes who already accept what would be the basic premise of evolutionary theory from a biological perspective: There is a causal relationship between the international environment or system, the internal composition or characteristics of units within it, and their subsequent behavior. Ultimately what most realists and liberals disagree over is not the idea of evolutionary adaptation per se, but over *how* adaptation occurs.

Natural Selection and the Status of Human Beings

Given that prior to Darwin there was already agreement within the scientific community that the environment was a cause for adaptation, what made Darwin revolutionary was his delineation of a particular selection mechanism. That is, he provided an argument that not only argued the environment caused adaptation but also delineated precisely how it encouraged, forced, or prompted organisms to adapt to it. His mechanism was called natural selection. Darwin argued that it was the struggle for existence within a zero-sum environment that prompted the adaptation process.[14] For any given population of species, the environment was zero-sum between species as well as within because natural resources and hence food supplies were not infinite, and in an environment of finite resources, populations could not survive and breed infinitely. This meant that all other organisms within the environment were potential competitors in either an indirect (consumption) or direct (predatory) manner. Hence the environment consisted not only of what was external to each organism (air, water, land, and so forth), but also all other organisms that were necessarily competitors for resources. Constant competition between and within species populations was the dynamic result, and Darwin argued that from it sprang the tremendous variety and diversification we see in the natural world.

This variety and diversification occurred because even organisms within the same population tended to have individual and entirely accidental characteristic variations. These individual variations could, in turn, be favored by the environment because those variations might allow the particular individual organism that had them to obtain greater access to the food supply. Greater access meant they would survive longer, in better health, and would therefore have a greater chance of breeding. In breeding, their characteristic variation would be transmitted to their offspring. Given that a portion of their offspring would have the variation, they too would gain greater access to food supplies, survive in better health, and have a better chance of breeding. In each succeeding surviving generation, there would be an increased tendency for the characteristic to be present and then gradually, but eventually, it would become dominant. The giraffe's long neck is a frequently used example:

> In the original population of grass-feeders, some individuals would by chance have longer than average necks, others shorter. When the grass began to disappear, those

with longer necks would be able to reach leaves on trees more easily; because they could exploit the alternative source of food more effectively, they would be healthier and able to breed more readily; their offspring would be more numerous and inherit the extra length of neck. Conversely, those animals with shorter necks would get less food and not breed so easily; in the extreme case they would die of starvation, although a difference in rate of reproduction is all the mechanism requires. It then follows that in the next generation more individuals will come from long-necked parents then from short. . . . (Bowler 1984: 157)

Not only would the inherited characteristic eventually cause a major changes in the species, but the selection mechanism would also lead to species differentiation and hence diversity because variations in characteristics would also allow different populations to exploit different resources.

One important conceptual point to highlight for the purposes of this discussion is that Darwin's mechanism of natural selection involved, as two separate steps, the impact of a zero-sum resource environment and the genetic inheritance of variations. There was a great deal of debate in the field of biology at the turn of the twentieth century, however, over how heredity actually worked. With the development of modern genetics it is easy to view these debates as part of the primitive understanding that existed about the subject at the time. In fact modern genetics was initially posed as an alternative to natural selection, and it was only gradually realized that the two could be synthesized (and subsequently have been) to make the case for Darwin's mechanism stronger.

This initial confusion encouraged an alternative perspective on heredity, based on J. Lamarck's argument for "in-use" inheritance, which exerted a great deal of influence on the development of evolutionary biological theories. Writing at the turn of the nineteenth century, Lamarck had argued for what is called "soft" heredity in which the characteristics favored by the environment were acquired as a result of *effort* within a given generation and could then be transmitted to the offspring that would spread the effect cumulatively throughout the population. In returning to the example of giraffes as a point of comparison, Lamarck's perspective on heredity suggested that:

. . . the short-necked ancestors of the modern giraffe were at some point in their history forced to begin feeding from trees. All the individuals stretched their necks upwards and as a result this part of the body grew in size. The next generation inherited the extra neck-length and stretched it even further, so that over a long period of time the giraffe gradually acquired the long neck we see today. (Bowler 1984: 81)

The work of Lamarck was seized upon by many of Darwin's critics as an alternative to natural selection because it avoided the nastier implications involved with competition for survival and breeding as central to environmental adaptation. According to a Lamarckian perspective the environment could still be one of finite resources that would encourage organisms to exploit various food supplies and in a variety of ways. But characteristics could be selected on the basis of use and disuse by the entire population, rather than having been selected out by the decline, failure to procreate, and death of those individuals within each generation who did not have the characteristic variation to begin with.

Moral and religious leaders who were uncomfortable with natural selection's implications for human beings were initially attracted to the writings of Lamarck as an alternative mechanism of selection. And although modern genetics has largely discounted in-use heredity as scientifically viable, the extent to which human beings may be unique in their adaptive capacities remains a point of contention among evolutionary biologists to this day. The problem, from an ontological perspective, is that natural selection involves a clear separation between structure and agent. The natural environment of air, water, sunlight, and so on, has an independent structural impact on the organism, and the response to that environment is then contained within the organism as an independent agent. Yet while it may be more or less accurate to posit a separate environment for other organisms (with regards to both consciousness of and ability to manipulate their environment), that proposition becomes much more problematic when applied to human beings who also exist in humanly created social and cultural environments. As O'Hear (1997: 212) puts it, "though we are indeed the products of natural and historical processes, our lives are largely lived on the level of what Oakeshott calls *inteligibilia*: that is to say practices through which we endow our behavior with meaning."

The two steps of natural selection are necessarily blurred for human beings as a result. This makes the ability to distinguish among potential causes for human behavior (genetics, cultural cross-fertilization, pure chance, reinvention?) as elusive to the evolutionary and sociobiologist as it remains for the IR theorist. The dilemma for sociobiologists in particular is, as Dennett (1994: 487) has put it, "If you are not totally idiotic, you don't need a genetic basis for any adaptation that you will pick up from your friends in any case." The resulting debates among evolutionary and sociobiologists over human evolution and its consequences for human behavior rage along a spectrum that continues to be informed by the earlier split between Darwinism and Lamarckism, which was itself informed by concerns over whether human beings were shaped *by* or alternatively shapers *of* their environment. Although evolutionary biologists would certainly not utilize these labels to describe this spectrum today, the terminology does manage to capture not only the essence of this ongoing debate but also its historical role within the development of biological evolutionary theory itself.

At one end of the spectrum lies Darwinism and its assumption that the separation between environment and organism remains relatively pure, even when the organisms in question are human beings. Hence it posits that human evolution occurred in a manner similar and is therefore comparable to the evolution of other organisms. The emphasis at this end of the spectrum is on human beings as organisms that have been genetically shaped by a separate environment and that shaping continues to have consequences for human behavior today. At the other end of the spectrum lies Lamarckism, which allows that the relationship between environment and human organism in particular is not as pure as Darwinism would suggest. Thus it posits that human evolution is dissimilar to and incomparable with the evolution of other organisms. The emphasis here is on human beings as shapers of their own environment and who exert greater control over their own evolution and destinies as a result.

The Human-Environment Relationship in IR Theory

What is striking about these debates within evolutionary biology are the parallels one can draw between Darwin's theory of natural selection and realism on the one hand, and a Lamarckian-type theory of in-use inheritance and liberalism on the other. These are alternative theories of the evolutionary mechanism of selection and their differences derive primarily from their alternative assumptions regarding the relationship between human beings and their environment. Like Darwinism, realism tends to emphasize the extent to which human beings are separate from and shaped by their environment. And liberalism, like Lamarck and other alternative selection theories, tends to emphasize the extent to which human beings are shapers of their environments.[15]

The difference in their emphasis can initially be traced to the different ways in which realism and liberalism define the environment. Both describe the environment of world politics as anarchic, meaning the absence of a common interstate government. But as Grieco (1990: 36–38) has pointed out, there is "a fundamental divergence in their interpretations of the basic meaning of international anarchy," with liberals emphasizing that "no agency can reliably enforce promises" and realists emphasizing that "there is no overarching authority to prevent others from using violence, or the threat of violence, to dominate or even destroy them." Why each theory interprets anarchy in different ways ultimately derives from their basic assumptions about the relationship between the anarchic environment and human beings.

In summarizing the realist assumption on this point, Mearsheimer (1994–1995: 41) manages to match it precisely to a Darwinian perspective: "Realists maintain that there is an objective and knowable world, which is separate from the observing individual." For realists, human beings remain distinct from their environment because anarchy is an essentially primordial realm with a central characteristic that exists independently of what human beings do. The realist fixation with survival is a reflection of this characteristic because the antithesis of survival is death. From the realist perspective, death is a primordial or natural feature of the environment in that it ultimately cannot be prevented by human activity. Nor is it necessarily related to human activity, since the physical substance of which human beings are comprised will expire regardless of human interaction, effort, or intervention. Copeland provides a useful example of this perspective:

> . . . individuals and societies can learn about the material implications of physical objects without any necessary interaction between them. Across all cultures, for example, individuals typically learn the concept "fire" through direct personal contact with the object—burning their hand as a child, watching a campfire turn logs into ashes, perhaps watching their home burn to the ground. Thus it is not surprising that across cultures, people have an understandable caution about things that would produce uncontrollable fires (and why people almost universally panic when trapped in a burning building). (1998: 14)

This fear can be generated without past socialization because it is the unknown quality and seeming finality of death that acts as a powerful motivator in its short-term avoidance. Hence according to realism it deserves pride of place among all other potential selection mechanisms in the environment, and it will deserve this place so as long as human beings remain subject to it. Ultimately it is this environmentally induced fear of death that drives human beings to create collectives and engage in social practices in the first place.

Although survival is frequently acknowledged as a prerequisite to the pursuit of all other interests in liberal theory, the fixation with death and survival is not replicated. Why this would be the case can again be traced to the theory's basic assumptions about the relationship between environment and human beings. From a liberal perspective it is because human beings have capacities far beyond those of other species and have developed more sophisticated ways of transmitting adaptive variations from one generation to the next (what Dennett (1995: 331) refers to as "the cultural transmission of information") that they may transcend an all-encompassing primordial fear of death. From a liberal perspective, the short-term emphasis on survival over all other goals varies according to context and can frequently be discounted for precisely this reason. In an off-handed manner, Keohane provides an excellent example of the difference between realists and liberals in this regard. In *After Hegemony*, he explicitly assumes that future rewards must be valued in order for cooperation to take place, and rejects the realist alternative that because players would "emphasize with Keynes that 'in the long run we're all dead,' they may prefer to defect to obtain better results in the present" (1984: 75–76).

Since liberalism largely discounts what is for realism a non-human and primarily causal characteristic of the environment, it is not surprising that its definition or interpretation of anarchy is very different as well. Anarchy does not constitute a force separate from what human beings do in liberalism. It is instead a vacuum at the global level that historically contained less human interaction and hence less human activity, processes, and institutions on aggregate than it does today. There is nothing about this vacuum that demands a short-term emphasis on survival, self-help, or violence. Wendt (1992) provides a good example of how these behavioral tendencies developed largely by accident to produce predation (an argument he explicitly presents in support of liberal IR Theory), although he also points out that once institutionalized materially and ideationally they become difficult to transcend. The anarchic global vacuum has become increasingly filled in the twentieth century thanks to the development of modern science and technology. This has contributed to the development of global interdependence in the generic sense of having "shrunk the geographic social, economic, and political distances that separate states and vastly multiplied the points at which their needs, interests, ideas, products, organizations and publics overlap" (Rosenau 1976: 38).

The importance of this for liberal theory is that it establishes a new systemic context or external environment for which realist theory is no longer appropriate. Realist theory is about human interaction prior to modern technology and the higher levels of "interaction capacity" that it has induced. Buzan, Little, and Jones (1993: 69) argue that this capacity must be considered a systemic variable in that "the evolution of technology continuously raises the absolute capability for interaction available within the system," and Ruggie (1998: chap. 5) offers a similar argument regarding "dynamic density." Modern technology has, in essence, shrunk the world so that action is impossible without interaction. In historical terms this is a new external context because human beings and the nation-states they created (as a dominant institutional form globally) were designed for an environment in which they could successfully obtain their interests autonomously. Their ability to do so in the new global environment of interdependence seriously compromises this ability. Existing institutions were adaptations to an entirely different environment and now human beings must adapt those institutions (both materially and ideationally) to another.[16]

The environment that confronts human beings is very different in each theory as a result. If anarchy is a primordial environment beyond human control in realism, it is for liberalism an environment composed of what human beings do. For realism the processes and institutions in which human beings engage are shaped by the environment. They serve as the means to survival in the environment and are not ends in and of themselves, although realism does anticipate cognitive and emotional attachments to form around the institutions and social practices human beings create.[17] But because the anarchic environment engenders a dominant, ongoing interest—the avoidance of death—the processes and institutions developed by human beings have been shaped by and are answers or responses to this interest in some way. The emphasis is on human practices as *acted* upon in realist theory, rather than as primarily or primordially causal.

For liberalism these same processes and institutions *are* the environment. They are not simply means to a particular end but ends in and of themselves and as such induce their own specific interests and identities. Thus there are multiple interests associated with different types of processes and institutions, such as (to name only a few) the realms of security, economics, ecology, and culture. The purposes of each set of processes and institutions varies, and they contain a logic of their own that the systemic condition of interdependence affects differently. Each must be examined from a perspective that, as Keohane and Nye (1977) had argued in *Power and Interdependence*, acknowledges the broad impact of interdependence but also recognizes what is specific and appropriate to each realm. When compared to realism, then, the emphasis is on human practices as *acting* upon in liberal theory, hence human processes are primarily or primordially causal.

The very different assumptions each theory makes with regards to the human-environment relationship produces very different assumptions about human nature and its consequences for political behaviors and practices as well. Although it remains unfashionable for IR scholars to attribute causality to a particular conception of human nature, alternative conceptions continue to implicitly inform the work of realists and liberals. In her study of the "consensual view of human nature and motivation" in realist texts, Freyberg-Inan (1999: 6; also Falger 1997; Shimko 1992: 286) provides ample evidence that realists continue to adopt a conception of human nature that is not only profoundly pessimistic but also assumes it is fixed and universal. Brooks (1997: 449; also Crawford 2000: 120–22) points out that this conception is present in neorealism, which relies on psychological fear as the primary cause for behavior and outcomes. Such a conception of human nature makes sense if one is also assuming, as realists do, that the environment in which human beings exist produces a fixed and universal fear of death in the species.

Alternatively, liberal IR theory relies upon an entirely different conception of human nature. As Michael Howard (1978: 11; also Shimko 1992: 285) has observed, liberals "have faith in the power of human reason and human action so to change [the world] that the inner potential of all human beings can be more fully realized." What liberal IR theorists have in common according to Zacher and Matthew (1995: 140), is the belief "that international politics is about the changing interests of the inhabitants of states (or other entities) and that the underlying forces of change are creating opportunities for increased cooperation and a greater realization of peace, welfare and justice." It is on this basis that Keohane (1990: 172) chastises both realism and Marxism for their determinism, which he argues is "an unsatisfactory doctrine for human beings," who are "agents in history." Hereto, such a conception of human nature makes sense if one is also assuming, as liberals do, that the environment in which human beings exist is primarily one of their own making and is therefore subject to human intent that is developing along normatively progressive lines.

This synopsis of each theory's perspective on environment is obviously a generalization. As such, it ignores some important differences within each paradigm as well as some important similarities (other than a shared rational choice methodology) that exist between them. The concept of interdependence, for example, is an implicit underlying condition for many strands of liberal theory, but for others (such as those concerned with the democratic-peace thesis) it is not. Thus the extent to which these general observations would apply to those strands may be limited as well. In a similar vein, many realist scholars accept a discount rate that places long-term before short-term interests, with ongoing disagreements among offensive and defensive realists involving the extent to which particular social practices and institutions might mitigate fear and the aggressive tendencies it produces.[18] This suggests that the realist-liberal distinction I have drawn about the human-environment relationship and some of my asserted paradigmatic ramifications may not be as sharp in practice. Indeed, Shimko (1992: 299) has argued that neo-realism is not that distinct from liberal IR theory (as classical realism was) because it is "philosophically antiseptic" about the human condition and so leaves open the possibility that its nastier attributes might yet be overcome. In making this argument, Shimko parallels a number of other works that suggest that the development of *all* IR theory has been informed by the predominantly liberal and optimistic values and beliefs of the American social milieu (such as Hoffmann 1995; Waever 1998).

In the context of a comparison of theoretical evolutionary tendencies, however, the alternative conceptions of environment and human nature remain relatively stark even if moderated in particular applications or paradigmatic variants. Ultimately what makes realism and liberalism so distinct (and leaves proponents of each theory talking past each other) is the alternative perspectives each adopts on the human-environment relationship and hence the different causal priority each gives to human activity within the anarchic environment. While some realists may be able to accept that particular institutions can mitigate violent behavior, ultimately differences among them still involve questions such as "how often—and not whether—actors are expected to behave in a highly cautious and conservative manner" in the anarchic environment (Brooks 1997: 473). And while some liberals may accept that uncertainty and fear can drive behavior in a functional security realm, they are united in their "emphasis on the cumulative effects of human action" and in their conviction that "people really do make their own history" (Keohane 1990: 173). Despite frequent calls to do so, there is little room for meeting in the middle since each theory views the relationship between the environment, human beings, and human-generated institutions and social practices in diametrically opposed terms.

THE SELECTION-BY-COMPETITION LOGIC OF REALISM

Since they have different assumptions about the relationship between the environment and human beings, realism and liberalism go onto explain how the environment encourages institutional adaptation in very different ways. These differences again parallel alternative theories of selection in evolutionary biology, with realism adopting a selection mechanism similar to Darwin's and liberalism adopting a selection mechanism similar to Lamarck's. Because realism concurs with Darwinism that the world contains finite resources and hence is zero-sum with regards to survival, human beings necessarily compete with one another. This intra-species struggle for survival encompasses all other struggles and all other interests. To put this another way, because competition for survival is the dominant logic, all human-created processes are adaptive variations within this ongoing context. In fact, according to realism, competitive struggle is the reason why human beings adapt at all, thus making the production of global social reality itself an adaptation resulting from and informed by the logic of competition.

Despite a common commitment to this selection-by-competition logic as a transhistorical boundary to human social activity, disagreement exists among realists over whether competitive behavior results from the zero-sum anarchic environment in which human beings find themselves or a particular genetic characteristic engendered by the environment such as power-lust.[19] The result is that in their emulation of the Darwinian selection mechanism realists have tended to treat environment and genetics as if they were alternative rather than interrelated causes (as modern evolutionary biology now recognizes them to be). Yet cutting across this divide is a common unit of analysis. Despite persistent claims by its critics that the nation-state is realism's primary interest, realist scholars have just as consistently pointed out that they are interested in the behavioral patterns of *any* group, be it "tribes, petty principalities, empires, nations, or street gangs" (Waltz 1979: 67; also Schweller and Priess 1997: 6). As Lapid (1996: 240) has observed, there is a "realist consensus concerning ontology (conflictual group fragmentation) and problematique (survival/war)." The reason for this interest in groups is not difficult to surmise. Individuals could expect to survive longer on aggregate within groups than not, so that the formation of groups as collective enterprises with their own binding social practices could be anticipated in the context of a zero-sum resource environment.

The question as to whether the tendency to form groups is genetically produced has remained largely unaddressed in the realist literature, although practitioners of yet a third variant known as "neoclassical" realism have explored the issue to some extent.[20] Mercer's (1995) reliance on social-identity theory, for example, argues that in-group favoritism and out-group discrimination is a basic biological parameter of social reality that supports realist expectations. [21] A selection-by-competition logic would explain the development of social practices encouraging intra-group identification, cooperation, and altruism, since these practices would facilitate group cohesion and hence its ability to access food supplies and procreate (see also Druckman 1994: 44–45; Hinde 1993: 31). And since competition for resources serves as the primary motivation for group formation, that same logic also indicates that the extension of cooperative processes across groups would be limited. Thus realism anticipates that intra-group interaction in a zero-sum environment would be primarily cooperative while inter-group interaction would remain primarily competitive. There is nothing in realist logic that demands this competition necessarily be violent, since resources and inter-group exposure varies. But because competition would remain a fundamental feature of inter-group interaction, it is no surprise from a realist perspective that competition frequently turns deadly.

The anarchic environment specified by realism also serves as a relatively dynamic force for institutional adaptation. This is because Darwin's mechanism of natural selection is not about *which* functions would be selected but *how* the environment promotes adaptation in the first place. A zero-sum resource environment is the mechanism necessary to overcome genetic complacency and sameness thereby inducing genetic innovation and diversity instead. Realism's reliance on a similar logic also allows it to explain why and how social practices are developed and adapted in general, although this same logic would limit its ability to predict the specific adaptations adopted by any given group.[22] Competition for survival would favor those groups that were willing or able to adapt their practices and institutions as changing circumstances warranted. It would, in turn, punish those groups that were or could not institutionally adapt. In other words, a zero-sum environment would promote experimentation of social practices for the purposes of group survival, and it would favor change in existing practices that appeared insufficient to the task.

Although innovation and experimentation with intra-group institutions and practices is always an option, the primary source for group "design revision" in realist theory is usually the imitation of one another's social practices (Resende-Santos 1996, 1999; Sterling-Folker 1997; Waltz 1999). The practices of the comparably more powerful groups are typically favored in this regard, since power indicates an ability to extract resources on behalf of the group. Realist logic also suggests that previously developed social practices and institutions would act as counterweights to institutional change precisely because they had been adopted as a means to survival in the first place (Gilpin 1996: 413). And because groups would avoid imitating those practices that they believed had failed to obtain the survival of other groups, adaptive institutional change *across* groups would occur within a band that was relatively narrow in comparison to the tremendous variation in human social practices and institutions that might be imagined *within* groups.

In this context, neorealism may be seen as a stand of realist theorizing that accepts the existence of this narrow band and is particularly interested in exploring competitive patterns of behavior and institutions within it. More specifically, it is interested in documenting why and how institutions (such as nation-states) and social practices (such as balance of power) that are associated with explicit group competition (in particular, war) are continually reproduced in a zero-sum environment and hence are a reoccurring feature of human existence. As Waltz puts it, his theory of international politics is meant to explain, "why the range of expected outcomes falls within certain limits . . . why patterns of behavior recur . . . why events repeat themselves" (1979: 69). Thus the emphasis in neorealist scholarship has been on exploring continuity in these particular types of social practices within the modern (usually twentieth century) period, rather than on examining how these practices have been adapted, modified, and changed throughout history. This is why its critics frequently assert that because it "contains only a reproductive logic, but no transformational logic," it simply cannot account for fundamental or constitutive changes in the political units within a global system (Ruggie 1998: 154).

Yet from an evolutionary perspective, the larger realist framework of which neorealism is a part is very much about institutional adaptation because it specifies a zero-sum environment which, as with Darwin's mechanism of natural selection, acts as a constant incentive for institutional adaptation and variation. Certainly it is the case that neorealist scholarship has been more interested in what cannot be changed within such an environment, namely that it is a selection-by-competition logic that induces institutional adaptation to begin with. But this hardly exhausts the potential adaptive implications that can be drawn from a realist (or even neorealist) theoretical framework. Kahler notes, for example, that:

> An evolutionary theory requires very little information about units and very few assumptions, if any about their behavior. Waltz's structural realism, rationalized and individualized by others, explicitly adopts selection as one of the key links between system and unit, and the only link that can explain change. Unfortunately Waltz himself and other neorealists have not extended this critical (and briefly remarked) feature of structural realism. (1997: 44, see also Kahler 1998: 925)

Extending this feature reveals that what a zero-sum environment would produce is certainly adaptation and hence change in an evolutionary sense. Much like the assumptive framework of natural selection, the selection-by-competition logic of realism is capable of accounting for change and variation in human social activities. Despite realism's reputation as a theory of stasis, from an evolutionary perspective it contains all the ingredients necessary to explain why, within limits promoted by the environment itself, institutional adaptation and variation would be a consistently anticipated characteristic of human activity.[23]

As with Darwin's theory of evolution it is also clear that realism places human beings squarely in the realm of nature, along with all other organisms. While human beings may have been more creative in their adaptations, the very reason why they adapt their institutions, and in so doing accept institutional change in the first place, is because they remain subject to the same environmental inducements to competition experienced by all other organisms. Thus the very institutions and social practices human beings have created are informed by a selection-in-competition logic that human beings cannot control. Particularly astute statesmen and policy-makers may be aware of this logic and seek to manipulate it in their favor, but a realist perspective indicates that conscious awareness of this logic is not required in order for human beings to conform their behavior and institutions to its demands.[24] The realist refusal to concur that human beings control their own species' destiny is undoubtedly one of the reasons it has remained a paradigmatic pariah in the American social scientific "Enlightenment" context, claims of theoretical dominance not withstanding.[25]

Of course all of these claims exceedingly rankle IR theorists of a postmodern bent, since they rest on an assumption that the environment works its effects on human practices in some sort of objective fashion, without human interpretation as a necessary, intervening mechanism. As one scholar has put it, "the problem with realism is that it validates only one interpretation of reality, or, said differently, it validates only one way of experiencing reality, denying the validity of others" (Wilmer 1996: 348). I believe this is yet another way in which realism and Darwinism parallel one another as theories of evolution, since Darwinism has been subject to similar criticisms. Bowler notes that it has been described by critics as "little more than a vacuous tautology" and that, "the whole concept of natural selection amounts to nothing more than a play on words" (1984: 327). And I suspect both realists and (philosophically minded) Darwinists would respond that their theories are hegemonic discourses for an "objective" reason, that is, they are about what exists independently of and so *a priori* shapes human interpretation.

THE SELECTION-BY-LEARNING LOGIC OF LIBERALISM

Liberalism can also be recast as a theory of global institutional evolution, but because it finds its parallels in evolutionary biology among theoretical alternatives arguing that the human-environment relationship is unique, its selection mechanism is very different from that of realism. There is no single, zero-sum environment separate from what human beings do and encompassing all others in liberal theory, although the functional environment of military-security can approximate this description at times. The anarchic environment is for liberalism a vacuum that historically allowed competitive adaptations to occur by chance rather than due to the inherently finite quality of resources in the environment itself. Numerous variables might affect the extent to which natural resources are finite and hence induce competition, and one of the most important variables in this regard is the capacity for human beings to innovate consciously and sometimes quite quickly (say within a single generation). Thus while resources could be zero-sum and promote the sort of competition highlighted by natural selection, from the liberal perspective there is no *a priori* reason why all resources everywhere need be so, particularly when human beings can control their own food supplies via agricultural cultivation and irrigation to such a large extent.

This theme of human control over human destiny informs all liberal IR theorizing (see, for example, Zacher and Matthew 1995). This does not mean that liberal IR scholars believe there is an automatic, perfect concordance among human beings, since some contexts may indeed involve zero-sum resources and hence competition for survival. Rather it is because human beings have the capacity to change the contexts in which they find themselves that they also have the capacity to harmonize their common interest in survival in a way that other organisms do not. As Lebow (1994: 275) puts it, "an understanding of structure creates the possibility of modifying it or of escaping from some of its apparent consequences. Human beings possess this capability." In other words, while liberalism accepts that human beings want to survive, it argues that competition with one another is not an inevitable outcome of that desire. The fact that human beings can manipulate the finite quality of their natural environment to such a large extent means that liberalism's preferred selection mechanism for evolution is quite similar to Lamarck's in-use inheritance, that is, adaptation occurs through human effort and, as Keohane (1990: 172) asserts, through "the effects of conscious human action."

Thus adaptation and change are not driven by a selection-by-competition logic in liberal theory. They depend instead on conscious and immediate innovation appropriate to the context at hand and this, in turn, depends on an appropriate cognitive recognition of the context. From a theoretical perspective this is actually a more demanding mechanism for adaptation than is natural selection because it involves a two-step learning process in which human beings must not only accurately understand their given contexts but also recognize the adaptations appropriate to them. Adler, Crawford, and Donnelly (1991: 28–29) call this learning mechanism "cognitive evolution," and describe it as "the process of intellectual innovation and political selection that occurs within and between institutional settings" when a new context leads to "the recognition that old interests . . . have become dysfunctional. In turn, this recognition could trigger a reevaluation process that ends up in new definitions of interests and the way they are pursued." The mechanism of adaptation for liberalism is a selection-by-learning logic that gives humans control over their institutional adaptations.

Given their differing perspectives on the relationship between environment and human beings, it is hardly surprising that realism and liberalism would also have such different perspectives on the role of learning and consciousness in adaptive change. These are central to a liberal mechanism of environmental adaptation, while realism is highly skeptical that learning and cognition need play any central role in institutional adaptation (Levy 1994). Or, to put this another way, according to realism adaptation can occur in the absence of an adequate understanding of one's environment. And if learning, in the sense of appropriate recognition of one's context, does play a role in realist adaptation it is as a cognitive revelation that one exists in an environment that requires selection-by-competition. Hence the most skillful politicians from a realist perspective are those who recognize the limitations imposed by a selection-by-competition logic and seek to manipulate institutions and social practices within its boundaries.

For liberalism, on the other hand, there are multiple environments in the twentieth century, all of which overlap and none of which can be ranked hierarchically (Keohane and Nye 1977: 25). These environments are comprised of the different processes in which human beings are engaged, and they can be categorized according to types of functional interest. Buzan, Jones, and Little (1993: 30–31) describe these environments as "sectors" that are "not subsystems in the normal sense of a subset of units located within a larger set," but as "selective lens that highlight one particular aspect of the relationship" or "different aspects of its reality." Because each sector is concerned with a different set of functional interests, adaptive change occurs according to a selection-by-learning logic unique to each. While interdependence affects all sectors, in that interests can no longer be obtained unilaterally, each sector also has a logic of its own that is what human beings must recognize if they are to adapt appropriately to the sector. They have to learn how interdependence has changed the sector so that they are now unable to unilaterally obtain interests in it, and they have to recognize what behavioral and institutional changes are now required by the sector.

Adler, Crawford, and Donnelly (1991: 38) sum up this logic with regards to interdependence in general, arguing that, "perceptions of interdependence can change decision makers' calculations about the usefulness of unilateral action in states' international relations," and "it can modify the calculations by which states choose to exercise their power." In a similar vein, according to Keohane and Nye (1977: 232) economic interdependence would require that nation-states "accept much more international participation in their decision-making processes than they have in the past," and that "the illusion that major macroeconomics policies can be purely domestic will have to be discarded, along with the search for total control over one's own economic system." This was because, as Rosenau (1976: 43–44) put it, interdependent interests "do not lend themselves so readily to unilateral action," and so "a modicum of cooperation with counterparts abroad" is necessary in order to obtain them. And Keohane (1990: 172) provides an interesting summation of issue areas that demand "conscious human action" including the avoidance of nuclear war, retarding nuclear proliferation, promoting equitable Third World development, protecting the global environment, and managing the joint pursuit of wealth in capitalist market. Finally, a common yet controversial assertion in liberal theory is that multilateralism is the appropriate, demanded institutional form in these newly interdependent sectoral environments.

As a result, liberal scholars are interested in how human beings will recognize the new process-based contexts in which they exist and in delineating what institutions would be appropriate to those contexts. There is an obvious danger of functional institutional teleology here, particularly when utilized as an explanation for international cooperation in the moment, but for many scholars the primary virtue of liberalism remains its prescriptive rather than explanatory capacities. Keohane (1990: 173 194; also 1989: 10, 158), for example, characterizes liberal IR theory as a "guide to choice" and asserts that, "liberalism holds out the prospect that we can affect, if not control, our fate, and thus encourages both better theory and improved practice. It constitutes an antidote to fatalism and a source of hope for the human race."

What undergirds this optimism is the belief that human beings can control their own adaptations, not only because they have capacities far beyond other organisms but because the environment(s) to which they must adapt are human constructions as well. This presumption aligns liberals with constructivists and, rather bizarrely, postmodernists—"bizarrely" because the enlightenment values to which liberalism subscribes are precisely postmodernism's target. Yet from an evolutionary perspective these theories have more in common than not, because each of them considers the institutions and social practices that human beings have created to *be* the only pertinent environment. Thus they tend to produce what Somit and Peterson (1999: 42, 1998) call a "political behavior is learning behavior" type of explanation that recognizes no causal space for anything that cannot be classified as either human consciousness and intent or accident and pure chance.

All of them are process-based theories as result, and realism remains an ontological alternative to each of them because it insists that biological parameters derived from an objectively separate natural environment continue to encompass and confine human social activity. Within the context of this evolutionary comparison Copeland's (1998: 20) observations regarding the difference between realism and constructivism hit the mark:

> It is perhaps even more fundamentally a divide between nature and nurture—between those building a universal theory on a few spare (and typically implicit) notions regarding the properties of humane existence and those building a historically-contingent theory of socialization through time.

Realism refuses to concur (critics would undoubtedly say "acknowledge") that anarchy is what human beings have made of it. It argues instead that the evolution of IR and global politics cannot be accounted for by reference to chance and human social practice alone.

DEBATES OVER THE PROCESS OF ADAPTATION IN EVOLUTIONARY BIOLOGY

The discussion to this point has focused on how the first step in Darwin's theory of natural selection—the environmental inducement for adaptation—compares to similar arguments in the two dominant paradigms of IR theory. The second step in Darwinism involved genetic inheritance and, as already noted, necessarily blurs with the first step when the subject is human beings and the evolution of their social practices. But it is important to examine the causal role that genetic inheritance plays within the theory of natural selection, because it involves conceptual issues that differ from those related to the first step. As such, these are issues that *any* evolutionary theory, regardless of discipline, must grapple with and address.

It is in Darwin's second step that the scientist is forced to grapple with the question of how exactly adaptation works in practice. The parameters initially appear to be straightforward. While the zero-sum resource environment would favor the variations of some individuals over others for the purposes of survival and breeding, Darwin posited that it was the inheritance of those variations that acted to preserve it in each subsequent generation. Darwin's initial perspective on heredity was "as a conservative force trying to maintain the original character of the species, while variation tried to disturb the process by introducing new characteristics" (Bowler 1984: 242). That perspective has since been superseded by the modern synthesis of natural selection and genetics in which heredity could both reinforce a particular variation *and* be the source for new characteristic variations in the future. In other words, as Darwinism developed in evolutionary biology, inheritance became not merely a conservative force but a force for "dynamic equilibria" because "populations do indeed contain substantial reservoirs of genetic variation that can be tapped under new conditions" (Bowler 1984: 298).

Thus one of the roles that genetic inheritance plays in biological evolutionary theory is as a simultaneous source for stasis and change. It explains how some characteristic variations can come to dominate over time so that the composition of the organism and hence the species becomes relatively stable. Yet it also explains from where new characteristic variations can come when conditions in the external environment change to encourage subsequent adaptations. It is, as a result, the pool from which subsequent organism innovation is tapped and, at the same time, a conservative force that keeps the organism within prescribed physical and behavioral boundaries. This suggests, in turn, that any evolutionary theory must address the issue of "dynamic equilibria" and be capable of accounting for both stasis and change in a theoretically coherent manner. In other words, it must strike a logical balance between what Modelski (1996: 336) calls "persistence of strategies" and "sources of variation which introduce innovation." Evolutionary theory too heavily skewed toward one or the other would produce explanation that would tend to argue either for persistence in everything or for innovation everywhere.

These are, in fact, the very grounds upon which critics of both realism and liberalism have frequently mounted their attacks. If, for example, the fear of death is a primary motivation, competition inevitable, and human institutions and social practices more effectual then causal, then why do any differences in human institutions exist and what serves as the source or inspiration for institutional change? By choosing an unchanging environmental inducement to competition as its selection mechanism, realism runs the risk of arguing that change simply directs groups to become functionally and institutionally similar. Waltz (1979: 97) implies as much in asserting that "each state duplicates the activities of other states at least to a considerable extent," and that "international politics consists of like units duplicating one another's activities." Thus realism is commonly characterized as a theory of stasis incapable of explaining how change occurs or why institutional differences exist between groups

Alternatively, if human beings are motivated by a myriad of interests, respond to contexts that are comprised of social practices, and can directly affect those contexts through their own actions, then why do so many practices and institutions look so similar and what are the sources for their institutional stasis? By choosing human cognition and learning as its selection mechanism, liberalism runs the risk of arguing that global institutional variations are infinite and subject to such rapid rates of change that it would be impossible to discuss or account for institutional similarity in a global or historical context. Indeed, it is not clear why, if liberals are correct that "human and state interests are shaped by a wide variety of domestic and international conditions" (Zacher and Matthew 1995: 119), we should witness any institutional stasis or convergence. Thus liberalism is sometimes characterized as a theory of institutional change incapable of explaining why there is any institutional convergence or stasis in global politics (Jackson and Nexon 1999).

Closer inspection reveals that there are attempts at a theoretical balance between institutional stasis and change in both realist and liberal explanations for how human institutions and social practices evolve. Whether these attempts are sufficient is the subject of considerable theoretical debate, of course, but in each case the institutions and social practices that human beings create serve as both a source of stasis as well as the resource pool from which subsequent institutional changes are drawn. Stasis occurs because both assume that institutions and social practices are collective creations that materially and ideationally reward individuals for having certain identities, interests, and behaviors. As Wendt (1992: 397) puts it, "actors acquire identities—relatively stable, role-specific understandings and expectations about self—by participating in such collective meanings." This assertion is neither a liberal nor realist one in its own right, as Wendt points out. Regarding self-help systems, he (1992: 412) notes that "the realist might concede that such systems are socially constructed and still argue that after the corresponding identities and interests have become institutionalized, they are almost impossible to transform." The difference, I would argue, is more fundamental (hinging on whether, even if we could wipe the slate clean, the environment's selection-by-competition logic would simply reinstitutionalize a self-help system), but Wendt is certainly correct in that the general concept of institutionalization is not purely liberal nor necessarily antithetical to realist theorizing.

Because the institutions human beings create as adaptive responses to their environment can be sources of stasis in both realism and liberalism, they accord with evolutionary biology's conclusion that "evolution can only work by modifying the structures available to it" (Bowler 1984: 182). That is, once a type of adaptation occurs (say, wings), genetic encodement becomes path-dependent. In much the same way realism and liberalism utilize concepts such as institutional path-dependency, historical contingency, imitation, and competition to explain why institutional similarity occurs. These same concepts also figure into their explanations for subsequent institutional change, although not surprisingly these concepts are utilized in different ways within each paradigm.

These differences parallel contemporary theoretical disagreements between evolutionary biologists and paleontologists, which arise because genetic inheritance is where the actual process of an organism's adaptation is delineated. It is with Darwinism's second step that the scientist shifts from how a specified environment encourages adaptation in general to how any particular organism has responded to that environment. As Eldredge puts it:

> Evolutionary *theory* is about how the evolutionary process works. And that, to a geneticist, means how genetic information, underlying the production of the physical appearance (and physiologies and behaviors) of organisms, comes to be modified over the course of time. " (1995: 2; emphasis original)

While evolutionary biologists and sociobiologists disagree over the degree to which human behavior can be traced to genetic orientations determined by natural selection, evolutionary biologists and paleontologists have squared off over how exactly the process of genetic adaptation occurs. Although these debates are not about the human evolutionary process specifically, they do have significant implications for that process and for how human beings adapt socially. Thus they are relevant to realist and liberal disagreements on this point as well.

The debates among evolutionary biologists and paleontologists have involved the issue of gradualism versus discontinuity in an organism's genetic adaptation. Darwinism argues that evolution is a gradual and continuous process in which accumulated, cascading inherited adaptations gradually drive species apart. While sudden mutations could occur because portions of present but under-utilized DNA could be unexpectedly expressed, they are not the stuff of subsequent inheritance or adaptation because they could not contribute to fitness. As Dennett describes metaphorically:

> Large leaps sideways *in a fitness landscape* will almost never be to your benefit; wherever you currently find yourself, you are where you are because this has been a good region of Design Space for your ancestors . . . so the bigger the step you take (jumping randomly, of course), the more likely you are to jump off a cliff. (1995: 288, emphasis original)

What disturbs many paleontologists, on the other hand, is that the fossil record often does not appear to conform to Darwinist expectations in "that species remain imperturbably, implacably resistant to change as a matter of course—often for millions of years" (Eldredge 1995: 3).

Eldredge and Gould (1972; Gould and Eldredge 1977) have argued instead for a model of "punctuated equilibrium" in which the evolutionary process is subject to episodes of rapid albeit infrequent change. They contend that the sudden appearance of a totally new mutation might channel an organism's evolution in an entirely new direction. A new characteristic might appear quite suddenly and by accident (due to genetic mutation) and would only then become subject to the forces of natural selection. As Bowler (1984: 325–26) puts this, "only the superficial character of the organ is molded to an adaptive purpose by selection," and "selection has acted to make adaptive use of the new structure once it had been formed in this way." Thus while they agree with evolutionary biologists that natural selection does play a role in the adaptive process, it does so only after a genetic characteristic has been spontaneously (albeit unconsciously) selected by the organism itself. The result is an emphasis on discontinuity over continuity and on historical contingency over path-dependency.

The theory of "punctuated equilibrium" has been subject to extensive criticism, and evolutionary biologists have mounted a major campaign against it in the form of convergence theory.[26] If organisms spontaneously generate their own response and historical contingency is so important then why, critics ask, is it relatively common to find physical and behavioral convergence among species that are unrelated? The answer, according to Morris (1998: 202), is that "all organisms are under constant scrutiny of natural selection," so that physical and chemical constraints "severely limit the action of all inhabitants of the biosphere." According to Angier, Morris notes that the role of contingency is important at some level because:

> We're all the product of one very, very lucky sperm. On the other hand, when you look at the broad structure of the history of life, you can't help but be impressed by the number of organisms that began at different starting points and have come together . . . The world is a rich and wonderful place, but its not one of untrammeled possibilities. (Angier 1998)

The repetition of physical patterns throughout the planet would remain inexplicable if genetic chance or accident played such a large a role in the process of adaptive evolution.

It is also interesting that one of the charges leveled at "punctuated equilibrium" returns us once again to the debate over the role of human activity in the process of human beings' own environmental adaptation. The organism's ability to spontaneously generate its own response revisits the Lamarckian issue of directed adaptation, since it involves the extent to which the environment imposes genetic outcomes on organisms, and this has obvious implications for human beings. Indeed, in his examination of Gould's entire body of theoretical work, Dennett (1995, chap. 10) argues that many of Gould's arguments are actually consistent with Darwinism. Dennett (1995: 299, 309) goes on to suggest that what actually offends Gould about Darwinism is its "predictable, mindless trudge up the slopes of Design Space," and that Gould's tendency to emphasize radical contingency over convergence in general is driven by "a desire to protect or restore the Mind-first, top-down vision of John Locke—at the very least to secure our place in the cosmos."

As a Darwinist, on the other hand, Dennett (1995: 311) argues that "punctuated equilibrium" would not "create any more elbow room for the power of contemporary events and personalities to shape and direct the actual path taken among myriad possibilities." One can see, in Dennett's response, a similarity to realist skepticism that it is ever possible to wipe the institutional slate clean of self-help processes and that interdependence has transformative effects in this regard. According to Waltz (1979: 145), those who argue otherwise "have discovered the complexity of processes and have lost sight of how processes are affected by structure." And Dennett's accusations directly touch upon the human-environment relationship assumed by liberal IR theory. In fact, the philosophical issues that are central to these scientific debates are also what distinguish realist and liberal explanations for how exactly the process of institutional adaptation works in practice.

THE PROCESS OF INSTITUTIONAL ADAPTATION IN REALIST AND LIBERAL THEORY

Despite the balance between stasis and change that both realism and liberalism attempt to strike in their accounts of the institutional adaptive process, alternative emphases on continuity or discontinuity remain. In part this is a function of the different chronological order in which they arrange causal concepts (with, for example, realism treating inter-group competition as a motivation for innovation and liberalism including it causally only after innovation has taken place). But these arrangements are, in turn, proscribed by their alternative selection logics and assumptions about the human-environment relationship. Thus the debates between evolutionary biologists and paleontologists have direct parallels to the debates between realists and liberals regarding the process by which political institutional adaptation occurs. Given its selection-by-competition logic, a realist process of institutional adaptation tends to approximate a Darwinian emphasis on gradualism, continuity, and convergence. And given its alternative selection-by-learning logic, a liberal process of adaptation tends to approximate the paleontological emphasis on suddenness, discontinuity, and contingency.

Realism's selection-by-competition logic implies that groups would not only accept but actively promote experimentation and change in their institutions. One of the primary sources for new ideas and alternative practices would be the social practices and institutions of other groups, particularly those who were very powerful. Institutional imitation driven by the competitive pressures of the environment (what Waltz called socialization) is one of the major reasons why group institutions tend to become similar over time (Resende-Santos 1996; Brooks 1997: 465). It is also why the practices and institutions of the most powerful groups in the system tend to become global hegemonic discourses (Thomson 1992; Schweller and Priess 1997: 12).

Yet it is from this tendency for institutional imitation among groups that realism also derives expectations regarding stasis and subsequent adaptation. Stasis would occur because domestic actors could be expected to develop vested identities and interests in imitated practices and institutions. Thus even when the environment subsequently exerted pressures for innovation, individuals and subgroups would exert pressure in the opposite direction in order to keep institutions as they were. Foreign policy analysts frequently lament that foreign policy is "inefficient" according to the demands of the international context (See, for example, Quandt 1988). Yet from a realist evolutionary perspective such lamentations are misplaced because foreign policy behavior results from a dual context and can only be understood and evaluated within it. The decision-maker is confronted with pressures for institutional change that emanate from the environment, yet these pressures are counteracted by existing group institutions and the decision-maker's own role and vested interests in them. That decision-makers would attempt to satisfy both pressures simultaneously, and to the complete satisfaction of neither, is to be expected.

Given the investment that individuals and subgroups would make in existing group social practices, the source for subsequent institutional innovation in realist theory derives from the act of imitation itself. Existing institutions and practices serve as a source of stasis, since the development of vested identities and interests in intra-group institutions would make them more difficult to modify and change over time. When institutional imitation does occur it cannot start with a clean slate and is instead amalgamated with or layered onto existing group processes to create a slightly different institutional variation with each act of imitation (Resende-Santos 1996; Posen 1984). In other words, the imitation would never produce identical institutions across groups, and the reason this is important is because if these variations appear successful to other groups they might then become the objects of imitation in the future. Institutional variants result from this formulation and these variants may become the subject of inter-group imitation at a later point in time. Thus a selection-by-competition logic simultaneously promotes intra-group commitment to existing institutions *and* inter-group institutional imitation.

The competitive anarchic environment would, for example, encourage weaker states to imitate the economic practices of the more powerful. But the replication would never be precisely identical because each state would already have existing institutions on top of which the imitation would be layered. From this perspective, realists would join many comparativists and scholars of the Third World in their skepticism that a liberal "one-size-fits-all" development model could ever work in practice (see, for example, Colclough and Manor 1991). Given its anticipation of a layering effect, realism would expect that each imitation of capitalist, free markets would create a slightly different institutional variant that would be similar but not identical to the economic liberalization efforts of other groups. And if one of these variants subsequently appeared to be relatively more successful at amassing capitalist wealth, its particulars would become the subject of inter-group institutional imitation. This same dynamic explains why, despite conscious imitation, no two democracies have precisely the same electoral institutions and practices.

Because the layering it entails and the variations it then produces could be imitated later and hence account for future rounds of adaptive institutional change, institutional imitation remains a crucial source for innovative change in the realist argument. The institutional variants that are created as a result of this layering serve as the "genetic" pool from which subsequent institutional imitations and hence process adaptations are drawn. Yet simultaneously the cognitive and functional investiture made in group social practices would provide a degree of institutional stasis. Thus in realist theory the particular ways in which the selection-by-competition logic affects institution-building itself is what accounts for both stasis and subsequent change in the social realities human beings create.

Liberalism's explanation for stasis and subsequent adaptation is very different. What provides the element of stasis in liberal theory are not the institutions in which individuals become invested but the functional interests that all human societies must address in some way. Human beings create institutions in order to meet these interests as efficiently as possible within their sectoral contexts. The desire to maximize economic welfare, for example, may be posited as a relatively timeless functional interest, but the most efficient institutions for obtaining this interest will vary according to environmental conditions that affect economic activity as a functional sector. Increases in technology levels and interaction capacities would produce a new economic sectoral environment that requires economic institutions appropriate to it, thus prompting the desire and search for new institutions.

It is at this stage that institutional experimentation takes place, but it is not contingent upon competition or imitation that are only important later in the adaptive process. Instead, the development of new institutions and hence adaptive variants to the new economic environment derive from the specific path dependencies of existing institutions and social practices. Spruyt's (1994: 25–26) arguments with regards to the development of the sovereign state in Europe provides a prime example, since the expansion in trade between 1100 and 1300 provided the external environmental change necessary to provoke new political relationships and coalitions among existing subgroups such as kings, aristocrats, burghers, and the church. These relationships had to be modified if new market opportunities were to be exploited, yet the extent to which they could be (and how) varied geographically (Spruyt 1994: 154). Several institutional variants in response to new environmental conditions were then developed simultaneously and included city-leagues, city-states, and sovereign territory states.

The development of these variants ultimately depended on cognitive evolution. As market participants in the early Middle Ages became increasingly dissatisfied with the performance of existing institutions and practices, their willingness to experiment with and change those institutions increased as well. According to Keohane (1984), time-lags between environmental and institutional changes would be anticipated, since sectoral environmental changes or institutional efficiencies would not be immediately obvious to all participants. But sectoral environmental changes eventually kick-off a round of institution-building, starting with those participants who early in the process become conscious of their inability to obtain interests in the new environment. Institutional changes are promoted and accepted irrespective of existing institutions, because functional interests are more important to institutional participants than existing (and ultimately inefficient) practices.

Thus unlike realist theory, the institutional variations occur in liberal theory *before* there is inter-group competition, and the selection of a specific institutional arrangement is initially driven by *intra*-group dynamics. It is after those arrangements have been established (historically the period between the 1300s and 1600s in Europe) that the process of *inter*-group institutional selection and the role of competition then begins. This sequencing is necessary because it is only once the new institutional variants have been created and are in the process of exploiting new market opportunities that their capacities for doing so effectively may be *consciously* compared. Eventually the territorial, sovereign state proved better at maximizing profit (and protecting profit obtained) than did the other institutional variants, and institutional selection across groups then occurred via institutional imitation, which Spruyt (1994: 158) refers to as deliberate mimicry and exit. In other words, a number of synchronic institutional variants had emerged as the "genetic" pool from which the subsequent round of imitative adaptation draws. The institution within this pool that demonstrated that it had a competitive advantage in obtaining the interest within the new environmental context then became the subject of imitation by others.

Stasis only becomes relevant again in the liberal argument after the competition among institutional forms has been resolved. Once the institutional variant more appropriate to the environment has been imitated by most groups, its appropriateness ensures its stability. Groups would have no reason to change the chosen institutions unless environmental changes make them inappropriate for the continued pursuit of economic profit. Thus the vested interests human beings have in their institutions derive from the ability of those institutions to meet particular functional demands. As long they do so in a relatively efficient manner, participants will remain loyal to them and will develop interests (or sunken costs) that make institutions difficult to modify. When environmental conditions change, however, participants will become increasingly dissatisfied with their institutions and social practices. Thus the cycle of institutional experimentation and competitive imitation begins anew, with a new institutional form eventually emerging to provide stasis thereafter.

The stark contrast between realist and liberal accounts for the process of institutional adaptation approximate the contemporary theoretical divisions between evolutionary biologists and paleontologists. In a realist account, all adaptations can be traced back to a selection-by-competition logic and all variations are subject to that logic. Competition is responsible for the development of social practices themselves, the cognitive commitment to intra-group institutions, the process of inter-group imitation and institutional innovation, and the dispersion of particular institutions and social practices on a global scale. Institutional evolution tends to be path-dependent in realist theory as a result, while the role of contingency remains relatively minor because adaptation occurs within boundaries proscribed by both an immutable natural environment and the social realities that have been created as the means to human survival in that environment.

The parallels here with Darwinism are striking. The role of institutional imitation, institutional layering, and unintentional variation in realist theory is similar in many respects to the gradual, continuous process of accumulated adaptation in the modern Darwinian synthesis. This puts realism on the side of continuity and convergence in the debate between evolutionary biologists and paleontologists. When Morris (1998: 2020) argues that, "put simply, convergence shows that in a real world not all things are possible," one can easily imagine most realists would readily concur given their assumptive framework.

Liberal accounts, on the other hand, rely on a selection-by-learning process that produces adaptive variations whittled down according to their competitive abilities within the particular sectoral environment. While inter-group competition drives the entire process of evolutionary adaptation and variation in realism, it serves in liberal theory only to select out a particular institutional form in the second stage of successive adaptation. And while path-dependency plays a role in the institutional variants that are created, historical contingency ultimately plays a far greater causal role in the final selection process. Those groups who will imitate are also willing to abandon their own institutional efforts for one that is functionally more efficient within the changed circumstances of the sector. Thus a particular institutional form comes to dominate globally in a relatively sudden, historically contingent manner.

In fact, it is no accident that in his account of European institutional change, Spruyt (1994: 24–25, 186) relies on Eldredge and Gould's theory of "punctuated equilibrium" as a more appropriate model than Darwin's theory of natural selection. In doing so he argues that, "whatever forms survive are not explained by reference to the types preceding the exogenous shock but by reference to the new environment and the now simultaneously existing forms which emerged after the shock" (Ibid.). In other words, human beings can and do consciously, purposefully abandon the institutional variations they had previously created. Thus we come full circle. Human beings remain in control of their own institutional adaptations in liberal theory in a way that they do not in realist theory. The similarities between liberal IR theory and Eldredge and Gould's "punctuated equlibrium," with its emphasis on discontinuity and historical contingency, are relatively obvious as a result.

EXAMPLES BY WAY OF CONCLUSIONS

In this concluding section I would like to highlight how this exploration of evolutionary tendencies has already provided a number of theoretical surprises. As noted earlier, the reconsideration of ongoing disagreements between realists and liberals in light of their evolutionary tendencies sheds more precise light on what it is they have been disagreeing about. Thus it should serve as a corrective to the growing tendency within the field to treat these theoretical paradigms as more similar than not on the basis of their common epistemology. As this discussion has repeatedly demonstrated, important substantive differences remain regarding the assumptions and causal organization within each theoretical framework. In addition, their reconceptualization as theories of global institutional evolution generates questions and answers which, given the way in which each theory is typically characterized, can be considered unexpected or even counter intuitive.

One of the interesting aspects of the process of adaptation derived from each theory, for example, is the common role that imitation plays in intra-group interaction and global institutional evolution. Both realism and liberalism assume groups become socially similar by imitating one another's institutions, however the concept of imitation is utilized differently. In realism the initial institutional similarity between groups is immediately modified because its layering onto existing institutions will actually produce institutional variation in practice. Alternatively, institutional variation is largely displaced by the act of imitation in liberal theory so that units become more alike than not thereafter. What makes this observation interesting is that realism is so often accused of treating groups as functionally alike, while liberalism is frequently cited for its capacity to include institutional domestic differences as causal. Yet an evolutionary perspective indicates that these characterizations may actually be reversed.

More specifically, institutional variation only acts as a causal force in liberal theory *after* the environment has prompted the need for subsequent adaptation, and those institutional variations actually drop out of the system once the competitive choice among them has been made. Theoretically, then, one has institutionally "like-units" in liberal theory until the environment promotes another round of institutional experimentation and change, which makes similarity and difference a chronological phenomenon in liberal IR theory. In realist theory, on the other hand, the institutional variations are always present and could be drawn upon for subsequent adaptations at any moment. Thus the extent to which units are alike and different is a simultaneous rather than chronological phenomenon in realism, a point which Waltz (1979, chap. 5) repeatedly underscores in his discussion of political structures. And although March and Olsen (1998: 956–57) read realism as a theory of functional teleology, from an evolutionary perspective there may actually be some compatibility between realism and the "new institutionalism" literature, since realism allows for institutional drag and path-dependency in a way that liberal IR theory does not.

In underscoring how an evolutionary approach produces new insights into old debates, it may also be pertinent to provide an explicit empirical example of how it can do so. For this purpose, the time and ink realists and liberals have spent mutually accusing one another of misunderstanding the dynamics at work in the European Union (EU), and in the present international system, is useful (see also Cornett and Caporaso 1992). These accusations are often phrased in rather unhelpful terms (by both camps) as a problem of maintaining "conceptual blinders," which inhibit the other from "seeing" reality for what it "really" is (or is becoming). Ultimately, however, the differences between them derive from their fundamentally divergent assumptions about the ability of human beings to control their own institutional adaptations. These differing assumptions produce very different interpretations of an empirical phenomenon like the EU.

It is no secret that liberal scholars have always had high hopes for the EU, which has grown from the original European Coal and Steel Community (ECSC) founded in 1951 between six European nation-states to encompass a vast number of functional issue areas and other nation-states. Early post-WWII liberal theorizing focused on the developing EU and took several forms including federalist theory, transactionalism, and neofunctionalism.[27] While the EU was largely abandoned as a liberal research topic after the 1960s, its efforts post-1990 to create a common currency encouraged a renewed liberal interest in the organization. Quite a number of scholars have since argued that the EU represents the transcendence of self-help social practices between its members (See, for example, Lebow 1994; Ruggie 1992: 561–63; Wendt 1992: 417–18, and 1994; Keohane 1993).

It is because European visionaries in the 1950s initiated the integrative steps that "would allow swords to be beaten into plowshares" that, according to Kegley (1991: 109), "today the prospect of an intra-European war is non-existent." While acknowledging that the end of European warfare might have multiple causes (112), Kegley suggests that based on the European integrative example, "We might derive policy principles with which the West can deal constructively with the multipolar world on the horizon" (113). In a similar vein, Jervis (1991–1992: 56) has argued that historical patterns of conflict will not reassert themselves in Europe because the EU is "filled with stable, democratic governments that have learned to cooperate and have developed a stake in each other's well-being." Such arguments are clearly informed by a liberal selection-by-learning logic in that human beings have the ability to shape their institutional contexts so that violent forms of competition can be consciously circumvented.

What triggered the selection-by-learning process among EU countries were the new environmental conditions in the twentieth century, although it varies among liberal scholars as to what those conditions entailed. Zacher (1992) provides a list of commonly cited environmental factors including the development of advanced communication technologies and nuclear weapons, increased economic interdependence, and the spread of Western democratic and cultural values. From a liberal evolutionary perspective these constituted a new international environment so that what we have been witnessing in the EU is the emergence of a new institutional adaptation in response to those changing conditions (Spruyt 1994: 189–91). While the precise form of this adaptation has been driven largely by the particulars of the region, we might look to other regions, nation-states, and even levels-of-analysis to discover different institutional adaptations to the same environment. From this perspective much of the neoliberal institutional literature can be reread as an argument about international regimes as alternative adaptations to this changing environment. Wendt (1994) provides another example of a possible institutional alternative in his discussion of the emerging "international state."

The extent to which liberal scholars have explored the next step of evolutionary competitive selection among these institutional alternatives has varied considerably. For some liberal scholars the EU constitutes the obvious choice, and so the future round of adaptive institutional imitation will involve the imitation of EU institutions and social practices. It is only within the context of a liberal evolutionary perspective that Francis Fukuyama's (1989: 14) assertion—"we are far more likely to see the 'Common Marketization' of world politics than the disintegration of the EEC into nineteenth-century competitiveness"—makes any sense. While regime theorists are generally more cautious about predictions of this sort, the liberal literature does appear united in the belief that whatever institutional form is eventually selected will necessarily involve multilateralism and a loss of nation-state autonomy (Zacher 1992).

A realist evolutionary perspective on the EU is, of course, very different. Realists typically explain European cooperation and the creation of the EU by expanding the time-horizon and dynamics of alliance cooperation. Under the unique conditions of bipolarity following WWII, European nation-states shared a common threat from the Soviet Union and a common benefactor in the United States. This mitigated the effects of anarchy by, in the first instance, reducing European fears of one another and, in the second instance, having a hegemonic arbiter and protector (Mearsheimer 1990: 47; Waltz 1979: 71; Grieco 1990: 40–47). These were unusual international circumstances that allowed Western Europeans to pursue cooperative and economic enterprises that would normally have been impossible in anarchy and other polarities (Snyder 1990: 11–12). Or, as Schweller and Priess

(1997: 18) put it, in a bipolar system "cooperative, although largely informal, institutional practices are likely to develop spontaneously as unintended by-products of the distribution of power."

With the end of bipolarity, realists expect that such cooperative ventures will decline and that the potential for competitive hostility among previously-cooperative states will resurface (Mearshiemer 1990; Layne 1993). Although liberal scholars are justified in pointing to the post-Cold War–EU development of the euro as a foil to the immediacy of this expectation, many realists lay claim (as liberals do with regards to cognitive awareness of environmental change) to institutional time-lags. Yet the question remains, why couldn't several decades of cooperative effort among EU countries change their sense of identity and purpose as liberalism asserts? Why is realism so insistent that atavism is a given? The reason derives from realism's selection-by-competition logic that maintains that group formation and inter-group competition is a means to species survival. This does not mean realism is arguing that group boundaries are immutable or that European nation-states could never form a larger union among themselves. Rather it is that such outcomes cannot be reached by ignoring, in spite of, or in the absence of competitive pressures. They can only be *the result of* competitive pressures, and if conscious institutional design is to play a role in the process it can only do so under particular circumstances.

To be more specific, realist logic indicates that it is when groups face an ongoing security threat and can only thwart it through inter-group union that conditions may be ripe for the transcendence of existing group identities. The possibility of such an outcome was actually greater during the Cold War, with the Soviet Union poised on their back-door steps, than it is in the post-Cold War period when a commonly shared threat has been absent. And from this perspective the extent to which conditions were ever that conducive during the Cold War is questionable, since the Western European nation-states actually relied on U.S. power to provide their security.[28] In other words, these nation-states did not depend on one another for the very thing that motivates group formation in the first place—survival.

According to Schweller and Priess (1997: 21), Western European cooperation under the US–NATO umbrella did produce a sense of "we-group" that explains the time-lag in institutional decline. Thus realism "predicts that some institutions will endure longer than the structural factors or threats that brought them into existence because of a shared sense of 'in-group' identity induced by prolonged, intense and focused threats." However this does not amount to a transformation from existing nation-state identities into a common or collective European identity. Inevitably, inter-group cooperative institutions decline in the absence of conducive environmental conditions. Europeans may continue to attempt unification in the absence of these conditions, but such a project is ultimately at the mercy of the environment in which groups exist. The pressure to compete in groups is inherent to human interaction itself and so it remains something that human beings cannot control. From the realist perspective any institutional project that seeks to deny or ignore this context is doomed to failure.

In summary, for liberals the EU represents a new institutional variant in response to new sectoral environments, and there is a possibility that it will serve as *the* institutional model for imitation in the future. From a liberal evolutionary perspective we are living in a period of conscious institutional adaptation induced by changed sectoral environmental conditions, and the EU is an empirical example of those adaptive efforts. For realists, on the other hand, the EU is an institutional adaptation to particular historical and geostrategic circumstances that have now disappeared. Certainly it may reflect the particulars of the European region as Grieco (1999) has argued, but in the absence of favorable geostrategic conditions the EU's ability to surmount intra-group differences and identities is not enhanced but rather worsened by the end of the Cold War. Because institution building is bounded by and subject to the logic of selection-by-competition, the ability of the EU to evolve further is determined by that logic and not the internal will of its participants. And because it is an institutional adaptation that never addressed the fundamental interest in survival that informs all group formation and inter-group behavior, it will eventually be selected out of the system simply because no other groups will imitate it.

While this account of each theory's interpretation of the EU will probably do nothing to quiet the criticisms each continues to level at the other, I believe it does manage to underscore not only why each theory characterizes the EU in such different ways, but also how each account is derived from alternative philosophical perspectives that can be labeled evolutionary in both form and content. The question remains, however, which version of events is correct? The answer must undoubtedly be, neither. This is because realists and liberals are grappling with philosophical issues involving "nature vs. nurture" that, as this review of biological evolutionary debates has indicated, have remained unresolved. In addition, realism and liberalism clearly occupy alternative ends of the philosophical spectrum. For realism "nature" remains paramount in that it considers human evolution to be subject to the same biological processes that have affected the evolution of all other organisms on the planet, and this then places identifiable boundaries around the act of institution-building itself. For liberalism, "nurture" remains paramount in that it assumes human evolution has preceded according to a different logic which allows "that behavior is conditioned by the social environment" (Bowler 1984: 315). Reality, however, is somewhere in the middle, which is why evolutionary biologists have increasingly rejected the "nature vs. nurture" dichotomy in favor of synthesis.

Perhaps both realism and liberalism can ultimately be faulted for continuing to provide "just-so stories" that merely reflect extreme perspectives on human nature. Indeed, Lebow (1994: 276–77) provides a particularly strident example of fault-finding in his accusations that the realist emphasis on nature instead of nurture is so misplaced that it is actually inhibiting human beings from exercising their capacities to evolve. This accusation is also common in much of the post-positivist IR literature (see, for example, Beer and Harriman 1996). Yet what these accusations amount to is an argument that Darwin's theory of natural selection itself and its relevance to global political activity has inhibited human institutional evolution and normatively desirable outcomes. The very idea of natural selection is what appears to be so dangerous to many scholars, which is why Dennett's (1995) review of reactions to Darwinism is so aptly entitled, "Darwin's Dangerous Idea." As he puts it:

> A review of all the major charges that have been leveled at Darwin's dangerous idea reveals a few surprisingly harmless heresies, a few sources of serious confusion, and one deep but misguided fear: if Darwinism is true of us, what happens to our autonomy?" (1995: 312)

As explanations for social phenomenon go, it may be equally possible to fault liberalism for placing far too much emphasis on nurture. Yet perhaps it is also the case that by placing the realist-liberal debate within an evolutionary context, we might move to a dialogue that attempts some balance between the two extremes and thus gives us better theoretical purchase on the empirical and global phenomenon in which we are interested.

NOTES

1. Insightful feedback and ideas for the development of this chapter came from Annette Freyberg-Inan, Patrick Thaddeus Jackson, Miriam Fendius Elman, Colin Elman, the participants at the ISP's Fall Seminar Series (BCSIA, Harvard University, October 1999), Bill Thompson, and the participants at the conference on "Evolutionary Approaches to International Relations" (Indiana University, December 1998).
2. These issues are discussed extensively by Wendt as well (1992; 1994), and the entire fiftieth anniversary issue of *International Organization* was organized around the theme of rationalism vs. constructivism, with neorealism and neoliberal institutionalism classified together as examples of the former (Katzenstein, et. al. 1998).
3. As this study will demonstrate, however, this asserted affinity between Social Darwinism but not Darwinism is deductively incorrect. Social Darwinism was an illogical amalgamation of elements from Darwinism and Lamarckism (Bowler 1984: 274), while IR realism clearly parallels Darwinian, not Lamarckian arguments.
4. Particularly interesting in this regard is Dennett's discussion of several philosophical "just so stories" from an evolutionary biological perspective, including Hobbes' *Leviathan*, Rawls' *Theory of Justice*, and Nietzsche's *Genealogy of Morals* (1995, chap. 16).
5. Denmark provides a useful overview of world-systems history (1999), and the ongoing work of Modelski and Thompson should be noted in particular (for example Modelski and Thompson 1999; Modelski and Poznanski 1996; Thompson 1997).

6. On the other hand, see Lebow (1994) for an analysis that considers both to have evolutionary tendencies, but is clearly informed by a normative bias for liberal rather than realist theory that then obscures the extent to which both are treated as viable theories of global institutional evolution. A "realist evolutionary" response that questions Lebow's obvious bias for liberal evolutionary theory may be found in Falger (1997: 169–71).

7. The Eugenics movement claimed that it was the state's duty to limit the multiplication of its least-fit citizens, while Social Darwinism was the notion that progress came through struggle so that the strongest nations and races were justified in dominating the weak. In his examination of the social implications of Darwinism, Bowler points out that Social Darwinism was not actually based on Darwin's theory of natural selection but on an amalgamation (and an illogical one) of alternative evolutionary theories, some of which specified entirely different mechanisms of selection (1984: 269–74). He also points out that evolutionary biological theories did not point to the accuracy or efficacy of perspectives such as Social Darwinism and other attempts at social engineering, but instead particular elements were drawn from theories of evolutionary biology in order to support preexisting perspectives and biases.

8. Sober provides a review of sociobiological arguments on cultural evolution and argues that the sociobiological position is " . . . genetic selection [that] has given our species the ability to engage in social learning. Once in place, this cultural transmission system allows characteristics to evolve that could not have evolved without it. In other words, it is only because the traits in question evolve in the context of a cultural transmission system that they are able to evolve at all" (1994: 487). As a result, sociobiologists are concerned with how this process of genetic selection combines with social learning to create particular social and physical consequences. But because it appears to have affinities with Social Darwinism and the like, the approach remains controversial and Eldredge (1995: 5) captures the more common perspective that, "sociobiology is an explicit application of ultra-Darwinian principles, asserting that social systems arise and evolve through competition for reproductive success." Critiques of some sociobiological excursions into IR theorizing may be found in Tickner (1999), Goldstein (1987) and Kitcher (1987).

9. This is one of Somit and Peterson's arguments for why biopolitical theorizing has failed to gain favor in American social scientific circles (1998, 1999). Others have noted the impact that American ideology has had on the content of social scientific and IR theorizing, including Waever (1998: 721–22); Winnerstig (1999); and Shimko (1992).

10. There are exceptions to this, including work by Masters (1983 for example); Falger (1997, 1994); Mercer (1995), Thayer (2000), and Fukuyama (1999, 1998).

11. Waltz (1979, ch. 2; 1959: 29–30). On this point see also Falger (1997: 156–63, 1994: 119–21); Shimko (1992); Guzzini (1998: 24–26, 126–28); and Spirtas (1996).

12. A sampling of works that exemplify this perspective include: Desch (1996); Gurr (1988); Hintze (1975); Rasler and Thompson (1994 1989); and Tilly (1975).

13. A sampling of works that exemplify this perspective include: Rogowski (1989, 1987); Gourevitch (1986); Katzenstein (1978); Milner (1988); Keohane and Milner (1996).

14. This description of natural selection is drawn from three sources: Bowler (1984); Dennett (1995); Sober (1994).

15. Sewell noted the direct link between liberal IR theories and Lamarckism in his 1966 study of functionalism, observing that Mitrany openly relied upon Lamarck's laws of evolution to explain the growth of functional unions (1966: 67–68). And this is

important because Mitrany's functionalism has remained a core component of all subsequent liberal IR theorizing (Sterling-Folker 2000).

16. For arguments along these lines see: Adler, Crawford, and Donnelly (1991); Held (1996); Keohane and Nye (1977, 1971); Keohane (1984); Rosecrance (1986); Rosenau (1976); and Zacher (1992).

17. In fact a great deal of realist scholarship has been devoted to the exploration of how perception or organizational culture can inhibit efficient responses to external threat. Reviews of realist works on these subjects, include Brooks (1997); Schweller and Priess (1997); Rose (1998); Zakaria (1992), and many of the neoclassical realist authors discussed in a later note.

18. Reviews of these contending realist categories and their differences may be found in Brooks (1997), Jervis (1999), Rose (1998), Schweller and Priess (1997), Spirtas (1996), Taliaferro (2000/01). Vasquez has claimed that these debates indicate degeneration of the realist paradigm itself (1998, 1997), but as Walt argues, "It is hardly evidence of degeneration when realists advance contradictory arguments or reach different conclusions, just as it is not a major issue whenever neo-Keynesian economists, Kinnerian psychologists, Darwinian sociobiologists, or quantum physics are at loggerheads" (1997: 933). See also Elman and Elman (1997b), Schweller (1999), and Buzan (1996).

19. Realists who believe that the selection-by-competition logic is induced by the environment are called "defensive" realists and Jervis includes under this label Herz, Waltz, Van Evera, Glaser and himself (1999: 49, 1998: 986). Spritas labels them "tragedy" realists and cites Herz, Waltz, Grieco, and Copeland as examples (1996). Realists who believe the logic is induced by genetic characteristics are called "offensive" realists, and Jervis cites as examples Schweller, Mearsheimer, and Gray (1999, 48–49, 1998: 986). Alternatively Spirtas labels them "evil" realists and cites Niebuhr, Morgenthau, and Schweller. See also Guzzini (1998: 203), and Thayer (2000).

20. Neoclassical realists are interested in how the domestic and individual levels of analysis act as filters for systemic pressures, and overviews of scholarly work that exemplifies this variant may be found in Rose (1998) and Schweller (1999). While the effects of domestic institutions is what interests many neoclassical realists, others are explicitly interested in how different biological parameters can affect foreign policy-making and international outcomes. The biological attributes of interest go far beyond the classical realism's power-lust, however, and include in-group/out-group distinctions (Mercer 1995; Schweller and Priess 1997), emotions and perceptions (Mercer 1999; Wohlforth 1994/5), and risk-aversion (Taliaferro 2000).

21. Many sociobiologists argue that it is inappropriate to generalize the concept of natural selection to the individual or group level because behaviors in the interest of survival and reproduction differ (and are in conflict) depending on whether one is discussing genes, individuals, or a group. This point remains debatable even among sociobiologists, however, in that natural selection might operate simultaneously on more than one level, so that groups were equivalent to individual competitors thereby making the existence of other groups relevant to group selection. Essays in Sober's collection (1984) that argue this issue include Williams, Wilson, Ruse and Wilson, Kitcher, and Sober.

22. In other words, realism can avoid positing functional institutional teleology if it recognizes that a Darwinist explanation can account for the evolutionary process but not necessarily the content of social practices and institutions. The issue of functional teleology is fundamental to Zakaria's 1992 review of Jack Snyder's *Myths*

of Empire, for example, and critiques of defensive realism, which appears to assume that the anarchic environment demands particular types of institutions and practices in order to fulfill particular types of functions. The resulting implications of this formulation would be a teleological end-point toward which nation-state institutions should be evolving, while Zakaria claims this is not realism's argument (1992: 194–96).

23. This is why the claim that neorealism needs a theory of the state in order to explain change is fundamentally misplaced. Hobden (1998: 69) and Wendt (1987: 342–44, 365–66) both make this argument, but it is greater explication of the implications of group formation in whatever historically contingent forms they take that is required instead. Thus while Hobden is correct that historical sociology cannot supply neorealism with a theory of the state (1998, 168), this is only because realism's Darwinist ontology allows it to subsume historical sociology as an approachap. The role of history in IR theorizing in general is considered in Jackson and Nexon (1999); Puchala (2000, 1995); Weber (1997); and a special symposium of *International Security* on "History and Theory" framed by Elman and Elman (1997a).

24. Waltz makes this argument in a number of places (1979: 76–77, 92–93, 118–119, 127–28), as does Zakaria (1992), and Levy notes that the role of learning "essentially has no independent explanatory power" in neorealist theory (1994: 297).

25. As Waever (1998: 724) points out, while neorealism may be hegemonic in security studies, this is "in contrast to general IR, where numerous articles are legitimized as critiques of the allegedly hegemonic neorealism, and critiques far out number the purported hegemon." Winnerstig provides ample evidence for this assertion (1999).

26. Angier (1998) provides an overview of recent work by various scientists on convergence theory, much of which is responding directly to Gould's (1989) *Wonderful Life.* See, in particular, Morris (1998).

27. The work of Karl Deutsch remains the best example of transactionalism, Ernst Haas and Leon Lindberg represent the neofunctionalist approach, and examples of federalism include the work of Altiero Spinelli and Peter Hay.

28. Added to this was the problem that, unlike the U.S. colonies, the EU did not contain states who had fought a common enemy together and was actually a combination of former allies and enemies who then faced a new common enemy in the Soviet Union. Thus there was a degree of security ambivalence toward one another that the U.S. presence managed to dampen but never put out, and it remains pertinent to the Franco-German relationship in particular. Thus many scholars have argued that French cooperation in the EU context is driven by its fear of German ascendance, which is the sort of competitive pressure realism would argue that the EU has done nothing to displace. See, for example, Gloannec (1992); Grieco (1995; 1996); Hopmann (1994).

REFERENCES

Adler, Emanuel, Beverly Crawford, and Jack Donnelly. 1991. Defining and Conceptualizing Progress in International Relations. In Emanuel Adler and Beverly Crawford, eds. *Progress in postwar international relations.* New York: Columbia University Press.

Almond, Gabriel A. 1989. The International-National Connection. *British Journal of Political Science* 19: 263–89.

Angier, Natalie. 1998. When Evolution Creates the Same Design Again and Again. *New York Times,* December 15.

Beer, Francis A. and Robert Hariman, eds. 1996. *Post-realism: The rhetorical turn in international relations.* East Lansing: Michigan State University Press.

Bowler, Peter J. 1984. *Evolution: The history of an idea.* Berkeley: University of California Press.

Brooks, Stephen G. 1997. Dueling Realisms. *International Organization* 51 (summer): 445–78.

Buzan, Barry. 1996. The Timeless Wisdom of Realism? In Steve Smith, Ken Booth, and Marysia Zalewski, eds. *International theory: Positivism and beyond.* Cambridge, U.K.: Cambridge University Press.

Buzan, Barry, Charles Jones, and Richard Little. 1993. *The logic of anarchy: Neorealism to structural realism.* New York: Columbia University Press.

Colclough, Christopher and James Manor, eds. 1991. *States or markets? Neo-liberalism and the development policy debate.* New York: Oxford University Press.

Copeland, Dale. 1998. Integrating Realism and Constructivism. Paper presented at the American Political Science Association, Annual Meeting, September 3–6, Boston, Massachusetts.

Cornett, Linda and James A. Caporaso. 1992. 'And Still it Moves!' State Interests and Social Forces in the European Community. In James N. Rosenau and Ernst-Otto Czempiel, eds. *Governance without government: Order and change in world politics.* Cambridge, U.K.: Cambridge University Press.

Crawford, Neta. 2000. The Passion of World Politics: Propositions on Emotion and Emotional Relationships. *International Security* 24 (spring): 120–22.

Darwin, Charles. 1859. *On the origin of species by means of natural selection.* London: Murray.

Denemark, Robert A. 1999. World System History: From Traditional International Politics to the Study of Global Relations. *International Studies Review* (1: 43–75).

Dennett, Daniel C. 1995. *Darwin's dangerous idea: Evolution and the meanings of life.* New York: Simon & Schuster.

Desch, Michael C. 1996. War and Strong States, Peace and Weak States? *International Organization* 50 (spring): 237–68

Druckman, Daniel. 1994. Nationalism, Patriotism, and Group Loyalty: A Social Psychological Perspective, *Mershon International Studies Review* 38 (April): 43–68.

Eldredge, Niles. 1995. *Reinventing Darwin: The great debate at the high table of evolutionary theory.* New York: John Wiley & Sons, Inc.

Eldredge, Niles and Stephen Jay Gould. 1972. Punctuated Equilibria: An Alternative to Phyletic Gradualism. In T. J. M Schopf, ed. *Models of paleobiology.* San Francisco: Freeman, Cooper, and Co.

Elman, Colin and Miriam Fendius Elman. 1997a. Diplomatic History and International Relations Theory: Respecting Difference and Crossing Boundaries. *International Security* 22 (summer): 5–21.

———. 1997b. Lakatos and Neorealism: A Reply to Vasquez. *American Political Science Review* 91(4): 899–912

Elman, Colin. 1996. Horses for Courses: Why *Not* Neorealist Theories of Foreign Policy. *Security Studies* 6 (autumn): 7–53.

Falger, Vincent S. E. 1997. Human Nature in Modern International Relations. Part I. Theoretical Backgrounds. *Research in Biopolitics* 5: 155–175.

———. 1994. Biopolitics and the Study of International Relations: Implications, Results and Perspectives, *Research in Biopolitics* 5: 115–34

Freyberg-Inan, Annette. 1999. Human Nature in International Relations Theory: An Analysis and Critique of Realist Assumptions About Motivation. Paper presented at the International Studies Association, Annual Meeting, February 16–20, Washington, D.C.

Fukuyama, Francis. 1999. *The great disruption: Human nature and the reconstitution of social order.* New York: Free Press.

———. 1998. Women and the Evolution of World Politics. *Foreign Affairs* 77, (5): 24–40.

———. 1989. The End of History? *The National Interest* 16 (summer): 3–18.

Gloannec, Ann-Marie Le. 1992. The Implications of German Unification for Western Europe. In Paul Stares, ed. *The new Germany and the new Europe.* Washington, D.C.: Brookings Institute.

Gilpin, Robert. 1996. Economic Evolution of National Systems. *International Studies Quarterly,* 40 (September): 411–31.

———. 1987. *The Political Economy of International Relations.* Princeton, New Jersey: Princeton University Press.

Goldstein, Joshua S. 1987. The Emperor's New Genes: Sociobiology and War. *International Studies Quarterly* 31 (March): 33–44.

Gould, Stephen Jay. 1989. *It's a wonderful life: The Burgess shale and the nature of history* New York: W. W. Norton and Company.

Gould, Stephen Jay and Niles Eldredge. 1977. Punctuated Equilibria: the Tempo and Mode of Evolution Reconsidered. *Paleobiology* 3: 115–51.

Gourevitch, Peter Alexis. 1986. *Politics in hard times: Comparative responses to international economic crises.* Ithaca, N.Y.: Cornell University Press.

———. 1978, The Second Image Reversed: The International Sources of Domestic Politics. *International Organization* 32 (autumn): 881–911.

Grieco, Joseph M. 1999. Realism and Regionalism: American Power and German and Japanese Institutional Strategies During and After the Cold War. In Ethan B. Kapstein and Michael Mastanduno, eds. *Unipolar politics: Realism and state strategies after the cold war.* New York: Columbia University Press.

———. 1996. State Interests and Institutional Rule Trajectories: A Neorealist Interpretation of the Maastricht Treaty and European Economic and Monetary Union. In *Security Studies,* 5 (Spring): 261–306.

———. 1995. The Maastricht Treaty, Economic and Monetary Union and the Neo-Realist Research Programme. *Review of International Studies* 21:21–40.

———. 1990. *Cooperation among nations: Europe, America, and non-tariff barriers to trade.* Ithaca, N.Y.: Cornell University Press.

Gurr, Ted R. 1988. War, Revolution and the Growth of the Coercive State. *Comparative Political Studies* 21: 45–65

Guzzini, Stefano. 1998. *Realism in international relations and international political economy: The continuing story of a death foretold.* London and New York: Routledge.

Hasenclever, Andreas, Peter Mayer, and Volker Rittberger. 1997. *Theories of international regimes.* Cambridge, U.K.: Cambridge University Press.

Held, David. 1996. The Decline of the Nation State. In Geoff Eley and Ronald Grigor Suny, eds. *Becoming national: A reader.* New York: Oxford University Press.

Hinde, Robert A. 1993. Aggression and War: Individuals, Groups, and States. In Philip E. Tetlock, et al., eds. *Behavior, society, and international conflict.* New York: Oxford University Press.

Hintze, Otto. 1975. Military Organization and the Organization of the State. In F. Gilbert, ed. *The historical essays of Otto Hintze.* New York: Oxford University Press

Hobden, Stephen. 1998. *International relations and historical sociology: Breaking down boundaries.* London: Routledge.

Hoffmann, Stanley. 1995. An American Social Science: International Relations (reprint). In James Der Derian, ed. *International theory: Critical investigations.* New York University Press.

Hopmann, P. Terrence. 1994. French Perspectives on International Relations After the Cold War. *Mershon International Studies Review* 38 (April): 69–93.

Howard, Michael. 1978. *War the liberal conscience.* London: Temple Smith.

Jackson, Patrick Thaddeus and Daniel H. Nexon. 1999. Relations Before States: Substance, Process, and the Study of World Politics. *European Journal of International Relations* 5 (3): 291–332.

Jervis, Robert. 1999. Realism, Neoliberalism and Cooperation: Understanding the Debate. *International Security* 24 (summer): 42–63.

———. 1998. Realism in the Study of World Politics. *International Organization* 52 (autumn): 971–91.

———. 1991–1992. The Future of World Politics: Will it Resemble the Past? *International Security* 16: 39–73.

Kahler, Miles. 1998. Rationality in International Relations. *International Organization* 52 (autumn): 919–41.

———. 1997. Inventing International Relations: International Relations Theory After 1945. In Michael W. Doyle and G. John Ikenberry, eds. *New thinking in international relations theory.* Boulder, Colo.: Westview Press.

Katzenstein, Peter, ed. 1978. *Between power and plenty: Foreign economic politics of advanced industrial states.* Madison: University of Wisconsin Press.

Katzenstein, Peter J. , Robert O. Keohane, and Stephen D. Krasner. 1998. *International Organization* at Fifty: Exploration and Contestation in the Study of World Politics. *International Organization* 52 (autumn).

Kegley, Charles W. Jr. 1991. The New Containment Myth: Realism and the Anomaly of European Integration. *Ethics and International Affairs* 5:99–114.

Keohane, Robert O. 1993. Institutional Theory and the Realist Challenge After the Cold War. In David A. Baldwin, ed. *Neorealism and neoliberalism: The contemporary debate.* New York: Columbia University Press.

———. 1990. International Liberalism Reconsidered. In John Dunn, ed. *The economic limits to modern politics.* Cambridge, U.K.: Cambridge University Press.

———. 1989. *International Institutions and State Power: Essays in International Relations Theory.* Boulder, Colo.: Westview Press.

———. 1984. *After hegemony: Cooperation and discord in the world political economy.* Princeton, N.J.: Princeton University Press.

Keohane, Robert O. and Helen Milner, eds. 1996. *Internationalization and domestic politics.* Cambridge, U.K.: Cambridge University Press.

Keohane, Robert O. and Joseph S. Nye. 1977. *Power and interdependence*, 1st ed. Glenview, Ill.: Scott, Foresman and Company.

———, eds. 1971. *Transnational relations and world politics.* Cambridge, Mass.: Harvard University Press

Kitcher, Philip. 1987. On the Crest of La Nouvelle Vague. *International Studies Quarterly* 31 (March): 45–52.

Lapid, Yosef. 1996. Nationalism and Realist Discourses of International Relations. In Francis A. Beer and Robert Hariman, eds. *Post-realism: The rhetorical turn in international relations.* East Lansing: Michigan State University Press.

Lapid, Yosef, and Friedrich Kratochwil. 1996. Revisiting the 'National': Toward and Identity Agenda in Neorealism? In Yosef Lapid and Friedrich Kratochwil, eds. *The return of culture and identity in IR theory.* Boulder, Colo.: Lynne Rienner Publishers.

Layne, Christopher. 1993. The Unipolar Illusion: Why New Great Powers Will Rise. *International Security* 17 (spring).

Lebow, Richard Ned. 1994. The Long Peace, the End of the Cold War, and the Failure of Realism. *International Organization* 48 (spring): 249–78.

Legro, Jeffrey, and Andrew Moravcsik. 1999. Is Anybody Still a Realist? *International Security* 24 (fall): 5–55.

Levy, Jack. 1994. Learning and Foreign Policy: Sweeping a Conceptual Minefield. *International Organization* 48 (spring): 279–312.

Little, Richard. 1996. The Growing Relevance of Pluralism? In Steve Smith, Ken Booth, and Marysia Zalewski, eds. *International theory: Positivism and beyond.* Cambridge, U.K.: Cambridge University Press.

March, James G. and Johan P. Olsen. 1998. The Institutional Dynamics of International Political Orders. *International Organization* 52 (autumn): 943–70.

Mearsheimer, John J. 1994–1995. The False Promise of International Institutions. *International Security* 19 (winter): 5–49.

———. 1990. Back to the Future: Instability in Europe After the Cold War. *International Security,* 15 (1): 5–56.

Mercer, Jonathan. 1999. Emotion Adds Life. Presented at the Annual Meeting of the International Studies Association, February 18–21, Washington, D.C.

———. 1995. Anarchy and Identity. *International Organization* 49 (2):229–52.

Milner, Helen. 1988. *Resisting protectionism: Global industries and the politics of international trade.* Princeton, N.J.: Princeton University Press.

Modelski, George. 1996. Evolutionary Paradigm for Global Politics. *International Studies Quarterly* 40 (September): 321–42.

Modelski, George and Kazimierz Poznanski. 1996. Evolutionary Paradigms in the Social Sciences. *International Studies Quarterly* 40 (September): 315–19.

Modelski, George and William R. Thompson. 1999. The Long and the Short of Global Politics in the Twenty-first Century: An Evolutionary Approach, *International Studies Review* 1 (summer).

Morris, Simon Conway. 1998. *The crucible of creation: The burgess shale and the rise of animals.* Oxford: Oxford University Press.

O'Hear, Anthony. 1997. *Beyond evolution: Human nature and the limits of evolutionary explanation.* Oxford, U.K.: Clarendon Press.

Posen, Barry. 1984. *The sources of military doctrine: France, Britain, and Germany between the world wars.* Ithaca, N.Y.: Cornell University Press.

Puchala, Donald J. 2000. Marking a Weberian Moment: Our Discipline Looks Ahead. *International Studies Perspectives* 1 (August): 133–44.

———. 1995. The Pragmatics of International History. *Mershon International Studies Review* 39 (April): 1–18.

Quandt, William B. 1988. The Electoral Cycle and the Conduct of American Foreign Policy. In Charles W. Kegley, Jr. and Eugene R. Wittkopf, eds. *The domestic sources of American foreign policy: Insights and evidence.* New York: St. Martin's Press.

Rasler, Karen A. and William R. Thompson. 1994. *The great powers and global struggle: 1490–1990.* Lexington: University Press of Kentucky

———. 1989. *War and state making: The shaping of the global powers.* Boston: Unwin Hyman.

Resende-Santos, Joao. 1999. Socialization and Emulation in International Relations Theory, presented at the Annual Meeting of the American Political Science Association, September, 2–5, Atlanta, Georgia.

———. 1996. Anarchy and the Emulation of Military Systems: Military Organization and Technology in South American, 1870–1914. In Benjamin Frankel, ed. *Realism: Restatements and renewal.* London: Frank Cass.

Rogowski, Ronald. 1989. *Coalitions and commerce: How trade affects domestic political alignments* . Princeton, N.J.: Princeton University Press.

Rose, Gideon. 1998. Neoclassical Realism and Theories of Foreign Policy. *World Politics* 51 (October): 144–72.

Rosecrance, Richard. 1986. *The rise of the trading state: Commerce and conquest in the modern world.* New York: Basic Books.

Rosecrance, Richard and Arthur A. Stein, eds. 1993. *The domestic bases of grand strategy.* Ithaca, N.Y.: Cornell University Press.

Rosenau, James N. 1981. *The study of political adaptation.* London: Frances Pinter.

———. 1976. Capabilities and Control in an Interdependent World. *International Security* (fall): 32–49.

Ruggie, John Gerard. 1998. *Constructing the world polity: Essays on international institutionalization.* New York: Routledge.

———. 1992. Multilateralism: The Anatomy of an Institution. *International Organization* 46 (summer): 561–98.

Schweller, Randall L. 1999. The Progressive Nature of Neoclassical Realism. Paper prepared for the Conference on Progress in International Relations Theory. Arizona State University, January 14–17.

Schweller, Randall L. and David Priess. 1997. A Tale of Two Realisms: Expanding the Institutions Debate. *Mershon International Studies Review* 41 (May): 1–32.

Sewell, James Patrick. 1966. *Functionalism and world politics: A study based on United Nations programs financing economic development.* Princeton, N.J.: Princeton University Press.

Shimko, Keith L. 1992. Realism, Neorealism, and American Liberalism. *The Review of Politics* (spring): 281–301.

Smith, Steve. 1996. Positivism and Beyond. In Steve Smith, Ken Booth, and Marysia Zalewski, eds. *International theory: Positivism and beyond.* Cambridge, U.K.: Cambridge University Press.

Snyder, Jack. 1990. Averting Anarchy in the New Europe. *International Security* 14 (spring): 5–41.

Spirtas, Michael. 1996. A House Divided: Tragedy and Evil in Realist Theory. In Benjamin Frankel, ed. *Realism: Restatements and renewals.* London: Frank Cass.

Sober, Elliott, ed. 1994. *Conceptual issues in evolutionary biology,* 2nd ed. Cambridge, Mass.: MIT Press.

Somit, Albert, and Steven A. Peterson. 1999. Rational Choice and Biopolitics: A (Darwinian) Tale of Two Theories. *PS: Political Science and Politics* 32 (March): 39–44.

———. 1998. Review Article: Biopolitics After Three Decades—A Balance Sheet. *British Journal of Political Science* 28 (July): 559–71.

Spruyt, Hendrik. 1994. *The sovereign state and its competitors: An analysis of systems change.* Princeton, N.J.: Princeton University Press.

Sterling-Folker, Jennifer. 2000. Competing Paradigms or Birds of a Feather? Constructivism and Neoliberal Institutionalism Compared. *International Studies Quarterly* 44 (March): 97–119.

———. 1997. Realist Environment, Liberal Process, and Domestic-Level Variables. *International Studies Quarterly* 41 (March): 1–26.

Taliaferro, Jeffrey W. 2000–2001. Security-Seeking Under Anarchy: Defensive Realism Revisited. *International Security* 25 (Winter), no. 3.

———. 2000. *Power politics and the balance of risk: Why do great powers fight peripheral wars.* Manuscript In Progress.

Thayer, Bradley. 2000. Evolutionary Theory and Realism, *International Security* 25 (2) (fall).

Thomson, Janice E. 1992. Explaining the Regulation of Transnational Practices: A State-Building Approach. In James N. Rosenau and Ernst-Otto Czempiel, eds. *Governance without government: Order and change in world politics.* Cambridge, U.K.: Cambridge University Press.

Thompson, William R. 1997. The Evolution of Political-Economic Challenges in the Active Zone. *Review of International Political Economy* 4: 286–318.

Tickner, J. Ann. 1999. Why Women Can't Run the World: International Politics According to Francis Fukuyama. *International Studies Review* 1 (fall): 3–12.

Tilly, Charles. 1975. Reflections on the History of European State Making. In Charles Tilly, ed. *The formation of national states in western Europe.* Princeton, N.J.: Princeton University Press.

Urwin, Derek. 1995. *The community of Europe: A history of European integration since 1945,* 2nd ed. London: Longman Group.

Vasquez, John A. 1998. *The power of power politics: From classical realism to neotraditionalism.* Cambridge, U.K.: Cambridge University Press.

———. 1997. The Realist Paradigm and Degenerative Versus Progressive Research Programs: An Appraisal of Neotraditional Research on Waltz's Balancing Proposition. *American Political Science Review* 91 (4): 899–912

Waever, Ole. 1998. The Sociology of a Not so International Discipline: American and European Developments in International Relations. *International Organization* 52 (autumn): 687–728.

Walt, Stephen M. 1997. The Progressive Power of Realism. *American Political Science Review* 91 (4): 899–912

Waltz, Kenneth. 1999. Globalization and Governance, *PS: Political Science and Politics* 33 (December): 693–700.

———. 1979. *Theory of International Politics.* New York: McGraw-Hill.

Weber, Steven. 1997. Institutions and Change. In Michael W. Doyle and G. John Ikenberry, eds. *New thinking in international relations theory.* Boulder, Colo.: Westview Press.

Wendt, Alexander. 1994. Collective Identity Formation and the International State. *American Political Science Review* 99 (June): 384–96.

———. 1992. Anarchy is What States Make of It: The Social Construction of Power Politics. *International Organization* 46 (spring): 391–425.

Wilmer, Franke. 1996. Indigenous Peoples, Marginal Sites, and the Changing Context of World Politics. In Francis A. Beer and Robert Hariman, eds. *Post-realism: The rhetorical turn in international relations.* East Lansing: Michigan State University Press.

Winnerstig, Michael. 1999. Dnacing the Master's Waltz: The Hidden Influence of Theory of International Politics. Paper presented at the Annual Meeting of the International Studies Association, Washington, D.C., February 16–20.

Wohlforth, William C. 1994–1995. Realism and the End of the Cold War. *International Security* 19 (Winter): 91–129.

Zacher, Mark W. 1992. The Decaying Pillars of the Westphalian Temple: Implications for International Order and Governance. In James N. Rosenau and Ernst-Otto Czempiel, eds. *Governance without government: Order and change in world politics.* Cambridge, U.K.: Cambridge University Press.

Zacher, Mark W. and Richard A. Matthew. 1995. Liberal International Theory: Common Threads, Divergent Strands. In Charles W. Kegley, Jr., ed. *Controversies in international relations theory: Realism and the neoliberal challenge.* New York: St. Martin's Press.

Zakaria, Fareed. 1992. Realism and Domestic Politics: A Review Essay. *International Security* 17 (1): 177–98.

chapter 5

Diversity or Uniformity in the Modern World?
Answers from Evolutionary Theory, Learning, and Social Adaptation

Hendrik Spruyt

INTRODUCTION

Is the world becoming ever more alike? Some of the most influential literature in political science suggests that international competition will lead to high degrees of uniformity in institutions and similarity of policies. Rivalry in security affairs will weed out those states that are too feeble to defend themselves or that engage in policies that jeopardize their own security. Globalization and economic competition will relegate inefficient nations to secondary status. Such arguments, explicitly or implicitly, rely on evolutionary models that stress environmental pressures and selection by relative fitness. Less competitive forms of government and less successful economic policies will be selected out. The result will be institutional convergence.

The argument that selection necessarily implies greater pressures for convergence and uniformity incorrectly applies insights from natural evolution. A closer reading of natural selection theory implies no such trend. In addition, where some degree of uniformity and similarity are observed, causal mechanisms other than selective forces might be at work. Empirical evidence of uniformity presents no *prima facie* evidence for the applicability of natural-selection models.

This is not to say that evolutionary theory has no relevance for social science theory. But evolutionary arguments borrowed from the biological sciences are more appropriately regarded as useful metaphors rather than as true models. Natural evolution differs in important ways from social evolution. While one might search for the social and cultural equivalents of genes and gene mutations, the heuristic analogies are hardly equivalents.

I argue, furthermore, that political scientists who wish to utilize evolutionary arguments should blend learning perspectives and sociological institutionalist arguments with evolutionary theory. Sociological institutionalism and learning perspectives suggest that convergence of institutions and behaviors are attributable to intentional patterns of behavior. Competitive selection over time is only one of the causal dynamics. Insofar as convergence occurs to signal credible commitments and to demonstrate conformity in preferences, institutions and behaviors might not be indicative of structural similarity (isomorph in the true sense) but instead reveal a pattern of mutual expectations. They will be pseudomorph, similar in outward appearance but in fact internally dissimilar. For example, it might appear that newly developing states (as some in the former Soviet Union) have adopted particular institutional types and practices popular in the West (democracy, market based economics). But they do so only to fit external expectations and images in order to gain aid or foreign capital. Internally, they lack domestic conditions to implement such institutions in practice.

I conclude that reasoning by evolutionary metaphors may be helpful for understanding certain phenomena but that the repertoire of heuristic images suggested by evolutionary theory, through which we might model the social world, is in fact richer than linear convergence arguments might suggest.

APPLICATIONS OF EVOLUTIONARY ARGUMENTS IN POLITICAL SCIENCE

Evolutionary theories have long influenced social science. Marx believed that his own work paralleled the insights of Charles Darwin, and sent him a copy of Das Kapital, where it remained—pages uncut—in Darwin's library. And, of course, Social Darwinism equally misapplied Darwin's insights to justify a variety of misguided policies.

More recently evolutionary theories have received renewed attention in a variety of fields within the social sciences. Particularly, three distinct bodies of scholarship explain similarity of form and behavior by invoking insights from evolutionary theory: competitive selection arguments in structural realism; globalization arguments in political economy; and theories that stress the convergence around certain norms.

Structural realism, particularly as articulated in Kenneth Waltz's seminal work (Waltz 1979), clearly uses an argument based on evolution and selective pressure to argue for similarity of behavior. In the structural realist perspective, the international system imposes environmental constraints on the units in the system. Some modes of behavior will be more successful strategies for surviving the rigorous demands of this predatorial environment. Less efficient or effective ones will prove unfit, and will fall by the wayside. Consequently, as in market environments, convergence results because "behaviors are selected for their consequences . . . individual entrepreneurs need not know how to increase their chances of turning a profit" (Waltz 1979: 76). Selection over time is the critical variable. In the anarchical realm of international politics, isomorphism is due to Darwinian dynamics, here interpreted as strong-form selection. Whether or not an individual unit (state) learns from other actors or not is essentially immaterial. The end-result will be the same: homogeneity of behavior among the units composing the system.[1]

Some arguments in international political economy look remarkably similar to structural realism (no surprise perhaps given Waltz's use of the market analogy).

Neoclassical economics takes the view that competition will induce actors to behave similarly or face their demise.

> Competitive forces will see that those who behave in a rational manner ... will survive, and those who do not will fail: and that therefore in a evolutionary competitive situation ... the behavior that will be continuously observed will be that of people who have acted according to such standards. (North 1990: 19)

Likewise, various perspectives submit that the contemporary globalization of trade and finance may lead to convergence of policies and institutions. The logic of explanation resembles Darwinian evolutionary arguments. The internationalization of trade and the increasingly fluid financial transactions across borders impose new environmental constraints and pressures on individual states and private actors. Indeed, David Andrews (1994) likens the changes in international financial flows to the structural condition of anarchy. In this new environment, certain routines, production techniques, and economic policies are more competitive than others. Actors that engage in less fit behaviors will be weeded out by competition, for example, when firms fail because others have taken over their consumer markets, or will be relegated to secondary status, and also in the instance of, when states fail to develop economically to the same extent as others do.

Over time one should see greater similarity in responses to the internationalization of trade and finance. Keohane and Milner, consequently, pose the question of whether we are witnessing a linear trend toward less government autonomy or whether domestic institutions and coalitions may channel and limit such external pressure (Keohane and Milner 1996: chap. 1, 22).[2]

A third strand of literature emphasizes how an evolutionary logic underlies the emergence of normative frameworks. In Robert Axelrod's analysis, certain norms prove to have long-run iterative benefits (Axelrod 1981, 1984, 1986). This will give the adherents to those norms benefits that nonadherents will not have. Given that even a small group in the population can accrue such long-term benefits, a small group may overcome the larger population in due time.

BUT WHAT DO WE EXACTLY TAKE OVER FROM EVOLUTIONARY THEORY?

Components of Evolutionary Theory

Biologists commonly identify several key variables to explain the rate and pattern of evolution. Variability, rate and character of mutation, length of generations, size of populations, and natural selection, are often adduced as the primary causal forces. Thus, while social scientists have incorporated evolutionary theories from the biological sciences by stressing the importance of selection, in the more comprehensive view of natural evolution it forms only one element among several.

Moreover, biologists disagree on the relative importance of selection vis-à-vis the other factors at work, and they dissent on the conjunction and interrelation of the various causal mechanisms.

Variability refers to the differences among individuals in genetic type and morphological structure. Variation can occur within species, in which case, natural selection of less-fit types leads to new offspring within the same species. Or variation can occur between species, in which case, selection works purely as a winnowing out of less-fit types.

Such inheritable variations occur through spontaneous and random mutations, which lack any specific generalizable cause. Since mutations occur between generations, the length of generations also influences the rate of evolutionary change. Statistically, the relative rate of mutation will be affected by the number of times that a mutation occurs. Given a random but fixed value of mutation the chances that a more adaptive trait will emerge that would affect the larger population go up as generational changes occur rapidly (that is, there will be more possibilities at success in a given environment).

Absolute population size matters as well. The larger the population, the greater the chances of a mutation becoming established in the population. Thus, if mutations arise once in a million, then in a population of ten million, the mutation will become established in twenty-five generations. But in a population of only ten thousand, it would take twenty-five thousand generations (Simpson 1984: 66. The example assumes a selective value of 0.01).

Finally, evolution is affected by natural selection. "An organism must be viable in an available environment in order to reproduce, and selection inevitably eliminates at least the most grossly inadaptive types of structure." (Simpson 1984: 74).

If most evolutionists can agree on the key ingredients of evolutionary theory they differ in the relative importance they place on each of these variables, how these causal variables interact or reinforce one another, and they differ in their interpretations of Darwinian theory.

Debates Among Biologists

One set of debates centers on the interpretation and importance of the concept of fitness. Fitness is the reproductive success of a genotype as compared to the progeny of other competing genotypes. In the original Darwinian formulation fitness referred to the relative ability of a complex organism to perform the functions demanded by the environment for survival. The greater the ability to meet such demands the greater the success at reproduction.

> Natural Selection acts exclusively by the preservation and accumulation of variations which are beneficial under the organic and inorganic conditions to which each creature is exposed.[3]

In original Darwinian theory natural selection constituted a struggle for existence, with those species most suited to particular environmental demands having the advantage in reproduction. In this sense fitness constituted adaptation. This was then the functionalist aspect to evolutionary theory.

Another biological perspective downplays the importance of adaptation for reproduction. Varieties of species that are not well adapted to particular environments may survive, even displace others, purely because of differential fertility and fecundity (Grant 1985: 92–94). For example, biologists who stress the key importance of adaptation would conjecture that long-neck giraffes displaced shorter-neck species variations because they were more adapted to the demands of the environment. Long-neck giraffes could reach farther up trees for edible vegetation. Thus they had an advantage in survival and could reproduce. Those biologists downplaying the importance of adaptation would argue that long-neck giraffes displaced the shorter-neck variation not because of their adaptation to the environment, but perhaps because their reproductive rate was simply much higher.[4]

In the Darwinian version fitness thus relates to the selection and winnowing of less fit. The organism that is more fit than others, that is more adapted to the environment, will continue to survive whereas those that cannot meet such demands in an absolute sense will die out in the long run. The rival version sees selection as less important, but stresses random mutation and reproduction.

The Darwinian view lends itself to interpreting evolution as directional and as progress (even if Darwin himself was of two minds on the matter).[5] If there is successive adaptation over time to a set environment, then evolution implies direction to greater perfectability. The alternative Darwinian view that stresses other factors besides natural selection, is less susceptible to being interpreted as directional. Evolution is undirected in lacking a general pattern of development, and is unpredictable. Random mutations and selection by exogenous events (such as cataclysmic natural events) drive evolutionary change.

Contrary to some popular interpretations of Darwinist theory, evolution thus does not entail progress. There is no reason to believe that later stages in evolutionary phases yield more complex, or more intricate solutions to environmental challenges. The visual conceptualization of an evolutionary ladder is mistaken. All evolution is contingent, and consists of random mutations to the external environment (Gould 1980, 1989).

Furthermore, while the external environment imposes material demands on the organisms in that environment there will be a multiplicity of mutations that will constitute fit responses to the environmental shift. For example, a drop in the global temperature might serve as an advantage for complex organisms that are more suited for cold climates (because of fur, layers of fat, and so forth). But these objective conditions may be met in various ways. Some species variations will survive because of their new migratory patterns, others because genetic variation in the species will lead them to burrow or hibernate, and so on. Multiple responses exist to such environmental demands. Not one variant in the species will proliferate following a speciation event but many.

Finally, biologists and paleontologists disagree among themselves on the importance of speciation events. Within evolutionary theory some adhere to a gradualist view of evolution while others see far more rapid change. Most recently the latter has become associated with the works of Gould and Eldredge, but arguably Goldschmidt had pioneered such ideas in the 1930s (Gould 1989; Simpson 1984: xv, xvi, 51f.). In Goldschmidt's views, dramatic variations in the genetic record, "hopeful monsters" could lead to dramatic and quick shifts. In the contemporary Punctuated Equilibrium model, critical changes in the environment will lead to dramatic and fast transformations, followed by long periods of relative stasis thereafter. Gradualists challenge such arguments by suggesting that incomplete taxonomies and lack of evidentiary proof of gradual change do not demonstrate that evolution does not work by long-term selection over sometimes minute differences.[6]

I do not weigh in on these debates. Nor is it my intention to clarify how close natural evolutionary processes and social evolution resemble each other, or how natural selection and theories of biological evolution should be more correctly understood. My intention has been merely to elucidate the various strands within biological debates on evolutionary theory, and to suggest how—by using specific interpretations of evolutionary theory—political scientists have consciously or unconsciously interpreted selection and homogeneity in a restricted manner. Indeed, the very complexity of such debates among the specialists of evolutionary research suggests that social scientists proceed with trepidation in adhering to any singular interpretation of evolution. I aim to expand the universe of metaphors that political science has borrowed from biological theory, and to suggest how other theories outside of evolutionary theory should contribute to explanations of convergence and homogeneity.

THE SELECTIVE USE OF EVOLUTIONARY METAPHORS IN POLITICAL SCIENCE

Evolutionary theory has gained recent adherence as a useful analogy to understand how competitive pressures lead to convergence.[7] In ascribing to states certain appropriate behavior in the face of security threats, structural realists assume that international systemic conditions will produce regular patterns of behavior. Certain behavior will be more fit than others. Similarly, economic arguments that globalization will lead to convergence assume a single uniformity of responses. Those types of arguments are mistaken on several grounds.

First, as suggested in our earlier discussion of evolutionary theory, natural evolution does not predict uniformity of responses. Only the strong-form selection perspective lends credence to that argument. The strong-form view of selection places a premium on centripetal dynamics.

> Selection is then entirely centripetal. It acts to eliminate the variant forms, and it ends to reduce variation in any direction and to concentrate the population around a point, the optimum condition. (Simpson 1984: 83)

Such selection thus reduces the variation in adaptive forms to only a few types, perhaps even to the point of singularity.

But this is only one of several dynamics at work (as I will later discuss in greater detail). Evolutionary theory does not presuppose such a trend to singularity, and, consequently, on theoretical grounds, one should not expect the competitive pressure of the international environment to lead to a uniform population of institutions and behavioral repertoires.

Conversely, if one were to observe such similarities it seems highly unlikely, given the variation among natural endowments, existing institutions, past historical track records, and the diversity of national cultures, that the similarities should be attributed solely to selective pressures. A correct reading of natural evolutionary theory would suggest variation.

Second, empirically, competitive selection and convergence has often not taken place in the manner suggested by the strict adherents of selection and fitness. There is little evidence that states have shown the uniform patterns of behavior that structural realism predicts. Indeed, the number of independent and sovereign states has increased dramatically in this century although the competitive environment, that is, the structural condition of anarchy, has not altered. Some of these independent states possess only insignificant military resources of their own and yet most of them are not likely to be selected out for the foreseeable future.

Moreover, as Robert Jervis has argued, if "falling by the wayside" merely means that states decline in rank, then internal factors are arguably as important as systemic pressures to conform to certain behavior (Jervis 1997: 106, 107). One might object to Jervis's argument that such an internal account of rank decline actually does conform with a competitive selection argument. States that for domestic reasons choose to engage in certain policies that make them less competitive will decline in rank. But if internal factors determine relative success then this suggests that agents consciously choose certain strategies in response to these pressures. Hence, this would collapse into an explanation based on learning and agent choices, rather than constitute one that is based on systemic and unintentional selection to some optimal point.

Such internal accounts further suggest that there is always a multiplicity of "fit" responses to certain pressures. Continuous and varied mutations spring up all the time. Threats to one's security can be met by alliances, collective security arrangements, internal balancing. Alliances can be loose or tight, even shade into hegemonic domination. Internal balancing can take the form of coercive extraction or negotiation.[8] It is impossible to determine one singular solution to security threats that was uniquely superior to all others at a given time. Success in war is only a weak indicator of institutional or policy fitness. Was Wilhelmine Germany institutionally or behaviorally "unfit" because it lost World War I? One might argue (D'Lugo and Rogowski 1993) that certain domestic institutions, for example, the British income tax, gave Germany's rivals a competitive advantage. Yet if Germany had succeeded early on in the Marne campaign, or in the offensives of 1918, or if England had stayed out of the war altogether, should those same German institutions now be regarded as competitively more fit?

More damning still, many states do not seem to engage in the competitive struggle that realism seems to presuppose. Sweden, Switzerland, and perhaps contemporary Japan, appear to have opted for different strategies for increasing their welfare than military competition.

The argument in political economy that globalization will lead to convergence of institutions and practices has proved incorrect as well. Some institutional practices, such as the independence of Central Banks, have indeed spread, even if not everywhere (Biersteker 1992). But factors other than competitive selection are the primary cause. The trend toward Central Bank independence has largely been instigated by international lending authorities (as the International Monetary Fund) and by the insistence of major private lenders. Hierarchical imposition, not blind selection, has been the key force. Governments that wish to attract foreign capital also wish to signal their credible commitment to a stable fiscal and monetary policy. Tying one's hands through granting Central Banks' independence from political authorities accomplishes this. A sociological institutional explanation, as well as rational-choice arguments, are thus more powerful explanations of this pattern of convergence than an evolutionary paradigm stressing competitive selection.

If strong-form selection did indeed hold we should expect to see convergence to similarly functioning institutions. Indeed, they might not even have to look alike provided they were equally effective and efficient. Ill-adapted forms would be weeded out. Conversely, if sociological dynamics and learning effects operate we might see similarity of institutions in external form but which are not necessarily equally effective or efficient. They would not perform the same functions in each country but serve simply as signalling devices or emerge in order to conform to external expectations. The institutions and policies will look alike but in fact be dissimilar. I would call such apparent similarity "pseudomorphism"—similar in appearance but not alike in function or meaning. They are the result of expected role patterns, rather than the competitive dynamics that would reward structural and functional similarity. In short, if we do see convergence, this need not be attributed to selective pressures.

Microlevel organizations (corporations) and macrolevel policies (national economies) thus continue to show variation. Historically developed domestic institutional arrangements, such as the existence of a powerful, interventionist state, determine the degree to which governments will tend to intervene in the future and how they intervene. Similarly, they also determine the degree to which markets are centralized and the reigning economic ideology will be key factors in generating specific corporate responses (Pauly and Reich 1997). At the macro level, national economies continue to show considerable variation as well (Gilpin 1996).

Adherents of natural selection arguments, who reject strong-form selection, would find little surprise in this multiplicity of responses. In this sense those arguing for convergence based on analogies to natural selection criteria simply misapply such criteria by unconsciously accepting strong selection views.

Conversely, one should not see such variation as proof that weak-form natural selection (which sees multiple responses to environmental pressure) is directly applicable to the social sciences. (This would thus validate the strict application of natural evolutionary models but in exactly the opposite manner of the strong-form selectionists.) The variation in responses does not constitute proof that evolutionary diversification in the face of external pressure is the key variable. As indicated above, the differences in such responses are caused by deliberate efforts at differentiation, not accidental variation. Actors try to utilize their comparative advantages. Moreover, the variation in responses has to do with differences in what individuals see as legitimate institutions and what types of institutions and behaviors have a taken-for-granted quality.[9] French and Japanese producers and consumers will continue to expect greater degrees of government intervention due to previous learning processes (which are only imperfectly understood as means/ends calculations) and ideological perspectives.

Arguments that certain norms spread in populations, as in Axelrod's model, resemble competitive selection arguments in some respects (Axelrod 1981; 1984; 1986). Where actors engage in certain patterns of behavior that prove to have long-term benefits, their success might be entirely unintentional. For example, cooperation between Amish farmers, might not be directed at increasing their overall competitiveness vis-à-vis non-Amish farmers, but their value structure might nevertheless give them such an advantage.

In most cases, however, it is likely that normative behaviors do take the reactions of others into account as well as the potential payoffs of such cooperation. Indeed, Axelrod's Tit-for-Tat model is based on the principle of reciprocity. In this sense, the selection mechanism once again deviates from an unintentional, natural selection model, and incorporates sociological institutionalist and learning arguments.

In sum, the bias toward strong-form selection theory is mistaken. A more correct reading of evolutionary theory reveals that such unilinear trends need not occur. Thus, when social scientists seek to incorporate insights from natural selection, they should, on theoretical grounds, expect greater variation. Moreover, on empirical grounds, the social world reveals greater variation than implied by strong selectionist perspectives. The reason for this variation lies in the differences between natural environments and social ones, and the intentionality of human agents.

INTEGRATING LEARNING, SOCIAL ADAPTATION, AND EVOLUTIONARY ARGUMENTS

Evolution in the natural world and in socially constructed environments differ in several important respects. These differences suggest how learning and institution-alist arguments need to be part of applications of evolutionary theory to the social sciences. Within biology the modification is generated at the genetic level. It is not clear what the equivalent of genetic variation is within social environments. Some scholars, who explore the parallels between evolutionary theory and economics, argue that the variation in behavior at the individual level is the analytic equivalent of genetic modification. Given the methodological individualism inherent in economic explanations this is hardly surprising.[10] Individuals might thus display a variety of behaviors in response to change in their economic environment, and markets will select among these variations of individual behaviors. Others suggest that larger aggregates are more relevant. One might thus use evolutionary arguments to discuss the selective advantage of firms, tribes, or even states (Cederman 1997; Spruyt 1994).

But whichever level is chosen—the individual or aggregates thereof—the mutation occurs in non-random fashion. Individuals learn, indeed anticipate in advance what the environment might look like. This differs from the random mutation and chance selection in the natural world.[11]

Moreover, the aggregate of such learning and instrumental adaptation will in turn affect, even create, the very environment that imposes constraints and opportunities on the other actors within that system. So not only is the modification intentionally induced, but the selective forces that come into play are similarly social creations. They are not material factors that simply present themselves to an ignorant genetic pool. So both modification and selection will work differently in the social environment. This non-random mutation and social construction of environments thus reinforces the relevance of the Lamarckian view of evolution in addition to the Darwinian perspective. (Indeed, biologists and paleontologists emphasize this perhaps more than social scientists. See, for example, Gould 1980.)

Finally, fitness for a particular social environment must be understood in different terms than fitness for a natural environment. Fitness need not refer to differential effectiveness, efficiency, or fecundity. Certain institutions or practices may become normatively and socially unacceptable. Slavery is one example. But certain practices of warfare might qualify as well. These practices might very well have survived were it not for changes in preferences and norms that altered the social environment in new directions.

Evolutionary arguments are thus only one theoretical approach that might explain convergence. Learning and sociological institutionalist arguments must be necessary components of arguments analyzing convergence and uniformity in a given population.

Learning

Social learning may be described as the ability of decision-makers and groups to distill particular lessons from the past and adjust their behavior, policies, and institutional arrangements to pursue their preferences. While there are a multitude of differences within this approach (for comprehensive discussions, see Levy 1994; Tetlock 1991) they share in common the belief that the process of change is deliberate and takes account of individual decision making. Scholars in security affairs thus argue that decision-makers can gain shared understandings of each other's strategic intentions (Nye 1987; Weber 1991). Perceptions and misperceptions that influence choices, and types of organizational structures that tend to inhibit learning, are critical facets of such a research program (Levy 1994; Sagan 1993).[12]

Another branch within this literature stresses learning as a process of networks of experts. Epistemic communities of specialists, who share similar perceptions and explanations, may create an international consensus on certain issues. For example, environmental experts made the public aware of ozone depletion and ultimately helped construct an international movement to ameliorate the problem through the Montreal protocol (Haas 1989; Haas 1992). Learning takes place among the network of experts, but also as a diffusionary process in which shared knowledge about certain cause-and-effect relations spreads to a larger population outside the initial network.

Certain aspects of this approach can be consistent with a competitive evolutionary perspective. Particularly if learning is defined as improving one's track record over time the complementarity would be quite large. When individuals and organizations engage in means/ends calculations that lead to greater efficiency or effectiveness of certain behaviors, they improve upon their own chances for survival. Learning is deemed to have occurred where such chances have indeed improved. Learning can thus incorporate competitive fitness and evolutionary arguments.

Much of the literature, however, does not view learning as the acquisition of means/ends knowledge (Breslauer 1987; Haas 1990; Levy 1994; Tetlock 1991: 35). Instead it argues that learning should be more properly understood as a change in belief systems, without any presupposition of greater effectiveness or efficiency. Learning in this sense is thus not defined by the improvement of chances of survival. Indeed, an individual or group may learn in terms of changing their beliefs, and yet be less fit to survive.

Conversely, the natural selection approach, particularly when it takes the strong-form selection view, does not incorporate intentional learning. Selection and learning are analytically distinct (Levitt and March 1988: 319). Whether actors learn is ultimately irrelevant for the final result. Those who did not learn will be weeded out over time, and the outcome will be the same as if the surviving actors had deliberately learned better ways to adapt. The literature on learning can thus incorporate a competitive evolutionary view, but the latter often does not incorporate the learning perspective. The natural evolutionists presuppose that a given environment will, over time, lead to an optimal outcome, irrespective of the ability of individuals and groups to learn, as long as no major changes have occurred in that environment.[13]

Sociological Institutionalism

Organizational sociology distinguishes between competitive and noncompetitive environments (DiMaggio and Powell 1983; Levitt and March 1988; Powell and DiMaggio 1991).[14] Uniformity and convergence among institutions can occur in both types of environments. While this literature focuses on institutional convergence, the same arguments may be extended to explain similarities of behavior.

In competitive environments homogeneity occurs through rivalry. Institutions tend to resemble each other because of selection among less-fit types. Competition weeds out those institutions that prove less efficient or less effective in a particular environment, and competitive isomorphism is the result. Institutions are alike in form and function.

Competitive isomorphism thus occurs because institutions are contested on means ends criteria. This can take place both at the micro- and macro-level. At the micro-level people choose institutions based on a rough cost benefit calculus. Herein sociological institutionalism deviates from the strong selection model, in that agent deliberations are explicitly part of the model, and it resembles learning in terms of acquisition of more accurate means/ends knowledge.

At the macro-level, the fit with evolutionary theory is closer. Darwinian selection eliminates less-fit choices (Carroll 1984). Macro-level sociological institutionalism focuses, thus, particularly on institutions operating in market environments. For example, it has tried to clarify why large companies in the United States tended to show comparable divisions of labor and similar organization (Fligstein 1991).

Noncompetitive isomorphism, by contrast, can occur, first, because of mimicry (DiMaggio and Powell 1983; Levitt and March 1988: 330). People create institutions and social practices in the mold of already existing ones. The process resembles learning as a change in beliefs, distinct from means/ends calculations. Actors do not engage in a full search for alternative institutions but take preexisting forms as given, on grounds of appropriateness. They adopt a "chameleon strategy."

This sociological perspective thus supplements views of strong-form selection and learning by clarifying how noncompetitive isomorphism can be the result of given sets of expectations or norms. Institutions operate in "organizational fields", networks of interrelated units (Scott and Meyer 1991; 120), where they have to fit in with previously existing formal and informal rules. Actors who create new institutions enter into preestablished networks of expectations and legitimations. Newcomers are socialized to particular behaviors and structures.

Noncompetitive isomorphism may also occur due to rigid cultural conditions or hierarchical lines of command. For example, public authorities will impose formal constraints on most private organizations. A given social culture might similarly dictate a particular institutional makeup.

The Complementarity of These Three Orientations

The consequences of emphasizing either a structural evolutionary approach or a learning model are not trivial. Competitive-selection arguments in social science often suggest that efficiency should weed out nonviable types. In so doing social scientists tacitly accept a strong-form evolutionary perspective. History marches in a particular direction. Given greater competition, larger exposure to global trading markets, expanding world financial systems, mutual military vulnerabilities, the units in the system should start to look more and more homogeneous in external form and internal arrangement.

A learning approach shades into such arguments if it understands learning in a strict means/ends sense. But even when learning refers to improvements in a means/ends sense there is no reason to expect that outcomes cannot be stuck in low-level equilibrium traps (Elster 1984; Caporaso 1989). Exactly because learning invokes deliberate choices on the part of agents, individuals may forego long-term efficiency gains to avoid short-run costs. Hence, a low-level equilibrium trap will occur, because actors cannot pass this equilibrium to a higher plateau. Cognitive factors (Jervis 1976) may similarly lead agents to prefer short run certain payoffs to long-run uncertain benefits, again leading actors to stagnate at a certain equilibrium level rather than transgress a low level trap.

If one understands learning in a broader sense, as in Jack Levy's view of learning, as a change in beliefs (Levy 1994), or as in Philip Tetlock's view of learning as the incorporation of greater complexity into one's belief structures (Breslauer 1987; Tetlock 1991), there is no reason to presuppose an evolutionary development toward a more efficient and more effective set of institutional arrangements.

However, once one surrenders the means/ends notion of learning this literature has a tough time accounting for institutional similarities. If selection is a relatively weak mechanism, and if there are cognitive reasons, as well as bureaucratic interests that create barriers to learning, then particular patterns of behavior or homogeneous institutional arrangements need not occur. There will be varied responses to the external stimuli.

Sociological theory, specifically in how it studies organizational behavior, can encompass both a learning and a competitive-selection perspective, and can add explanatory power to both perspectives. It can supplement both those perspectives by showing how agent choices in the long run structurally constrain the range of options of their successors and thus limit the variety in learning repertoires (Spruyt 1994). It clarifies how relative fitness must also be understood in sociological terms. Over time institutional choices become more difficult to dislodge for material as well as ideological reasons. Institutions will assume a taken-for-granted nature. They will not only influence cost-benefit calculations but will define the very framework through which actors will define and understand their preferences (Meyer, Boli, and Thomas 1987).

Sociological theory has, consequently, moved away from differentiating competitive environments and noncompetitive environments. Isomorphism due to competitive selection and isomorphism due to shared expectations and rules, are not as distinct as once thought. Both processes tend to operate coterminously. What at face value seemed like a pure competitive environment—for example, rivalry among corporations in the market place—turned out to evince some similar patterns of behavior as not-for-profit, non-competitive environments. Isomorphism occurred not just by competition and selection but equally by constraints imposed by government and society, by hierarchical dictate and normative expectations—usually attributed to noncompetitive dynamics. Research demonstrated, for example, that antitrust laws required corporate strategies to diversify rather than expand horizontally and vertically within the same sector (Fligstein 1991). Governmental hierarchy induced institutional isomorphism. Furthermore, in order for companies to attract employees, they had to fit certain social and cultural preconceptions of what constituted a good company to work for (normatively induced uniformity). Management and personnel strategies were thus partially determined by the larger social environment and established set of perceptions, and were not immediately reducible to profit oriented means ends calculations. Other work demonstrated how non-profit and for-profit health organizations showed very similar institutional characteristics despite their variant environments (Clarke and Estes 1992).

From the other side, institutional isomorphism previously attributed to established social rules and norms, turned out to be partially driven by competitive dynamics. Non-profit organizations competed for private funding. Associations sought to attract scarce members from rival associations. Museums vied for attention of a discerning public.

In short, the traditional distinction that competitive isomorphism occurs in non-hierarchical, and hence "rule-less" environments, and that noncompetitive isomorphism occurs in organizational fields structured by shared rules and norms, no longer seems analytically fruitful. Competitive selection, learning, and networks of societal constraints all interact. The initial choices of elites and social groups for particular institutional forms might be tenuous. Over time, however, continued interaction based on those institutions becomes habitual and actors will infer particular modes of behavior from each other. This externalization of the initial institutional choice will then present itself as an objective fact to subsequent elites and social groups.[15]

The synthesis that I propose between the various perspectives also means that the perceptions of individuals of their environment may be as important as the "objective" conditions imposed by that environment. Take the argument regarding "globalization." The very perception that the international economy is becoming ever more integrated and is thus posing new constraints on autonomous national economic policies, brings about that very condition of "globalization." If actors operate with a belief system that the international environment presents objective constraints (such as increasing international trade and capital flows), and if social discourse reinforces that cognitive framework, their subsequent behaviors in adjusting to such perceptions may create those very conditions for themselves and other actors.

EXPANDING THE RANGE OF METAPHORS
FROM EVOLUTIONARY THEORY

I have argued, then, that political science has selectively appropriated the insights of evolutionary theory from biology. This appropriation has bordered on misappropriation.

It has overemphasized natural selection as virtually the only component of evolutionary theory. It has, furthermore, stressed, within natural selection arguments, largely the strong-form selection view, that there is likely to be only one fit solution. And within that view it has accepted the centripetal perspective that dynamic pressures force solutions to a modal point. In so doing, political scientists can argue that state behaviors and institutions are converging, and adapting to environmental constraints. But as argued above the biological views of evolution see natural selection as only one element of the theory. Chance mutations of many forms continue to survive, and selection to some most adaptive type is highly questionable and depends on many variables (population size, mutation rate, and so forth). I argue, therefore, that by taking one view of selection we invoke an image of convergence that is even missing in the biological world. Hence, the argument for convergence might hold on empirical grounds but not because the evolutionary metaphor holds as an analogy.

The gradations within natural selection provide other metaphors that are potentially more useful for understanding social phenomena. What happens if, contrary to strong-form, centripetal dynamics, centrifugal forces are equally powerful causal mechanisms? Centrifugal logic holds that in response to environmental pressure one does not see a move toward a modal point, but a radical shift away in multiple directions (that is, a move toward multiple biological responses when the environment changes). Say that an existing modal condition becomes highly ill-adapted. Many mutations will then be superior to the existing one, and a flight from the modal point will occur. Weak-form selection will generate a gradual set of mutations emanating from the modal condition to some new set of states, whereas strong-form selection will show a dramatic flight to other conditions where no

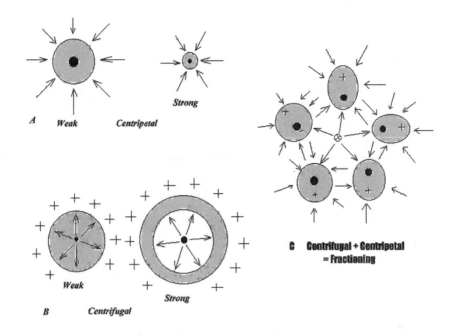

Figure 5.1 Models of Biological Evolution

form will resemble anything close to the older modal condition. In strong-form selection, with centrifugal dynamics, the ill-adapted type is completely exterminated (resulting in the hollow doughnut model).

In political and social environments both processes would seem to operate together, and indeed might provide a useful metaphor to think through contemporary state policies, institutional behaviors, and corporate strategies. Centrifugal forces are at work insofar as mutations move away from the previous modal point. Actors start to diverge from the previous status quo or particular mode of doing things, and try new strategies and behaviors. Centripetal forces come into play in sorting out the variety of responses that try to occupy the same space (not all the new experiments will be successful in the long run).

An example of such a process in the contemporary social world might be the variation in types of states and state behaviors we are witnessing today. For a variety of reasons there has been a trend toward state centralization and territorial sovereignty (Tilly 1990; Spruyt 1994). Partially related to institutional efficiencies and scale economies, the number of states declined quite rapidly from fifteen hundred on. Currently, however, that trend seems interrupted and many small states (Singapore) have fared well. This "small state strategy" to pursue economic gains rather than military ones or territorial aggrandizement, seems like one viable option. At the same time states can also pursue greater efficiencies of scale through tighter integration (the European Union for example). Similarly, not all states engage to the same extent in military competition, balancing behavior, and so forth (centrifugal selection).

Rather than expect convergence among these distinct types, the appropriate image might rather be one of differential state strategies. States choose to occupy different niches (the centrifugal dynamic) and only compete with others within that niche (centripetal selection within those niches). Small states that face similar environmental challenges might thus over time look alike. Other states that prefer scale efficiencies as their predominant strategy, might compete with other states who prefer a similar strategy (there might be successful and unsuccessful regional organizations). Clusters of convergence might thus occur with multiple approximations around modal points, rather than some linear trend to any singular optimal point. Utilizing different evolutionary perspectives leads thus to different heuristic images and different expectations. This set of views would predict less convergence than one might expect from strong-form selection.

This argument is also compatible with Kim and Hart's analysis of competition in this volume. Rather than expect one response to economic competition, firms and states will vary their responses depending on where they see their comparative advantage, and depending on the social, historical legacies that inform their economic policies. They will adopt various strategies (centrifugal responses to a changing economic environment) and will compete within their niche with other actors who have adopted similar practices (centripetal dynamics).

Similarly, there might be various strategies for states to pursue economic gains (a European corporatist model, an East Asian interventionist model, or American liberalism). But not all corporatist models will be equally successful, and, hence competition, learning, and adaptation will lead to pressures within this niche of corporatist states to follow the leader of the group, the most efficient type. The same dynamic will occur within the various niches of East Asian developmental states, and so on.

I am thus not questioning the use value of metaphors, quite the contrary. Ironically, even progress in evolutionary theory in the biological sciences partially depended on metaphors borrowed from the social world. Darwin thought his selection of the fittest to be similar to market competition. (He also drew from geology—Lyell's work—and population theory—Malthus.) But we do need to examine their implications and validity for explaining political events. I argue, consequently, for greater variation in the metaphors we invoke to think about questions of convergence in state institutions and behavior or corporate strategies.

We have already usefully introduced natural evolution perspectives with some success in political science. The Punctuated Equilibrium model has resonated with political scientists who argue that the notion of sudden dramatic change, even if debated by students of natural evolution, provides a plausible account for dramatic social transitions.[16] Similar to speciation events in the natural world, dramatic changes in the international environment, as crises and wars, seem to precipitate periods of rapid changes in institutions and policies. These cataclysmic periods are then followed by relatively stable periods. After an initial period of experimentation with various "species types" (that is, multiple institutions or policies) the more fit type will displace the others and dominate the scene for some time. After initial variance convergence occurs on a particular type.

The reason why major policy and institutional changes are relatively infrequent is because institutions and policies represent sunk costs and learned repertoires. New institutions impose starting-up costs, information barriers, and create collective action problems. And perhaps most importantly past policies and institutions serve particular interests and coalitions. In order for change to occur some dramatic change has to take place to open up the political space to unseat existing coalitions and powers-that-be. Without such change actors will also be inclined to run standard operating procedures even if they are potentially less efficient in the long run.[17]

CONCLUSION: WHAT USE ARE EVOLUTIONARY PERSPECTIVES?

In this essay I have suggested that incorporating sociological institutionalist arguments and learning perspectives with evolutionary views, provides a better explanation of whether convergence will occur and why it occurs. Convergence might be due to path dependency, and lock-in, not by continuous adaptation and selection through environmental demands. Convergence may also occur on grounds of appropriateness and cultural preferences, rather than competitive efficiency or effectiveness. Some institutions and practices might continue even if they are demonstrably less adapted to changed circumstances. And where we do find convergence it might not be caused by selective pressures.

I have also suggested that in our selective appropriation of evolutionary theory, particularly when we try to link the consequences of competition with expectations about uniformity, we have adopted the strong-form selective view. We have also overemphasized centripetal dynamic processes. Alternatively, evolution might show weak-form selection, with far less disastrous consequences for less fit types. Stronger even, centrifugal forces might suggest a multiplicity of responses to environmental pressures rather than singularity. In other words, the images we hold influence the explanations we adopt. Let us expand the range of our imagination.

Even the Punctuated Equilibrium model must be treated as a useful metaphor rather than as the strict application of insights of biological evolutionary theory. In natural evolution, punctuation events are indeterminate, and their effects on genetic variation unclear. The bewildering variety of fauna and flora exemplifies the plethora of responses. With social events, speciation changes are at least partially driven by the agents themselves who are affected by such events. Indeed, agents react to and even create the events. Social "speciation events" are not exogenous to agent variation as natural phenomena are with regards to biological species.

It is also inherently difficult, for the latter reason, to determine *a priori* what a speciation event is. In the natural world cataclysmic events (a giant meteorite hitting earth; huge volcanic eruptions; shifts in global temperature) will likely yield great variation. In the social world, speciation events are seldom identifiable before their observed consequences. Furthermore, unlike the natural world, the appropriate unit of analysis is unclear. At what level of aggregation does the speciation event work to produce variation? Finally, stasis is at all times incomplete, and partially determined by the chosen unit of analysis. The greater the abstraction of the macro structural phenomena, the easier it is to argue for relative stability in history.

Let me conclude with the suggestion that the biological understanding of change in political science has several benefits over misplaced mechanistic conceptualizations of politics. Unlike the physical sciences, biology pays less heed to the criterion of predictability. Indeed, dramatic changes in species and populations are only explained after the fact. Yet few would argue that therefore biology is scientifically invalid. The argument that social scientific theories do not predict well (such as foreseeing events as the end of the Cold War or the dissolution of the Soviet Union) should not serve as a litmus test to repudiate theories. A less mechanistic view of the universe will also avoid Alfred Whitehead's fallacy of "misplaced concreteness," assigning more credence to forecasts and expectations than warranted, rather than acknowledging the wide range of probabilities and possibilities that confront us in the social world.

NOTES

1. Out of fairness to Waltz, one should recognize that he also draws attention to the more intentional dynamic of socialization (Waltz 1979: 74–77). Actors learn from others which strategies are better than others. However, this introduces several elements that do not fit with a strict evolutionary framework; intentionality in modification, social learning, and cumulative adaptation to the environment as an organizational effort. If his view of socialization means the emergence of surviving patterns of behavior, it collapses back into a competitive-selection argument.
2. Consequently, scholars have sought to account for the convergence around similar economic policies and domestic structures (Bennett 1991; Biersteker 1992; Kahler 1992), as well as explain their continued differences, if any. This debate on the causes and consequences of policy convergence can be extended to institutions.
3. See Darwin (1859/1952), ch. 4: 60.
4. Darwin invoked the long necked giraffe as evidence of his theory of survival of the fittest. See Darwin (1859/1952), ch. 7: 104.
5. See Gould (1996).
6. See discussions in Simpson (1984) and Somit and Peterson (1992: 3f).
7. Indeed, some argue for a very stong analogy between biological evolution of systems and the evolution of social systems (see Runciman 1989).
8. For the variety of responses to external military pressure, see Tilly (1990) and Downing (1992).
9. For a discussion of taken-for-grantedness, see DiMaggio and Powell (1983).
10. For parallels between the two, see Krugman (1996).

11. I would like to thank Robert Jervis for raising several of these points during the evolutionary IR conference (Bloomington, Indiana, December 1998).
12. By contrast, Goldstein and Keohane (1993: 6–7) distinguish their analysis of the impact of ideas from learning approaches. They focus on the effects of ideas rather than on the causes of beliefs.
13. For discussions, see Moe (1984: 746); Garrett and Weingast (1993); and Thelen and Steinmo (1992).
14. The sociological literature tends to denote noncompetitive isomorphism as institutional isomorphism. Since I use the latter term to denote instiutional similarity in general, regardless of whether competitive pressures were the primary cause, I have used a different terminology without altering the explanatory logic of organizational analysis.
15. This formulation resembles Peter Berger's views on the institutionalization of role behavior. See the discussion thereof in Abercrombie (1986).
16. Dodd (1994), Krasner (1989), Spruyt (1994) and a variety of approaches in Somit and Peterson (1992).
17. For the notion of external events opening up domestic political space for reform, see Keohane and Milner (1996).

REFERENCES

Abercrombie, Nicholas. 1986. Knowledge, Order and Human Autonomy. In James Hunter and Stephen Ainlay, eds. *Making sense of modern times*. New York: Routledge.
Andrews, David. 1994. Capital Mobility and State Autonomy: Toward a Structural Theory of International Monetary Relations. *International Studies Quarterly* 38 (2):193–218.
Axelrod, Robert. 1981. The Evolution of Cooperation Among Egoists. *American Political Science Review* 75:306–18.
———. 1984. *The evolution of cooperation*. New York: Basic Books.
———. 1986. An Evolutionary Approach to Norms. *American Political Science Review* 80:1095–1112.
Bennett, Colin. 1991. Review Article: What is Policy Convergence and What Causes It? *British Journal of Political Science* 21: 215–33.
Bermeo, Nancy. 1992. Democracy and the Lessons of Dictatorship. *Comparative Politics* 24: 273–91.
Biersteker, Thomas. 1992. The 'Triumph' of Neoclassical Economics in the Developing World: Policy Convergence and Bases of Governance in the International Economic Order. In James Rosenau and Ernst-Otto Czempiel, ed. *Governance without government: Order and change in world politics*. New York: Cambridge University Press.
———. 1994. Globalization as a Mode of Operation. Presented at the annual meeting of the American Political Science Association, New York.
Breslauer, George. 1987. Ideology and Learning in Soviet Third World Policy. *World Politics* 39:429–48.
Breslauer, George and Philip Tetlock, eds. 1991. *Learning in U.S. and Soviet foreign policy*. Boulder, Colo.: Westview Press.
Bryant, Ralph. 1987. *International financial intermediation*. Washington: The Brookings Institution.
Buzan, Barry, Charles Jones, and Richard Little. 1993. *The logic of anarchy*. New York: Columbia University Press.

Cammack, Paul. 1992. The New Institutionalism: Predatory Rule, Institutional Persistence, and Macro-Structural Change. *Economy and Society* 21:397–429.

Caporaso, James. 1989. Microeconomics and International Political Economy: The Neoclassical Approach to Institutions. In Ernst Otto-Czempiel and James Rosenau, eds. *Global changes and theoretical challenges.* Lexington, Mass.: D.C. Heath.

Carroll, Glenn. 1984. Organizational Ecology. *Annual Review of Sociology* 10:71–93.

Cederman, Lars-Erik. 1997. *Emergent actors in world politics.* Princeton, N.J.: Princeton University Press.

Clarke, Lee and Carroll Estes. 1992. Sociological and Economic Theories of Markets and Nonprofits: Evidence from Home Health Organizations. *American Journal of Sociology* 97:945–69.

Cornett, Linda and James Caporaso. 1992. 'And Still It Moves!' State Interests and Social Forces in the European Community. In James Rosenau and Ernst-Otto Czempiel, eds. *Governance without government: Order and change in world politics.* New York: Cambridge University Press.

Cowhey, Peter. 1993. Domestic Institutions and the Credibility of International Commitments: Japan and the United States. *International Organization* 47:299–326.

Darwin, Charles. 1952. *The origin of species.* Chicago: University of Chicago/Encyclopaedia Britannica. First published 1859.

D'Lugo, David, and Ronald Rogowski. 1993. The Anglo-German Naval Race and Comparative Constitutional 'Fitness'." In Richard Rosecrance and Arthur Stein, eds. *The domestic bases of grand strategy.* Ithaca, N.Y.: Cornell University Press.

Dodd, Lawrence. 1994. *The dynamics of american politics.* Boulder, Colo.: Westview Press.

DiMaggio, Paul, and Walter Powell. 1983. The Iron Cage Revisited: Institutional Isomorphism and Collective Rationality in Organizational Fields. *American Sociological Review* 48:147–60.

Downing, Brian. 1992. *The military revolution and political change.* Princeton, N.J.: Princeton University Press.

Eggertson, Thrain. 1990. *Economic behavior and institutions.* New York: Cambridge University Press.

Elster, Jon. 1984. *Nuts and bolts.* Cambridge, U.K.: Cambridge University Press.

Fligstein, Neil. 1991. The Structural Transformation of American Industry: An Institutional Account of the Causes of Diversification in the Largest Firms 1919–1979. In Walter Powell and Paul DiMaggio, eds. *The new institutionalism in organizational analysis.* Chicago: University of Chicago Press.

Garrett, Geoffrey and Barry Weingast. 1993. Ideas, Interests and Institutions: Constructing the European Community's Internal Market. In Judith Goldstein and Robert Keohane, eds. *Ideas and Foreign Policy.* Ithaca, N.Y.: Cornell University Press.

Gilpin, Robert. 1996. Economic Evolution of National Systems. *International Studies Quarterly* 40: 411–32.

Goldstein, Judith and Robert Keohane, eds. 1993. *Ideas and foreign policy.* Ithaca: Cornell University Press.

Gould, Stephen Jay. 1980. *The panda's thumb.* New York: W.W. Norton.

———. 1989. *Wonderful life.* New York: W. W. Norton.

———. 1996. Why Darwin. *New York Review of Books* 43, 6:10–14.

Gourevitch, Peter. 1986. *Politics in hard times.* Ithaca, N.Y.: Cornell University Press.

Grant, Verne. 1985. *The evolutionary process.* New York: Columbia University Press.

Haas, Ernst. 1990. *When knowledge is power.* Berkeley: University of California Press.

Haas, Peter. 1989. Do Regimes Matter? Epistemic Communities and Mediterranean Pollution Control. *International Organization* 43:377–403.

———. 1992. Introduction: Epistemic Communities and International Policy Coordination. *International Organization* 46:1–36.

Hall, Peter, ed. 1989. *The political power of economic ideas*. Princeton, N.J.: Princeton University Press.

Hintze, Otto. 1975. *The historical essays of Otto Hintze*, ed. Felix Gilbert. New York: Oxford University Press.

Hirschman, Albert. 1970. *Exit, voice, and loyalty*. Cambridge, Mass.: Harvard University Press.

Hirst, Paul, and Grahame Thompson. 1992. The Problem of 'Globalization': International Economic Relations, National Economic Management and the Formation of Trading Blocs. *Economy and Society* 21:357–96.

———. 1976. *Perception and Misperception in International Politics*. Princeton, N.J.: Princeton University Press.

Jervis, Robert. 1997. *System effects*. Princeton, N.J.: Princeton University Press.

Kahler, Miles. 1992. External Influence, Conditionality, and the Politics of Adjustment. In Stephan Haggard and Robert Kaufman, eds. *The politics of economic adjustment*. Princeton, N.J.: Princeton University Press.

Keohane, Robert and Helen Milner. 1996. eds. *Internationalization and domestic politics*. New York: Cambridge University Press.

Krasner, Stephen. 1989. Sovereignty: An Institutional Perspective. In James Caporaso, ed. *The elusive state*. Newbury Park, Calif.: Sage.

———. 1993. Westphalia and All That. In Judith Goldstein and Robert Keohane, eds. *Ideas and foreign policy*. Ithaca, N.Y.: Cornell University Press.

Krugman, Paul. 1996. What Economists Can Learn From Evolutionary Theorists. Presentation before the European Association for Evolutionary Political Economy.

Levitt, Barbara, and James March. 1988. Organizational Learning. *Annual Review of Sociology* 14:319–40.

Levy, Jack. 1994. Learning and Foreign Policy: Sweeping a Conceptual Minefield. *International Organization* 48:279–312.

March, James and Johan Olsen 1984. The New Institutionalism: Organizational Factors in Political Life. *American Political Science Review* 78:734–49.

McNeely, Connie. 1992. The Determination of Statehood in the United Nations. In *Research in political sociology*, Vol. 6. Greenwich, Conn.: JAI Press.

Meyer, John, John Boli and George Thomas. 1987. Ontology and Rationalization in the Western Cultural Account. In George Thomas, et.al., eds. *Institutional structure*. Newbury Park, Calif.: Sage.

Milner, Helen. 1991. The Assumption of Anarchy in International Relations Theory: A Critique. *Review of International Studies* 17:67–85.

Moe, Terry. 1984. New Economics of Organization. *American Journal of Political Science* 28:739–777.

Nelson, Richard. 1994. Recent Evolutionary Theorizing About Economic Change. Columbia University. Typescript.

Nettl, J. P. 1968. The State as a Conceptual Variable. *World Politics* 20:559–92.

North, Douglass. 1981. *Structure and change in economic history*. New York: W. W. Norton.

———. 1990. *Institutions, institutional change and economic performance*. New York: Cambridge University Press.

North, Douglass and Robert Thomas. 1973. *The rise of the western world*. Cambridge, U.K.: Cambridge University Press.

North, Douglass and Barry Weingast. 1989. Constitutions and Commitment: The Evolution of Institutions Governing Public Choice in 17th Century England. *Journal of Economic History* 49:803–32.

Nye, Joseph. 1987. Nuclear Learning and U.S.-Soviet Security Regimes. *International Organization* 41:371–402.

Oye, Kenneth, ed. 1986. *Cooperation under anarchy.* Princeton, N.J.: Princeton University Press.

Pauly, Louis and Simon Reich. 1997. National Structures and Multinational Corporate Behavior: Enduring Differences in the Age of Globalization. *International Organization* 51:1–30.

Posen, Barry. 1993. Nationalism, the Mass Army and Political Power. *International Security* 18:118.

Powell, Walter. 1991. Expanding the Scope of Institutional Analysis. In Walter Powell and Paul DiMaggio, eds. *The new institutionalism in organizational analysis.* Chicago: University of Chicago Press.

Reich, Robert. 1991. *The work of nations.* New York: Alfred Knopf.

Robertson, Roland. 1992. *Globalization.* Newbury Park, Calif.: Sage.

Runciman, Walter. 1989. *A treatise on social theory,* Vol .2. Cambridge, U.K.: Cambridge University Press.

Sagan, Scott. 1993. *The limits of safety.* Princeton, N.J.: Princeton University Press.

Scott, Richard and John Meyer. 1991. The Organization of Societal Sectors: Propositions and Early Evidence. In Walter Powell and Paul DiMaggio, eds. *The new institutionalism in organizational analysis.* Chicago: University of Chicago Press.

Simpson, George. 1984. *Tempo and mode of evolution.* New York: Columbia University Press. First published 1944.

Somit, Albert and Steven Peterson, ed. 1992. *The dynamics of evolution.* Ithaca, N.Y.: Cornell University Press.

Spruyt, Hendrik. 1994. *The sovereign state and its competitors.* Princeton, N.J.: Princeton University Press.

Strang, David. 1991. Anomaly and Commonplace in European Political Expansion: Realist and Institutional Accounts. *International Organization* 45:143–62.

Tetlock, Philip. 1991. In Search of an Elusive Concept. In George Breslauer and Philip Tetlock, eds. *Learning in U.S. and soviet foreign policy.* Boulder, Colo.: Westview Press.

Thelen, Kathleen, and Sven Steinmo. 1992. Historical Institutionalism in Comparative Politics. In Sven Steinmo, Kathleen Thelen, and Frank Longstreth, eds. *Structuring politics.* New York: Cambridge University Press.

Thomas, George, and John Meyer. 1984. The Expansion of the State. *Annual Review of Sociology* 10:461–82.

Tilly, Charles, ed. 1975. *The formation of national states in western Europe.* Princeton, N.J.: Princeton University Press.

Tilly, Charles. 1990. *Coercion, capital, and European states, AD 990–1990.* Cambridge, Mass.: Basil Blackwell 1990.

Waltz, Kenneth. 1979. *Theory of international politics.* New York: Random House.

Weber, Steven. 1991. Interactive Learning in U.S.-Soviet Arms Control. In George Breslauer and Philip Tetlock, eds. *Learning in U.S. and Soviet foreign policy.* Boulder, Colo.: Westview Press.

Wendt, Alexander. 1987. The Agent-Structure Problem in International Relations Theory. *International Organization* 41:335–70.

———. 1994. Collective Identity Formation and the International State. American Political Science Review 88:384–96.

Zacher, Mark. 1992. The Decaying Pillars of the Westphalian Temple: Implications for International Order and Governance. In James Rosenau and Ernst-Otto Czempiel, eds. *Governance without government: Order and change in world politics.* New York: Cambridge University Press.

chapter 6

The Evolution of International Norms
Choice, Learning, Power, and Identity

Stewart Patrick

> What has been is what will be,
> And what has been done is what will be done;
> There is nothing new under the sun.
> Is there a thing of which it is said,
> "See, this is new"?
> It has been already,
> In the ages before us.
> —Ecclesiastes 1: 9–10

INTRODUCTION

The words of Ecclesiastes notwithstanding, the sudden and dramatic end of the Cold War a decade ago provided striking evidence that qualitative transformations do occur in world politics. Political scientists, recognizing the inability of static conceptual frameworks to explain new patterns of interaction among international actors, have begun to turn to evolutionary paradigms to understand the "descent, with modification" of the global system (Modelski 1990, 1996; Adler 1991; Florini 1996). Simultaneously, they have begun to realize that when fundamental change occurs in international relations, it "usually reflects new ideas" (Jackson 1993: 112).

Thus the 1990s witnessed an upsurge of research on the role of beliefs and norms in the construction of state identities, the formulation of national interests and foreign policies, and the shaping of international outcomes (Lapid and Kratochwil 1995; Katzenstein 1996; Checkel 1998). Nevertheless, political science still lacks convincing answers to some very basic questions: Where do norms come from? How do they evolve and change? How do they become institutionalized? What is the relationship between ideational change, per se, and normative evolution?

Combining cognitive and evolutionary perspectives, this chapter attributes changing practices in foreign policy to evolving standards of conduct within international society. It proposes a "selective retention" model of norm evolution to elucidate how and why these shared understandings arise, spread, endure, and disappear. Building on insights from population genetics and cultural evolutionary theory, this model identifies the (1) units of inheritance, (2) sources of variation,

(3) mechanisms of transmission, and (4) forces of transformation that shape the origin and persistence of global norms. The chapter compares and evaluates the importance of five potential selective forces responsible for international normative change: (a) natural selection, (b) rational choice, (c) learning, (d) power, and (e) socialization.

The chapter concludes by offering several hypotheses: First, *normative selection*, or the differential replication of international norms, is the primary explanation for changing patterns of interstate behavior. Second, international selection operates mainly on norms themselves, rather than on norm carriers. Third, the cognitive processes of learning, socialization, and hegemonic legitimation are more important in the retention and elimination of norms than are pure rational choice or natural selection. Fourth, the importance of learning and socialization in normative selection depends on the stage of a norm's life cycle. Fifth, the "fitness" of new principled beliefs is constrained by current identity commitments and logics of appropriateness. Finally, dominant states may influence the evolution of global norms by legitimating their preponderance.

CONSTRUCTIVISM AND INTERNATIONAL NORMS

The dominant American approaches to world politics have failed to anticipate or to explain pacific international change (Gaddis 1992, 1993). This shortcoming has both methodological and conceptual origins. Espousing a positivist research agenda more appropriate to the natural than to the social sciences, neorealism and neoliberalism share a primitive conception of interstate anarchy, a narrow view of interest-formation, and an unwarranted skepticism about the impact of collective norms on foreign policy choices. Both perspectives depict the world as an essentially asocial landscape populated by rational state actors maximizing expected utility across a range of consistently ordered, exogenously given preferences. Moreover, both cling to a static conception of international politics that discourages them from thinking in evolutionary terms.

According to neorealists, the topography of power channels national goals, constrains human creativity, and restricts global change to the repetition of cyclical patterns. Policy shifts reflect only mechanistic adaptation to new environmental circumstances; international rules and institutions are but a thin veneer atop the underlying distribution of power; and compliance with norms reflects expedient concerns of state survival (Gilpin 1981: 35–36; Vayrynen 1987; Grieco 1988). By concentrating on enduring regularities and stable equilibria rather than on human agency and historical contingency, neorealists ignore the irreversible sequences and unrepeatable events that continually inject novelty into world politics. In short, they deny that international society is always in the process of "becoming" (Ruggie 1986; Walker 1987; and Cox 1992).

Although neoliberals share similar neoutilitarian assumptions, they concede that ideas, norms, and institutions may affect international outcomes. A state's regime type may shape its foreign policy choices; states may learn within international institutions; and global regimes may alter incentives to cooperate by lowering transaction costs and diminishing relative gains considerations. New worldviews and causal or principled beliefs provide road maps for action or focal points for coordination in situations of multiple equilibria (or in debates over where to settle on the Pareto frontier). Once entrenched in institutions, these principles, norms, and conventions may be de-coupled (temporarily) from underlying structures of power or cost-benefit calculations of material interest, securing compliance even as their initial bases erode (Goldstein and Keohane 1993: 12–13).

Nevertheless, the neoliberals' institutionalism remains "bounded." As functional frameworks serve the needs of rational egoists, rule-governed practices and norms do not alter actor identities and ends (Keohane 1996). Neoliberals elide the issue of how new values, subjective interpretations, and social institutions constitute actor identities, frame premises for action, and enter state utility functions (North 1990: 23–24). In so doing, they neglect critical sources of variation in foreign policies and global outcomes.

Positivism creates the impression of "hard" science, but its individualist and rationalist premises overlook the fact that social reality depends on the collective interpretations and meanings that human beings give to experience. It is not enough to say that states behave "rationally" by maximizing expected utility within structural constraints. As John Ruggie (1998: 19) writes, "A core constructivist research concern is what happens *before* the neoutilitarian model purportedly kicks in." Constructivists take an alternative, hermeneutic approach. They perceive states to be engaged in value-laden social action within an intersubjective matrix of mutual expectations and principles of practice. Rather than treating identities and interests as nontheorized initial conditions (or deducing these from behavior), constructivists deepen the analysis of motivation and choice by examining the normative, epistemic, and institutional context in which states acquire perceptions of themselves and international society. Constructivists seek to document how "social facts," shared knowledge, and historical legacies constitute actor identities and preferences.

This sociological approach is consistent with the "International Society" tradition in international relations (IR) theory. The (so-called) "English School" rejects neorealism's dichotomy between "governed" domestic systems and the "decentralized and anarchic" international system (Waltz 1979: 88). The society of states may lack a single legitimate authority, but its members share elements of a common culture, as well as "common interests in the elementary goals of social life; rules prescribing behavior that sustains these goals; and institutions that help to make these rules effective" (Bull 1977: 65; Milner 1993)[1] *Norms,* or "collective expectations for the proper behavior of actors with a given identity" (Katzenstein 1996: 5) distinguish this society from a mere "system." Intersubjective understandings about legitimate conduct embody shared social purpose; they reflect not only what states *do* but also what they *should* do. As nonmaterial elements of structure, norms exercise a "compliance pull" distinct from power constraints and particularist interest (Kratochwil and Ruggie 1986: 764; Hasenclever, Mayer, and Rittberger 1997: 170).

Material structures obviously impinge upon state action, but only after being given content and meaning. This suggests that the conventional distinctions between "idealism and materialism" are "utterly misconceived" (Hall 1993: 39). As Robert Jackson (1993: 112) reminds us, national interests are "concepts and therefore ideas." Thus power politics is just one historically conditioned, socially constructed response to anarchy (Wendt 1992). Between structure and volition lies *interpretation*: existing identities, norms, and values-condition state choices about appropriate ends and means (Hall 1993: 39; Haggard and Simmons 1987: 511).[2]

Scholars have identified four basic categories of norms: *constitutive* norms define the identity of an actor and the essence of the game being played; *regulative* norms specify legitimate behavior for these actors and the rights and obligations inherent in a particular game; *evaluative* norms establish moral standards, judgments, and prescriptions; and *practical* norms provide commonly accepted "best solutions"— like Greenwich Mean Time. (Individual norms may fall into more than one category.) Norms have meaning only if they can be negated by an alternative norm (or norms). Thus "free trade" negates "autarky," just as "citizenship" negates "subjecthood." By definition, norms are considered legitimate by their carriers.

International norms vary along multiple dimensions, including their universality of application; their connection with "justice;" their mode of transmission; and their degree of internalization and enforcement. Norms influence actor behavior by constituting identities; constraining policies; shaping perceptions of possibilities; providing coordinating mechanisms; and becoming entrenched in bureaucracies. As ideational phenomena, they can be observed only indirectly in the language of international conventions; in the rules of formal organizations; in patterns of custom and practice; in legal and philosophical discourse; or in communications among states—including justifications for violations of custom (Kowert and Legro 1996: 452). Convergent expectations about acceptable behavior and desirable goals lay a foundation for international institutions, whether "fundamental" ones like sovereignty and diplomacy or issue-specific "regimes." Through regularized interaction, states (re)produce the normative structures of international society (Wendt and Duvall 1990: 52–5)

When combined with the managerial role of the great powers, norms foster *governance*, or "purposive order" within international society (Rosenau 1992). There are makers, takers, and breakers of norms. "[O]ccupy[ing] the inner circle," the European great powers and the twentieth century United States played a leading role historically in articulating and promoting the "normative assumptions and behavioral expectations required for full membership" (Armstrong 1992: 20). Dissatisfied or recalcitrant states have championed alternative principles of world order.

Constructivists document multiple norms that have influenced state conduct and transformed international society. A partial inventory would include reciprocity, transparency, sovereign equality, free trade, embedded liberalism, national self-determination, decolonization, racial equality, nonintervention, arms control, the laws of war, diplomacy, the abolition of slavery, collective security, human rights, women's suffrage, humanitarian intervention, foreign assistance, chemical and nuclear weapons taboos, and (even) the obsolescence of war.[3] Certain norms like sovereignty command universal respect; the dimensions of others (like human rights) remain hotly contested.

By and large, however, scholars have been unable to explain how collective understandings emerge and spread. Partly, this reflects a status quo bias. Constructivists call for an equal emphasis on structure and agency, but their accounts typically privilege the former. Just as neorealists attribute foreign policies and international outcomes to the current distribution of power, so constructivists attribute these to the current distribution of norms and identities. The question remains: How does this distribution change?

To account for both continuity and transformation, constructivists must embrace an evolutionary approach that gives appropriate weight to human agency. Such a perspective might help unravel two conceptual puzzles: (1) the distinction between "norms" and "principled beliefs" (Goldstein and Keohane 1993); and (2) the relationship between "weak cognitivism" and "strong cognitivism." (Hasenclever, Mayer, and Ritttberger 1997: 136–210).[4]

First, although norms are by definition consensual, ironically they evolve through *contestation* with rival norms (Finnemore 1996a: 160). Presumably, then, there exists a stage in their evolution in which norms (or the "proto"-norms that give rise to them) are not "collective" in any meaningful sense. This article contends that norms emerge first as principled ideas that subsequently spread globally. These "shared ideas" eventually become "collective expectations" when embedded in institutions and internalized by members of international society.

Second, most cognitivist (or constructivist) approaches fall into one of two categories. According to cognitivism's *weak* variant, the demand for international regimes arises through "complex learning." In effect, new consensual knowledge or shared understandings about past experiences and current problems spur states to reformulate national interests and the means to achieve these (Nye 1987: 373). In contexts of uncertainty, "epistemic communities" introduce new cognitive frameworks by disseminating authoritative, policy-relevant knowledge and influencing state agendas. One can imagine a plausible division of labor between "weak cognitivism" and rational choice theory: The former would focus on preference-formation and the latter on the subsequent pursuit of value- or knowledge-laden interests (Hasenclever, Mayer, and Rittberger 1997: 136–210).

Cognitivism's *strong* version is less easily reconciled with rational choice, for the former insists that mutual expectations and intersubjective understandings constitute identities as well as interests. Regimes depend upon collective principles of order and systems of meaning. Whereas cognitivism's weak variant emphasizes agency, the strong version privileges structure. A simple matrix (see Figure 6.1) can distinguish the two. Its poles represent *agency* and *structure* (on the one hand) and *material* and *ideational* factors (on the other). Weak cognitivism occupies the upper right quadrant, strong cognitivism the lower right.[5] A third quadrant embraces structural materialist perspectives, including Waltzian structural realism and conventional (non-Gramscian) Marxism. A fourth quadrant encompasses conventional rational choice; it sees agents maximizing interests defined in material terms.

As a static description of ideal types, the matrix lacks any temporal dimension. We can introduce dynamism—and bridge the gap between the two forms of cognitivism—by hypothesizing that the role of ideas may change over time. It seems plausible that new principled and/or causal beliefs first arise because they offer solutions to current dilemmas. With the aid of epistemic communities, intellectual

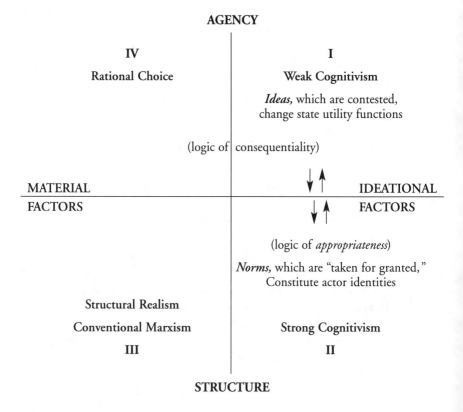

Figure 6.1 Sources of State Behavior—Four Approaches

entrepreneurs, and transnational channels, contested beliefs may gain political traction and compete successfully with rival ideas at both domestic and international levels. Over time, these beliefs may spread through various processes of socialization and become embedded in institutions, organizational structures, and law, acquiring a "taken-for granted" quality as collectively held "norms" of international society. In terms of the matrix, this would entail a migration from Quadrant I to Quadrant II. Whereas actors initially embraced ideas out of the logic of *consequentiality*, they now conform to norms out of the logic of *appropriateness*.

"Embedded liberalism" provides an historical example about how this transformation might occur. In the years surrounding 1945, several major industrialized states came to similar conclusions about the proper role of the state in the domestic and international economy. Once institutionalized within the principles, norms, rules, organizational structures, and decision-making procedures of global trade and monetary regimes, these concepts became part of the fabric of international life (Ruggie 1982). Put simply, weak cognitivism may be more useful in explaining how regimes arise, whereas strong cognitivism may be better at explaining how regimes subsequently shape identity and interest-formation. "Thus, theoretical debates about the degree to which norm-based behavior is driven by choice or habit . . . often turn out to hinge on the stage of the norm's evolution [that] one examines" (Finnemore and Sikkink 1998: 12). As Hasenclever, Mayer, and Rittberger (1997: 187) observe, "[E]goistic motivations may play an important role in the early stages of regime-building, but, over time . . . the parties [may] acquire more collective identities." Thus an Atlantic "security community" has emerged from a set of multilateral military and economic arrangements initially constructed for functional reasons during the early Cold War years (Risse-Kappen 1996).

According to strong cognitivists, the arrows of influence work in the opposite direction, too. That is, existing norms and institutions will impinge upon the creation of (and compliance with) specific regimes. Although it is difficult to document such connections, the emergence of new principled and causal ideas and their consolidation as new collective standards of behavior is likely to be mediated by existing logics of appropriateness (as well as anticipated consequences). As David Lumsdaine (1993: 5, 22) writes, "Many kinds of regimes and practices display a long-term evolution guided by their implicit social and moral meanings." Finally, history records instances when venerable institutions like slavery or colonialism have once again become controversial, migrating from the status of "norm" to contested (and ultimately rejected) "idea."

TOWARD AN EVOLUTIONARY APPROACH

Neorealists and neoliberals address what one might label an *explanatory* dimension of world politics, showing how "given" interests guide state decisions in particular choice environments. This approach is "ecological" insofar as it addresses the (synchronic) determinants of state "fitness" at a single point in time and ignores the (diachronic) question of how the system came to be. Constructivists add an *interpretive* dimension by showing how different identities and shared understandings inform actor interests—and how practice influences regnant norms (Hollis and Smith 1990). With few exceptions, however, constructivists fail to engage an *evolutionary* dimension to account for how norms arise, gain prominence, diffuse, persist, change, and disappear.[6] (See Figure 6.2.)

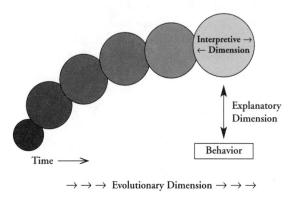

Figure 6.2 Evolving Norm Pool

Consider, for example, John Mueller's (1994: 68) hopeful contention that armed warfare is following "once-fashionable dueling" into "terminal disrepute." This is an intriguing hypothesis, but it lacks a causal mechanism. "[S]ocial ideas and attitudes seem to change themselves," complains Carl Kaysen (1994: 87, 97). "[W]hat governed the pace of change in the social evaluation of war?"

Most constructivists continue to treat norms as "exogenously given." To demonstrate that norms transcend mere descriptions of state practice or intervening variables between power and outcomes, constructivists must show how new "definitions of appropriateness" gain prominence, win adherents, and become entrenched in discourses, customs, identities, and formal organizations. "Having demonstrated the possibility of system transformation at the macro level," Ruggie (cited in Finnemore and Sikkink 1998: 10–11) writes, "corresponding micropractices that may have transformative effects must be identified and inventoried." Likewise, Eyre and Suchman (1996: 89) speculate that normative evolution may resemble "speciation in the biological world."

Political scientists offer few insights about the cognitive microfoundations of normative transformation. Fortuitously, anthropologists have constructed sophisticated models of cultural change, based on analogies with Darwinian evolution, that may shed light on the evolution of principled beliefs in international society. Let us turn to these now.

Evolution in the Biological and Social Sciences

Evolution means "cumulative and transmissible change" (Durham 1991: 20–22). The present evolutionary framework of the biological sciences is the legacy of Charles Darwin, whose *On the Origin of Species* (1859) concluded that living organisms were not "immutable" but in fact the "lineal descendants of some other and generally extinct species." Most importantly, Darwin proposed a new mechanism for evolution, or the "descent, with modification from ancestral forms." Downplaying the "inheritance of acquired characteristics" described by his predecessor Lamarck (1984: 112–13), Darwin identified "Natural Selection [as] the main but not exclusive means of modification." In conditions of high fecundity and resource scarcity, organisms with varying, heritable traits faced a "struggle for existence." Such competition generated "the preservation of favorable variations and the rejection of injurious variations" (Darwin 1964 [1859]: 6, 11, 132). Given time and isolation, changes in morphology, physiology, and behavior accumulated in response to local adaptation, producing distinct species. Complemented by Mendelian and molecular genetics, natural selection forms the core of biology's "modern synthesis."

Although Darwin owed a debt to social theory, social science never fully embraced the evolutionary paradigm.[7] For decades, scholars of "cultural evolution" followed the lead not of Darwin but of his contemporary, the social philosopher Herbert Spencer. Instead of arranging cultures in branching phylogenies showing ancestral affinity, early anthropologists like Lewis Henry Morgan "employed an analogy with a developing organism" and ranked societies according to their particular stage (savagery, barbarism, or civilization) on the linear ladder of human "progress" (Blute 1979: 46–47). These teleological models offered (pseudo)scientific justifications for racialism and imperialism at the turn of the century. Despite the excesses of "Social Spencerism," this developmentalist tradition proved resilient.

Wary of those who conflate evolution with development (and of more recent sociobiologists who confound society with biology), social scientists began only recently to apply Darwinian principles to cultural change (Rindos 1985: 66). These scholars point out that humanity is unique among animals in possessing a second (nongenetic) track of inheritance composed of cultural beliefs. As an "emergent" from organic evolution, cultural capacity gives humans an extra-somatic means to adapt—and a way to transmit information—far more efficiently than the slow mechanisms of genetic replication and natural selection that set the entire process in motion.

Human nature does not exist independently of culture (Geertz 1966: 108–15). A symbolically encoded set of ideational instructions, culture shapes how humans perceive the world, the meanings they place upon their existence, and the goals they choose to pursue. Culture is acquired and transmitted by processes of social learning, modeling, reinforcement, and trial and error. Although our myths, values, theories, technologies, and symphonies are products of the mind, they develop autonomous reality as (what Karl Popper calls) "World 3" phenomena. Once communicated, they enter humanity's collective understanding and shape the lives of their creators (Popper 1982).

A Selective Model of Cultural Evolution

If we define evolution as "the sequential transformation of a system of replicating entities," it becomes clear that culture is subject to evolutionary analysis. Think of the total concepts of any society as a unique "cultural pool." Like a gene pool, these "plans, recipes, rules and instructions" code for specific phenotypes, including standards of behavior. This "social heredity" changes continually from previous forms (Geertz 1973: 44; Ruyle 1973). Significantly, culture possesses the five generic properties of a "selective retention" system. These include (1) *units of inheritance*, or "self-description units"; (2) *sources of variation,* or the continual appearance of new variants upon which selection can act; (3) *mechanisms of transmission,* or means by which the units are reproduced; (4) *processes of transformation,* which explain the retention or rejection of alternative variants over time; and (5) *means of isolation,* which permit accumulating differences to result in divergence (Campbell 1965; Durham 1991). Cultural evolution occurs through *cultural selection,* or the differential replication of cultural units over time.

Note that cultural evolution is not based upon genetic evolution. Rather, both systems evolve because in each case the phenotypic consequences of variation result in the differential replication of units of inheritance (Dunnell 1980). There are of course enormous differences between the two evolutionary processes. The most important reflect the role of human intentionality. Organic evolution is a ramshackle, opportunistic process. A "tinkerer" rather than an "engineer," natural selection acts on undirected variation to cobble new attributes onto pre-existing architecture. Since selection can only "track" a constantly changing environment, adaptation is entirely contingent (Gould and Lewontin 1978). In contrast, cultural adaptation may result from purposeful selection and transmission of inventions designed to serve human desires. Table 6.1 compares genetic and cultural evolution.

Evolutionarily minded anthropologists contend that cultural systems evolve through the "selective retention" of shared beliefs and values (Hill 1978; Boehm 1982; Durham 1991).[8] The assumption uniting this research is that microevolutionary processes can explain the origin and persistence of ideas, customs, and institutions and account (ultimately) for macroscopic patterns of cultural change.

Cultural evolution denotes the sequential transformation of replicating units of symbolic information. The cultural **unit of inheritance** is the *meme* (Dawkins 1976: 203–15) an ideational "functional equivalent" of the gene.[9] Replicated and trans-

Table 6.1 Properties of Genetic and Cultural Evolution Compared

System Properties	Genetic Evolution	Cultural Evolution
(1) **units of inheritance**	genes (alternative alleles in population's gene pool)	memes (alternative beliefs in society's concept pool)
(2) **sources of variation**	random mutation or recombination; migration	deliberate or random innovation, synthesis, diffusion, migration
(3) **transmission mechanism**	sexual reproduction ("vertical" parent-offspring transmission)	social communication (many modes and ratios of "teachers" and "learners")
(4) **transforming forces**	*Primary:* natural selection *Secondary:* organic constraints; mutation, migration, and drift	*primary:* cultural selection (choice, imposition, socialization, learning, natural selection) *secondary:* biased transmission, social constraints; drift, diffusion, and migration
(5) **means of isolation**	Geographic, behavioral	geographic, social, behavioral

(*Modified from Durham 1991*)

mitted among carriers, memes structure minds, inform worldviews, and generate phenotypic effects in the form of behaviors, customs, artifacts, and institutions. Like genes, memes exist in alternative alleles, whether binary opposition pairs (like us/other or Hindu/Moslem) or points on a spectrum (like fashionable skirt length).

As *holons*, memes are simultaneously "(1) *parts of* a greater system and therefore subject to its constraints, and (2) *parts from* that system, and thus capable of independent change" (Durham 1991: 422). Their scope ranges from single customs (like whether to shake hands or bow in greeting strangers) to entire cosmologies. A large meme like Catholicism may encompass lesser concepts like the doctrine of transubstantiation. Like genes, memes frequently act in concert. Moreover, selection on a phenotype may affect memes for structurally or functionally related traits.

Variation among replicating units supplies the raw material for selection in evolving systems. The ultimate source of genetic variation is "blind" mutation. Cultural analogs exist in accidental invention (like the discovery of penicillin) or random copy error (like linguistic mistranslation, textual mistranscription, or faulty memory). Cultural analogs of migration, gene flow, and genetic drift also exist. Social groups may relocate, carrying unique memes with them; beliefs and customs may diffuse to adjacent societies; and small, unrepresentative populations may become isolated.

Unlike mutation, however, cultural innovation is often conscious. Selective retention occurs whenever variable, heritable traits have differential consequences; there is "no requirement that the original source of variation be random with respect to selection" (Richerson and Boyd, in Rindos 1985: 83). Possessing foresight and creativity, humans learn from experience, modify existing practices, synthesize old habits, and invent novel solutions to current or anticipated necessity.[10] Intentionality gives cultural evolution an "explosive rapidity and cumulative directionality" that biological evolution lacks. Culture may be *driven* towards "progress" (Gould 1996: 219–30).

How effectively new memes spread depends upon the actual **mechanisms of transmission.** Cultural exchange bears scant resemblance to the slow intergenerational process of genetic inheritance. The transfer of heredity through gametogenesis and fertilization, governed by the principles of Segregation and Independent Assortment, is a conservative processs. According to the Hardy-Weinberg Law of population genetics, sexual reproduction itself will not (*ceteris paribus*) alter the allelic frequencies of a breeding population or *deme* (Ayala 1982: 55–56).

Cultural transmission is by contrast fast, flexible, and continuous. Involving imitation and social learning, it exploits the ever-proliferating avenues of human communication and the variable "mating systems" of cultural exchange. Unrestricted to parent-child transmission, cultural transfer involves various ratios of "teachers" and "learners."[11] Lamarckian rather than Mendelian, cultural transmission permits inheritance of acquired characteristics; both "parent" (teacher) and "offspring" (learner) participate actively in the exchange of memes. Variation may be *guided,* as the experienced transmit acquired knowledge to "naive" individuals. Learners may imitate successful models on the basis of perceived attributes— "direct bias"—or out of conformity with a locally favored variant—"frequency-dependent bias" (Boyd and Richerson 1985: 1–18). Biased transmission and multiple modes and ratios imply that the mechanics cultural reproduction themselves can alter the frequencies of heritable "replicators." Change in a society's concept pool may be profound if many people adopt the ideas of a single individual (Gandhi or Hitler, for example).

Mechanisms of transmission explain the *descent* but not the *modification* of replicating entities. To understand why particular memes are retained or eliminated, we must look beyond *who* says what to *whom* and examine potential **forces of selection.** As there are more ways for cultural (than genetic) information to be transmitted, so there are more ways for culture to be differentially replicated. If "cultural selection" is the differential replication of memes, *cultural fitness* measures the relative transmission success of particular belief variants.[12] As in genetic evolution, fitness depends on the replicator's consequences for "carriers." But whereas humans cannot (yet) choose their own genes, they *can* determine the fortunes of their memes.

First, memes are selected for compatibility with the existing cultural environment. Cultural selection is no mere "tinkerer," but "constraints of inherited form" can bias cultural (like biological) evolution. Current technology can determine the feasibility of cultural innovations, just as current understandings may render some plausible options socially inconceivable.

Second, natural selection may alter the frequency of allomemes through the differential reproductive success of meme carriers. Natural selection can act on any heritable, transmissible trait that influences inclusive fitness, whether or not the mechanism of inheritance is genetic or cultural. Thus the struggle for biological survival should encourage the spread of myths, meanings, values, and systems of logic that generate adaptive behaviors. One can contrast the fates of Catholicism and Mormonism, which have outstripped religious competitors partly by fostering fecundity and transmitting memes to children, with the fate of the Shakers, a nearly extinct sect committed to celibacy (Alland 1969). This is *selection by consequences*: Societies do not "solve problems" intentionally or "observe particular practices in order that the group will be more likely to survive." Rather, they maintain adaptive practices "because groups which induced their members to do so survived and transmitted them." In other words, "circumstances select the cultural practices which yield a solution" (Skinner 1981: 503).

Although logically consistent, the natural selection model limits cultural diversity to output generated by impersonal forces. This weakness is shared by a third perspective, which portrays memes as *"active replicators."* Richard Dawkins, employing an analogy with "selfish genes," posits that cultural units "hijack" their human vehicles to foster their own replication. This is a racy but implausible thesis. Surely, catch phrases, fashion styles, and snappy tunes occasionally prove irresistible and accumulate like "junk DNA" (Dawkins 1982: 81–83, 109; 1976: 203–15). But as a passive copying model, the "selfish meme" hypothesis overlooks the conscious intervention of the mind in cultural transmission and selection. Intentionality and volition permit conceptual spring cleaning; human beings can filter their cultures on adaptive, hedonic, ethical, or aesthetic grounds.

Both the natural selection and selfish meme models treat humans as short-sighted automatons with little role in the selective process. Doing so ignores that "[c]ultural behavior is the conscious, meaningful activity of human beings, who create ideas in order to satisfy their own needs" (Ruyle et. al. 1977: 55). Faced with environmental exigencies, groups often *adapt* rather than wait to *become adapted*. Agency and ingenuity allow human beings to anticipate the consequences of their beliefs and actions in particular settings. Within the constraints of history, power, cultural appropriateness, and bounded rationality, they can select memes *according to* consequences. "Rational pre-selection" permits human beings to *"to solve problems rapidly and to come up with novel solutions handily"* (Boehm 1982: 112–14, emphasis mine).[13] Neither computing machines nor blind ignoramuses, human beings can learn from mistakes and fine-tune their culture to realize locally valued goals.

Still, human interaction and adaptive choice within any society is constrained, enabled, and mediated by current identity commitments and prevailing standards about security and prosperity. Existing institutions—both formal and informal bundles of conventions, codes, and norms of behavior—generate mutual expectations and permit habit-driven action. Since actors make decisions on the basis of historically shaped understandings and identities and in pursuit of locally valued ends, behavior may diverge from instrumental rationality and bias social evolution in idiosyncratic directions.

Finally, cultural choices are not always voluntary. Within any society, competition for scarce resources (to further security, wealth, or prestige) creates disparities in *social power*. Privileged elites or classes use coercion, authority, and agenda-setting capacity to control cultural transmission, constrain the choices of the weak, and impose their own beliefs, practices, and institutions. Diffuse social pressures, including psychological needs to "fit in" and fears of antagonizing authorities, likewise discourage innovation, deviance, and dissent.

These several selective pressures account for the sequential transformation of a single lineage (or sympatric evolution). But cultural divergence requires an additional factor: **isolation**. Geographical and social separation permit small differences to accumulate between cultural pools and incipient "cultural species" to diverge. Given the malleability of cultural identity, diversity cannot *persist* without some continued isolation. Modern history provides ample evidence that local memes may be swamped by a globalizing culture.

THE EVOLUTION OF INTERNATIONAL NORMS

If we accept the existence of a "society of states," we should predict similar processes of cultural generation, reproduction, and transformation at the global level. Principled beliefs about standards of international behavior are an important subset of memes. A cognitivist/constructivist evolutionary approach implies that international values, conventions, and institutions coevolve with humanity's cognitive universe. The pattern of norm evolution should reflect the emergence, transmission, differential selection, and internalization of new behavioral standards within the population of sovereign states.

As Figure 6.3 depicts, an evolutionary theory of norms links historical changes in state practice (P_t) to the sequential transformation of cognitions about appropriate behavior (N_t). Thus $\Delta P_t = f(\Delta N_t)$, where P_t, the distribution of state practices, is a function of the "norm pool" (N_t), or the distribution of allonorms (principled beliefs and their variants) within international society at time t. The symbol I_a refers to the influence of existing norms and institutions on state practices; I_b refers to the reciprocal influence (Kratochwil 1989: 217) of these practices (for example, sovereignty or multilateral diplomacy) on the differential replication of norms—a process mediated by various forces of transformation—including

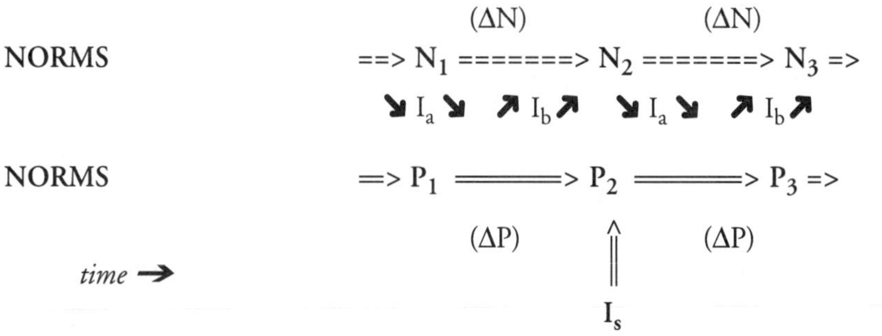

$$\begin{array}{ccc} & (\Delta N) & (\Delta N) \\ \text{NORMS} \quad & ==> N_1 ========> N_2 ========> N_3 => \\ & \searrow I_a \searrow \quad \nearrow I_b \nearrow \quad \searrow I_a \searrow \quad \nearrow I_b \nearrow \end{array}$$

$$\begin{array}{ccc} \text{NORMS} \quad & => P_1 =======> P_2 =======> P_3 => \\ & (\Delta P) \quad \Big\uparrow \quad (\Delta P) \\ time \rightarrow & \Big\| \\ & I_s \end{array}$$

Figure 6.3 The Interaction between an Evolving Norm Pool (N_t) and State Practice (P_t)

direct copying, rational choice, social learning, external imposition, and socialization. The arrows depicting normative influence are multiple, since the normative "code" is inherited continually and changed frequently. Selection pressures act directly on the norm (a form of "replicator selection"), but the environment may also reward or punish norm "vehicles"—whether individuals, bureaucracies, states, or rival international societies. (The symbol I_s shows selection acting directly on vehicles.)

(1) Norms as "Units of Inheritance"

The unit of inheritance, naturally, will be the *norm*. A particular subset of memes, norms are intersubjective understandings about standards of legitimate conduct in specific areas of international relations. Although they are ideational, norms code (like genes) for behavioral phenotypes. To use an analogy with a sacrament, state behavior is the "outward and visible sign"; its associated norm is the "inward and spiritual grace."

When they embody shared social purpose and collective intentionality, norms can facilitate policy convergence. Thus the norm of collective security obligates adherents to respond "against the unknown enemy . . . on behalf of the unknown victim" (Ruggie 1993: 10). Likewise, the norm of commercial multilateralism obligates adherents to pursue reciprocity and nondiscrimination in trade relations. However, convergent expectations need not produce harmony. Indeed, shared racialist assumptions justified the "New Imperialism" and the glorification of warfare a century ago, just as the beggar-thy-neighbor economic nationalism of the 1930s rested on common zero-sum assessments about global economic competition (Koch 1984).

Is it legitimate, one might ask, to treat norms in atomistic fashion? After all, they are frequently bundled together in the fabric of international society, and complex institutions like sovereignty (or the balance of power) may consist of multiple behavioral expectations. Still, treating norms as single units makes analytic sense, since it offers insights into how institutions evolve through the selective retention of their constituent norms.[14] As North observes, "institutions typically change incrementally," through "changes in norms at the margins" (1990: 4, 6, 83, 89).

Prior to becoming institutionalized and "taken for granted," normative beliefs typically exist as contested alternatives. The allonorms of commercial multilateralism, for example, include autarky and bilateralism (or preference). At any time, the population of states may be "polymorphic": different governments may espouse alternative allonorms. One state may oscillate between different standards of conduct (like mercantilism and free trade). The sum of all allonorms constitutes the global "norm pool." International society evolves as allonorm frequencies change.

(2) The Sources of Norm Variation

Variation among normative beliefs provides raw material for the global selection of international standards of conduct. But from where do new allonorms come? New principled beliefs emerge and gain international prominence through the activities of important actors, including states, international organizations and, increasingly, nongovernmental organizations (NGOs). Such beliefs may arise through "top-down" or "bottom-up" processes. At the systemic level, sovereign governments may propose new behavioral standards. Alternatively, NGOs and issue-advocacy networks may frame policy issues and mobilize domestic and international forces in support of new principles. The British development NGO Oxfam, for instance, has raised the salience of debt relief by coordinating a global campaign of pressure on bilateral and multilateral donors.

Historically, most successful norms have enjoyed the political sponsorship of at least one state. Because world politics involves "two-level games," potential norms must survive "selective retention" at *both* domestic and international levels. Within pluralist states, domestic purposes emerge through competition among social and political forces. The normative beliefs that survive are transmitted globally as sources of variation, as states compete to shape international order to their national predilections (Nau 1990: 18, 29).[15]

The innate qualities of innovative ideas are not sufficient to ensure their rise to domestic and international prominence. To influence a state's foreign policy choices, ideas must acquire political power by offering practical or ethical solutions to past mistakes or current problems and by demonstrating epistemic, administrative, and political viability. Potential norms must win over relevant experts and moral authorities within government and civil society on the basis of their theoretical appeal, ethical resonance, or practical relevance. Any new causal and principled understandings must accommodate (or overwhelm) current biases and power configurations, and "captured" agencies must have the practical capacity to implement new policies. Finally, the new norms must advance the agendas of ruling parties or mobilize new coalitions of political forces. National differences in these categories of "viability" help explain the uneven spread of ideas (Hall 1989: 361–90; Kahler 1990: 57).

New normative beliefs may sometimes arise blindly, but scholars should not dismiss the role of learning, thoughtful reflection, and moral sentiments.[16] Actors may adopt new ideas through the "trial" half of trial and error, or they may construct ideas "on the basis of prior experience and a theory about what is likely to work in the future" (Axelrod 1984: 170). Such "pre-selection" may be guided by anticipated consequences, local standards of appropriateness, or by both. Concerned that a lack of transparency might lead to nuclear holocaust, the United States and the Soviet Union tacitly accepted a Cold War regime of reconnaissance satellites permitting verification of compliance with stated intentions (Gaddis 1987). Normative innovation implies human reasoning, but the latter is shaped by knowledge, interpretations, and concepts of legitimacy.

Besides innovation, other sources of normative variation include synthesis and diffusion. The most-favored nation (MFN) principle, for example, emerged by fusing norms of reciprocity and nondiscrimination. Likewise, many attributes of contemporary nation-states reflect the undirected diffusion of political customs, economic practices, and cultural values (Strang and Meyer 1993).

(3) Mechanisms of Norm Transmission

Historically, most new standards of international behavior have benefited from "norm entrepreneurs" who "frame" policy debates and press other actors to change their utility functions. These entrepreneurs endeavor to transform contested, subjective ideas into collectively held, intersubjective norms (Finnemore and Sikkink 1998). Historically, great powers have taken the lead in (de)legitimizing standards of international conduct. Thus nineteenth century Great Britain pushed for free trade—and an end to the slave trade. Likewise, during and after World War II, U.S. officials pursued a reciprocal, nondiscriminatory international order based on collective security, open commerce, free trade, national self-determination, and the free flow of ideas. The spread of this multilateral vision since 1945 has reflected not only U.S. material preponderance but also America's vigorous epistemic communities and dominance over global communication.

Even without great power sponsorship, epistemic communities and "transnational moral entrepreneurs" can influence the global transmission of new normative beliefs. Peter Haas has documented the role of "networks of knowledge-based experts" in "articulating cause-and-effect relationships of complex problems, helping states identify their interests, framing the issues for collective debate, proposing specific policies, and identifying salient points for negotiation" (Haas 1992: 2–3). For example, the Bretton Woods accords for postwar monetary relations reflected a transatlantic alliance of American and British economists committed to both Keynesian domestic policies and commercial multilateralism (Ikenberry 1993).

Transnational NGOs like the World Wildlife Fund, Amnesty International, and Greenpeace exploit organizational platforms to shame violators of existing norms and to press for new standards on issues such as endangered species, human rights, or nuclear testing (Finnemore and Sikkink 1998). "Global prohibition regimes" often arise from the work of "transnational moral entrepreneurs" who mobilize domestic and foreign public support, sponsor "like-minded organizations" abroad, and "elevat[e] their objective beyond . . . the national interests of their government" (Nadelman 1990: 482).

A recent, spectacular example of this phenomenon is the International Campaign to Ban Land Mines (ICBL), which in a few brief years mobilized more than one thousand NGOs and Intergovernmental Organizations (IGOS) (from the Anglican Church to *Medecins Sans Frontieres* to UNICEF). Assisted by individual moral entrepreneurs (like Senator Pat Leahy of Vermont) and medium-sized "moral powers" (like Canada and Norway), the ICBL bypassed the stalled, consensus-based disarmament negotiations, sidestepped American opposition, and successfully pursued a global ban through the multilateral Ottawa Process (Price 1998).

International financial institutions and international organizations serve as additional sources of new global norms. In designing technical advice, lending activities, and aid conditions, the World Bank and the International Monetary Fund (IMF) now push recipients to meet standards of "good governance"—as well as to conform to the neoclassical economic orthodoxy of the "Washington consensus." Similarly, the multiple departments, programs, and agencies of the United Nations actively promote new norms in spheres like environmental protection, humanitarian assistance, sustainable development, and human rights.

Many approaches to normative evolution focus on the transmission process itself, rather than on the content or consequences of the transmitted message. Transmission theorists depict meme/norm transfer as a straightforward process of *imitation*: The naive simply "copy" the phenotypic traits of the more experienced (Boyd and Richerson 1985). According to Florini:

> The evolutionary argument is based on a fundamental assumption that human "choices" about behavior are based far more on simple imitation, encoded in the form of a norm, than on deliberate weighing of well-considered and well-understood options. (1996: 378)

Faced with incomplete information in complex situations, actors may simply imitate to avoid the "cognitively difficult" effort of "decid[ing] one's own optimal strategy." Rather than "actually *learning* from other people's experiences," policymakers may be unaware of "what the [other actor's] goal was and whether it was achieved."[17]

There are at least two problems with the simple imitation thesis. As this article argues, the *principled ideas* that later become "norms" arise and spread initially as contested responses to current dilemmas or questions (such as: "How should we organize our trade relations with other countries?" or "How should we treat people who look different?"). New beliefs change the utility functions of actors making choices; only later do these ideas take on the status of collective norms. Second, the capacity for rationality suggests that human actors are more likely to "emulate" others through observational learning than to "imitate" them unconsciously.

By treating norm spread as a simple matter of "contact" or "contagion," transmission theorists can employ epidemiological methods and make complex predictions about group behavior (Cavalli-Sforza and Feldman 1981). But this methodological simplification overlooks the dynamics of human choice. By concentrating on what actors *do* rather than how they *think*, what they *believe*, or how they *feel*, such copying models ignore volition, judgment, and sentiment and have little to say about the content or meaning of cultural or normative shifts. Finally, cultural contact models assume a radical individualism, depicting cultural change as the statistical aggregation of innumerable imitation events by autonomous individuals. There is little appreciation of social power and the ways that conflicts of interest, coercion, and structural asymmetries can bias the transmission and adoption of norms.

Transmission theories do provide some insights about how normative beliefs attain global prominence. The question remains: What forces of selection operate on the variation injected into the international arena?

(4) Forces of International Selection

This essay predicts that the main process of transformation in international society is *normative selection*, or "the differential replication of international norms." Selection can operate either directly on normative beliefs or indirectly on norm carriers at several levels—individuals, bureaucratic structures, states, or (even) "societies of states."[18] This section evaluates five selective forces that might potentially filter the global pool of norms and determine the fitness of particular allonorms. These are (a) natural selection, (b) rational choice, (c) learning, (d) social power, and (e) socialization. (See Table 6.2.)

(A) Natural Selection

Neorealists depict the evolution of global norms as the outcome of natural selection. Within the self-help international system, structures of power "act as a selector" by "rewarding some behaviors and punishing others." Kenneth Waltz describes anarchy as a "constraining and disposing force" that "shape[s] and shove[s]" states toward adaptive behaviors through the dual processes of "competition" and "socialization." As in markets and ecosystems, competition sorts actors

Table 6.2 Potential Forces of Norm Selection

MODEL	EXPLANATION FOR NORM CHANGE
(A) Natural Selection (Structural Realism)	*Selection by consequences:* The differential survival or success of state actors possessing particular norms. (An unconscious process.)
(B) Rational Choice (Neoliberalism)	*Selection according to consequences:* The conscious promotion or acceptance of norms to advance specific interests in situations of strategic choice or bargaining, according to the logic of consequentiality and the shadow of the future.
(C) Learning (Weak Cognitivism)	*Knowledge (or experience) informed selection according to consequences:* New causal and principled beliefs shape state utility functions. Choices reflect endogenous learning; emulation; analogical reasoning; or new values.
(D) Social Power (Hegemonic Socialization)	*Hegemonic socialization:* Dominant states secure subordinate compliance through an initial exercise of power (whether manipulation of incentives, structural power, or conquest). Hegemonic rule is legitimated as weaker states internalize dominant norms through normative persuasion; external inducement; internal reconstruction; or popular socialization.
(E) Socialization (Strong Cognitivism)	*Selection according to appropriateness:* States select and comply with norms based upon identity commitments and perceived "fit" between new behavioral standards and the fundamental rules, institutions, and concepts of legitimacy/justice in international society. New identities and norms emerge through the expansion of international society; "norm cascades"; practical discourses; and institutionalization within organizations, rules and law.

according to "fitness." Even if states rarely go extinct—though some, like the Soviet Union, occasionally do—some nonetheless fare better than others. "Their competitors will emulate them or fall by the wayside." Regardless of their internal predilections, the units that survive and thrive eventually resemble one another (Waltz 1979: 69, 73–77; Axelrod 1984: 50).

Waltz's discussion of "socialization" is less satisfying. He asserts that societies "establish norms of behavior," but he fails to identify any mutual expectations that operate at the international level. He argues that that societies praise conformity and punish deviancy, but he provides no insight into the content of global norms and the social purposes these serve. The "system" Waltz (1979: 74–76, 127–28) describes is devoid of social content. He uses the word "socialization," but he describes behavioral conditioning.

This generative grammar of world politics suffers because Waltz neglects nonmaterial elements of the international "structure." The claim that "competition spurs the actors to accommodate their ways to the *socially most acceptable* [emphasis mine] and successful practices," for example, begs attention to collective standards of legitimacy. Instead, Waltz (1979: 77, 128) treats "global conventions" as behavioral regularities produced by the functional imperatives of interstate competition. ("It is this 'sameness,' an effect of the system, that is so often attributed to so-called rules of state behavior.") Intentionality, moreover, is irrelevant: "Where selection according to consequences rules, patterns emerge and endure" without conscious design; "order may prevail without an orderer; adjustments may be made without an adjuster; tasks may be allocated without an allocator." (Waltz uses the phrase "selection according to consequences," but he means "behavioral conditioning.") The positional pursuit of power is an Evolutionarily Stable Strategy (ESS): it cannot be defeated by an alternative strategy.

International political economy (IPE) scholars have applied natural selection to the global economy. Systemic market forces reward or punish states depending on their commercial orientations, so that "only the 'fittest' are likely to survive." The successful are those that "adapt their economic policies to respond receptively (both flexibly and favorably) to . . . changing global conditions." The inefficient must "innovate or else face economic extinction"—or at least marginalization (Biersteker 1992: 112–13; Gilpin 1987: 67). These competitive pressures reduce state-market relations to a single model—a phenomenon Cox terms "the internationalization of the state" (Cox 1987: 253).

A "first image" variant of this natural selection thesis links policy change to the differential "survival" not of states but of statesmen holding particular beliefs. According to Andrew Farkas, foreign policy evolves as domestic political systems reward or punish *policy-makers* according to the consequences of the alternative courses of action that they recommend (for example, "constructive engagement" vs. economic sanctions). Whether statesmen actually understand the international environment or simply choose fortuitously, those advocating successful courses are promoted and leave more "intellectual offspring."[19] The survival of the "fittest" policymakers shapes the goals, causal beliefs, and policy choices of subsequent political "generations"—and makes policies appear more rational than they actually are (Farkas 1996). Although this mechanism may occasionally operate, it is likely to produce frequent maladaptation because of the unavoidable time lag before selection operates and the over-generalization of earlier "lessons" like Munich or Vietnam (Khong 1992).

(B) Rational Choice

The "natural selection" approach is a primitive conception of state behavior. By depicting states as simply "tracking" an often malevolent environment, structural realism overlooks that human beings, possessing foresight, may prejudge the impact of a given norm on their own fortunes. As rational choice theorists point out, human beings may select or reject beliefs *according to* likely consequences long before their overt behavior is selected *by* those consequences (Durham 1991).[20] This might be thought of as rational "self-selection."

Biologists define "fitness" as effective design for survival and reproduction. An *adaptation* is a fitness-enhancing trait naturally selected for its current function.[21] Some ecological anthropologists contend that culture is generally adaptive because human beings consciously select memes based on reproductive implications. Accordingly, the memes with the highest "cultural fitness" (or replication success) ought to be those that enhance the "inclusive fitness" (total reproductive success) of their carriers (Durham 1976 1991).[22] Applied to IR theory, this hypothesis jibes with the rational choice view that actors accept or reject norms on the basis of perceived consequences for state welfare. As Strang and Meyer (1993: 488) observe, "A core idea [of diffusion literature] is that practices are adopted to the extent that they appear more effective or efficient than the alternatives."

More attuned than structural realists to the implications of Lamarckian inheritance, neoliberals portray norms as useful instruments consciously created and maintained to help utility-maximizing states overcome coordination obstacles. The neoliberal account for international institutions (of which norms are an important component) is ultimately a functional one: "Institutions exist because they could have reasonably been expected to increase the welfare of their creators" (Keohane 1984: 80). In particular, institutions reduce uncertainty and transaction costs by providing information and stabilizing expectations (Keohane 1996: 195–99).

Unfortunately, functional explanations are not particularly successful at explaining the emergence of norms (like Social Darwinism) that manifestly hinder cooperation among states. Nor do they account for why norms arise in some issue areas but not in others where they may be equally urgent (Haggard and Simmons 1987: 506–09). These shortcomings arise in part because rational choice approaches "bracket off" issues of preference-formation, and particularly the role of knowledge and identity in shaping state interests. Neoliberals also overlook the role of social power in the creation, persistence, and erosion of frameworks for international cooperation. Neorealists, in contrast, are inclined to ask of international regimes: "functional" *for whom*? (Grieco 1988). For example, Janice Thomson (1992: 199) predicts that "a transnational practice will be delegitimated when strong states see it as an internal or external threat to their power or control."

In general, rational choice theory tends to overestimate human reasoning powers and to underestimate the constraints on adaptive decision-making. Potential sources of maladaptation include imperfect information; emotional or irrational behavior; imposition by powerful actors; social pressures to conform; time lags; environmental unpredictability or malevolence; over-generalization; novel social-ecological contexts; reification (or undue weighting); and misperception. In addition, norms may change in response to selection operating on functionally related norms or at higher levels (for example, the collapse of an entire world view).

Finally, current technological capabilities (and scientific breakthroughs) may influence the fitness of new norms. Thus advances in satellite reconnaissance have encouraged transparency in military affairs. Since sovereign states can no longer defend their "right" to secrecy in military preparations, they find it easier to embrace mutual verification.

(C) Learning

The most fundamental shortcoming of rational choice approaches, however, is their inattention to the role of knowledge, experience, and values in mediating actor interests and decisions. Weak cognitivists, in contrast, point to the role of learning in shaping state utility functions and the selection of international norms. Learning refers to "the development of new beliefs, skills, or procedures as a result of the observation and interpretation of experience" (Levy 1994: 283, 291; Nye 1987). A two-step process, it denotes (first) the redefinition of interests in the light of new causal and principled understandings and (second) the subsequent adjustment of behavior. This is a more nuanced portrait than depicted in conventional rational choice literature, which treats learning as invariant adjustment to the changing payoff matrix of a volatile environment. For weak cognitivists, the international environment does not *instruct* states so much as *challenge* them.

Learning occurs when new ideas about efficiency and justice and novel "images of the future bounded by what is physically, humanly, and socially possible" provide a new foundation for state action (Adler 1991: 52–53). Learning can be *endogenous*, as states arrive at norms independently through direct experiential learning. States may employ different strategies over time and stick with the most satisfying ones. According to Axelrod and Keohane (1985), most efforts to "gain acceptance for new norms" have been "experimental, trial-and-error efforts to improve the current situation based on recent experience" (Axelrod 1984: 50, 170).

Alternatively, learning may take the form of *emulation*, as states seek to replicate the success of others. This differs from crude copying; after all, "imitation holds little value if the blind lead the blind." Learning occurs only "if others are monitored not as role models for imitation but instead as natural experiments" (Cosmides and Tooby 1987: 295). Adaptation requires observers to attribute reasons for others' triumphs and failures.

More generally, inferences about past events can shape current beliefs, policy preferences, and decisions. Dramatic failures—like depressions or military defeats—can overcome institutional inertia, encourage a turnover of political leadership, and stimulate violent reaction against past policies (Levy 1994: 301–06). Likewise, policymakers may look for parallels between contemporary and historical situations, relying on analogies to interpret their predicament and to guide their selection of ends and means (Khong 1992).

Still, the "lessons of history" are often ambiguous. Why are some lessons learned but not others? Why do some ideas acquire influence over policy? Epistemic communities and other networks of policy specialists often facilitate international learning by transmitting "both the cognitive content of their causal models and values and a compressed interpretation of their historical experience." Learning thus underpins "rational choice" (Adler and Haas 1992: 386).

Trial and error, emulation, and epistemic communities all played a role in the "triumph" of neoclassical economics in the developing world during the 1980s. Many less-developed countries, frustrated by the failures of import substitution strategies, hoped to replicate the export-oriented growth of the East Asian "tigers." These direct and vicarious experiences fostered a political climate favorable to the policy prescriptions of economists advocating stabilization, privatization, and liberalization. Successful early converts to structural adjustment and market liberalization, like Chile, became models to emulate. Although power considerations (including U.S. pressure and IMF conditionality) encouraged this shift, experiential learning and expert consensus determined the timing of this "policy bandwagoning" (Kahler 1990; Biersteker 1992).

(D) Social Power

Normative selection need not begin as a voluntary process. As states (and other actors) compete to establish the standards of international conduct, they are likely to face resistance from recalcitrant or revolutionary states holding contrary beliefs, rejecting universal norms, or advocating alternative standards of legitimacy. In such circumstances, assuring compliance with new standards may require the exercise of social power. Most obviously, a hegemon or great power concert can manipulate tangible punishments and rewards to secure conformity with international norms. At the Congress of Vienna, for example, the Grand Alliance restored the French monarchy and forced France to abide by the principles of the Concert of Europe. More recently, the U.N. Security Council has tried (with limited success) to compel Iraq to terminate its programs for weapons of mass destruction.

Besides employing "relational" power, of course, great powers structure the very framework of international politics by setting the agenda, establishing the institutions, and controlling the organizations that govern the international political economy. Prior to actual bargaining, dominant states use their *structural power* to determine the norms, principles, rules, and decision-making procedures that constitute international regimes. Within established organizations, weighted voting allows the strong to block distasteful initiatives and to redirect resources to preferred priorities. In other words, "[S]ome issues are organized into politics while others are organized out" (Gaventa 1980: 9; Guzzini 1993: 471). More generally, great powers dominate the security, production, financial, and knowledge "structures" of the international political economy (Strange 1988: 24–25, 115–17).

Thus acquiescence to international norms may reflect not shared principles but the use of sanctions or the perceived lack of alternatives. Mere compliance, however, is a fragile basis for international governance; it requires persistent structural asymmetries, continual supervision, and occasional enforcement. A more lasting expression of power is achieved not by manipulating incentives or structuring options but by shaping another's very wants (Lukes 1974: 23–31). Social conformity becomes enduring when actors identify with the source of behavioral standards and (especially) internalize the norms themselves (Aronson 1984: 35–37).

Neorealists distinguish between anarchical international systems and hierarchical domestic ones, but the society of states has always been either *hegemonic* or *oligopolistic*: either a single state or an "international aristocracy" has enjoyed special privileges and shouldered obligations to maintain order (Aron 1966: 95; Bull 1977: 206–07; Clark 1989). The principal socializing agents have been the European great powers and, more recently, the United States; they have determined the criteria of international legitimacy and transmitted behavioral expectations to the wider world. Recognizing that durable governance requires legitimacy as well as preponderance, global power wielders like domestic rulers have tried to justify their dominion by winning support for shared purposes (Ikenberry and Kupchan 1990a and 1990b).

How do dominant states transform the pragmatic acquiescence of subordinates into the loyal participation of "followers"? (Cooper, Higgott, and Nossal 1991). First, great powers have used *normative persuasion* to convince others of the worthiness of their goals. The inherent attractiveness of norms and the credibility of their advocates may lead weaker states to internalize new standards (even in the absence of material incentives). During World War II, for example, President Franklin Roosevelt used moral appeals to win allied sympathy for an open postwar world. Second, subordinate states may internalize norms following sustained, materially-beneficial interaction in international frameworks (Ikenberry and Kupchan 1990b: 290–94). If normative persuasion is akin to "love at first sight," *external inducement* begins as a "marriage of convenience." During the first decade after 1945, the United States provided its European allies with financial assistance (the Marshall Plan) and military protection (in NATO) to win general commitments to a liberal, interdependent world economy. In addition, Washington incubated elite support for multilateralism within Atlantic institutions to coordinate Free World economic and security policy (Maier 1989a: 273–76). Initially, subordinate state elites may adopt new policies for instrumental reasons. To gain the benefits of membership in the World Trade Organization (WTO), for example, China must agree to accept nondiscrimination and reciprocity and to protect intellectual property. Eventually, they embrace the normative logic of these regimes—whether to achieve cognitive consistency or to avoid the appearance of capitulation.

Third, a hegemon or great power concert may impose institutions and policies on a defeated enemy through a process of *internal reconstruction*. Local political forces, particularly opponents of the defeated regime, may internalize the values these frameworks embody. A "shotgun wedding," in other words, precedes the eventual "love affair." In both West Germany and Japan, military occupation permitted the United States (and its allies) to restore democracy; to transform economic, societal, and (to a degree) cultural institutions; and to integrate former enemies into international political, security, and economic institutions. Short on legitimacy, both states were susceptible to U.S. norms (Muravchik 1991: 91–108; Ikenberry and Kupchan 1990b: 303–07).

Whereas the preceding scenarios focus on elites, legitimation of hegemonic power might also occur through *popular socialization* at the level of mass publics. By controlling the form and content of global information—what Susan Strange (1988: 115–34) terms the "knowledge structure"—powerful states can bias the construction of sociocultural reality and foster solidarity within "security communities" (Deutsch 1957). The present age of instantaneous communication offers multiple mechanisms to transmit values, providing a dynamic engine for sociocultural evolution. The unprecedented volume, velocity, and intrusiveness of American culture have turned the United States into the universal referent for the political-economic development of foreign societies and the dynamic source of many of their tastes, products, and habits. Arguably, public acculturation has facilitated U.S. leadership (Russett 1985: 228–30).

One need not posit manipulated consensus (Ashley 1990: 267) to regard ideas as important sources of social power. Although neorealists dismiss the normative underpinnings of international authority as "barely one step removed from capability" (Waltz 1979: 88), state capacities may take subtler, "softer" forms (Nye 1990: 188). According to Weber, "willingness to submit to an order . . . always in some sense implies a belief in the legitimate *authority* of the source imposing it" (Weber 1947: 132). Dominant states that articulate attractive, universal norms; possess an accessible culture; make credible commitments; and institutionalize their purposes may create consensual systems of governance based on "right" as well as "might," transforming a situation of potential or actual conflict into one of convergent interests (Ikenberry and Kupchan 1990b: 283–87). If weak states regard this leadership as principled and justified, they may choose to "follow" rather than to submit or acquiesce (Cooper, Higgott, and Nossal 1991: 395–99). Structural and relational capacities confer *power over* actors and outcomes; but legitimation gives a hegemon *"power to"*—"capacity to construct a higher degree, or alternative form, of political 'order' than would have existed in its absence" (Maier 1989b: 2–3).

(E) Socialization

It is likely, however, that socialization is a more general process within international society. By raising issues of identity and legitimacy, proponents of "hegemonic socialization" open the door for inquiry into the role of social (rather than material) structures in the selective retention of standards of state conduct. Socialization occurs when new principled understandings, articulated by various proponents (including states, IOs, or NGOs), are incorporated into actor identities and institutionalized in informal conventions, formal law, and the rules of international organizations.

According to strong cognitivists, states select and comply with new principled beliefs according to the latters' perceived "fit" with existing identity commitments and the fundamental institutions, rules and, concepts of legitimacy in international society. Norm change is governed less by the logic of consequentiality (and the "shadow of the future") than by the logic of appropriateness (and the "shadow of institutions").

States formulate national interests and foreign policies not through pure rational choice but through subjective standards. Decisions are shaped by rules of thumb, proverbs, conventions, ethical principles, and enduring habits. Thus, as David Packenham shows, America's foreign assistance policy during the Cold War was mediated by four unspoken assumptions derived from the country's liberal-exceptionalist political culture: "change and development are easy"; "all good things go together"; "radicalism and revolution are bad"; and "distributing power is more important than accumulating power" (1973: 20). Identity commitments give valence to the "national interest" and establish the boundaries of acceptable behavior for self and others.

Since the "reception and interpretation" of new ideas is inevitably "affected by . . . prior beliefs" (Nye 1987: 333), global norms should be partly self-selecting. That is, new standards will be favored according to their logical and effective continuity with existing ones. This is clearest in international law, where existing conventions and precedents determine the status of new rules.

Like genes, moreover, norms may be mutually reinforcing or "co-adapted." The norm of transparency, for instance, presupposes a prior commitment to reciprocity and nondiscrimination. Likewise, the principles of nonintervention and diplomatic immunity rest on a prior commitment to sovereign equality. Normative selection is no mere "tinkerer," but it is affected by "constraints of inherited form." Universal human rights standards could not have arisen during the Age of Exploration, when European jurists defined land occupied by hunter-gatherers as *territorium nullius*. National self-determination could not have spread when the principle of political legitimacy was still dynastic (rather than republican). Since World War II, the global application of national self-determination and racial equality have delegitimated European colonialism and (recently) racial *apartheid*, making their reappearance inconceivable.

Normative evolution, being contingent on historical precedents and accumulated cultural inheritance, is also likely to be path dependent. Rather than an inevitable march toward "progress," global change will reflect the presence of multiple equilibria, the unanticipated downstream effects of chance events, and the high costs of alternative courses (North 1990: 94–95, 100).

Strong cognitivism has a status quo bias. The global social structure should encourage conformity with existing standards, as *"rationalizing"* actors resist change to protect identity commitments (Aronson 1984: 119). But how do *new* standards of appropriate behavior arise (as opposed to the reproduction of current norms)? Four possibilities suggest themselves.

First, international norms have spread during the long, ongoing "expansion of international society" from a European core, a process fostered by exploration, colonial expansion, political competition, and commercial exchange (Bull and Watson 1984). Consistent with interaction role theory, norms and identities have emerged to distinguish "in" and "out" groups. This process has divided international society into concentric and overlapping circles, according to states' acceptance of particular allonorms (Goldgeir and McFaul 1992). Historically, aspirants to the society of states have gained membership by adjusting and adapting, voluntarily or involuntarily, to fundamental principles and practices like sovereignty and diplomacy. One result is that "international" law reflects Western standards of jurisprudence and, indeed, "the values and interests of Western civilization" (Gilpin 1981: 35–36). Peripheral polities like Turkey, Russia, Japan, and China were integrated gradually as they met a Western-defined "standard of civilization" (Gong 1984; Buzan 1993). As the Opium Wars and other conflicts attest, coercion has often accompanied integration. Failure to meet membership criteria has justified unequal treatment, as evinced by changing norms of humanitarian intervention: In the 1820s, great powers intervened in Greece to protect fellow Christians; today, the United Nations is as likely to intervene on behalf of Muslim Bosniacs or Kurds (Finnemore 1996a).

How do identities and norms actually change? It is possible that international society "evolves functionally from the logic of anarchy." According to Adam Watson, "[T]he regulating rules and institutions of a system usually, and perhaps inexorably, develop to the point where the members become conscious of common values and the system becomes a society." Barry Buzan suggests a more complex process, whereby "unlike units in anarchy" begin to form a society when they accept "a set of rules that legitimize the differentiation of units and establish a distribution of rights and responsibilities among functionally differentiated actors." Social solidarity subsequently emerges through the organic forces of trade, war, the balance of power, technological transfer, migration, and travel.[23] More dramatically, world-historical shocks like war or depression may cause the "breakdown of consensus about identity commitments"; stimulate the "critical examination of old ideas about self and other"; and culminate in the adoption of "new practice" (Wendt 1992: 420–21). Finally, new identities may emerge through communicative action among actors possessing rival interpretations; such "practical discourses" may generate convergent expectations about norms and their specific application. Thomas Risse documents such a process of discursive validation in the gradual (and grudging) acceptance of human rights standards by authoritarian states (1998).

A second, potentially complementary approach to socialization envisions a "tipping point" phenomenon, whereby outsiders rapidly internalize a new behavioral standard once the latter is accepted by a critical mass of states. According to Finnemore and Sikkink (1998), a "norm cascade" typically occurs only after at least one third of all states have adopted the proto-norm. Socialization is based not on rational anticipation of likely consequences but on identity commitments: Simply put, the norm has become inherent in the identity of "statehood" (or in a narrower identity like "liberal" or "Islamic" state). Such a norm cascade seems to have accompanied the global spread of both women's suffrage and the land mine ban. One could imagine similar processes accompanying the abolition of the death penalty among European states or the adoption by NATO of a "no first use" policy regarding nuclear weapons (currently under discussion). Once the "cascade" phase begins, domestic politics and mass movements play a lesser role in state decisions than do "demonstration effects," peer pressure, legitimacy concerns, and self-esteem considerations.

A third force for international socialization is the influence of formal international organizations (IOs). First, IOs promote like-mindedness through the *engrenage* (or "grinding together") of elites who cooperate on functional tasks—as neofunctionalists anticipated would occur in European integration (Haas 1958). Second, such entities "serve as more than opportunities for communication ... they are designed specifically to promote the homogenization of their members around models of progressive policy" (Strang and Meyer 1993: 491). Thus the International Labor Organization (ILO) promotes new labor standards among industrialized countries; the UN High Commission for Human Rights (UNHCHR) presses countries to abide by universal conventions; and the Organization of Economic Cooperation Development's (OECD) Development Assistance Committee promotes common donor positions on issues like post-conflict aid or "excessive" military expenditures. More broadly, the United Nations organizes multilateral conferences to create norms, adopt "action plans," and establish monitoring systems for cooperation in various issue areas, including the environment (Rio 1992); human rights (Vienna 1993); population and development (Cairo 1994); social development (Copenhagen 1995), women and development (Beijing 1995), human settlements (Istanbul 1996), food security (Rome 1996), and climate change (Kyoto 1997).

Finally, international law provides a potent source of new global norms. As the product of successive, authoritative decisions about competing claims about values, law changes at the margins through the emergence of new cases and precedents. International jurists distinguish between *lex lata*—or codified (and binding) "hard" law—and *lex ferenda*—or law that is coming into being (Beck 1996, 14–19). Of particular relevance to international norms is "customary international law," or law that emerges from the stable behavior of states over time. The conventions of diplomatic immunity, for example, arose from the practice of treating representatives of foreign states as immune from the jurisdictional enforcement of host nations. In addition, treaties that have been ratified and implemented by most countries "may . . . create a prevalent pattern of behavior which, as 'customary law,' obligates states that have not accepted the treaty." The compliance pull of international law derives from perceived legitimacy: State obligations are concomitants of membership in the international community (Franck 1990, 189–99). Arguably, as Finnemore and Sikkink (1998) contend, "customary international law *is* norms."

International legal rules help constitute international society by enshrining the doctrine of sovereignty, establishing criteria for membership, providing a language for diplomacy, giving normative value to state actions, and providing guidance about legitimate norms and procedures. Moreover, international law has the advantage of flexibility. "[I]t allows norms and principles to be introduced . . . to be given formal expression, and gradually to be hardened into binding rules that are capable of giving rise to specific duties and obligations (Hurrell 1996: 208–14).

Hypotheses about the Forces of Normative Selection

Figure 6.4 summarizes the forces that together filter the global norm pool. These include (1) consistency with current norms; (2) simple imitation; (3) natural selection; (4) rational choice; (5) learning; (6) social power; and (7) socialization.

An example may help clarify the differences among them. Imagine an initial distribution of allonorms, N_1, pertaining to commercial exchange. Most states

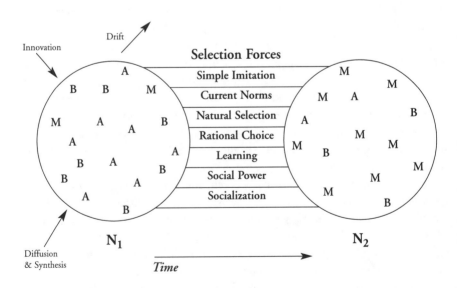

Figure 6.4 Forces of Normative Selection in International Society

pursue either economic autarky (A) or bilateral trade relations (B). Multilateral (M) strategies have arisen by innovation or diffusion but are initially rare. What forces might account for changes in the frequency of norm variants? First, reciprocity and nondiscrimination might be more compatible with existing international norms (like collective security) and identity commitments (like democratic governance). Second, in keeping with simple "transmission" models, states might differentially imitate a norm that had gained prominence through the activities of a powerful country. Third, countries pursuing autarky or bilateralism might fail to compete with free traders and "fall by the wayside" (according to Waltzian natural selection). Fourth, states might rationally calculate the fitness consequences of alternative norms and choose multilateralism to maximize utilities defined in terms of material interest. Fifth, states might alter their preferences through processes of learning (as shaped by the acquisition of new knowledge, direct or vicarious experiences, analogical reasoning, or new values). Sixth, great powers might impose open commercial orientations on weaker states through incentives, conquest, or structural dominance; subsequently, subordinates might embrace open trade as principled and justified. Finally, states might be socialized to adopt multilateralism—whether through entry into international society, through their involvement in international organizations, through the spread of international legal rules, through processes of social communication (and practical discourses), or through the phenomenon of "norm cascade."

Doubtless these categories overlap in practice. Learning may inform "rational" choice, for example, just as the exercise of power may be a prelude to socialization. It will be the task of future research to address the intriguing implications of multiple selection pressures operating simultaneously on the transmission of international norms. Several questions spring to mind: Are the various forces competing or complementary? If selection dynamics push in opposite directions, what determines which one has the greatest impact? Most importantly, under what circumstances does the logic of appropriateness outweigh the logic of consequentiality?

Addressing the issue of institutional change generally, Douglass North hypothesizes that values (rather than rational choice) guide behavior only when the material costs of doing so are low. Conversely, when the price of expressing "ideology, or norms or preferences is extremely high," these factors will play a lesser role in human behavior. The problem with North's formulation is that it privileges material constraints, overlooking the role of collective understandings in constituting identities and creating the intersubjective "realities" upon which actors base their decisions.

The several selective forces identified above are unlikely to possess equivalent importance for the global evolution of norms. To determine their relative weight, investigators will need to conduct qualitative research on historical instances of normative change. In anticipation of such case studies, I offer the following tentative hypotheses:

Hypothesis 1: The main but not exclusive means of modification of international behavior is "normative selection," or the differential replication of international norms. Changes in state behavior will covary with the cognitive universe of state leaders. By implication, new collective expectations of appropriate behavior will introduce novel patterns of state interaction.

Hypothesis 2: Normative selection operates primarily on norms themselves, rather than upon norm carriers (whether these are individuals, bureaucracies, states, or groups of states). This is a claim about the unit of selection: Although norm "vehicles" are occasionally eliminated, the global norm pool evolves largely through the selective retention of alternative normative beliefs.

Hypothesis 3: The principal forces of normative selection are the cognitive processes of (a) learning, (b) socialization, and (c) the legitimation of hegemonic power. By contrast, (i) simple imitation, (ii) natural selection, and (iii) pure rational choice are rarely responsible for the selective retention of international norms.

Hypothesis 4: The relative importance of learning (weak cognitivism) and socialization (strong cognitivism) varies with the stage in the norm's life cycle. Norms arise initially as contested principled beliefs that address practical and ethical dilemmas. These subjective beliefs become collective expectations when embedded in actor identities, international institutions, organizational structures, and law (whereupon they acquire a "taken for granted" quality).

Hypothesis 5: The fitness of new normative beliefs will be influenced by existing logics of appropriateness and identity commitments. The direction of normative change (and the consolidation of protonorms into new collective standards) will be mediated by the norm's logical, affective, and moral continuity with current institutions and identities. Thus, norms will tend to be highly self-selecting.

Hypothesis 6: Dominant states may influence the selection of international norms by legitimating their dominion over weaker states through several processes of hegemonic socialization. These processes include normative persuasion, external inducement, internal reconstruction, and popular socialization.

CONCLUSION

Evolution is a critical, missing dimension in IR theory. Conventional IR approaches like neorealism, neoliberalism, and game theory focus on the "ecology" of the state system, describing strategic interaction and the synchronic determinants of state "fitness" in an asocial environment at a given moment in time. Constructivism has added an "interpretive" element by embedding states in an intersubjective anarchical society where they discover identities and purposes through meaningful social interaction. Evolution adds a dynamic perspective, showing how the norms that guide behavior originate, diffuse, and change.

Building upon an evolutionary theory of culture, this chapter attributes changing patterns of behavior in international society to microevolutionary processes—and specifically to the differential replication of normative beliefs about appropriate state conduct. It hypothesizes that three selective forces are especially important in the selective retention of international norms: learning, socialization, and hegemonic power. Such a microevolutionary approach promises to bring greater precision to the wooly concept of an "international society." It will allow scholars to account for the emergence, spread, persistence, and elimination of specific norms like free trade, national self-determination, or noncombatant immunity.

Before closing, I wish to register two caveats about the proposed model. First, the tempo and mode of normative evolution is likely to include not only gradual change but also abrupt, macroevolutionary events. Second, historical patterns of normative evolution may be irrevocably altered by the accelerating forces of globalization.

The microevolutionary approach developed in this chapter is consistent with the view that "institutional change . . . is overwhelmingly incremental" (North 1990). However, scholars should consider the possibility that normative change occurs not only through of *phyletic gradualism* but also through large-scale events akin to *punctuated equilibria* in biological systems (Gould and Eldredge 1977). Anthropolologists have documented instances of "quantum adjustment" in sociocultural evolution (Diener 1980). IR theorists, so drawn to historical "turning points" and cataclysmic events like war, may uncover similar instances of discontinuous normative change.

In addition, scholars should contemplate the impact of globalization on international normative change. Branching evolution occurs only if selection operates on distinct populations: otherwise, "swamping" will prevent divergence. In past centuries, time and distance permitted the coexistence of relatively autonomous states (and groups of states) possessing unique norms that were transmitted by traditional mechanisms and shaped by local selection pressures.

The end of geographical and social isolation bodes ill for human cultural, political, and economic diversity. Sociology's institutionalists document the spread of "a global, all-encompassing world culture." The spread of the Western capitalist state has "bureaucratized, marketized, and individuated the world," eradicating distinct social spaces and ways of life.[24] By fostering the internationalization not only of the state but also of civil society itself, global integration may herald movement from a "pluralist" international society based on the nation-state to a "solidarist" world society based on the individual (Bull 1977). Normative evolution would continue within such a world community, but it would be restricted to *anagenesis*—sequential transformation within a single lineage—rather than *cladogenesis*—the branching of lineages from common stock.[25]

NOTES

I would like to thank Rosemary Foot, Shepard Forman, Cesare Romano, Andrew Walter, Emanuel Adler, and Alexander Wendt for comments on earlier versions of this chapter. I am profoundly grateful to William H. Durham for his inspiration and for his supervision of my unpublished 1987 thesis "Towards a Systematic Evolutionary View of Human Culture." This chapter draws heavily on the selective-retention model developed in that work.

1. Globally, this society remains "unevenly distributed." Solidarity is strongest among core states, united by organic bonds of "sentiment, experience, and identity," such "we-feeling" is lacking in the periphery, where society must be consciously constructed for functional reasons (Buzan 1993: 349–50).

2. Sophisticated versions of rational choice theory can accommodate this insight by accepting that human beings maximize value-laden preferences (Wendt 1992).

3. On these norms (respectively) see Keohane 1986; Florini 1996; James 1986; Cox 1987; Ruggie 1982; Mayal 1990; Jackson 1993; Klotz 1995; Vincent 1974; Nye 1987; Walzer 1977; Der Derian 1987; Ray 1989; Weber 1993; Risse 1998; Finnemore and Sikkink 1998; Finnemore 1996a; Lumsdaine 1993; Price and Tannewald 1996; and Mueller 1989.

4. Goldstein and Keohan (1993) divide ideas into "world views" and " causal" and "principled" beliefs, but these three categories may overlap into a single idea like "embedded liberalism." Hasenclever, Mayer, and Rittberger (1997: 136–210) introduce the term "cognitivist" to refer to those approaches to international relations theory that emphasize ideas and knowledge, as opposed to interest (neoliberalism) or power (neorealism). This chapter treats cognitivism as synonymous with "constructivism."

5. For an alternative view placing constructivism at the intersection of the two axes, see Adler (1997).

6. The major exception is the innovative work of Emanuel Adler (1991), who uses the framework of "evolutionary epistemology" to explain cognitive change and "progress" in international relations. On evolutionary epistemology, see E. Haas (1982). See also Nadelman (1990) and Florini (1996).

7. On Malthus' influence, see Darwin (1859/1964: 63). As Marx wrote Engels in June 1862, "It is remarkable how Darwin recognizes among beast and plants his English society with its division of labor, competition, opening up of new markets, 'inventions' and the Malthusian 'struggle for existence' " (Smith 1987: 239).

8. Philosophers of science perceive similar patterns in the selective retention and elimination of scientific hypotheses, paradigms, and practices (Toulmin 1981).

9. The unit of cultural inheritance is *ideational* rather than behavioral or material because social practices and cultural artifacts are both "phenotypic" translations of a conceptual code (Stuart-Fox 1986: 73).

10. Biologists thus ask *how* a given trait evolved; social scientists, *why* (Flannery 1986: 4).

11. Memes flow vertically (between parent and offspring), horizontally (within each generation), and obliquely (between unrelated individuals of different generations). Transmission ratios may include many-to-one; one-to-few; or one-to-many (Cavalli-Sforza and Feldman 1981; Cavalli-Sforza 1986).

12. An alternative definition of "cultural fitness" would measure an *individual's* ability to reproduce cultural copies of him/herself (to become a "cultural parent").

13. For Durham (1976: 91), "Culture is generally adaptive in the biological sense" because human beings selectively retain those *cultural* beliefs and values that increase fitness.

14. *Institutions* are "related complexes of rules and norms" that "prescribe behavioral roles, constrain activity, and shape expectations" (Keohane 1996: 191–92).
15. On units as the ultimate source of systems change, see Ruggie (1986: 152).
16. Florini (1996: 371–74) considers the source of norm variation irrelevant, since all norms are subject to selection, but this perspective overlooks the potential of "guided" variation to bias the direction of norm evolution.
17. Finally, Florini (1996: 379–80) wonders "how, if at all, does 'learning' apply to changes of moral or social norms, where the questions of success or failure in the instrumental sense does not arise?" This argument neglects that many norms, like multilateralism, have both normative and instrumental dimensions.
18. Biologists likewise dispute whether the gene, organism, population, or species is the unit of selection.
19. Of course, the human penchant for claiming credit often makes it difficult to assign paternity. "Victory has a hundred fathers," President Kennedy noted after the Bay of Pigs debacle, whereas "defeat is an orphan."
20. Keohane (1984: 80–81) dismisses the "hard" Darwinian arguments of structural realists on the grounds that "states rarely disappear."
21. Biologists use the term *exaptation* for an adaptive trait not initially selected for its current function.
22. Evolutionary psychologists believe culture is adaptive because human decision-making criteria are derived from innate (naturally selected) psychological structures. "The evolutionary function of the human," write Cosmides and Tooby (1987: 282), "to process information in ways that lead to adaptive behavior." But differences between current and ancestral environments may produce maladaptation (Wright 1994).
23. Watson, cited in Buzan (1993: 335–52).
24. Traditional political and economic institutions have "become unimaginable" as "global cultural norms make similar behavior claims on dissimilar actors" (Finnemore 1996b: 329). States may try to block the transmission of dominant memes (by jamming broadcasts, banning satellite dishes, and regulating imports), but such "reproductive isolating mechanisms" face insuperable obstacles in the age of global communication.
25. One should not exaggerate current levels of normative homogenization, of course, nor ignore local resistance to globalization. Twentieth century Western (and American) values have been both alluring and despised, and cultural diversity continues to limit the camaraderie required of a moral community based on Kantian reciprocity and shared conceptions of legitimacy. Huntington (1996) presents an alarmist view.

REFERENCES

Adler, Emanuel. 1991. Cognitive Evolution: A Dynamic Approach for the Study of International Relations and their Progress. In Emanuel Adler and Beverly Crawford, eds. *Progress in postwar international relations.* New York: Columbia University Press.

———. (1992. The Emergence of Cooperation: National Epistemic Communities and the International Evolution of the Idea of Nuclear Arms Control. *International Organization* 46: 101–46.

———. 1997. Seizing the Middle Ground: Constructivism in World Politics. *European Journal of International Relations* 3: 319–63.

Adler, Emanuel, and Peter M. Haas. 1992. Conclusion: Epistemic Communities, World

Order, and the Creation of a Reflective Research Program. *International Organization* 46: 367–90.

Alland, Alexander, Jr. 1969. Darwinian Sociology without Social Darwinism? *Social Research* 36: 549–61.

Armstrong, David. 1994. The Socialisation of States. Paper presented at the annual meetings of the International Studies Association.

Aron, Raymond. 1966. *Peace and war: A theory of international relations.* London: Weidenfeld and Nicolson.

Aronson, Elliot. 1984. *The social animal.* New York: W. H. Freeman.

Ashley, Richard K. 1990. Imposing International Purpose: Notes on a Problematic of Governance. In Ernst-Otto Czempiel and James N. Rosenau, eds. *Global changes and theoretical challenges.* Lexington, Mass.: Lexington Books.

Axelrod, Robert. 1984. *The evolution of cooperation.* New York: Basic Books.

Axelrod, Robert, and Robert O. Keohane. 1985. Achieving Cooperation under Anarchy: Strategies and Institutions. *World Politics* 38: 226–54.

Ayala, Francisco. 1982. *Population and evolutionary genetics.* London: Benjamin/Cummings.

Beck, Robert J. 1996. International Law and International Relations: The Prospects for Interdisciplinary Collaboration. In Robert J. Beck, Anthony Clark Arend, and Robert D. Vander Lugt, eds. *International rules: Approaches from international law and international relations.* New York: Oxford University Press.

Biersteker, Thomas J. 1992. The 'Triumph' of Neoclassical Economics in the Developing World: Policy Convergence and Bases of Governance in the International Economic Order. In James N. Rosenau and Ernst-Otto Czempiel, eds. *Governance without government: Order and change in world politics.* Cambridge, U.K.: Cambridge University Press.

Blute, Marion. 1979. Sociocultural Evolutionism: An Untried Theory. *Behavioral Science* 24: 46–59.

Boehm, Christopher. 1982. A Fresh Outlook on Cultural Selection. *American Anthropologist* 84: 105–25.

Boyd, Robert, and Peter J. Richerson. 1985. *Culture and the evolutionary process.* Chicago: University of Chicago Press.

Bull, Hedley. 1977. *The anarchical society: A study of order in world politics.* London: MacMillan.

Bull, Hedley, and Adam Watson. 1984. *The expansion of international society.* Oxford: Clarendon Press.

Buzan, Barry. 1993. From International System to International Society: Structural Realism and Regime Theory Meet the English School. *International Organization* 47: 327–52.

Campbell, Donald T. 1965. Variation and Selective Retention in Socio-Cultural Evolution. In G. Blanksten and R. Mack, eds. *Social change in developing areas.* Cambridge, Mass.: Schenkiman.

Cavalli-Sforza, L. L. and M. W. Feldman. 1981. *Cultural transmission and evolution: A quantitative approach.* Princeton, N.J.: Princeton University Press.

Cavalli-Sforza, Luigi L. 1986. Cultural evolution. *American Zoologist* 26: 845–55.

Checkel, Jeffrey. 1998. The Constructivist Turn in International Relations Theory. *World Politics* 50: 324–48.

Clark, Ian. 1989. *The hierarchy of states: Reform and resistance in the international order.* Cambridge, U.K.: Cambridge University Press.

Cooper, Andrew Fenton, Richard A. Higgott, and Kim Richard Nossal. 1991. Bound to

Follow? Leadership and Followership in the Gulf Conflict. *Political Science Quarterly* 106: 391–410.

Cosmides, Leda, and John Tooby. 1987. From Evolution to Behavior: Evolutionary Psychology as the Missing Link. In John Dupre, ed. *The latest on the best: Essays on evolution and optimality.* Cambridge, Mass.: MIT Press.

Cowhey, Peter F. 1993. Elect Locally—Order Globally: Domestic Politics and Multilateral Cooperation. In John Gerard Ruggie, ed., *Multilateralism matters: The theory and praxis of an institutional form.* New York: Columbia University Press.

Cox, Robert W. 1987. *Power, production and world order.* New York: Columbia University Press.

———. 1992. Multilateralism and World Order. *Review of International Studies* 18: 161–80.

Darwin, Charles. 1964 [1859]. *On the origin of species.* Cambridge, Mass.: Harvard University Press.

Dawkins, Richard. 1976. *The Selfish gene.* Oxford: Oxford University Press.

———. 1982. *The Extended phenotype.* Oxford: Oxford University Press.

Der Derian, James. 1987. *On diplomacy.* Oxford: Basil Blackwell.

Deutsch, Karl W. 1957. *Political community and the North Atlantic area: International organization in the light of historical experience.* Princeton, N.J.: Princeton University Press.

Diener, Paul. 1980. Quantum Adjustment, Macroevolution, and the Social Field: Some Comments on Evolution and Culture. *Current Anthropology* 21: 423–44.

Dunnell, Robert C. 1980. Evolutionary Theory and Archeology. *Advances in Archeological Method and Theory* 3: 36–99.

Durham, William H. 1976. The Adaptive Significance of Cultural Behavior. *Human Ecology* 4(2): 89–117.

———. 1991. *Coevolution: Genes, culture, and human diversity.* Stanford, Calif.: Stanford University Press.

Eyre, Dana P., and Mark C. Suchman. 1996. Status, Norms, and the Proliferation of Conventional Weapons: An Institutional Theory Approach. In Peter J. Katzenstein, ed. *The Culture of national security: Norms and identity in international relations.* New York: Columbia University Press.

Farkas, Andrew. 1996. Evolutionary Models in Foreign Policy Analysis. *International Studies Quarterly* 40: 343–61.

Finnemore, Martha. 1996a. Constructing Norms of Humanitarian Intervention. In Peter J. Katzenstein, ed. *The Culture of national security: Norms and identity in international relations.* New York: Columbia University Press.

———. 1996b. Norms, Culture, and World Politics: Insights from Sociology's Institutionalism. *International Organization* 50: 325–47.

Finnemore, Martha, and Kathryn Sikkink. 1998. International Norm Dynamics and Political Change. Paper presented at Princeton University workshop on Ideas and Culture in Political Analysis.

Flannery, Kent. 1986. The Research Problem. In Kent V. Flannery, ed., *Guilla Naquitz.* New York: Academic Press.

Florini, Ann. 1996. The Evolution of International Norms. *International Studies Quarterly* 40: 363–89.

Franck, Thomas M. 1990. *The Power of legitimacy among nations.* New York: Oxford University Press.

Gaddis, John Lewis. 1987. Learning to Live with Transparency: The Emergence of a Reconnaissance Satellite Regime. In John Lewis Gaddis, ed. *The Long peace: Inquiries into the history of the cold war.* New York: Oxford University Press.

Gaddis, John Lewis. 1992/1993. International Relations Theory and the End of the Cold War. *International Security* 17: 5–58.

Gaventa, John P. . 1980. *Power and powerlessness: Quiescence and rebellion in an Appalachian Valley.* Oxford: Clarendon Press.

Geertz, Clifford. 1966. The Impact of the Concept of Culture on the Concept of Man. In J. Platt, ed. *New views of the nature of man.* Chicago: University of Chicago Press.

———. 1973. *The Interpretation of cultures: Selected essays.* New York: Basic Books.

Gilpin, Robert. 1981. *War and change in world politics.* New York: Cambridge University Press.

Goldgeir, James M., and Michael McFaul. 1992. A Tale of Two Worlds: Core and Periphery in the Post-Cold War Era. *International Organization* 46: 467–91.

Goldstein, Judith, and Robert O. Keohane. 1993. *Ideas and foreign policy: Beliefs, institutions, and political change.* Ithaca, N.Y.: Cornell University Press.

Gong, Gerrit. 1984. *The standard of civilization in international society.* Oxford: Clarendon Press.

Gould, Stephen Jay. 1996. *Full House: The Spread of excellence from Plato to Darwin.* New York: Harmony Books.

———, and Niles Eldredge. 1977. Punctuated Equilibria: The Tempo and Mode of Evolution Reconsidered. *Paleobiology* 3: 115–51.

———, and Richard Lewontin. 1978. The Spandrels of San Marco and the Panglosssian Paradigm: A Critique of the Adaptationist Programme. *Proceedings of the Royal Academy of London* 205: 581–98.

Grieco, Joseph M. 1988. Anarchy and the Limits of Cooperation: A Realist Critique of the Newest Liberal Institutionalism. *International Organization* 42: 485–507.

Guzzini, Stefano. 1993. Structural Power: The Limits of Neorealist Power Analysis. *International Organization* 47: 443–78.

Haas, Ernst. 1982. Words Can Hurt You; or Who Said What to Whom About Regimes. *International Organization* 36: 207–43

———. 1958. *The uniting of Europe.* Stanford, Calif.: Stanford University Press.

Haas, Peter M. 1992. Introduction: Epistemic Communities and International Policy Coordination. *International Organization* 46: 1–35.

Haggard, Stephan, and Beth A. Simmons. 1987. Theories of International Regimes. *International Organization* 41: 491–517.

Hall, John A. 1993. Ideas and the Social Sciences, in Judith Goldstein and Robert O. Keohane, eds. *Ideas and foreign policy: Beliefs, institutions, and political change.* Ithaca, N.Y.: Cornell University Press.

Hall, Peter A. 1989. *The political power of economic ideas: Keynesianism across nations.* Princeton, N.J.: Princeton University Press.

Hasenclever, Andreas, Peter Mayer, and Volker Rittberger. 1997. *Theories of international regimes.* Cambridge, U.K.: Cambridge University Press.

Hill, Jack. 1978. The Origin of Sociocultural Evolution. *Journal of Social and Biological Structures* 1: 377–86.

Hollis, Martin, and Steve Smith. 1990. *Explaining and understanding international relations.* Oxford: Clarendon Press.

Huntington, Samuel. 1996. *The Clash of civilizations and the remaking of world order.* New York: Simon and Schuster.

Hurrell, Andrew. 1996. International Rules and the Study of Regimes: A Reflective Approach. In Robert J. Beck, Anthony Clark Arend, and Robert D. Vander Lugt, eds. *International rules: Approaches from international law and international relations.* New York: Oxford University Press.

Ikenberry, G. John. 1993. Creating Yesterday's New World Order: Keynesian New Thinking and the Anglo-American Postwar Settlement. In Judith Goldstein and Robert O. Keohane, eds. *Ideas and foreign policy: Beliefs, institutions, and political change*: 57–86. Ithaca, N.Y.: Cornell University Press.

Ikenberry, G. John, and Charles A. Kupchan. 1990a. The Legitimation of Hegemonic Power. In David P. Rapkin, ed. *World leadership and hegemony*. Boulder, Col.: Lynne Rienner.

———. 1990b. Socialization and Hegemonic Power. *International Organization* 44: 283–315.

Jackson, Robert H. 1993. The Weight of Ideas in Decolonization: Normative Change in International Relations. In Judith Goldstein and Robert O. Keohane, eds. *Ideas and foreign policy: Beliefs, institutions, and political change*. Ithaca, N.Y.: Cornell University Press.

James, Alan. 1986. *Sovereign statehood: The basis of international society*. London: Allen and Unwin.

Kahler, Miles. 1990. Orthodoxy and its Alternatives: Explaining Approaches to Stabilization and Adjustment. In Joan M. Nelson, ed. *Economic crisis and policy choice: The politics of adjustment in the third world*. Princeton, N.J.: Princeton University Press.

Katzenstein, Peter J. 1996. Introduction: Alternative Perspectives on National Security. In Peter J. Katzenstein, ed. *The Culture of national security: Norms and identity in international relations*. New York: Columbia University Press.

Kaysen, Carl. 1994. Is War Obsolete? A Review Essay. In Sean M. Lynn-Jones and Steven E. Miller, eds. *The Cold War and After: Prospects for Peace*. Cambridge, Mass.: MIT Press.

Keohane, Robert O. 1984. *After hegemony: Cooperation and discord in the world political economy*. Princeton, N.J.: Princeton University Press.

———. 1986. Reciprocity in International Relations. *International Organization* 40: 1–27.

———. 1996. International Institutions: Two Approaches. In Robert J. Beck, Anthony Clark Arend, and Robert D. Vander Lugt, eds. *International rules: Approaches from international law and international relations*. New York: Oxford University Press.

Khong, Yuen Foong. 1992. *Analogies at war: Korea, Munich, Dien Bien Phu, and the Vietnam decisions of 1965*. Princeton, N.J.: Princeton University Press.

Klotz, Audie. 1995. Norms Reconstituting Interests: Global Racial Equality and U.S. Sanctions against South Africa. *International Organization* 49: 451–78.

Koch, H. W. 1984. Social Darwinism as a Factor in the 'New Imperialism.' In H. W. Koch, ed. *The origins of the first world war: Great power rivalry and German war aims*. London: Macmillan.

Paul Kowert and Jeffrey Legro. 1996. Norms, Identity, and their Limits: A Theoretical Reprise. In Peter J. Katzenstein, ed. *The culture of national security: Norms and identity in international relations*. New York: Columbia University Press.

Kratochwil, Friedrich. 1989. *Rules, norms, and decisions: On the conditions of practical reasoning in international relations and domestic affairs*. Cambridge, U.K.: Cambridge University Press.

Kratochwil, Friedrich, and John Gerard Ruggie. 1986. International Organization: A State of the Art on an Art of the State. *International Organization* 40: 753–75.

Lamarck, Jean-Baptiste. 1984. *Zoological philosophy*. Chicago: University of Chicago Press.

Lapid, Yosef, and Friedrich Kratochwil. 1995. *The Return of culture and identity in IR theory*. Boulder, Col.: Lynne Rienner.

Lears, T. J. Jackson. 1985. The Concept of Cultural Hegemony: Problems and Possibilities. *American Historical Review* 90: 567–93.

Levy, Jack S. 1994. Learning and Foreign Policy: Sweeping a Conceptual Minefield. *International Organization* 48: 279–312.

Lukes, Steven. 1974. *Power: A radical view.* London: MacMillan.

Lumsdaine, David H. 1993. *Moral vision in international politics.* Princeton, N.J.: Princeton University Press.

Maier, Charles S. 1989a. Alliance and Autonomy: European Identity and U.S. Foreign Policy Objectives in the Truman Years. In Michael J. Lacey, ed. *The Truman presidency.* Cambridge, U.K.: Cambridge University Press.

———. 1989b. Analog of Empire: Constitutive Moments of United States Ascendancy after World War II. Unpublished Wilson Center paper.

Mayall, James. 1990. *Nationalism and international society.* Cambridge, U.K.: Cambridge University Press.

Milner, Helen. 1993. The Assumption of Anarchy in International Relations Theory: A Critique. In David A. Baldwin, ed. *Neorealism and neoliberalism: The Contemporary debate.* New York: Columbia University Press.

Modelski, George. 1990. Is World Politics Evolutionary Learning? *International Organization* 44: 1–24.

———. 1996. Evolutionary Paradigm for Global Politics. *International Studies Quarterly* 40: 321–42.

Mueller, John. 1989. *Retreat from doomsday: The obsolescence of major war.* New York: Basic Books.

———. 1994. The Essential Irrelevance of Nuclear Weapons: Stability in the Postwar World. In Sean M. Lynn-Jones and Steven E. Miller, eds. *The Cold War and after: Prospects for peace.* Cambridge, Mass.: MIT Press.

Muravchik, Joshua. 1991. *Exporting democracy: Fulfilling America's destiny.* Washington, D.C.: AEI Press.

Nadelman, Ethan A. . 1990. Global Prohibition Regimes: The Evolution of Norms in International Society. *International Organization* 44: 479–526.

Nau, Henry. 1990. *The Myth of America's decline: Leading the world economy into the 1990s.* Oxford: Oxford University Press.

North, Douglass C. . 1990. *Institutions, institutional change and economic performance.* New York: Cambridge University Press.

Nye, Joseph S., Jr. 1987. Nuclear Learning and the U.S.-Soviet Security Regimes. *International Security* 41: 371–402.

———. 1990. *Bound to lead: The Changing nature of American power.* New York: Basic Books.

Packenham, Robert. 1973. *Liberal America and the third world: Political development ideas in foreign aid and social science.* Princeton, N.J.: Princeton University Press.

Popper, Karl. 1982. The Place of Mind in Nature. In Richard O. Elvee, ed. *Mind in Nature.* New York: Harper and Row.

Price, Richard. 1998. Reversing the Gun Sights: Transnational Civil Society Targets Land Mines. *International Organization* 52: 613–44.

———, and Nina Tanenwald. 1996. Norms and Deterrence: The Nuclear and Chemical Weapons Taboos. In Peter J. Katzenstein, ed. *The Culture of national security: Norms and identity in international relations.* New York: Columbia University Press.

Ray, James Lee. 1989. The Abolition of Slavery and the End of War. *International Organization* 43: 405–39.

Rindos, David. 1985. Darwinian selection, symbolic variation, and the evolution of culture. *Current Anthropology* 26: 65–88.

Risse, Thomas. 1998. Human Rights, European Identity and the Diffusion of Principled Ideas. Paper presented at Princeton University workshop on Ideas and Culture in Political Analysis.

Risse-Kappen. 1996. Collective Identity in a Democratic Community: The Case of NATO. In Peter J. Katzenstein, ed. *The Culture of national security: Norms and identity in international relations*. New York: Columbia University Press.

Rosenau, James N. 1992. Governance, Order, and Change in World Politics. In James N. Rosenau and Ernst-Otto Czempiel, eds. *Governance without government: Order and change in world politics*. Cambridge, U.K.: Cambridge University Press.

Ruggie, John Gerard. 1982. International Regimes, Transactions, and Change: Embedded Liberalism in the Post-War Economic Order. *International Organization* 36: 195–231.

———. 1986. Continuity and Transformation in the World Polity: Toward a Neorealist Synthesis. In Robert O. Keohane, ed. *Neorealism and its critics*. New York: Columbia University Press.

———. 1993. Multilateralism: The Anatomy of an Institution. In John Gerard Ruggie, ed. *Multilateralism matters: The theory and praxis of an institutional form*. New York: Columbia University Press.

———. 1998. *Constructing the world polity: Essays on international institutionalization*. New York and London: Routledge.

Russett, Bruce. 1985. The Mysterious Case of Vanishing Hegemony; Or, is Mark Twain Rally Dead? *International Organization* 39: 207–31.

Ruyle, Eugene E. 1973. Genetic and Cultural Pools: Some Suggestions for a Unified Theory of Biocultural Evolution. *Human Ecology* 1: 201–215.

Ruyle, Eugene E., F. T. Cloak, Jr., L. B. Slobodkin, and William H. Durham. 1977. The Adaptive Significance of Cultural Behavior: Comments and Reply. *Human Ecology* 5: 49–68.

Skinner, B. F. 1981. Selection by Consequences. *Science* 213: 501–04.

Smith, Eric Alden. 1987. Optimization Theory in Anthropology: Applications and Critiques. In John Dupre, ed. *The Latest on the best: Essays on evolution and optimality*. Cambridge, Mass.: MIT Press.

Stuart-Fox, M. 1986. The Unit of Replication in Sociocultural Evolution. *Journal of Social and Biological Structures* 9: 67–89.

Strange, Susan. 1988. *States and markets*. London: Pinter.

Strang, David, and John W. Meyer. 1993. Institutional Conditions for Diffusion. *Theory and Society* 22: 487–511.

Thomson, Janice. 1992. Explaining the Regulation of Transnational Practices: A State-Building Approach. In by James N. Rosenau and Ernst-Otto Czempiel, eds. *Governance without government: Order and change in world politics*. Cambridge, U.K.: Cambridge University Press.

Toulmin, Stephen. 1981. Evolution, Adaptation, and Human Understanding. In Marilynn B. Brewer and Barry E. Collins, eds. *Scientific inquiry and the social sciences*. San Francisco: Jossey-Bass.

Vayrynen, Raimo. 1987. Global Power Dynamics and Collective Violence. In Raimo Vayrynen, ed. *The Quest For Peace*. London: Sage.

Vincent, R. J. 1974. *Non-Intervention and international order*. Princeton, N.J.: Princeton University Press.

Walker, R. B. J. 1987. Realism, Change, and International Political Theory. *International Studies Quarterly* 31: 65–86.

Waltz, Kenneth N. 1979. *Theory of international politics*. New York: Random House.

Walzer, Michael. 1977. *Just and unjust wars*. New York: Basic Books.

Weber, Max. 1947. *The Theory of social and economic organization.* London: MacMillan.

Weber, Steve. 1993. Shaping the Postwar Balance of Power: Multilateralism in NATO. In by John Gerard Ruggie, ed. *Multilateralism matters: The Theory and praxis of an institutional form.* Columbia: Columbia University Press.

Wendt, Alexander. 1992. Anarchy Is What States Make of It: The Social Construction of Power Politics. *International Organization* 46: 391–425.

Wendt, Alexander, and Raymond Duvall. 1990. Institutions and International Order, in Ernst-Otto Czempiel and James N. Rosenau, eds. *Global changes and theoretical challenges.* Lexington, Mass.: Lexington Press.

Wright, Robert. 1994. *The Moral animal: Evolutionary psychology and everyday life.* New York: Pantheon.

part III

Applications to Conflict and Cooperation

chapter 7

Evolution in Domestic Politics and the Development of Rivalry
The Bolivia-Paraguay Case

Paul R. Hensel

Evolutionary approaches have long been important in the study of biological and anthropological phenomena, but evolution and related concepts have generally been ignored in the social sciences. Possible explanations for this lack of attention include the controversial status of evolution in popular society, the rejection of biological or genetic factors as sources of human behavior, and the belief that the biological sciences are not an appropriate source of ideas for social scientific research. Social scientists are finally beginning to proclaim the merits of evolutionary approaches in studying social phenomena, though, as suggested by a 1996 special issue of *International Studies Quarterly*. This chapter uses evolutionary concepts to develop a model of militarized interstate rivalry, focusing on evolution with the domestic political systems of two adversary nation-states.

Militarized interstate rivalry refers to a longstanding, competitive relationship between two adversaries who engage in numerous militarized confrontations (Goertz and Diehl 1993, Diehl and Goertz 2000; Hensel 1996, 1999). Although there have been relatively few rivalries in the modern era, enduring rival adversaries account for one-fourth of all interstate wars and territorial changes since 1816, roughly 40 percent of all militarized interstate disputes and violent territorial changes, and approximately half of all international crises (Goertz and Diehl 1992, Diehl and Goertz 2000; Hensel 1998a). Relations between rivals have been argued to be more conflictual than relations between other types of states, largely because of the distrust and hostility that are said to characterize rivalry. Despite the apparent importance of the rivalry concept, though, little systematic research has addressed the origins of rivalries, with most research focusing on the dynamics of established rivalries or on the termination of rivalry (including the Thompson and Rasler contributions to this volume). Perhaps the most prominent explanation of interstate rivalry suggests that most rivalries can be explained by preexisting structural or environmental factors or by "shocks" in the external environment (for example, Goertz and Diehl 1995).

Despite the emphasis on preexisting factors in the current rivalry literature, the central elements of a traditional biological approach to evolution offer important insights into the development of conflictual relationships between nation-states. In particular, the notions of fitness, adaptation, and selection offer useful insights into the identity of state leaders and the foreign policies that they implement. After describing the basic elements of an evolutionary approach, this chapter uses these elements to develop a model to account for the evolution of conflictual relationships between nation-states. It then examines the utility of this model with a brief case study of the rivalry between Bolivia and Paraguay, and with an examination of recent quantitative evidence on the origins and dynamics of rivalry. This chapter concludes by discussing the implications of the evolutionary approach for future research in international relations.

EVOLUTIONARY APPROACHES

The concept of evolution has been used most widely in the natural sciences. Evolutionary approaches are commonly used to study such phenomena as adaptive change within established species (sometimes termed vertical evolution), the increasing diversity of populations and development of new species (horizontal evolution), and the development of societal behaviors or means of organization (social or cultural evolution). The next section of this chapter identifies the central themes of such evolutionary approaches from the natural sciences, with the goal of developing an evolutionary approach that is relevant to the social sciences in general and the study of interstate rivalry more specifically.[1]

One important characteristic of evolutionary approaches is the rejection of determinism as an explanation for observed phenomena, in favor of evolutionary processes reflecting unfolding, cumulative processes of change over time. Systems or populations in evolutionary theory are seen as changing over time in response to environmental challenges, reaching their particular state or condition at any given point in time through a series of changes. The study of evolution, then, involves replacing such static questions as "what is it" or "how does it work?" (whether this refers to a species' bodily structure, a domestic political system, or a competitive international relationship) with more dynamic, process-oriented questions like "how did it come to work that way and not some other way?"

A second characteristic of most evolutionary approaches—despite the emphasis on cumulative processes of change—is the absence of teleological ends, or the rejection of progress- or perfection-directed change. Thus, while a given evolutionary adaptation may improve an organism's fitness and improve its ability to survive in its current environment, there is no guarantee that the adaptation represents ultimate "progress," movement toward "perfection," or fulfillment of any grand cosmic design. Indeed, the same adaptation that improves fitness in one set of environmental conditions may actually reduce fitness in a subsequent set of conditions.

Beyond these two central assumptions, explanations of evolutionary change typically revolve around the notions of the organism, the environment, variation, fitness, adaptation, and natural selection. The organism in evolutionary stories—the entity facing an evolutionary challenge—is generally a species, a specific individual, or a social grouping. The "environment" refers to the setting in which this organism lives and works, and typically includes such elements as food, shelter, climate, and predators. Changes in this environment produce the need for evolution, by making it difficult for the organism to survive in its current form. Typical evolutionary challenges from the environment include the introduction of a new predator, a shortage in the supply of food or shelter, or changes in the climate.

When such environmental challenges arise, survival becomes a contest between different individuals or species. "Variation" refers to the traits or behaviors that distinguish between individuals or species; it is this variation that allows certain individuals or species to deal with evolutionary challenges better than others. "Fitness" generally refers to the ability to survive and reproduce in a particular environment or the probabilistic expected time to extinction for an organism or species given a particular time and environment (Beatty 1992); the relative fitness of organisms is influenced by their variation in relevant traits and behaviors.

A serious environmental challenge to an organism or species may culminate in several different outcomes. The first, evolutionary "adaptation," refers to alterations in the traits or capacities of the organism that enable it to solve (or to improve on previous solutions for) problems posed by the environment, in such a way as to increase its relative fitness or likelihood of survival (Burian 1992; West-Eberhard 1992). Examples might include the development of a new physical attribute or a behavior modification, which would allow the organism to avoid or defend against predators or to obtain scarce food or shelter.

An organism that fails to adapt to environmental challenges, though, may fall victim to "natural selection." Originally articulated by Darwin in *The Origin of Species,* the selection process begins with competing organisms that differ from each other in one or more ways (that is, there must be some type of variation in traits). Natural selection refers to a process by which organisms with better fitness are more likely to survive and reproduce successfully than other organisms, generally leading to the preservation of organisms with favorable variations and the rejection of organisms with less favorable variations—essentially, a process of the "survival of the fittest" (Darwin 1859/1968: 130–31; Endler 1992; Hodge 1992). An organism that does not adapt to deal with the changes in the environment, then, may be "selected out" in favor of competitors that are better able to deal with the environment.

Although each of these evolutionary concepts was originally developed in the natural sciences, many of them also offer useful insights for the social sciences. The next section of this chapter develops an evolutionary approach to interstate rivalry, focusing on domestic politics in two potential rival nation-states. Despite important differences in the subject matter between the evolution of species and the evolution of rivalry, evolutionary concepts such as fitness, adaptation, and selection can help us to understand the processes and interactions that lead to interstate rivalry and the consequences of rivalry for world politics.

APPLYING EVOLUTION TO INTERSTATE RIVALRY

Perhaps the most prominent theoretical model of interstate rivalry is Goertz and Diehl's "basic rivalry level" or "punctuated equilibrium" model, which does not allow for any systematic evolutionary change in potential or actual rivalry relationships. As described by Goertz and Diehl (1995, Diehl and Goertz 2000; Diehl and Hensel 1998), conflictual relationships between states are assumed to fluctuate in intensity or severity around some basic rivalry level (BRL) that varies from dyad to dyad. Certain rivalries have more conflict-prone or more escalatory BRLs than others, with the differences largely predetermined by structural or exogenous factors before each rivalry begins. Each rivalry is assumed to "lock in" around its BRL quickly, with adversaries that will eventually become enduring rivals recognizing each other as such early in their relationship. These adversaries then treat each other as enduring rivals from that lock-in point until the end of their rivalry, with little variation in the intensity of their relationship while the rivalry is ongoing.[2] Interactions between the adversaries during their ongoing rivalry are not assumed to affect the relationship in any meaningful or systematic way.

Unfortunately, this model concentrates much more on conflict behavior within rivalry than on the origins of rivalry itself. Goertz and Diehl have not specified the determinants of rivalry BRLs (and thus the factors that lead to rivalry), leaving them unable to account for the sources of BRL variation between rivalries or the differences between dyads that become rivalries and those that do not. In his most detailed statement on the subject (Diehl and Hensel 1998), Diehl speculates that BRL variation may be due to factors such as characteristics of the interstate system (for example, polarity), dyad (for example, joint democracy, geographic proximity, or relative capabilities), or nation-states (for example, wealth)—most of which appear to be influences on conflict behavior arising for other reasons, rather than causes of the rivalry itself.[3] Dissatisfaction with Goertz and Diehl's BRL model led Hensel (1996, 1999) to propose an evolutionary approach to interstate rivalry, which attempts to account for both the origins of rivalry and variation in conflict behavior within ongoing rivalries. The next portion of this chapter examines the basis for a general evolutionary approach to world politics, before applying this approach to the explanation of recurrent interstate conflict and rivalry.

EVOLUTIONARY CONCEPTS AND WORLD POLITICS

An evolutionary approach in the social sciences must begin by recognizing that there will be undeniable differences from applications of evolutionary theory in the natural sciences. Rather than genes or species, an evolutionary approach in the social sciences must deal with human beings or political collectivities. Rather than a time frame spanning generations or millennia, evolution in the social sciences generally involves a time frame of years or decades. Also, whereas unsuccessful species may become extinct because of their inability to adapt, the consequences in the social sciences may range from the removal of a leader from office to the disintegration of a political system. With these caveats, though, many evolutionary concepts from the natural sciences are relevant to interstate conflict and rivalry, offering important insights into the origins and development of conflictual relationships between nation-states.

As noted earlier, evolutionary approaches generally reject deterministic explanations in favor of more dynamic models. In contrast to the near-determinism of the BRL model, then, an evolutionary model of rivalry begins with the premise that rivalry—rather than being predetermined by structural conditions—is a dynamic phenomenon that comes into being over time as the cumulative result of interactions between two states. The eventual result of this evolutionary process—whether two adversary states become enduring rivals or manage to settle their differences short of protracted militarized competition—can not be known (by the participants or by outside observers) with any certainty at the start of the process or at any point during the process. This is not to say that structural conditions are irrelevant and do not affect relations between adversaries. Rather, this approach argues that the interactive, changing relationship between two adversaries is also very important, above and beyond the impact of any relevant structural conditions.[4]

It was also noted that evolutionary models generally reject teleological ends as the outcomes of evolutionary processes. Similarly, an evolutionary approach to interstate rivalry makes no assumption of movement toward perfection or toward some ultimate progressive goal of peace, prosperity, or justice. Domestic political systems or international relationships may evolve in a way that leads to more enlightened domestic and foreign policies, or they may evolve in a way that leads to protracted relationships characterized by death, destruction, and the transfer of resources from social purposes to the military.

One important difference between biological applications and the evolutionary approach to rivalry is the nature of the actors and their environments. Whereas biological applications of evolution tend to focus on individuals or species as the organisms facing evolutionary challenges, this chapter's evolutionary approach to rivalry focuses on the political leadership within each of two nation-states. Each state is assumed to have a single chief executive who is ultimately responsible for making decisions on foreign policy issues.[5] It is this chief executive who faces evolutionary pressures from the environment.

The environment includes both domestic and external influences on the chief executive. One domestic influence involves other governmental actors who are responsible for approving, ratifying, or implementing the chief executive's decisions, who must be convinced to support the leader's foreign policy decisions before they can be put into effect (see, for example, Putnam 1988; Hagan 1993). A leader who fails to consider this policy ratification constraint is unlikely to be able to achieve his or her goals, as decisions are likely to be overturned or ignored and never ratified or carried out. The other primary domestic influence involves the "selectorate," which is made up of those political actors with the authority to select the political leader—such as the electorate in democracies, or the military or official political party in authoritarian states (see, Bueno de Mesquita and Siverson 1995; Hagan 1993). The selectorate has the power to remove or replace the chief executive (through elections, a coup, or some other means) if his or her policies are seen as undesirable or ineffective.

The primary international influence in the environment involves the state's adversary, which can block or assist the leader's attempts to achieve his or her goals. Even if the leader is able to satisfy other domestic actors associated with policy ratification and leader selection, foreign policy success depends on the actions and characteristics of the potential rival state. A peaceful agreement requires that the adversary be willing to negotiate and be flexible enough to agree to a settlement that both sides can accept, and unilateral action be the adversary that may block both peaceful and conflictual attempts to achieve goals. This combination of domestic and external influences forms the evolutionary "environment" in which political leaders operate, and which affects their prospects for survival in office (and for achieving their desired policy goals). A leader who is able to deal with the pressures and constraints offered by the environment is likely to achieve many of his or her political goals, and is likely to remain in power.[6]

In biological settings, individuals' fitness is linked to variation in physical characteristics and/or behavioral patterns, which may increase or decrease an individual's prospects for surviving, reproducing, and thus passing their favorable variations to future generations. With regard to world politics, leaders and their political opponents will vary in preferred policy goals and/or preferred behavioral paths to policy formulation and implementation.[7] This variation may give certain individuals greater political "fitness" or ability to remain in office and pursue desired policies. To the extent that these policies are acceptable to the selectorate and to other domestic actors who are responsible for approving or implementing policies—and to the extent that these policies appear to be successful in achieving the leader's policy goals—the chief executive should be able to remain in power and continue pursuing similar policies.

It must be emphasized, though, that not all policy preferences are equally relevant at all times and in all places. As in the natural sciences, a leader's "fitness" can only be considered in the context of a specific environment, which has already been noted as including both domestic and international elements. In certain spatial-temporal contexts, such as peace-time periods with no perceived foreign threat, the relevant environment will be primarily domestic in nature, and the leader's preferred foreign policy goals or competence may not be very important contributors to his or her political fitness. In different contexts, such as during an ongoing war, the relevant environment may be primarily foreign in nature, and the leader's direction of the war effort may be much more important to his or her political fitness than any set of domestic policies. A leader who is seen as effective and "fit" in one type of environment may be seen in an entirely different light in another context; Winston Churchill and George Bush come to mind as examples of leaders who were seen as very effective in foreign war-making but were removed from office by citizens who began to focus on domestic policy.

In biological applications of evolutionary models, an organism facing environmental challenges must either adapt to deal with the challenges or risk being the victim of natural selection in favor of more "fit" competitors. Chief executives in world politics face a similar set of options as they confront challenges from the (domestic or international) environment. Adaptation for a chief executive involves changing his or her preferred policies or preferred path to achieving those policies, as when a formerly hawkish leader begins to pursue a peaceful settlement with a former enemy. The alternative to adapting one's own preferences to be more in line with the preferences of the selectorate and other domestic actors is the risk of natural selection, which in this case involves the leader's replacement with a more suitable (more "fit") individual through democratic elections, a coup d'etat, or some other means.

EVOLUTIONARY CONCEPTS AND MILITARIZED RIVALRY

The above discussion of evolutionary concepts in world politics is general enough to suggest a complete model of foreign policy making. The preferred foreign policies that help to determine a given leader's political fitness may involve military policies regarding a long-time rival state, economic policies regarding trade or integration with neighboring states, or any number of other types of policies involving other international actors. The focus of the present chapter, though, is an evolutionary model of militarized interstate rivalry. As a result, the evolutionary model being developed here emphasizes relations with a particular rival nation-state adversary, leaving for future research the task of extending this model to more peaceful or cooperative dimensions of world politics.

The evolutionary model begins by noting that relations between nation-states result from choices made by each state's political decision-makers. To understand rivalry, then, we should attempt to understand how two states' political systems can produce decisions leading to a longstanding competitive relationship between states that features frequent militarized confrontations. Given the general evolutionary assumption that outcomes are not predetermined by structural or other factors, but rather that outcomes are reached as the result of cumulative changes over time, this approach suggests that the decisions that lead states toward or away from rivalry are influenced by the changing (international and domestic) political environment.

Before two adversaries begin to engage in militarized conflict and approach enduring rivalry, it is likely that most domestic political actors are concerned with domestic economic and social issues, and that the international adversary does not pose a severe constraint on action for the chief executive. This is consistent with research on public opinion, which generally indicates that foreign policy is not a day-to-day concern of most citizens. At least in the United States, the public generally treats foreign policy issues as confusing or uninteresting, and public opinion is best described as "latent"—having the potential for expression, but only if activated by an international crisis, war, or other serious event (see Holsti 1996; Powlick and Katz 1998; Stimson 1991).

As a result, when there is little or no history of recent conflict with an adversary, the primary determinants of a leader's political fitness should involve his or her domestic policies. A leader facing a new adversary thus has little to worry about from the domestic political scene in reaction to foreign policy initiatives, unless the leader dramatically bungles foreign relations in such as way as to bring on an unintended war or to give away what is perceived as an important national interest. The leader's popularity and ability to remain in office, in short, should be affected primarily by domestic policies (which are beyond the scope of the current model).

Foreign policy is likely to become more important, though, when it creates the perception that individuals' personal safety or interests are at stake. Militarized interstate rivalry is typically described as involving decades of competition between the same actors, with each side perceiving that the other poses a serious security threat to important interests (see, for example, Goertz and Diehl 1992; Vasquez 1993; Hensel 1996, 1999). Rivalries often feature dozens of militarized confrontations, some of which may escalate to full-scale war, and even in peacetime each rival will generally pay close attention to the actions and military deployments of the other. This combination of a decades-long threat from a specific adversary, frequent confrontations (perhaps leading to the death or injury of friends or relatives), and constant military vigilance and preparations (perhaps leading to military stationing abroad) is likely to create the perception that one's own safety and interests are at stake in the rivalry, thereby making the management of the rivalry directly relevant to one's own well-being.

As two adversaries come to see each other as serious security threats, more domestic actors on each side are likely to see their chief executive's foreign policy behavior as an important indicator of his or her competence. Foreign policy issues, particularly those involving the rival, should then be more important sources of the leader's political fitness, with regard to both policy ratification and leader selection or deselection.[8] Unlike a non-rivalry context, in which the management of foreign relations has little impact on the leader's fitness, the domestic and international environment in a context of rivalry is much more threatening politically—potentially leading the leader to reevaluate his or her desired policies in light of recent events and recent trends in public attitudes (adaptation) or to risk removal from office in favor of a more desirable leader (selection).[9]

The next section of this chapter attempts to elaborate on this general statement of an evolutionary model of foreign policy. In particular, what is needed is a set of factors related to a developing conflictual relationship that might be expected to lead to the political activation of domestic political actors, along with specific expectations about how this activation might be expected to affect the relationship. Consistent with the earlier evolutionary assumptions that evolutionary processes are not unidirectional or teleological, it must be emphasized that not all of these factors will have effects in the same direction. Indeed, as will be seen, different factors may have different effects on foreign policy toward the rival, and even a single event can produce several competing effects in opposite directions. Three types of factors are examined: the nature of the contentious issues dividing the two states, the general context of recent relations between them, and specific details of past interactions between the states.

Contentious Issues

The first factor that must be considered is the nature of the issues at stake between two adversary states. As several scholars have argued (Holsti 1991; Vasquez 1993; Hensel 2000), conflict—military or diplomatic—occurs for a reason, and the specific issues or stakes behind a given conflict can be an important influence on the course and consequences of that conflict. From an evolutionary perspective, domestic political activation—and therefore domestic constraints on policy-makers—is likely to be greatest when highly salient issues are at stake.

The salience of an issue for any given actor depends on that actor's evaluation of the value of that issue, whether for him/herself or for the country as a whole. An example of a generally low-salience issue might be a question of foreign default on a debt owed to a bank or individual; although this may be important for the bank or individual whose money was not repaid, the average citizen is unlikely to see the issue as worthy of attention or as deserving any great sacrifice. A higher-salience issue might involve territory that the state has historically claimed or occupied, and which contains valuable resources and strategic military positions; Vasquez (1993) describes territory as perhaps the most salient type of issue. Many citizens would be affected by the loss of such territory to an enemy, in terms of both lost resource revenue and the enemy's newly threatening military positions, although the effects would be strongest for citizens whose careers depend on extracting or using those resources and for those who live near the territory.

Low-salience issues are likely to have little impact on domestic political activation, as most citizens, legislators, and other actors perceive that even a total defeat over the issue is unlikely to carry high costs for themselves or for the country. Because of their greater perceived importance to more actors, though, high-salience issues are likely to be followed by many different political actors. As a result, leaders are likely to face much greater domestic constraints when dealing with high-salience issues than when dealing with low-salience issues, and policy failures over high-salience issues are more likely to lead to the replacement of the leader. Unlike many of the other factors discussed herein, the political activation effect of high-salience issues may be felt almost from the beginning of contention over the issue, at least to the extent that the public recognizes that a high-salience issue is under contention. As two or more adversary states continue to contend over high-salience issues, more and more people are likely to become aware of the issue, thereby increasing the constraints on leaders attempting to manage the issue (and making it much more difficult for them to settle the issue when large portions of the selectorate or other political groups are agitating for success over the issue).

The General Context of Past Relations

A central tenet of the evolutionary approach to rivalry, with its emphasis on cumulative changes over time, is that the context of relations between states changes in response to earlier events between those states. Hensel (1996, 1998a, 1999) describes two distinct types of evolutionary factors that help to account for movement toward or away from rivalry, beyond the impact of contentious issues or control variables like relative military capabilities or political democracy. The first type of factor is the general context of past relations, with relations expected to become more conflictual as two adversaries accumulate a longer history of militarized conflict or more cooperative as they build up a longer history of friendship and cooperation. The second type involves specific details of past interactions, such as the outcomes and severity levels of specific militarized confrontations.

Before two states become involved in a string of recurrent militarized conflict, they are unlikely to recognize each other as primary security threats or as primary obstacles to the achievement of desired goals. Although journalists, political activists, or individual members of government may warn about the dangers posed by the adversary, it is unlikely to be seen as a serious rival in the military sense by most of the population or the government. For example, books appeared in the 1980s proclaiming "the coming war with Japan" and similar arguments are being made today about "the future U.S.-Chinese war" or the future rivalry between the West and the Islamic world, but most current observers view such proclamations as alarmist and not as prudent bases for policy making. As noted earlier, a variety of public opinion literature suggests that foreign affairs are of little day-to-day consequence to the average citizen, at least until his or her personal interests are perceived as being threatened. In the absence of a clear military rival, then, this chapter's evolutionary approach suggests that the primary determinants of a leader's popularity and prospects for remaining in power are domestic in nature (typically involving social or economic policy). A leader may thus pursue foreign policy goals with little risk of domestic backlash, at least as long as the leader is able to avoid a dramatic misadventure such as a costly or unsuccessful war (Bueno de Mesquita and Siverson 1995).

As two adversaries begin to confront each other militarily, however, foreign policy vis-à-vis the rival is likely to become more important as an influence on both the selectorate and the chief executive. Each confrontation between two adversaries is likely to lead to a general deterioration in relations due to increased feelings of hostility, distrust, or enmity, as well as any death or losses that may have resulted. Beyond these direct effects on the chief executive, a longer history of conflict is likely to lead to the political activation of a larger portion of the selectorate, for whom foreign affairs are becoming more menacing. Any confrontation that has led to fatalities or to the extended stationing of military forces in harm's way is likely to create the perception of a threat to personal interests for the soldiers and their friends and families, and any domestic social or economic hardships as a result of the budding rivalry are likely to have a similar (if less intense) effect on a wider scale. As a result, the leader's policies regarding the rival state are likely to be seen as an important indicator of his or her overall quality of leadership, and a leader with unpopular policies must either change the policies (that is, undergo evolutionary adaptation) or risk being removed from office by the selectorate (that is, risk being "selected out" in favor of a more "fit" political competitor).

It is important to note that past interactions may influence domestic political actors—and, as a consequence, the foreign policy-making process—in either a more conflictual or a more cooperative direction. A longer history of conflict and distrust should be expected to produce more suspicion and conflict, as the history of past conflict leads to self-fulfilling prophecies that the enemy can not be trusted and must be stopped by force if needed. Indeed, each successive confrontation that occurs should have such an effect, all else being equal; it is difficult to imagine a circumstance where confronting an adversary militarily improves relations with the adversary (although characteristics of the confrontation, such as its outcome, may produce this effect; see below). A longer history of cooperative interactions—such as arms-control agreements, confidence-building measures, or attempts to settle disputed issues peacefully through negotiations— should be expected to produce more cooperation in the future, perhaps helping bring a long-time rivalry to a close. This is consistent with the result of U.S. opinion polls taken during the Cold War that show the U.S. public seeing the Soviets as more trustworthy (and cooperation as more likely) in periods such as detente, when recent history seemed to show successful examples of U.S.-Soviet cooperation (Holsti 1996: 66 ff). Similarly, the perception of the Soviet Union as trustworthy tended to decline with each new Cold War incident or crisis, which Holsti (1996: 67) illustrates by juxtaposing a list of early Cold War incidents with the decreasing popular perception of Soviet trustworthiness from 1945 to 1949.

Specific Details of Past Relations

Beyond the general contextual effects discussed above, the unfolding processes of change that characterize the evolutionary approach are also influenced by specific details of past interactions. With regard to past episodes of militarized conflict, relevant details include the outcomes and severity levels of each past confrontation, which may exacerbate the conflictual effect of the confrontation itself or may help to counterbalance it in a more cooperative direction. For example, a confrontation that ends in a stalemate is likely to increase distrust and hostility between two adversaries without resolving any of their disputed issues to either side's satisfaction. In contrast, a confrontation ending in a negotiated compromise may settle some or all of the disputed issues and may create a more cooperative atmosphere. A decisive victory for one side may be able to settle the issues if the loser should recognize the futility in continued contention against a demonstrably stronger adversary; even if contention is not abandoned altogether, a substantial period of time may be required before the loser begins to feel confident in its ability to reverse its earlier losses.

Focusing more specifically on domestic actors beyond the chief executive, the impact of past conflict outcomes may also depend on the political activation of relevant domestic actors. If most domestic actors are uninterested in the rivalry or the issue(s) under contention, then leaders face few constraints on policy-making, and defeat might not be enough to spur a disinterested selectorate to remove a leader from power. To the extent that domestic actors are activated (either by the outcome itself or by events occurring before the confrontation), though, the impact of dispute outcomes on policy should be much greater. For example, an outcome in which the state was defeated by its rival and lost control of disputed territory appears likely to activate more of the public by convincing them that the rival poses a serious threat to their interests (and that the leader's policies were ineffective). If the defeat was so overwhelming as to indicate that even a more effective leader is unlikely to achieve better results against this adversary, though, domestic political actors may begin to prefer a more accommodationist strategy vis-à-vis the rival, and may pressure future leaders in that direction.

The severity level reached in a previous confrontation between two adversaries may also affect their subsequent relations, independent of the outcome of the confrontation. If a confrontation reaches a high level of escalation, the involved nations may need to rearm or replace the loss of much of their military hardware or trained military personnel. Public opinion may develop an aversion to belligerent foreign policies as the result of previous experiences with wars or perhaps crises that raised the strong possibility of escalation to war. Either separately or in conjunction with the effects of public opinion, a state's policy-makers may develop a similar aversion to war that will lead them to hesitate before seeking to initiate another confrontation, often referred to as a "war-weariness" or "negative reinforcement" effect. A previous confrontation that led to heavy losses could lead policy-makers to reevaluate or abandon the policies that led to those losses, as the leader attempts to adapt his or her policy preferences or is replaced by a new leader favoring a less hard-line policy. Alternatively, a confrontation that ended with few or no losses may contribute to more aggressive foreign policy actions in its aftermath, relative to confrontations that produced heavier losses in men or material.

The present chapter's emphasis on domestic actors also suggests that such a dramatic international event as a full-scale war is likely to lead to the political activation of a large segment of domestic society, because so many people's interests were likely affected by the war. In general, then, the evolutionary model suggests that especially severe conflicts between two rivals should have the twin effects of activating a sizable portion of the public and generating opposition to such costly conflict in the future. The result should be that the government will be less belligerent in the near future after the war, because of the high political costs of pursuing a belligerent policy that the public is likely to oppose.[10] It is instructive that Bueno de Mesquita and Siverson (1995) find that involvement in a costly war increases a government's likelihood of losing political power, whether the war ended in victory or defeat.

Returning to more cooperative forms of interaction, we might also expect specific details to have important effects. As noted earlier, we should generally expect a history of cooperation to increase the prospects for future cooperation. Yet not all negotiations or other peaceful interactions will have the same effect, and some may work in the opposite direction. Negotiations that produce successful treaties that are ratified and carried out are likely to produce a positive effect on future relations. The opposite result is likely, though, for talks that end without agreement or for agreements that are not ratified or carried out by one or both sides. Such cases may indicate to one or both sides that the other side can not be trusted or has no interest in reaching a genuine peaceful settlement of their contentious issue(s), rendering future cooperation more difficult.

Summary

This basic evolutionary model suggests that interstate rivalry can be understood as both the product and an agent of evolution in domestic politics. Most previous studies of rivalry—particularly those that consider the impact of domestic politics (see for example, Mor 1997; Rasler, this volume; Thompson, this volume)—have treated rivalry as a given and focused on the management or termination of ongoing rivalries. In contrast, this evolutionary approach allows us to begin to understand how rivalries develop initially, and how rivalries—once developed—affect the nature and consequences of domestic politics.

Under this model, rivalries are likely to begin over issues that are seen as salient by important portions of the political system, such as control over strategic or otherwise valuable territory. Relatively trivial issues would appear to be unlikely to lead chief executives into chains of recurrent militarized confrontations, or to lead to the political activation of other domestic political actors in such a way as to push leaders toward aggression or away from more cooperative initiatives. More salient issues would appear to be more likely to generate hard-line policies by leaders initially, as well as activating the political opposition and the selectorate in such a way as to reward tough policies vis-à-vis the rival and to punish what are seen as policies of weakness or appeasement.

Beyond issue salience, interactions between two potential rival states can also generate pressures leading toward (or away from) rivalry. A longer history of conflict or a highly visible outcome related to it—such as a decisive victory or loss in a military confrontation, or a bloody confrontation with the adversary—is likely to attract greater public attention to the rivalry, making it more difficult for the leader to back down or to end the rivalry without suffering domestic political consequences. Alternatively, a longer history of cooperation (such as a series of confidence-building measures, arms control treaties, or agreements involving some or all of the contentious issues between the adversaries) may help to convince both the leader and his or her constituents that cooperation is both possible and desirable. Political shocks—whether related to the rivalry or external in nature—may produce either of these effects, depending on the nature of the shock and the way that it is perceived by political actors; if the leader is blamed for the occurrence or impact of the shock, it may increase the political constraints against him or her (see also Rasler, this volume; Thompson, this volume).

Of course, this is not to say that these evolutionary explanations are the only factors that affect the development of potential interstate rivalries. The combination of salient issues and a history of conflictual interactions may greatly increase the prospects for future conflict and rivalry, but other factors may intervene. For example, if both sides are political democracies, they may be able to settle their differences peacefully even when highly salient issues are at stake (see, for example, Dixon 1993, 1994). Similarly, if the two sides are highly unequal in military capabilities, their disagreements may be ended quickly through a decisive military victory by the stronger side or a capitulation by the weaker side in the face of overwhelming odds. Any test of this or any other model of rivalry should control for such elements, in order to obtain the most accurate understanding of the role of evolutionary or other factors in the development of rivalries.

THE BOLIVIA-PARAGUAY RIVALRY

Having presented an evolutionary model to account for the origins and development of militarized rivalry, it is now important to evaluate this model to determine its relevance to interstate rivalry. Two forms of evaluation are used, beginning with a brief case study of the rivalry between Bolivia and Paraguay in the late nineteenth and early twentieth centuries. After this case has been examined, the recent quantitative evidence on rivalry is examined, in order to determine the extent to which this evidence is consistent with the evolutionary model or with its competitors.

The Bolivia-Paraguay rivalry offers a useful case to examine for these purposes. Most case studies of rivalries in the decade or so that rivalry has been a systematic topic of study have focused on rivalries between major powers (such as the Cold War) or on rivalries that were closely tied to major power rivalries (such as the Arab-Israeli rivalries). Little is known about rivalries between minor powers that generally avoided direct major power involvement, as was the case for Bolivia and Paraguay. Whether or not such a case provides substantial support for the evolutionary model proposed herein, we can conclude with some confidence that we are getting a fair picture of the role of evolutionary dynamics in the rivalry. With a case such as the Israel-Egypt rivalry that was tightly interconnected with the Cold War, it would be easy to dismiss negative or inconclusive results as an artifact of the Cold War, rather than as an indication of the irrelevance of evolutionary considerations. Similarly, with a major power rivalry such as the Cold War itself, it would be easy to dismiss weak results as an artifact of the centrality of the rivalry in world politics; perhaps the system's two superpowers have higher concerns or are affected by so many additional factors beyond their own rivalry that evolution would not operate as expected in such a case.

HISTORICAL BACKGROUND

The rivalry between Bolivia and Paraguay involved competing territorial claims to the Chaco Boreal region between the two countries. After independence from Spain in the early nineteenth century, both states claimed the territory on the basis of incomplete and contradictory Spanish records. By the end of the century, both sides were exploring the region and building ever-advancing lines of military outposts to protect their claims. Bilateral talks between Bolivia and Paraguay in the late nineteenth century failed to produce an agreement that could be ratified by both sides, and further talks in the early twentieth century failed even to produce an agreement that could be submitted for ratification. Military patrols from the two sides' Chaco outposts began to encounter each other in the 1920s, leading to a number of militarized incidents and failed attempts to settle the competing claims. One set of incidents spawned the bloody Chaco War of 1932 to 1935, in which Paraguay captured most of the region. After three years of difficult postwar negotiations and renewed incidents in the Chaco, Bolivia and Paraguay agreed to a final settlement of the Chaco that recognized most of Paraguay's gains from the war (for more detail see Hensel 1996).

Table 7.1 summarizes the major military and diplomatic events between Bolivia and Paraguay, from 1850 (shortly after both sides were recognized as sovereign nation-states) to the 1938 settlement of the Chaco issue. The first column lists militarized interstate disputes (Jones, et al. 1996) between Bolivia and Paraguay, indicating which confrontations were severe enough to lead to fatalities among the participants. The second column lists peaceful attempts to settle the Chaco Boreal territorial claim, including both bilateral negotiations and talks involving third party assistance (for example, good offices or mediation). This column also addresses the effectiveness of each attempt, indicating failed talks that never led to an agreement between the participants, as well as failed agreements that were never ratified or were never carried out by at least one of the participants.

Bolivia and Paraguay managed to avoid militarized conflict for much of their disagreement over the Chaco. At first, both states were concerned with other international issues (for Bolivia the War of the Pacific and its aftermath, for Paraguay the War of the Triple Alliance and its aftermath), the Chaco was not seen as central to either state's existence, and both sides were plagued by internal political and economic troubles. The few incidents that did occur were neither frequent nor serious until the 1920s, at which point the Bolivia-Paraguay relationship would be classified as an enduring rivalry by most quantitative measures. Diplomatically, the Chaco question was largely ignored throughout the nineteenth century, with a few negotiations producing treaties that were never ratified or carried out. The pace of diplomacy picked up in the twentieth century,

Table 7.1 Timeline of the Bolivia-Paraguay Rivalry

	Militarized Conflict	Negotiations
1850–1879:		1878–79 Treaty (not ratified)
1880–1889:	1886 Fuerte Olimpo Militarization	1887 Treaty (not ratified)
	1887–88 Puerto Pacheco Seizure	
1890–1899:		1894 Treaty (not ratified)
1900–1904:		1901 Talks (no agreement)
1905–1909:	1906 Chaco Fortifications	1906 Arg. Good Offices (no agreement)
		1906–07 Arg. Good Offices—Treaty (not ratified)
1910–1914:		1912–13 Procedural Treaty (not carried out)
1915–1919:	1918 Chaco Fortifications	1915 Procedural Treaty (not carried out)
		1916 Procedural Treaty (not carried out)
		1917 Procedural Treaty (not carried out)
		1918 Procedural Treaty (not carried out)
		1919 Procedural Talks (no agreement)
1920–1924:	1921 Chaco Fortifications	1921 Procedural Talks (no agreement)
	1922 Chaco Fortifications	1923 Uru. Good Offices (no agreement)
	1923 Chaco Fortifications	1924 Procedural Talks (no agreement)
	1924 Mennonite Incidents	
1925–1929:	1927 Fortín Sorpresa Incident	1927 Arg. Good Offices (no agreement)
	1927 Oil Rumors Buildup	1928 Arg. Good Offices (no agreement)
	1928–29 Vanguardia Clashes*	1928–29 Good Offices (procedural agreement)
		1929–30 Arg. Good Offices (no agreement)
1930–1934:	1930 Bolivian Attack Plans Crisis*	1931–32 Good Offices (no agreement)
	1931–35 Chaco War*	1932–33 Good Offices (no agreement)
		1933 Mediation (no agreement)
		1933–34 League Fact-Finding (no agreement)
		1933 Mediation (no agreement)
		1934 Mediation (no agreement)
		1934 League Fact-Finding (no agreement)
1935–1938:	1935 Demarcation Line Patrols	1935 Mediation (ceasefire/troop withdrawal)
	1936–37 Chaco Road Incident	1935–37 Mediation (no agreement)
	1936 Chaco Clashes*	1936 Mediation (no agreement)
	1937 Chaco Road Occupation	1936–37 Mediation (agreement not carried out)
	1937 Chaco Patrols	1938 U.S. Mediation (no agreement)
	1937 Pre-Treaty Incidents	1938 Mediation—Final Settlement
		1938 Arbitration—Final Settlement

* Indicates militarized disputes that led to at least one dispute-related fatality among the participants.

Sources: COW Militarized Interstate Dispute data (Jones, Bremer and Singer 1996); ICOW Territorial Claims data (Hensel 2000).

beginning with further unsuccessful bilateral talks between Bolivia and Paraguay and occasional talks under Argentine good offices. As serious militarized incidents began to accumulate, drawing foreign attention and concern to a previously ignored portion of the world, third parties became involved diplomatically as well. Particularly after the near-war crisis of 1928 and the Chaco War in the 1930s, the League of Nations, the United States, and neighboring Latin American states offered good offices and mediation with great frequency, generally failing to reach agreement but eventually producing the final 1938 settlement.

CONTENTIOUS ISSUES

The rivalry between Bolivia and Paraguay centered around territory in the Chaco Boreal, a desert region lying between them. Perceptions of the disputed territory changed during the rivalry, with the Chaco coming to be seen as much more salient later in the rivalry than it had been earlier. At the initial independence of both Bolivia and Paraguay, the Chaco was not seen as especially vital to the well-being of either state. Selected leaders and scholars on each side knew about their countries' claims to the Chaco, but the mass public neither knew nor cared about the Chaco (Warren 1949; Rout 1970). Both sides maintained a presence in the region to some extent during the nineteenth century, in the form of small military bases ("fortines"), explorations, small settlements, and missionaries. Yet neither made a concerted effort to establish undisputed sovereignty over the territory until later in their relationship, when the perceived value of the Chaco had been increased by both sides' losses in previous wars and by economic conditions.

Upon achieving independence, Bolivia's economy and foreign policy were oriented westward toward the Pacific Ocean through its coastal territory, ports, and nitrate mines. In the 1879 to 1883 War of the Pacific, however, Chile captured Bolivia's Litoral province, which contained all of Bolivia's nitrate mines and ocean ports. Decades of postwar diplomacy failed to return the Litoral province or to acquire rights from Chile to the formerly Peruvian areas of Tacna or Arica, leaving Bolivia a landlocked state without direct access to the sea (and without its valuable nitrate mines). By the time Peru and Chile resolved the Tacna-Arica question in July of 1929, giving Tacna to Chile and Arica to Peru, it had become clear that Bolivia would not be able to recover any Pacific coastland, and the Bolivian government began to look elsewhere for access to the sea.

The rivers in Bolivia were not deep enough to allow oceangoing vessels, but Bolivia saw a suitable opportunity in the Río Paraguay, which ran through Brazil and the Paraguayan Chaco. This river was deep enough for oceangoing vessels, and Bolivia had historical claims to the Chaco dating back to the early days of Spanish rule. The loss of Bolivia's Pacific coastland thus led Bolivia to devote much greater effort to its previous claims to the Chaco (Abecía Baldivieso 1979; Arze Quiroga 1991; Fernandez 1956; Garner 1966; Rout 1970).

The importance of the Chaco to Bolivia also increased dramatically with the discovery of oil. Bolivia's economy, which had been dependent on tin exports since losing the nitrate industry to Chile, was crippled by the 1920s collapse of the world tin market. The recent discovery of oil in Bolivian-occupied portions of the Chaco offered the prospect of improving the economy through oil exports. According to Abecía Baldivieso (1979: II, 480; my translation), "If for Baptista in 1904 the Chaco was a useless territory, for Salamanca in 1920 it was the route to a port and the possibility of exporting oil. The Chaco War could no longer be only a question of frontiers for Bolivia; it was now a question of sovereignty over the Río Paraguay." Furthermore, as Rout (1970: 25) and Garner (1966: 33–34) note, the oil issue complicated the already-complex Chaco problem by making compromise less tolerable to Bolivia. Negotiating with Paraguay for the right to build a pipeline to the Río Paraguay would mean tacit acceptance of Paraguay's claims to the Chaco and diversion of some of the tax revenues that would result from the oil exports, neither of which was desirable in view of the 1920s deterioration of Bolivian-Paraguayan relations and of Bolivia's economic situation.

Like Bolivia, Paraguay was motivated by the desire to avoid further losses of territory. After the disastrous War of the Triple Alliance from 1865 to 1870, Paraguay had lost the disputed Apa region to Brazil and the disputed Chaco Central region to Argentina. Already having lost territory to two of its neighbors, the Paraguayan government felt it absolutely necessary to maintain Paraguayan possession of the Chaco Boreal, particularly in light of the perceived economic importance of the region (and because the Chaco made up over half of Paraguay's remaining territory). The Chaco contained valuable quebracho timber and ample space for cattle ranches and agriculture, and began to attract foreign investors in the late nineteenth century and early twentieth century. Paraguay granted numerous concessions to American, British, and Argentine businessmen to exploit the Chaco's land and resources for cattle ranching, quebracho timber, and tannin extract. The importance to Paraguay of revenue from these concessions made the Chaco an asset to be retained at all costs, leading to active measures to ensure continued Paraguayan ownership as the Bolivian and Paraguayan lines of settlements and military outposts began to come into contact in the middle of the Chaco (Rout 1970: 18–21).

DOMESTIC POLITICS IN BOLIVIA AND PARAGUAY

The Bolivian and Paraguayan political systems during much of the rivalry were nominally democratic, with leaders being selected through elections and with checks and balances among the executive, legislative, and judicial branches of government. Realistically, though, neither system met modern standards of democracy. Elections in both systems were limited to a very small electorate, generally the literate upper classes. Furthermore, elections in both systems tended to be rigged in favor of the ruling party, marked by the frequent threat or use of violence to keep supporters of opposition parties from voting. As a result, Bolivia was ruled by a president from the Conservative Party from 1880 to 1899, the Liberal Party from 1899 to 1920, and the Republican Party from 1920 to 1934; Paraguay was ruled by the Colorado Party from 1878 to 1904, and the Liberal Party from 1904 to 1936. Opposition parties occasionally acquired significant representation in the legislature, including a majority for the opposition Liberal Party in the Bolivian legislature under Republican President Daniel Salamanca (1931 to 1934), but in each period the presidential dominance of the ruling party was only ended by a coup or revolution (Fifer 1972; Klein 1969, 1992; Lewis 1993; Roett and Sacks 1991; Warren 1949, 1985).

The political process in Bolivia during the rivalry—including numerous coups, revolts, and other instability as well as the more routine selection of leaders and policy formulation—was influenced primarily by domestic concerns most of the time (Fifer 1972; Klein 1969, 1992). These concerns included the relative influence of silver and tin miners, the restriction of rights for Bolivia's indigenous peoples, large budget problems, and an often dissatisfied or unpaid military, and the personal greed of individual leaders (indeed, President Melgarejo has been accused of sacrificing much of Bolivia's Pacific coast to Chile for personal profit). Up to the 1920s, the few exceptions where international factors affected Bolivian politics generally involved Chile, including the overthrow of President Daza during the War of the Pacific in 1879, public discontent over negotiations or treaties that seemed to award formerly Bolivian territory to Chile, and a 1918 attempt by the political opposition to raise the Chilean question in order to weaken the hold of the ruling party. It was not until the 1920s that the Bolivian mass public and political opposition (and the government itself) began to seize on relations with Paraguay as a vital issue affecting the Bolivian political process. Klein (1969: 102) notes that the question of the Pacific dominated Bolivian newspapers until December 1926, when stories on the Chaco first began to appear.

Similarly, in Paraguay, the budding rivalry with Bolivia apparently failed to capture the attention of the mass public until the mid- to late-1920s (Lewis 1993; Roett and Sacks 1991; Warren 1949, 1985). Throughout the 1870s and 1880s, Paraguay was recovering from its catastrophic loss of over half of its population in the War of the Triple Alliance (López War), and was the subject of frequent postwar interference by its Argentine and Brazilian opponents. In subsequent decades, Paraguay's political situation was preoccupied with domestic political, economic, and social concerns, including frequent splits within each political party as well as the expected disagreements between the parties.

SOURCES OF POLITICAL ACTIVATION

Public opinion on each side of the rivalry was activated in large part by the efforts of the political opposition, the mass media, and interest groups. Warren (1949) notes that opposition parties and newspapers on both sides were very effective at keeping up agitation, supporting their country's claims to the Chaco, rejecting the rival's claim, criticizing perceived governmental inaction, warning against tricks by the rival, and urging military preparation. Similarly, beginning in the 1890s and accelerating in the 1920s, academics and other scholars—many of whom would later reach the presidency or other political offices—published numerous well-received books supporting their own country's claims and rejecting those of the rival (Warren 1949; Rout 1970). Together, these opinion leaders essentially converted geographic features like the Río Paraguay into sacred national symbols, and created a psychological climate in which concession to the rival became tantamount to treason. After leaving office, Paraguayan President José Guggiari (1928 to 1932) declared that the Bolivian menace in the Chaco provided the principal issue for Paraguayan opposition parties; Bolivians went so far as to claim that the Chaco dispute was the one cohesive factor holding Paraguay together as a nation (Warren 1949: 290).

This political activation was most effective for the masses after Bolivia and Paraguay had started to engage in serious militarized confrontations. The incidents of the late nineteenth and early twentieth century tended to be minor, involving threats or protests over both sides' military expansion into largely uninhabited portions of the Chaco. Beginning in the late 1920s, though, these incidents took a more serious turn as the military front lines started to encounter each other, leading to the first fatalities in the rivalry and offering fertile ground for political activation.

The first bloodshed came in February 1927, when a clash between patrols at Fortín Sorpresa resulted in the death of a Paraguayan lieutenant. With his death, "an outburst of nationalist emotion" swept through students and the military, leading to numerous angry demonstrations (Lewis 1993: 142) and causing "emotions in La Paz and Asunción to rise to fever pitch" (Fifer 1972: 208). Lewis (1993: 145) goes so far as to claim that Paraguayan public opinion was so inflamed by the incident that war was only averted through Argentine diplomatic intervention. This incident also sparked the rapid rise of opposition newspapers and political movements, with the primary goals of spreading awareness of the Bolivian threat and pressuring the government to do more to meet this threat (Lewis 1993). Talks over the Fortín Sorpresa incident—conducted with Argentine assistance—lasted until July 1928, but ended without a positive decision. This failure of diplomacy, coupled with the intense nationalism inspired by the incident itself, led to the hardening of attitudes over negotiation as both sides began to abandon compromise in favor of more extreme demands (Rout 1970; Fifer 1972; Lewis 1993).

Intense clashes in December 1928, led to the capture of the Bolivian outpost Fortín Vanguardia and the Paraguayan Fortín Boquerón. These incidents "inflamed public passion to a dangerous degree" in Paraguay, bringing the Chaco issue to the attention of the entire country (Warren 1949: 298). Similarly, the clashes had an "overwhelming" impact on Bolivia, immediately uniting all political parties behind the government (albeit temporarily) and prompting three days of mass popular demonstrations (Klein 1969: 105–06). Fifer (1972: 209 ff) notes that with these clashes, both Bolivian and Paraguayan "national honor became identified with the small, apparently worthless plot of ground which had changed hands in the Chaco"; subsequently, both Bolivian and Paraguayan public opinion would react violently against any Chaco concession that might be seen as weakness.

The 1928 incident also intensified political problems within Paraguay, as the troop mobilization during the crisis revealed shortages of weapons, ammunition, uniforms, medical supplies, and food. The political opposition criticized the administration of President José Guggiari for its lack of preparation and demanded a rapid military buildup. Opposition increased in January 1929, when Guggiari accepted the terms of the International Conference of American States on Conciliation and Arbitration, which named Paraguay as the aggressor in the 1928 crisis and ordered Paraguay to rebuild Bolivia's Fortín Vanguardia. Guggiari's administration would subsequently be associated with appeasement, and a coup by the disaffected military appears to have been avoided only by the lack of a willing leader (Lewis 1993). Bolivian President Siles would also suffer political fallout from the 1928 crisis and its aftermath, being attacked by the opposition for his "cowardliness" in the Chaco and for "selling out national sovereignty to the Paraguayans" when he refused to order a general mobilization during the crisis (only calling up several draft classes) and attempted to avoid war by agreeing to the 1929 settlement (Klein 1969: 105–06, 112).

Another incident in September 1931 resulted in the Bolivian capture of Paraguay's Fortín Masamaclay (Agua Rica). After a failed attempt to recapture the outpost, Paraguay's military leadership and President José Guggiari were willing to accept the loss because of Bolivia's overwhelming military superiority in the Chaco at the time. The Paraguayan government tried to keep the loss secret by suppressing the news, but a month later word leaked out and enraged the public; the public anger over the loss was only compounded by the government's attempt to cover up the incident. The political opposition demanded action, criticizing Guggiari's alleged pacifism and inaction. A "mob of excited super patriots" rioted in Asunción in October, led by students and intellectuals. The government refused to talk with the mob and attempted to disperse the crowd; eleven protesters were killed while marching on the presidential palace, leading to the establishment of martial law and the arrest or deportation of major opposition leaders. Most of the cabinet resigned or was replaced, Guggiari was forced to step down during a Congressional investigation (he would be exonerated because the opposition had already withdrawn all of their legislators), and serious revolt was averted only because the armed forces remained loyal (Warren 1949; Lewis 1993). By this point, the Chaco was seen as vitally important by a politically activated public and political opposition, and weak or ineffective leadership on the Chaco would likely lead to the loss of political power.

Incidents continued in 1932, creating continued pressure on both sides' political leaders (Fifer 1972; Klein 1969, 1992; Lewis 1993; Warren 1949). A Bolivian force occupied a Paraguayan position at Laguna Chuquisaca and beat off several counterattacks before being defeated in July. Paraguayan President Eusebio Ayala, who took power in August 1932, would quickly be "heckled and goaded by fiery nationalists" for his moderation over the Chaco dispute and "pilloried by the mob" for his hesitation in declaring war (Warren 1949: 301). Indeed, president-elect Ayala had called on Congress to vote down war credits in June, convinced that Argentina and Brazil would force Bolivia—recently branded as the aggressor by the Inter-American Conference in Washington—to stop shooting and pull back its Chaco forces. After his August inauguration, Ayala proposed a ceasefire and the creation of a demilitarized zone, but incidents continued and escalated into full-scale war in September (Lewis 1993). By this point, Fifer (1972: 212) argues, both governments were "committed too far to withdraw without loss of national prestige," making war in the Chaco seem "both inconceivable and inevitable."

Once the war began, public opinion generally followed battlefield results. Paraguayan successes in the Chaco translated into national unity behind President Ayala and the military; Warren (1949: 303) notes that "even those discontented elements who had no love for Ayala" refrained from a revolt that would have disrupted the national unity and allowed Bolivia to take advantage of a divided enemy. Once the war ended, however, dissatisfaction with the ruling Liberal Party's prewar diplomacy and management of the war came to the surface. The Liberals were blamed for poor diplomacy that allowed the war to begin and that had failed to make adequate military preparations, for repressing popular protests (including the killing of ten students in an October 1931 mob), for agreeing to a 1934 ceasefire that allowed the Bolivian military to regroup and resupply, and for stopping the war when a much greater victory appeared to be in reach (Roett and Sacks 1991; Lewis 1993). After the war ended, Ayala ordered a large-scale demobilization to cut expenses from an empty treasury, leading to angry protests from the opposition because no peace treaty had yet been signed to end the threat from Bolivia. This discrediting of Liberal party rule helped to ensure the downfall of the party after decades of rule, and prepared the way for military rule after a 1936 coup.

Bolivian losses in the Chaco helped to turn the people against President Daniel Salamanca. As the war began, literate public opinion in Bolivia was already disturbed by the political use that Salamanca was making of the Chaco situation; feelings of doubt and opposition quickly spread to the rest of society as the Bolivian army suffered several early defeats. Several weeks into the war, twenty thousand rioters demanded Salamanca's resignation, and several leading military officers soon demanded his dismissal. Salamanca survived these protests, but he was forced to ask the opposition Liberal party to join him in a coalition government. Talks with the Liberals broke down with a further Bolivian defeat, leading to opposition attacks on Salamanca, government-encouraged mob violence against opposition newspapers, and the banning of all unions and labor organizations (Klein 1992: 191; 1969: 169–84). Salamanca would eventually be overthrown in a 1934 coup as the war (and Bolivia's losses) continued.

In each of these cases, interactions between Bolivia and Paraguay contributed to the political activation of domestic political actors with regard to the rivalry. Early in the relationship, when leaders' attention was elsewhere and there had been little direct confrontation, most of the populace in both states paid little attention. With each successive military clash in the 1920s, though, more and more of the public came to see the Chaco dispute as highly salient for each country (and as an indicator of the effectiveness of their chief executive). The next section addresses the impact of this activation on decision-making on each side of the rivalry.

IMPACT OF DOMESTIC POLITICS ON FOREIGN POLICY

As political actors on both sides became increasingly activated politically, the rivalry over the Chaco came to exert an increasingly important influence on policy-making in both Bolivia and Paraguay. Two specific forms of this influence are examined, centered around the two primary types of domestic constraints on political decision-makers discussed earlier: leader selection and policy ratification. Special consideration is given to the timing of the influence in rivalry, emphasizing changes in political activation.

Leader Selection

Leader selection refers to the replacement of a political leader by the "selectorate," which could involve the military, political parties, or the voting public and could occur through elections, coups, revolutions, or other means. In both Bolivia and Paraguay, leader selection at the outset of competition over the Chaco was not influenced by the Bolivian-Paraguayan relationship. To the extent that foreign policy affected leader selection, the impact came from relations with other countries; both sides experienced changes in leadership around the time of their nineteenth century wars. For example, Bolivian President Hilarión Daza was over-thrown in an 1879 revolution involving both citizens and the military, following political and military blundering that helped lead to the War of the Pacific and that led to disastrous military defeats by Chile (Klein 1992). Similarly, Paraguayan dictator Francisco Solano López was killed in battle in 1869 during the War of the Triple Alliance, and the selection of Paraguayan leaders over the next decade was heavily influenced by Brazil and Argentina in unilateral attempts to gain political advantage following the war (Warren 1978). Outside of these war-related cases, both Bolivian and Paraguayan leaders in the nineteenth and early twentieth centuries were generally selected (or removed from power) on the basis of domestic political and economic issues.

Once the rivalry became active and led to full-scale war, though, both Bolivia and Paraguay saw leaders removed from office largely because of perceived foreign policy failures relating to the rivalry. Paraguay's president during the Chaco War, Dr. Eusebio Ayala, was overthrown by Colonel Rafael Franco in February 1936 because of alleged weakness at the postwar peace table. In particular, beyond the alleged misconduct of the war that has already been noted, Ayala had inflamed nationalist opinion by agreeing to release all seventeen thousand captured Bolivian soldiers in exchange for the only twenty-five hundred captured Paraguayans. Many nationalists had sought a one-for-one exchange, with the remaining Bolivians to be used as bargaining chips in future negotiations, and Ayala's actions were seen as confirming their suspicions about his lack of patriotism (Warren 1949; Rout 1970; Lewis 1993).

Franco's government committed itself to a more militant defense of Paraguayan interests, including the rejection of new concessions at the Chaco Peace Conference (Warren 1949; Rout 1970). Yet Franco made an important concession in January 1937, agreeing to withdraw from forward positions controlling a strategic Chaco road in order to allow the passage of Bolivian supply trucks. Although neutral observers would continue to monitor the road, Franco's concession was seen as appeasement. Paraguayan forces in the Chaco—already dissatisfied due to supply shortages—refused to abandon the road, and another coup in August 1937 overthrew Franco.

Bolivia also experienced an important change in leadership due to the rivalry with Paraguay. Bolivian President Daniel Salamanca was widely perceived to have started the Chaco War for personal gain after deceiving the public and overcoming military objections. After a series of Bolivian military defeats in the war, Salamanca lost the widespread popular support that had accompanied the march to war. Finally, the Bolivian army removed Salamanca from power in November 1934, temporarily uniting the country again politically and socially (Klein 1969, 1992). Indeed, Klein (1992: 199) notes that by the end of the war Bolivians were so frustrated by poor leadership and military defeat that they were showing much hostility toward their own leaders and surprisingly little hatred toward Paraguay.

Policy Ratification

Policy ratification refers to constraints by domestic political actors on the policy-making process, rather than on the selection or deselection of leaders. Policy ratification constraints are most visible when political actors refuse to ratify or implement a policy chosen by the chief executive, as when a legislature refuses to ratify a treaty or a government agency refuses to carry out the policy. Less visible, but at least as important, is the situation in which the chief executive is aware of potential policy ratification problems and formulates policies with ratification in mind. There are numerous examples of policy ratification problems in the Bolivia-Paraguay rivalry; as with leader-selection constraints, these problems became most prominent after the rivalry had become active and blood had been spilled.

The Bolivia-Paraguay rivalry offers many examples of ratification problems, where the Bolivian and Paraguayan leadership signed four treaties over their territorial dispute that subsequently failed to achieve ratification in one or both countries (Rout 1970). The 1879 Quijarro-Decoud Treaty was signed after what were termed very smooth negotiations, with neither side presenting the extreme demands that would characterize later negotiations. Seeking to settle the Chaco question peacefully and without the resort to arbitration, Paraguay agreed to give Bolivia half of the territory that it would eventually acquire through the Chaco War. However, fearing popular opposition, the Paraguayan government attempted to keep the details of the treaty secret until Congress could convene to ratify it. Paraguayan President Cándido Bareiro, who had supported the treaty, died in office in 1880; his successor, Bernardino Caballero, was much less inclined to be generous with Bolivia. The Bolivian National Assembly ratified the treaty in August 1881, with the additional provision that Paraguay cede Bolivia one or two ports on the Río Pilcomayo above flood level, which Paraguay refused to accept. Bolivia finally ratified the treaty without any reservations in 1886, but the seven-year time limit for ratification of the treaty had passed (Rout 1970; Warren 1985).

Miguel Suárez Arana, a Bolivian developer, built a port called Puerto Pacheco at Bahía Negra on the Río Paraguay in 1885; the Paraguayan government had granted Arana permission, although reserving Paraguay's territorial rights in the area. Puerto Pacheco lay in an area claimed by Paraguay, although well north of the line that Paraguay had agreed to in the (never ratified) 1879 Quijarro-Decoud treaty. With Arana in deep financial trouble, the Bolivian government nationalized Puerto Pacheco in 1885, later sending a troop detachment to the port and raising the Bolivian flag. Bolivia sent Dr. Isaac Tamayo to Paraguay to negotiate either the ratification of the Quijarro-Decoud treaty or the signature of a new treaty, but the Bolivian exercise of sovereignty in territory still claimed by Paraguay (and not yet given to Bolivia because the 1879 treaty remained unratified) was increasing opposition in the Paraguayan Congress and press. Paraguay remilitarized Fuerte Olimpo, a colonial-era fort on the Río Paraguay, in August of 1886, to help protect Paraguay's interests in the area; Bolivia protested and rejected Paraguay's exercise of sovereignty in the area. In December 1887 and January 1888, Paraguayan military authorities seized Puerto Pacheco and declared the entire west bank of the Río Paraguay up to Bahía Negra to be Paraguayan, creating a serious international incident and blocking timely ratification of the 1887 Tamayo-Aceval Treaty (Rout 1970; Warren 1985).

The Paraguayan remilitarization of Fuerte Olimpo and seizure of Puerto Pacheco aroused war fears in both Argentina and Brazil, prompting both to offer their good offices to ease the situation. Neither Bolivia's nor Paraguay's leaders apparently felt ready for war, though, and neither side's public appeared to desire war. Paraguay's press treated Bolivia in a conciliatory fashion, referring to Bolivian chargé Claudio Pinilla as a modest and prudent diplomat and a perfect gentleman. Even Paraguayan Foreign Minister Juan Crisóstomo Centurión, while publicly defending the Paraguayan actions, was privately annoyed by the Pacheco incident (Warren 1985: 156–57).

The Tamayo-Aceval Treaty had been signed in February of 1887 after a smooth round of negotiations, and was even more favorable to Bolivia than the 1879 treaty had been. This treaty divided the Chaco into three segments, with the middle segment to be submitted to King Leopold of Belgium for arbitration; even with a favorable arbitral decision, Paraguay would receive only one-third of the total area of the Chaco. Bolivia's legislature ratified the treaty in November of 1888, although apparently after the time limit for ratification had already passed. Paraguayan President Escobar strongly defended the treaty, but it was rejected overwhelmingly in 1889 by the legislature as "an outrageous giveaway of Paraguayan territory" (Warren 1985: 155). After waiting in vain for Paraguay's ratification, Pinilla wrote a scorching January 1889 letter in the Paraguayan newspaper La Razón that claimed for Bolivia the entire Chaco region, far beyond any previous Bolivian claims; Warren (1985: 157) notes that the Chaco dispute "had taken an ugly turn."

In 1891, the Paraguayan press openly editorialized in favor of new diplomatic efforts to settle the Chaco issue, prompting Bolivia to dispatch another envoy to Asunción. The envoy, Bolivian Vice President Mariano Baptista, was unable even to convince the Paraguayan government to discuss the Chaco. Despite additional editorials favoring negotiations and even Paraguayan concessions in the name of peace, the government refused to meet with Baptista, who left Paraguay in October after several fruitless months (Warren 1985).

Renewed talks in 1894 led to the Ichazo-Benítez treaty in November. As in previous treaties, Paraguay agreed to surrender a large portion of its Chaco claim, an unpopular decision. Paraguayan President Egusquiza recommended ratification, recognizing the need "to harmonize the rights of Paraguay with economic interests and the cause of American fraternity" (Warren 1985: 159; Rout 1970). Paraguay's legislature only agreed to appoint a commission to study the treaty, though, and Bolivia's president then refused even to send the treaty to the Bolivian legislature. Paraguayan press and opposition sources blamed Argentina or Brazil for the terms of the treaty, with the editor of *El Pueblo* charging that the Colorado Party had allowed Paraguay to become a Brazilian protectorate (Warren 1985). An 1896 attempt by Bolivia to obtain ratification of the treaty failed due to opposition from the Liberal Party and opposition newspapers. Paraguay's legislature stalled when pressed on the issue, appointing a commission to study Paraguay's title to the disputed territory and postponing future negotiations. The commission issued its report in April of 1898, recommending rejection of the treaty and opposing any concession to Bolivia (Warren 1985).

An American developer, E. F. Swan, obtained a Bolivian concession in early 1897 to build a railway and communications lines from the Río Paraguay to Santa Cruz, prompting immediate Paraguayan protests. Paraguay then sent reinforcements to Fuerte Olimpo and Puerto Pacheco, Congress secretly authorized calling out the national guard, and many young Paraguayans volunteered for military duty. Brazil's minister to Asunción reported that there was no war fever in the air, although Warren (1985: 160) notes that the Chaco question was now taking a more serious turn, with both Bolivia and Paraguay adopting more extreme positions that would be difficult to modify. Bolivia replied to the Paraguayan protests in a relatively conciliatory manner, leading to a series of talks, but Paraguay continued reinforcing its positions and encouraged new efforts to populate the Chaco with missionaries and agricultural colonies. Bolivia's press began a serious campaign against Paraguay, using insulting language and charging that it was useless to negotiate with a country that resorted to such means as Paraguay had been using. Some Bolivian journalists went so far as to recommend attacking Paraguay, leading to equally bellicose statements in the Paraguayan press (Warren 1985). In this tense atmosphere, both governments continued to encourage exploration, settlement, and development of the Chaco, and newspapers on both sides continued to publish jingoistic articles (Warren 1985).

New movement came under Paraguayan President Benigno Ferreira (1906 to 1908), whom Lewis (1993: 101) describes as "the first president, save for Egusquiza, to recognize that Bolivia had designs on the Chaco and to begin preparing Paraguay for the upcoming fight." Ferreira took a strong line with Bolivia, leading to the 1907 Pinilla-Soler Protocol, which ceded about one-fourth of the Chaco to each side and provided for arbitration over the remaining half. Bolivia also promised not to advance any further into the Chaco, and Argentina guaranteed the status quo. The Paraguayan Congress quickly ratified this protocol, but the Bolivian Congress refused to ratify it. Bolivia then demanded modifications that Paraguay found unacceptable, and efforts to revise the protocol ended in deadlock (Rout 1970; Warren 1985; Lewis 1993).

Renewed talks in 1913 led to the Ayala-Mujía Protocol, in which both Bolivia and Paraguay promised to maintain the status quo established in the 1907 accord and agreed to submit their claims to arbitration if a bilateral settlement could not be reached within two years. Paraguay's Foreign Minister, Eusebio Ayala, intentionally overlooked recent Bolivian violations of the status quo in an attempt to reach a peaceful settlement by being conciliatory, but many Paraguayan citizens felt that the government was giving away too much. One of these critics, former president Emilio Aceval, formed a nonpartisan "Patriotic Union" to raise awareness and opposition among people from all political parties and factions (Lewis 1993). The terms of this treaty (involving foreign arbitration) were never carried out, and a series of additional treaties (in 1915, 1916, 1917, 1918, 1919, and 1921) extending the time for implementation similarly failed to be carried out (Rout 1970; Lewis 1993).

Given the history of past ratification troubles on both sides, the final peace treaty of 1938 was accompanied by careful planning on both sides. Paraguay's chief representative at the final peace talks in 1938 was General José Félix Estigarribia, the war hero who had led Paraguay's military in the Chaco. Estigarribia "knew the advantages of a definite settlement" to the Chaco conflict and "did not hesitate to sign a treaty when opposition was certain to appear in Asunción"; Warren (1949: 324) considered his involvement to have "saved the treaty from going the way of all previous efforts." Similarly, Rout (1970: 211) argues that the war hero Estigarribia was "perhaps the only person with sufficient prestige to make concessions and still escape denunciation as a traitor." Estigarribia replaced Gerónimo Zubizarreta, who had opposed any Paraguayan concessions at the conference, frustrating the neutral conference participants (Argentina, Brazil, Chile, Peru, and the United States) and leading Bolivia to threaten a renewal of the war. Once the treaty was signed, the combination of Estigarribia's involvement and a strong public desire for peace overcame opposition from Zubizarreta and others, and a plebiscite ratified it by an overwhelming margin.

On the Bolivian side, the government of Colonel Germán Busch had also recognized that compromise would be necessary for any lasting peace settlement. Previous Bolivian leaders had demanded a useful littoral on the Río Paraguay, and public opposition to any major concessions would likely have meant the loss of political power after signing an agreement that failed to produce such a littoral. Busch, in contrast, recognized that what was most important was the psychological value of a littoral on the Río Paraguay (rather than a length of coast that could actually be useful economically), and expressed a willingness to pay for it. Additionally, a top priority for Busch was the withdrawal of Paraguayan forces safely beyond Bolivian oil fields, which was accomplished without the need for Bolivia to pay an additional sum (Rout 1970). In short, the final 1938 treaty "was neither moral, impartial, nor faithful to previously state goals; instead it was an agreement that all interested parties could accept" (Rout 1970: 216).

DISCUSSION

This brief examination of the Bolivian-Paraguayan rivalry fits very well with the general model presented earlier. The rivalry centered around a territorial issue, competing claims to the Chaco Boreal region, which is consistent with the expectation that most rivalries will require a highly salient issue. This issue changed in salience over time, though, beginning as a largely unpopulated and unknown area and later developing a vital attachment to the two states' economies and national psyches. This increasing perceived salience of the Chaco also generally corresponds with leaders' willingness to risk more aggressive policies in pursuit of their goals, and appears to have contributed to the political activation of large segments of both societies.

Interactions over the Chaco also appear to have contributed to political activation, as suggested by the evolutionary model. Early in the competition over the Chaco, attempts to settle the territorial question peacefully generally failed due to legislative opposition, occasionally backed by popular criticism. For example, after the aggressive incidents of the late 1880s and the subsequent failure of negotiations, the public and media on both sides generally appeared to oppose a military solution. As further negotiations failed, though, the media began to lobby for more aggressive actions and against any appeasement of the adversary. This media pressure, when combined with the militarized clashes of the late 1920s, helped to create very interested—and very bellicose—public sentiments on both sides.

Both military and diplomatic interactions over the Chaco produced international evolutionary challenges to each side's chief executives, as the other side prevented each leader from accomplishing his goals over the Chaco (through a peaceful settlement or through the simple occupation of claimed territory). The political activation of domestic actors compounded these international evolutionary challenges by offering additional domestic challenges to the environment. Several leaders on each side were removed because of their management of the rivalry (particularly once it had led to full-scale war), and many others found themselves under serious political pressure from domestic opponents displeased with their lack of firmness (or lack of success) in dealing with the rival.

Even when leaders were not directly threatened with removal from office, chief executives on both sides encountered great difficulties with policy ratification, particularly when attempting to manage the rivalry or to settle the Chaco issue peacefully. For every Salamanca who attempted to use aggressive action in the rivalry for personal political benefit, there were several Guggiaris or Ayalas who encountered strong domestic pressure to abandon their more accommodative stances in favor of a stronger defense of national interests in the Chaco. As might be suggested by this evolutionary model, many leaders in such a position ended up adapting their policies to be more in line with these international and domestic pressures—which usually kept them in power until the term of office had ended (or at least prevented their removal on the basis of foreign policy issues), although it failed to produce enlightened policy-making that might have avoided the one-hundred thousand or more deaths suffered during the Chaco War. It is also worth noting that these constraints existed in two political systems that never approached modern standards of democracy during the rivalry, with very small electorates and the frequent use of violence or intimidation to control elections, and with the only changes of power between parties coming through coups or revolutions. Although constraints might be greater in fully functioning democratic political systems, the Bolivia-Paraguay case indicates that they can still affect policy-making in important ways in much less open systems.

QUANTITATIVE EVIDENCE ON EVOLUTION AND RIVALRY

The Bolivia-Paraguay case suggests that this evolutionary model appears to be quite useful as an explanation of the development of militarized interstate rivalry. Yet a single case study, particularly one as brief as this, should not be taken as scientific evidence of the overall validity of a model. The final section of this paper examines the results of more scientific research on rivalry, in order to determine the extent to which these results support or oppose the evolutionary model of rivalry (as well as its competitors). As will be seen, several recent quantitative studies have addressed questions related to the evolutionary and BRL models of rivalry, producing limited evidence in support of each model but being unable to reject either approach in favor of the other. This section reviews evidence on the two models of rivalry, including studies of the origins of rivalry and of conflict behavior within rivalry.

Origins of Rivalry

Several empirical studies have examined the sources of rivalry, in order to determine whether the origins of rivalry are more consistent with the evolutionary or BRL models. With regard to Goertz and Diehl's BRL model, very few empirical tests of the origins of rivalry have been possible because of the lack of explicit theoretical expectations about the sources of rivalry. In one of the few empirical tests of this approach, Goertz and Diehl (1995) find that 87.7 percent of all enduring rivalries begin within ten years of a political "shock," or a dramatic change in the internal or external environment. Particularly important shocks are the political independence of one or both rivals (45.5 percent of all rivalries in their study began within a decade of independence), civil war within one or both (28.9 percent), and world wars (28.9 percent).[11] Diehl and Goertz (2000: chapter 11) find similar results with updated data on militarized disputes and rivalries, with 95.2 percent of all enduring rivalries beginning within a decade of some type of political shock.

Another test of the BRL model involves identifying specific factors that might contribute to a dyadic basic rivalry level, and thus account for the outbreak of rivalries. Sowers and Hensel (1997) examine all dyadic relationships that included at least one militarized interstate dispute, in order to distinguish those that went on to become enduring rivals from those that stopped short. Contention over territorial issues proves to be a powerful predictor, accounting for the probability of eventual enduring rivalry as well as for such other measures as the eventual number of militarized disputes between the adversaries, the duration of the conflictual relationship, and the probability of at least one full-scale war. Relationships beginning less than a decade after the independence of one or both states are also significantly more likely than other relationships to become full-fledged enduring rivalries, although the effect is somewhat weaker than for contention over territory. Similarly, Hensel and Sowers (1998) find that dyads contending over territorial issues and dyads composed of two major power adversaries are significantly more dangerous than other types of adversaries, with more than twice the probability of fighting at least one war and three times the probability of reaching the intermediate or advanced phase of rivalry (analogous to the levels of "proto-rivalry" or enduring rivalry). It appears, then, that factors at the start of a conflictual relationship are very helpful in predicting the course of that relationship, which is consistent with the expectations of the BRL model.

Yet these empirical tests of the BRL model generally fail to control for factors associated with the evolutionary approach. Hensel (1996, 1998a, 1999) finds evidence of evolution in militarized interaction along the path to rivalry. In particular, two adversaries are more likely to become involved in recurrent militarized conflict after the conclusion of one militarized dispute when they have a longer history of past conflict. Recurrent conflict occurs after around half of all disputes in the "early phase" of rivalry, as compared to over two-thirds of all disputes in the "intermediate phase" and almost ninety percent of all disputes in the "advanced phase" (with the phases determined by the number of recent militarized confrontations between the same adversaries and the advanced phase corresponding to the time that a relationship begins to qualify as an "enduring rivalry"). The likelihood of experiencing a tenth dispute after the conclusion of the ninth dispute between two rivals is much greater than the likelihood of a fourth dispute after the conclusion of a third, which in turn is greater than the likelihood of a second dispute between two adversaries that have just concluded their first confrontation. A longer legacy of conflict thus contributes greatly to the renewal of conflict, making it more difficult over time to resolve the contentious issues, tension, and hostility that separate two adversaries.

Beyond simply establishing that subsequent conflict becomes more likely as two adversaries accumulate a longer history of past conflict, Hensel (1996, 1999) attempts to account for the evolution of adversaries toward full-fledged enduring rivalry. The recurrence of conflict is found to be much more likely after a dispute that ended in a stalemated outcome than after a dispute that ended in a compromise or decisive outcome, and much more likely after a dispute that involved territorial issues than after a dispute over nonterritorial issues. Even after controlling for the impact of specific details of past conflict and for other relevant variables such as military capabilities and political regime type, the general rivalry context remains important; dispute recurrence is much more likely between adversaries with a longer history of militarized conflict.[12] Furthermore, Sowers and Hensel (1997) find that evolutionary factors such as past conflict outcomes and severity levels remain important in the hypothesized directions after controlling for the impact of supposed BRL factors (contention over territory, recent independence, major power status) and other relevant control variables.

The rivalry context in which a confrontation occurs thus has a large effect on subsequent relations between the adversaries. As two adversaries accumulate a longer history of confrontation, they become much more likely to engage in renewed conflict in the immediate future. In other words, conflict begets conflict, and adversaries that are not careful to resolve their differences early face a great risk of becoming trapped in a protracted string of conflict. These results are very consistent with the evolutionary model of rivalry, with its emphasis on change over time due to previous interactions and confrontations between two adversaries. Overall, the available evidence on the origins of rivalry offers support for both the BRL and evolutionary models. Indeed, in the only study so far to take both models into account (Sowers and Hensel 1997), factors from each model remain highly significant in the expected directions after controlling for the effect of factors from the other model. Although future research should attempt to identify conditions under which each model is more useful, it seems clear that both models are useful and neither can be rejected on the basis of the current evidence.

Conflict Behavior within Rivalry

Several additional studies focus on conflict behavior within relationships that eventually become enduring rivalries, in order to identify patterns or trends in conflict severity. Diehl and Goertz (2000: Chapter 9) find that most enduring rivalries do not appear to develop through an evolutionary pattern of ever-increasing conflict severity. The majority of Goertz and Diehl's cases fit the null model of no secular trend in conflict severity, consistent with the BRL model, with relatively few cases fitting the "volcano model" (a pattern of rising conflict severity culminating in war). Additionally, Hensel (1996) finds little evidence of a pattern of ever-increasing conflict severity within rivalries, and both Hensel and McLaughlin (1996) and Diehl and Hensel (1998) find that militarized disputes in later phases of rivalry are significantly less escalatory than disputes in earlier phases. These results appear to offer little systematic support for an evolutionary approach's general expectation of increasing conflict escalation in developing interstate rivalries—although the finding of significant decreases in escalation is equally inconsistent with the BRL model's general prediction of stability in conflict patterns across the duration of rivalry. Furthermore, many of the specific effects hypothesized by the evolutionary approach appear to be relevant, with previous conflict outcomes and severity levels affecting subsequent conflict escalation patterns in the hypothesized ways (Hensel and McLaughlin 1996; Sowers and Hensel 1996).

On the basis of the above results, it seems clear that not all rivalries show evolution in the sense of ever-increasing conflict severity, at least with the indicators that have been studied so far. More likely, there are probably several different patterns of evolution, each involving different dynamics and having different effects on conflict severity. It may be, for example, that major power rivalries involve different dynamics than do minor power rivalries. It may also be that rivalries involving certain types of issues (perhaps those involving territorial issues) are especially likely to show rapid escalation in their early years and throughout the period of rivalry, while rivalries over less inflammatory stakes may take longer to reach high levels of escalation (if they reach these levels at all).

It should also be noted that empirical analyses are not limited to only the militarized dimensions of world politics. Focusing on relations below the threshold of militarized conflict, Hensel (1997) finds that nonmilitarized interaction between rivals shows evidence of evolution in several ways. Disaggregated analysis of the conflictual and cooperative dimensions of interstate relations reveals that relations between rivals become both more intensely cooperative and more intensely conflictual in later phases of rivalry. Additionally, when conflictual and cooperative relations are aggregated together, overall relations between rivals become much more conflictual in later phases of rivalry.

Moving from conflict behavior to the continuation or termination of rivalries, the current evidence offers support for both the evolutionary and BRL models. Goertz and Diehl (1995, Diehl and Goertz 2000) find that most rivalries end shortly after a political shock, and that the impact of shocks is particularly strong for civil war in one of the rivals and for periods of large-scale global territorial change. In a more rigorous research design, Bennett (1998) finds that periods of global territorial change or world war increase the probability that rivalries will end, although other shocks such as civil wars have little impact.[13] Issue salience appears closely connected to rivalry continuation, with contention over highly salient issues such as territory lengthening the expected duration of rivalry in rivalry-level analyses (Bennett 1998) as well as in analyses of annual interactions within individual rivalries (Hensel 1996, 1999). This importance of shocks and of issues suggests support for the BRL model, because certain types of issues appear to produce more conflictual "basic rivalry levels" that make rivalry more difficult to end and because external shocks may be needed to disrupt the stability of an ongoing rivalry.

Yet additional evidence suggests that the continuation or ending of rivalries is also strongly affected by interactions between the rivals, as the evolutionary model suggests. Focusing on the aftermath of specific militarized confrontations, Hensel (1996, 1999) finds that both compromises and decisive outcomes to militarized disputes increase the likelihood of rivalry termination (or decrease the likelihood of conflict recurrence) relative to stalemates; dispute severity appears to have little systematic impact. These results hold both for interactions along the road to rivalry (that is, in the "early phase" or "intermediate phase" of a conflictual relationship) and for interactions once enduring rivalry has been reached (that is, in the "advanced phase"). Additionally, while Bennett (1998) finds an increasing hazard rate for the termination of enduring rivalries that have lasted for a number of decades, Hensel (1996, 1999) finds that a longer history of conflict—as indicated by the number of past militarized confrontations—makes rivalry more difficult to end at any given point in time.[14] The available evidence, then, supports the evolutionary model's arguments about both the general contextual effect of past relations and some of the more specific details of past conflict (particularly conflict outcomes).

Summary

In conclusion, recent research offers some empirical support for both the BRL and evolutionary models of the origins and dynamics of rivalry. Many rivalries appear to begin within a decade of one or more political shocks, supporting the punctuated equilibrium model. Yet the approach to rivalry—whether or not a shock has recently occurred—appears to be influenced heavily by evolutionary considerations, with the overall history of past conflict and specific effects of previous confrontations both significantly increasing the likelihood of renewed militarized conflict. Similarly, most rivalries do not appear to emerge through increasingly escalatory militarized confrontations, with little systematic trend in conflict severity along the road to many rivalries. Yet evolutionary analysis has shown that conflict behavior within enduring rivalries is not necessarily constant over time, with general (nonmilitarized) relations between adversaries becoming more conflictual with a longer history of conflict, and with the outcomes and severity levels of previous confrontations affecting conflict severity levels along the road to rivalry.

One difficulty in evaluating the BRL/punctuated equilibrium and evolutionary models of rivalry is that few of the studies discussed here have considered potential explanatory factors from both models. Sowers and Hensel (1997) and Hensel and Sowers (1998) have begun to do so, examining several factors that are consistent with the BRL model as well as factors drawn from the evolutionary model, in order to study whether or not each model's effects hold up while controlling for factors from the other model and whether or not certain BRL-type factors lead to evolutionary behavior while others produce a simple BRL with little subsequent variation. Future work along these lines is necessary, both to test the two models head-to-head and to refine each model (for example, by indicating situations in which it is expected to be most important or situations in which it is expected to play little role).

CONCLUSIONS AND IMPLICATIONS

This chapter has used evolutionary concepts to develop an evolutionary model of interstate rivalry. Notions of fitness, adaptation, and natural selection have helped to formulate a model of rivalry that focuses on the identity and policy preferences of state leaders. Before rivalry begins, foreign affairs are unlikely to play much of a role in the selection of state leaders; domestic considerations are likely to be most important. As conflict begins to accumulate between two states, though, relations with the rival are likely to become important in domestic political debate. A leader with unpopular or unsuccessful policies must attempt to adapt his or her policy preferences in order to deal with the changing (international and domestic) environment, or the leader may be selected out of office; specific outcomes of past confrontations and the salience of the issues under contention between the rivals may exacerbate or mitigate this effect.

The evolutionary approach suggested herein appears to tell a plausible story about some of the domestic political processes that accompany (and help to guide states along) the road toward or away from rivalry. A brief case study suggests that the course of the Bolivia-Paraguay rivalry was largely consistent with this model, with early events in the rivalry activating the political scene in both rival states and thus complicating later efforts to manage or resolve the rivalry. This evolutionary model is also very different from the competing basic rivalry level or punctuated equilibrium model, offering a very different view of the world and very different hypotheses on the origins and dynamics of rivalry. A review of evidence from recent studies of rivalry suggests that many expectations of this evolutionary model are supported by the empirical evidence, although many expectations of the BRL model also receive support, particularly with regard to conflict behavior within rivalry.

DIRECTIONS FOR FUTURE RESEARCH

What is needed next is more detailed work to follow up on the preliminary tests that have been conducted thus far, in order to distinguish better between the two models of rivalry and to help identify areas where each model can be refined. One area for improvement in the evolutionary model involves the question of how long it takes for evolution to take effect. Past studies of evolution have measured the evolutionary rivalry context simply by the number of recent militarized disputes between two adversaries, implicitly assuming that each dispute carries equal weight in the evolutionary process and that each dyad reaches the "advanced phase" of rivalry after the same number of disputes. Yet the evolutionary hypotheses laid out here suggest that certain factors may hasten or impede this process, including conflict outcomes, severity levels, and changes in the nature of the issues between two rival states; political shocks may also play a similar role. Ideally, the evolutionary model can be improved to provide better guidance on the expected time frame of evolution, taking into account characteristics of past conflicts as well as their frequency.

A second area for improvement involves the question of the specific makeup of the domestic political situation, including both the chief executive and other political actors. The present evolutionary model leaves these details unresolved, treating the preferences of the selectorate and other political actors only implicitly and ignoring the possibility of variations in political settings. A hard-line, militaristic leader at the beginning of a potential rivalry relationship may produce very different evolutionary dynamics than a more pacifistic, accommodationist leader, and popular support for the leader may depend on the specific political views of the selectorate (or as suggested earlier, the specific views of several selecting agents within the political system). Future extensions of this model should address the impact of specific policy preferences of leaders and other other domestic political actors.[15]

A third area in which the model can be extended involves the deescalation and termination of rivalry. The present model emphasizes the path to rivalry, focusing on processes that lead two states to enduring rivalry or that allow these states to stop short of rivalry. Once two adversaries become rivals, this model would primarily suggest that domestic politics would make a resolution of the rivalry difficult to achieve. To the extent that resolution is possible, this model would suggest that interactions during the rivalry (such as the outcomes or severity levels of confrontations) may offer the needed incentives to end it. The Rasler and Thompson contributions in this volume offer much greater detail on the processes and factors that can help produce rivalry deescalation or termination than has been possible here; future research would do well to integrate such ideas more closely with the present model.

Beyond militarized interstate rivalry, this model can also be extended to nonmilitarized dimensions of world politics. There is no reason that evolutionary dynamics in domestic politics must be confined to militarized conflict and rivalry. Similar dynamics would appear likely to affect such processes as international economic relations or negotiations over any number of potential issues between states (whether or not there is a threat of militarized action). The case study in this chapter appears to suggest an evolutionary dynamic in the negotiations over the Chaco that existed even before Bolivia and Paraguay began their climactic series of confrontations in the 1920s. Elsewhere (Hensel 2000) I apply the basic outlines of this model to study both militarized and nonmilitarized interactions over territorial claims, and find evidence that the history of both militarized conflict and peaceful settlement attempts between two adversaries affects their prospects for settling their issues peacefully.

It is possible that such improvements may introduce overwhelming complications in the basic conceptual model, outweighing the benefits of a simplifying model. It is also possible that such improvements may exacerbate the (already great) difficulties of testing the model empirically in a meaningful and appropriate fashion. Yet future theoretical and empirical work on evolution is strongly encouraged, both with regard to interstate rivalry and in the study of world politics more generally. There have already been great payoffs in terms of theoretical contributions beyond competing models and empirical support in a variety of tests; it is to be hoped that scholars will help to advance the evolutionary study of world politics even further in the future.

NOTES

1. Useful natural-science sources on evolution that were consulted include Darwin (1859/1968), Eldredge (1985), Keller and Lloyd (1992), Mayr (1988), and Minkoff (1983).
2. Goertz and Diehl describe this as a "punctuated equilibrium" model, largely because of its explanation for rivalry termination. Once a rivalry has been established by exogenous factors, the stability of interactions within rivalry lasts until the rivalry is terminated abruptly by some type of environmental "shock" in the international system, a specific geographic region, or one or both rival states.
3. Hensel (1996) suggests several other potential determinants of BRLs and thus sources of rivalry, including geopolitical position (along the lines of Mahan and Mackinder), superpower status in an anarchic system (following neorealists such as Waltz), and disagreement over territorial and ethnonationalist issues.
4. Indeed, future research might profitably address the linkages between structural and evolutionary factors, covering questions such as whether evolutionary paths can be "bounded" by previously existing structural conditions, and under which conditions evolutionary paths can overcome structural constraints on the adversaries. Hensel and Sowers (1998; Sowers and Hensel 1997) have begun to investigate such linkages in the origins and dynamics of rivalry.
5. See Hensel (1998b) for more detail on the domestic political aspects of this model. The chief executive is also responsible for making domestic policy decisions, although the purpose of this model is to study foreign policy. It should be noted that this assumption of a single chief executive is common in political science research, and is meant to include any type of political system (whether a democracy, monarchy, dictatorship, or other type).
6. Even in the presence of term limits that prevent a given leader from remaining in power indefinitely, such a leader is more likely than an ineffective leader to see his

or her preferred successor come to power, which will maximize the continuity of the leader's preferred policies.

7. Although leaders (or candidates) may show variation on many policy dimensions, including domestic social, political, or economic policies, the dimension of interest here involves policies relating to the rival. Some leaders favor hard-line policies toward the rival, preferring the risks inherent in coercion to the possibility of negotiations or accommodation, while others favor more accommodative policies (see also Vasquez 1993).

8. During a rivalry, the leader's policies vis-à-vis the rival are not the only influence on his or her prospects for remaining in office, but they are important. If the leader is unable to please the selectorate with policies regarding the rival, then removal from office is likely. Even if the leader is able to please the selectorate, he or she can still be removed from office for other (social, economic, political, or other) reasons.

9. It should be noted that several different "selectorates" may exist for a given leader or political system, each of which may have different policy preferences. For example, a leader in a weak democratic system may be voted out of office in the next election, or may be overthrown by a coup or revolution. Policies that please the voting public may alienate the military or other groups with the power to select leaders (and vice versa), resulting in a greater probability of losing office. For now the model assumes the existence of a single unified selectorate, but future research could benefit by expanding this assumption to consider multiple selecting actors.

10. If the issue at stake is highly salient and the bloody confrontation did not result in overwhelming defeat, losses of life may actually product the opposite impact, as leaders and other actors decide that the deaths of their countrymen must not be in vain. Such an effect is likely to be rare, though, depending on a sufficiently salient issue and sufficiently low-expected future costs that the issue is seen as worth risking further bloodshed.

11. It is useful to keep in mind, though, that political shocks are common events. Using Goertz and Diehl's (1995: 41) list of shocks, only forty-three years between 1816 and 1976 (26.7 percent) did not fall within ten years of a system-level shock, and many of these forty-three years fall within ten years of the 225 national-level independence or civil war shocks that Goertz and Diehl study.

12. By the time two adversaries reach the advanced phase of rivalry, the legacy of past conflict comes to dominate their relationship, with dispute outcomes and contentious issues showing greatly reduced effects on subsequent conflict behavior. Even the least conflict-prone outcomes or issues in Hensel's (1996, 1998a, 1999) "advanced phase" of rivalry are more likely to be followed by recurrent conflict than the most conflictual outcomes or issues in the "early phase."

13. Bennett (1998) also finds that the impact of shocks depends heavily on specific measurement issues, including both the time period after the shock and the potential of high collinearity among the various shocks included in the model.

14. Part of the difference may be accounted for by different units of measurement. Bennett (1998) examines rivalry termination in five-year periods, while Hensel (1996, 1999) examines the probability of conflict recurrence in each year after the end of the previous militarized confrontation between two states, for up to fifteen years (the time in which a new militarized dispute would be considered to extend the period of rivalry.

15. It is also possible that different types of political systems may work differently, as well. Although democratic and authoritarian systems in all of their variants feature some type of selectorate and some set of actors that may be able to ratify or veto policy decisions by the chief executive, there may be important differences that should be addressed in future research.

REFERENCES

Abecía Baldivieso, Valentin. 1979. *Las Relaciónes Internacionales en la Historia de Bolivia*, vol. 2, parts 1 and 2. La Paz: Editorial "Los Amigos Del Libro."

Arze Quiroga, Eduardo. 1991. *Las Relaciónes Internacionales de Bolivia, 1825–1990*. La Paz: Editorial Los Amigos del Libro.

Beatty, John. 1992. Fitness: Theoretical Contexts. In E. F. Keller and E. A. Lloyd, eds. *Keywords in evolutionary biology*. Cambridge, Mass.: Harvard University Press, pp. 115–19.

Bennett, D. Scott. 1998. Integrating and Testing Models of Rivalry Duration. *American Journal of Political Science* 42, 4 (October): 1200–32.

Bueno de Mesquita, Bruce, and Randolph M. Siverson. 1995. War and the Fate of Political Leaders: A Comparative Study of Regime Types and Political Accountability. *American Political Science Review* 89: 841–55.

Burian, Richard M. 1992. Adaptation: Historical Perspectives. In E. F. Keller and E. A. Lloyd, eds. *Keywords in evolutionary biology*. Cambridge, Mass.: Harvard University Press, pp. 7–12.

Darwin, Charles (1859/1968). *The Origin of species*. New York: Penguin Books.

Diehl, Paul F., and Gary Goertz. 2000. *War and peace in international rivalry*. Ann Arbor: University of Michigan Press.

Diehl, Paul F., and Paul R. Hensel. 1998. Punctuated Equilibrium or Evolution?: A Research Note on Models of Rivalry Development. Paper presented at the Annual Meeting of the Peace Science Society (International), New Brunswick, N.J.

Dixon, William J. 1993. Democracy and the Management of International Conflict. *Journal of Conflict Resolution* 37,1 (March): 42–68.

———. 1994. Democracy and the Peaceful Settlement of International Conflict. *American Political Science Review* 88, 1 (March): 14–32.

Eldredge, Niles. 1985. *Time frames: The Evolution of punctuated equilibria*. Princeton, N.J.: Princeton University Press.

Endler, John A. 1992. Natural Selection: Current Usages. In Evelyn Fox Keller and Elisabeth A. Lloyd, eds. *Keywords in evolutionary biology*. Cambridge, Mass.: Harvard University Press, pp. 220–224.

Fernandez, Carlos Jose. 1956. *La Guerra del Chaco, vol. I: Boquerón*. Buenos Aires: Impresora Oeste.

Fifer, J. Valerie. 1972. *Bolivia: Land, location, and politics since 1825*. Cambridge, U.K.: Cambridge University Press.

Garner, William R. 1966. *The Chaco dispute*. Washington, D.C.: Public Affairs Press.

Goertz, Gary, and Paul F. Diehl. 1992. The Empirical Importance of Enduring Rivalries. *International Interactions* 18, 2: 151–63.

———. 1993. Enduring Rivalries: Theoretical Constructs and Empirical Patterns. *International Studies Quarterly* 37, 2 (June): 147–71.

———. 1995. The Initiation and Termination of Enduring Rivalries: The Impact of Political Shocks. *American Journal of Political Science* 39, 1 (February): 30–52.

Hagan, Joe D. 1993. *Political opposition and foreign policy in comparative perspective*. Boulder, Col.: Lynne Rienner.

Hensel, Paul R. 1996. *The Evolution of interstate rivalry*. Ph.D. dissertation, University of Illinois.

———. 1997. What Do They Do When They Aren't Fighting?: Event Data and Non-Militarized Dimensions of Interstate Rivalry. Draft manuscript, Florida State University.

———. 1998a. Interstate Rivalry and the Study of Militarized Conflict. In Frank P.

Harvey and Ben D. Mor, eds. *Conflict in world politics: Advances in the study of crisis, war, and peace.* London: Macmillan, pp. 162–204.

———. 1998b. Domestic Politics and Interstate Conflict. Paper presented at the annual meeting of the American Political Science Association, Boston.

———. 1999. An Evolutionary Approach to the Study of Interstate Rivalry. *Conflict Management and Peace Science* 17, 2 (fall 1999): 179–206.

———. 2000. Contentious Issues and World Politics: The Management of Territorial Claims in the Americas, 1816–1996. Draft manuscript, Florida State University.

Hensel, Paul R. and Sara McLaughlin. 1996. Power Transitions and Dispute Escalation in Evolving Interstate Rivalries. Paper presented at the Annual Meeting of the American Political Science Association, San Francisco.

Hensel, Paul R. and Thomas Sowers. 1998. Territorial Claims, Major Power Competition, and the Origins of Enduring Rivalry. Paper presented at the joint meeting of the International Studies Association and the European Standing Group on International Relations, Vienna.

Hodge, M. J. S. 1992. Natural Selection: Historical Perspectives. In E. F. Keller and E. A. Lloyd, eds. *Keywords in evolutionary biology.* Cambridge, Mass.: Harvard University Press, pp. 212–19.

Holsti, Kalevi J. 1991. *Peace and war: Armed conflicts and international order, 1648–1989.* New York: Cambridge University Press.

Holsti, Ole R. 1996. *Public opinion and American foreign policy.* Ann Arbor: University of Michigan Press.

Jones, Daniel M., Stuart A. Bremer, and J. David Singer. 1996. Militarized Interstate Disputes, 1816–1992: Rationale, Coding Rules, and Empirical Patterns. *Conflict Management and Peace Science* 15, 2 (summer): 163–213.

Keller, Evelyn Fox, and Elisabeth A. Lloyd, eds. 1992. *Keywords in evolutionary biology.* Cambridge, Mass.: Harvard University Press.

Klein, Herbert S. 1969. *Parties and political change in Bolivia, 1880–1952.* Cambridge, U.K.: Cambridge University Press.

———. 1992. *Bolivia: The Evolution of a multi-ethnic society.* Oxford: Oxford University Press.

Lewis, Paul H. 1993. *Political parties and generations in Paraguay's liberal era, 1869–1940.* Chapel Hill: University of North Carolina Press.

Mayr, Ernst. 1988. *Toward a new philosophy of biology: Observations of an evolutionist.* Cambridge, Mass.: Harvard University Press.

Minkoff, Eli C. 1983. *Evolutionary Biology.* Reading, Mass.: Addison-Wesley Publishing Co.

Mor, Ben D. 1997. Peace Initiatives and Public Opinion: The Domestic Context of Conflict Resolution. *Journal of Peace Research* 34, 2 (May): 197–215.

Powlick, Philip J., and Andrew Z. Katz. 1998. Defining the American Public Opinion/Foreign Policy Nexus. *Mershon International Studies Review* 42, 1 (May): 29–61.

Putnam, Robert D. 1988. Diplomacy and Domestic Politics: The Logic of Two-Level Games. *International Organization* 42, 3 (summer): 427–460.

Rasler, Karen. 2001. Political Shock and the Deescalation of Protracted Conflicts: The Israeli-Palestinian Case. In William R. Thompson, ed. *Evolutionary interpretations of world politics.* New York and London: Routledge, pp. 240–60.

Roett, Riordan, and Richard Scott Sacks. 1991. *Paraguay: The Personalist legacy.* Boulder, Col.: Westview Press.

Rout, Leslie B., Jr. 1970. *Politics of the Chaco peace conference 1935–1939.* Austin: University of Texas Press.

Sowers, Thomas, and Paul R. Hensel. 1997. Parity, Disputed Issues, and the Evolution of Interstate Rivalry. Paper presented at the Annual Meeting of the Peace Science Society (International), Indianapolis, November 1997.

Stimson, James A. 1991. *Public opinion in America: Moods, cycles, and swings.* Boulder, Col.: Westview Press.

Thompson, William R. 2001. Expectancy Theory, Strategic Rivalry Deescalation and the Evolution of the Sino-Soviet Case. In William R. Thompson, ed. *Evolutionary interpretation of world politics.* New York and London: Routledge, pp. 218–39.

Vasquez, John A. 1993. *The War puzzle.* Cambridge, U.K.: Cambridge University Press.

Warren, Harris Gaylord. 1985. *Rebirth of the Paraguayan republic: The First Colorado era, 1878–1904.* Pittsburgh: University of Pittsburgh Press.

———. 1949. *Paraguay: An Informal history.* Norman: University of Oklahoma Press.

West-Eberhard, Mary Jane. 1992. Adaptation: Current Usages. In E. F. Keller and E. A. Lloyd, eds. *Keywords in evolutionary biology.* Cambridge, Mass.: Harvard University Press, pp. 13–18.

chapter 8

Expectancy Theory, Strategic Rivalry Deescalation, and the Evolution of the Sino-Soviet Case

William R. Thompson

Interstate disputes come and go. When they are active, we tend to assume that they will go on forever. When they wind down in a seemingly abrupt fashion, we are often surprised. When they are inactive, we tend to ignore them. These three tendencies suggest some awkwardness at conceptualizing disputes as ongoing processes. We argue a great deal about why they come about (both specifically and in general) and how many may be in existence at any point in time. But we have been slow to look upon them as phenomena that have life cycles. They are relationships that are born, wax and wane, sometimes die, or become something else. Put another way, they evolve—presumably in ways that can be analyzed systematically.

One useful prerequisite of systematic analysis is theory development. In this chapter a theory of rivalry deescalation and termination is constructed and illustrated by a discussion of the Sino-Soviet dispute. An illustration falls short of a test of the theory. The idea is to explore the plausibility and utility of some of the theoretical implications in a concrete context. If the theory has no applicability to the Sino-Soviet case, the illustration should provide a very quick reality check. More likely than a complete failure, however, is an outcome in which the case sheds some light on how useful the theory is and whether it seems advisable to proceed to more rigorous examinations with more cases.

Moreover, the theory developed in this chapter is expected to do double duty. Its second mission is to contribute to a bridging of the environment-agent gap in evolutionary perspectives in international relations. The development of an evolutionary paradigm pertaining to such subjects as war and peace, international political economy, and change and complexity is a welcome departure from often sterile debates between realists and liberals. Nonetheless, the attractiveness of evolutionary interpretations will be highly constricted if we cannot break free of the biology-inspired notion that agents simply respond to environmental change through blind mutation, variable rates of reproductive success, and natural selection. What may work for one discipline is not necessarily helpful to others without suitable translation.

For evolutionary perspectives to be successful in international relations (IR), we need to be able to deal with evolution at several levels of analysis and temporal frames. The applicability of evolutionary themes to change at the system level over the long term may be most obvious. Less obvious is how one should go about analyzing decision-makers operating in the short term. The expectancy theory developed in this chapter is one possible way to tackle shorter-term phenomena at the decision-maker level. It also appears to have the capability to serve as both a foundation and bridge to longer-term movements and evolutionary change. While the theory has been constructed specifically to deal with the problem of rivalry deescalation, it is not without some potential for more general statements about international (and domestic) politics.

The strategy that will be pursued in this chapter has three components. After a brief discussion of the nature of the rivalry deescalation problem, an expectancy theory is advanced as a set of assumptions and propositions, accompanied by a set of derived hypotheses. The hypotheses are applied to the Sino-Soviet case with a primary focus on events in the 1970s, 1980s, and 1990s. The main idea is not to create a novel explanation of the Sino-Soviet case as much as it is to take what we think we know about this case and assess the extent to which an expectancy theory is helpful in structuring an explanation. Following an answer to this question, the third section of the chapter proceeds to offer a consideration of some of the implications of this analysis for the development of an evolutionary paradigm in IR.

THE RIVALRY DEESCALATION PROBLEM

Strategic rivalries involve the identification of competitors as unusually menacing because they invoke some potential for military threat that is not associated with other competitors (Thompson 1998). Once they begin, they tend to have long lives, but they do not persist infinitely. Rivalries die. Frequently, they do so in such a drawn-out fashion that it is difficult to pin down the exact date of termination. Nevertheless, we can usually tell which ones are alive and which ones are dead or dormant. The question to be addressed here is why do some rivalries become extinct or at least experience significant deescalation?

The basic paradigmatic perspective adopted in this chapter is an evolutionary one. By this I mean that I begin with the assumption that why change occurs is and should be a primary focus and problematique. Following Modelski's (1996) lead somewhat loosely, it is changes in strategies that provide a concrete focus.[1] Moreover, strategies evolve as a consequence of selection processes operating in a context characterized by variety. Selected strategies do not necessarily improve anything. They need not be progressive. Nor are they necessarily the "best" option from the variety menu. Whether change is gradual or abrupt is an empirical question. The answer is likely to be some of both.

But if strategies are the unit of analysis, someone must devise and adopt them. Decision-makers cannot grow longer beaks or develop better night vision through sexual reproduction. They must choose change in strategies in some sense—even if they do not always know exactly what they are doing when they do it. That means that we need some linkage between individuals and strategy choices. Following Adler (1991a, 1991b) and Young (1998), individual expectations link to analytical choice.[2] This choice places some emphasis on the cognitive level but it does not focus exclusively on that level of analysis. Why people change their minds is certainly an interesting and challenging question. But it is also one that will be left in the spirit of divisions of labor to other analysts better equipped to deal with these complexities (see, for example, the literature on changes in cognitive schema cited in Stein 1995). The question here is not so much why some individuals change their minds about strategies, rather, the specific question is why are some rivalries deescalated? Also, why do decision-makers sometimes move to defuse long-standing conflictual relations with a major adversary? Why do they change their strategies toward enemies?

Whatever cognitive processes are involved are, for the most part, blackboxed. It is assumed that expectations are subject to considerable inertia but why that is the case is not something that will be pursued theoretically or empirically. The preferred question is what environmental changes (externally and internally) are required to initiate the search for different strategies? The main answer consists of a combination of certain types of environmental shock(s) and policy entrepreneurs with adequate control over their own governments, in conjunction with elements of reciprocity and reinforcement. Such an approach is not all that substantively novel in the area of rivalry deescalation. While no conscious effort was made to synthesize the existing literature, the elements of shock + policy entrepreneur + reciprocity + reinforcement do not represent marked substantive departures from earlier foci. What is different is their bundling into one theory. Other analysts have emphasized some of the elements or at least one, but earlier approaches have normally taken the form of isolated hypotheses.

Space considerations preclude an extensive literature review. Two of the stronger earlier efforts will have to suffice as examples.[3] Much of Armstrong's (1993) argument relates to tactics to be employed in negotiations once two rivals begin to explore the prospect of rapprochement. Negotiation tactics are not emphasized in the deescalation theory that is developed in this chapter, but Armstrong (1993: 134) does begin his five proposition model with two generalizations about the "international circumstances" that encourage both sides to come to the table in the first place. Improved relations with an adversary are more likely to succeed when the following conditions are present for both governments: (1) the general strategic and/or diplomatic situation threatens to deteriorate and continued hostility obstructs the governments' ability to address the problem, and (2) expectations of the nonviability of the adversary regime have been replaced by expectations of viability for the foreseeable regime.

Note first that Armstrong's emphasis is on the likelihood of rapprochement success whereas the emphasis in this chapter will be on the likelihood of significant rivalry deescalation that may stop short of rapprochement. Significant rivalry deescalation may also be finite in duration. Nevertheless, the first condition relates to environmental deterioration that implies a change in strategies to meet more effectively. While Armstrong focuses on perceptions of impending deterioration, the theory that is developed in this chapter will stress the advent of shocks as a more general conceptualization of environmental deterioration. A second difference is that the shocks must actually occur. The possibility of near future shocks is very difficult to pin down with any precision.

Both of Armstrong's conditions introduce the idea of expectations—albeit not very explicitly. His first condition speaks to expectations of strategic deterioration. His second addresses expectations about an adversary's viability in a context of abandoning earlier hopes that the other side might solve one side's problems by conveniently collapsing. While this factor does appear in some cases, it is not clear that it shows up in enough cases to make it a compelling explanatory element. Still, one could argue that Armstrong's conditions are anchored in decision-maker expectations and that at least one of the two conditions overlaps with the shock component of the expectancy theory.

Another approach is taken by Lebow (1995: 181) who hypothesizes that conciliatory accommodation between two adversarial states is most likely when leaders:

1. are committed to internal reforms that require or are expected to benefit from improved relations with an adversary;
2. recognize that confrontation has been counterproductive in the past; and
3. expect their adversaries to respond positively to conciliatory overtures.

Lebow refers to these conditions as propositions about pathways to accommodation. He believes (1995: 182) that other pathways also exist and suggests that "mutual fear of a third party" and "economic incentives" may also play some role. In a subsequent article (1997: 165) he adds a new condition relating to the domestic feasibility of mobilizing support for conciliatory foreign policy. Moreover, implicit to both of his treatments is a very strong focus on the leaders involved. The ending of the Cold War was very much a Gorbachev story. The deescalation of Egyptian-Israeli tensions was very much a Sadat story, and so on. Yet in both analyses, Lebow (1997: 175) also makes sure to stress that his hypotheses "represent a tentative step toward a more comprehensive theoretical explanation . . . and need to be incorporated into a broader theory that more fully specifies the . . . other conditions. . . ."

The expectancy theory that will be put forward is intended to approximate that broader theory to which Lebow refers, even though it may not be exactly what he had in mind. A variant on his first condition (commitment to domestic reforms) is incorporated as one of several sources of shock—as are his suggestions of third-party threat and economic incentives. His second condition does not appear in the theory in any explicit way (essentially, it is taken for granted that innovative policy entrepreneurs are dissatisfied with the old ways of doing things) but his third condition (expected reciprocity) is one of the main components. The idiosyncratic element of leadership is translated into a strong version of policy entrepreneurship. Finally, his fourth domestic support condition plays the role of one source of continued reinforcement for what is seen as a gradual process of deescalation.

Thus there are a few points that can be made based on this very selective and brief sample of the literature on rivalry deescalation. One is that earlier efforts have been content, for the most part, to advance hypotheses. The need for a broader and more comprehensive treatment has not gone unrecognized. Second, the substantive arguments relied upon in earlier efforts need not be abandoned. No effort need be made to incorporate every possible proposition, but it is quite likely that a more comprehensive theory will overlap substantially with earlier hypotheses. The difference is that the theory needs to tie the components together in some coherent fashion. It also needs to generalize as much as possible the conditions that are thought to influence deescalation efforts. That may mean using different language to convey (and to cover) similar types of behavior as are discussed in earlier propositions. Finally, the Armstrong and Lebow "sample" highlight the standard mode of analysis on rivalry deescalation. Things change in decision-makers' environments that lead them to revise either their view of the adversary or the wisdom of their existing strategy for coping with the adversary. This theme constitutes the core of the expectancy theory developed below. Changing decision-makers' minds is critical and necessary to creating situations in which deescalatory negotiations between rivals can begin. But, it will be argued, these changes are not sufficient to bring about rivalry deescalation

AN EXPECTANCY THEORY
OF RIVALRY DEESCALATION AND TERMINATION

A preliminary step to theory construction is the matter of delineating assumptions, seven need to be articulated at this point. The first one declares a preference for a liberal perspective on state-group interactions. The second assumption eschews a rational cost-benefit calculus. Assumption three takes a position on how rivals are identified. The last four assumptions introduce the roles played by, and the interrelationships between, expectations, strategies, and behavior.

Theory Assumptions:

1. Actors rarely function as unitary decision-makers in pursuit of fixed national interests. Various domestic groups, including important governmental agencies, have different agendas and attempt to influence governmental agendas and behavior. When feasible, groups will seek to capture the government in order to monopolize its agenda and behavior. Government leaders who wish to stay in power must attempt to juggle these internal demands within the context of external demands on governmental behavior. One of the principal ways in which this can be done is to organize and maintain a coalition of domestic groups. Coalition maintenance requires the pursuit of interests and agendas that appeal to the coalition in question. Hence, foreign policy will reflect to variable degrees the identity of the ruling domestic coalition. As the coalition identity undergoes change, so too will the interests and agendas that are pursued.

2. Actors are not hyperational. They operate with imperfect information, have hazy ideas about their own values and preference schedules, and do not necessarily weigh all options and then proceed with the least costly, most advantageous alternative. Instead, foreign policy formulation and execution is likely to be a process of trial-and-error in which policies emerge after a number of experimental probes in different directions. Just which direction will be privileged is not always clear. However, actor leaderships do monitor their environment for threats and opportunities. They also attempt, variably, to respond to perceived changes in threats and opportunities.

3. Actors distinguish other actors into competitor and noncompetitor categories. Competitors are further distinguished according to whether they represent some possibility of physical attack over conflicted interests. While noncompetitors may also be threatening, external competitors that are potential attackers are considered strategic interstate rivals.

4. Actors develop strategies to deal with rivals (either internal or external) on the basis of expectations concerning what other actors are likely to do and what their own capabilities to deal with rivals is likely to be.

5. Expectations are predicated in part on what rivals have done in the past and are currently doing, and in part on what nonrivals have done and are doing. These expectations are not easy to change once developed because people are reluctant to revise cognitive filters for interpreting stimuli.

6. Strategies are plans for coping with adversarial behavior that are developed in response to interpretations of an opponent's behavior, within the context of other environmental considerations (for example, other threats and opportunities, domestic coalition preference schedules, allies, capability calculations, and competing demands for resource allocations).

7. Expectations, strategies, and behavior are not identical phenomena. One does not necessarily translate into another without some distortion but the three should be related via a rough expectation → strategy → behavior causal chain.

The crux of the theory revolves around the assumption that expectations—once formulated—are highly resistant to change. We create these mental filters to economize on processing external stimuli. Individuals are often more likely to disregard or suppress incoming information that conflicts with their beliefs than to alter those beliefs. But, expectations can be changed. Otherwise, old disputes would remain around forever. Something must change in decision-makers' environments in a way that at least some individuals are encouraged to rethink the way they do things. If these individuals are in a position to do something about their proposed innovations in strategy, we may anticipate some movement toward changes in the relationships between rivals. Still, it will take movement on both sides of the relationship, although not necessarily of equal scale, for the movement to be translated *eventually* into a concrete outcome on the order of significant deescalation. The emphasis is on *eventually* since these deescalatory affairs are rarely abrupt phenomena. Expectations are unlikely to change abruptly. There may also be limits to how far expectations about adversaries can change within a specific period of time. It is one thing to downgrade the threatening status of an enemy. It is quite another to begin trusting the former enemy. A policy entrepreneur's monopoly over decision-making is frequently tentative and finite. Environmental conditions that initially facilitated the possibility of deescalation can revert to earlier circumstances that inhibited deescalation. All of these considerations suggest that rivalry termination is apt to be a protracted process—not unlike the protracted nature of the conflict that characterized the rivalry in the first place.

Theory Propositions

1. Actor expectations, strategies, and behavior tend to be characterized by inertia.
2. Expectational and strategic inertia are subjected to repeated shocks of varying magnitude. In the abstract, any shock may be viewed as an opportunity for expectational and strategic revision. However, inertial constraints usually are difficult to overcome. To tip expectations (and thus strategy and behavior) from one established routine to another requires fundamental alterations in expectations. In turn, fundamental alterations are made more probable by major shocks that force actors to reevaluate the accuracy and appropriateness of their existing expectations and associated strategies.
3. The types of shocks that have the most impact are those that either alter how threatening the adversary appears and/or how efficacious one's own side is likely to be in coping with the adversary.
4. The more entrenched the expectations (and the greater the strategic inertia), the greater are the shocks needed to tip expectations in a different direction. No matter how great the shock, though, there may still be variable lags between revisions in "sticky" expectations, strategies, and behavior.
5. Shocks must be interpreted. The same shock may be viewed positively or nega-

tively vis-à-vis prevailing expectations. As a consequence, it is unlikely that shocks are sufficient for expectational revisions. Equally important are changes in actor leaderships (on one side or both) that go beyond mere personnel changes. To be effective, the leadership changes must also remove or neutralize sufficiently governmental and domestic elite opposition to revisions in expectations, strategy, and behavior.

6. Third party pressure for revision may reduce the need for domestic policy entrepreneurship but is unlikely to be successful in the absence of fundamental revisions in expectations and leaderships.

7. A further necessary ingredient in the revision process is some auxiliary expectation that an adversary will reciprocate at some level any initial concessions made as part of an overture toward strategic and behavioral revisions.

8. Once expectations (and strategies and behavior) have tipped from one regime or routine to another (or are in the process of tipping), it cannot be assumed that the new relationship is stable. On the contrary, new relationships emerge haltingly. Constant reinforcement of expectational revisions is necessary to prevent lapses back to the previous relationships still favored by historical conditioning.

This expectancy theory appears to have potential for expansion to other topics that could lead to a variety of hypotheses. In the specific context of rivalry deescalation, the two main hypotheses are:

1. Significant rivalry deescalation and termination (as an instance of mutual strategic revision) requires a combination of:
   a. major shocks,
   b. expectational revision,
   c. domestic policy entrepreneurship with sufficient political control to overcome internal commitments to older strategies,
   d. some level of reciprocity, and
   e. continual reinforcement.

2. Third party pressure can contribute to significant rivalry deescalation but it is neither necessary nor sufficient.

While the expectancy theory can generate several hypotheses, its main derivation can be summarized in the following equation:

$$\text{Deescalation} = \text{Shocks} + \text{Expectancy Revision} + \text{Consolidated Policy Entrepreneurship} + \text{Reciprocity} + \text{Reinforcement}$$

All five may be necessary factors, although it is certainly conceivable that the levels that are manifested will vary from case to case. It is also conceivable that all five are not fully necessary. But of the five factors, only policy entrepreneurship may be dispensable. If shock or expectancy revision are unnecessary, the basic validity and utility of the theoretical apparatus would be jeopardized. It is also difficult to imagine continuing deescalation without some minimal level of reciprocity and reinforcement. At the same time, it is quite clear that none of the five factors is likely to be singularly sufficient.

The main focus is on the relationship between shock and expectancy revision. It is helpful to avoid specifying too narrowly precisely what is viewed as shock. Yet there is no reason to accept any environmental turbulence as likely to have a shocking effect. But some perceived change in the domestic or external environment—usually involving either a significant change in the threatening nature of the enemy and/or the ability to compete with that enemy—can lead to revisions in expectations about a rival. The shocks can also be ignored or interpreted in such a way that they do not lead to changes in expectations. Shocks, then, do not determine psychological revisions. They do increase the probability of revision and, presumably, the greater the shock(s), the greater the probability that some people will *begin to see things differently.*

The emphasis here is on *begin to see things differently.* It would be naive to think that events in the real world lead directly to revolutions in perceptions. More likely is that some events—shocks—have sufficient impact to initiate searches for alternative ways of interpreting the outside world. Those people most affected do not suddenly see what was once black as now white. Rather, they grope about in a process highly familiar to evolutionary arguments as a trial-and-error search for new ways of thinking. There may be some lag, therefore, in the linkage between shock and expectational revisionary outcome.

It is not necessary that everyone alter their expectations about the rival but elites with some degree of access to government decision-making must do so for it to make any difference. Unless the "revisionists" are or develop sufficient control over their own governments, they will be unable to implement the implications of their new way of thinking. Capturing the chief executive position is unlikely to suffice for "sufficient control." It will probably also be necessary to eliminate or neutralize, intentionally or otherwise, significant portions of the bureaucracy committed to the older ways of thinking about rivals. Otherwise, the battle between old and new expectations and strategies within the government is likely to continue. To the extent that it does continue, mixed signals will be sent to the rival that will interfere with successful deescalation.

Some minimal level of reciprocity and reinforcement are facilitative factors that are indispensable. Overtures or concessions made by one side with no appropriate response can not be expected to contribute to a deescalatory process. Continued external reciprocity (beyond being open to an initial step) is critical to reinforcement and continuing deescalation. So, too, is continued internal reinforcement that can evaporate if the policy entrepreneurship disappears, is replaced, or overwhelmed by dissension within the government and prevailing ruling coalition. The point here is that rivalry deescalation is not usually an abrupt process that happens literally overnight. It is more likely to be a lingering or protracted conflict that may even be as protracted as the conflict that it is deescalating. Once deescalation is initiated, there are no guarantees that it will continue. New shocks and expectations, as well as different policy entrepreneurs, can reverse the process, just as dwindling reciprocity and diminishing reinforcement can slow it to a standstill that may also contribute to movement back to earlier expectations and strategies.

THE SINO-SOVIET CASE

The immediate question is whether this perspective helps to account for the ups and downs of Sino-Soviet relations since 1969 when their rift peaked with relatively large scale border clashes. Since that time, China first moved closer to the United States in the 1970s seeking some external protection and then attempted to distance itself from both the Soviet Union and the United States in the 1980s. In the 1990s, China and Russia give the appearance of moving back toward a more cooperative relationship that probably will stop short of recreating the alliance of the early 1950s. During this same period, the Chinese initially upgraded the Soviet Union to the role of its principal rival (supplanting the United States), deescalated its rivalry with the United States, and then proceeded slowly to deescalate its rivalry with the Soviet Union. At the present time, the Soviet Union is no more but then so are the rivalries among the United States, Russia, and China. While it might be most appropriate to tackle the simultaneous deescalation of the U.S.–U.S.S.R., U.S.–China, and China–U.S.S.R. rivalries, the scope of such a task is too great for a single chapter. Focusing on one of the three, the Sino-Soviet rivalry deescalation, will suffice for present purposes. At the same time, the issue of whether these rivalries are dead or simply dormant will also be dodged. It is sufficient that they have deescalated significantly to the point that most observers acknowledge an absence of strategic rivalry existing among them.

The Sino-Soviet dispute has a reasonably long and complicated history. One might easily start with the initial Sino-Russian clashes that date back to Russian expansion into Siberia in the seventeenth century. The Russian encroachments on Chinese territory in the nineteenth century were part of the same historical process. The most recent phase of Sino-Russian conflict dates back to the brief interlude between the late 1940s and 1950s. The alliance of the Soviet Union and China appeared to represent a Eurasian monolith threatening to expand to the west, the east, and the south. In fact, Sino-Soviet cooperation was very short-lived. After the death of Stalin and the emergence of a new Soviet approach to dealing with the west, Mao and China began to distance themselves from the Khruschev-led, Soviet preference for coexistence. On the one hand, the dispute was about Marxist ideology and policy in the East-West struggle, with the Chinese holding out for a harder line. This dimension turned into a competition for leadership within the Communist international system. But it was also about dyadic subordination. The Chinese resented playing the role of the weaker partner. China needed technology, financial assistance, arms, and protection. The Soviet Union was prepared to offer these things but at a price that included acknowledging Soviet superiority in the relationship.

The Chinese began to move away from accepting the Soviet lead after 1956. By the early 1960s, the rift was out in the open. By the end of the 1960s, the probability of war between the two states seemed high. In reaction, the Chinese sought a new relationship with the state that had formerly presided as the principal Chinese adversary, the United States. Still seeking protection, technology, financial assistance, and arms, a Sino-American rapprochement seemed the answer. Such an arrangement served American purposes in Southeast Asia and in terms of its Soviet containment objectives. Yet as the Sino-American courtship seemed to be intensifying, the perceived threat to the Chinese from the Soviet Union was receding. This change facilitated a change in Chinese strategy that involved maintaining some distance from both the United States and the Soviet Union while, at the same time, continuing to negotiate/cooperate with both superpowers on a selective basis.

The Soviet Union appeared to be ready to negotiate at least some of its differences with China, albeit on its own terms, as early as 1969/1970. Several Soviet initiatives were advanced in the form of proposals for a nonaggression pact, presumably with the intention of lessening the high level of threat perceived by Chinese decision-makers. The Chinese remained unresponsive throughout most of the 1970s. Chinese probes toward patching up its differences with the Soviet Union began in 1979 (Chi Su 1993: 49). The initial Soviet response was cautious, preferring to focus first on nonpolitical exchanges of students and delegations. In particular, U.S.S.R. decision-makers were reluctant to discuss what they regarded as third-party situations in Cambodia and Afghanistan while Chinese decision-makers posed these issues as major stumbling blocks (the "Three Obstacles," which included troop-level and boundary concerns along their mutual border) to further progress.

Soviet receptivity began to be manifested more clearly in the early 1980s even though Pi-Ying-hsien (1989b) describes the Brezhnev Tashkent gesture as a compromise between hard-liners and moderates. After the ascension of Gorbachev in 1985, Soviet receptivity became even more clear. By 1985, the Chinese were also wavering a bit on the extent to which the Three Obstacles were genuine barriers. Alternatively put, the Chinese had signaled that compromise on one of the three, the Cambodian issue, might suffice. Yet the two states seemed unable to come to terms until 1989—a full decade after the initiation of overtures toward deescalation from both sides. Why did the process take so long to reach fruition when both sides appeared interested in reaching some form of accommodation?

Table 8.1 provides some sense of the flow of interaction between the Chinese and the Soviets across three decades. The reported interactions do not represent a systematic inventory of interactions. Instead, they constitute events reported in the literature on the Sino-Soviet rapprochement and thus should be viewed as a form of purposive sampling undertaken by informed specialists on the subject.

The main question to address is the relation between shocks and changes in expectations. Table 8.2 summarizes the seven hypothesized shocks ranging from external threat perceptions to military defeat. As many as four are found in the Sino-Soviet case. The Chinese downgraded their perceptions of the likelihood of a Soviet military attack in 1979 prior to the Chinese overtures for reduced tensions (Shambaugh 1994: 204 and Robinson 1994: 572, although Nelson 1989: 139 says the downgrading came later). Apparently, the argument was that if the Soviets were going to attack, they would have done so already. Since they had not done so, the probability of an attack was increasingly less likely. It is not clear that Soviet decision-makers ever anticipated a Chinese attack per se. Their security concerns were always more long term in anticipation of increased conflict with a large Chinese population needing more space in northeast Asia and/or attempting to regain northern territory once part of the Chinese Empire. These concerns do not appear to have completely vanished from the Russian policy scene.

The other three shocks are closely interrelated. Both sides moved toward a posture that emphasized the need for a peaceful external environment while maximal energies could be focused on domestic reforms and rebuilding. China moved first, in 1979, as articulated in Deng's Four Modernizations. The Soviet Union followed after 1985 with Gorbachev's perestroika movement. This convergence (Legvold 1993: 81) comes under the "domestic preferences emphasizing domestic concerns" heading.

While this convergence was crucial, it also had two implications. Soviet perestroika stemmed from an interpretation that Soviet capabilities had fallen behind those of the West and that radical reform was necessary to stay in the competition. The Chinese agreed with this assessment. At one point, when their own sense of Soviet threat was acute, Chinese decision-makers portrayed the Soviet Union as surpassing U.S. capabilities. In the 1980s, that assessment was scaled back to a view that the United States had renewed its own capabilities and had pulled ahead (Dittmer 1992: 231). A weakened Soviet Union not only meant less threat to China, it also meant that Chinese capabilities relative to those of the Soviet Union were no longer so asymmetrical. Chinese weakness was reduced by Soviet weakness. To the extent that Chinese decision-makers had been reluctant to negotiate with the Soviet Union prior to 1979 from a position of relative dyadic weakness (see Chi Su 1993: 49 and Goldstein 1994: 241), this attribute of the bargaining situation had been altered substantially (that is, a "change in relative economic capabilities").

Table 8.1 Selected Sino-Soviet Interactions, 1960s–1990s

Dates	Venue	Outcome
2–8/1964	border talks in Beijing	No agreement
6/1969		U.S.S.R. proposes no first attack policy
6–8/1969	river navig. commission	Some agreement
10–12/1969	border talks in Beijing	No agreement
1–4/1970	border talks in Beijing	U.S.S.R. conciliatory; no agreement
2/1970		U.S.S.R. proposes both sides make no territorial claims and accept status quo
5/1970	river navig. commission	Some agreement
1–summer/1971	border talks in Beijing	U.S.S.R. offers concessions, including nonaggression pact; no agreement
12/1971–3/1972	river navig. commission	No agreement
3–7/1972	border talks in Beijing	No agreement
1–3/1973	river navig. commission	No agreement
3–6/1973	border talks in Beijing	U.S.S.R. offers nonaggression pact again; no agreement
2–3/1974	river navig. commission	No agreement
6–8/1974	border talks in Beijing	China conciliatory if U.S.S.R. will agree to mutual withdrawal from disputed areas; no agreement
10/1974		U.S.S.R. offers nonaggression pact again
11/1974		China offers to accept nonaggression pact if coupled to mutual withdrawal from disputed territories
2–5/1975	border talks in Beijing	No agreement
1/1976		Death of Zhou
4/1976		Ouster of Deng Xiaoping
9/1976		Death of Mao
10/1976		Ouster of Gang of Four
11/1976–2/1977	border talks in Beijing	U.S.S.R. conciliatory; no agreement
7/1977		Deng Xiaoping assumes power; talks on river navigation resumed
7–10/1977	river navig. commission	Some agreement
2/1978		U.S.S.R. proposes joint statement of principles
5–6/1978	border talks in Beijing	Agreement to suspend talks
2–3/1979	river navig. commission	Some agreement
4/1979		China proposes general negotiations after declining to renew 1950 alliance
9–11/1979	normalization talks in Moscow normalization	China establishes 3 preconditions/ obstacles to (troop reductions along border, withdrawal from Outer Mongolia, and end support for Vietnam in Cambodia; U.S.S.R. proposes expansion of nonpolitical interactions
3/1980	river navig. commission	No outcome
2–3/1981	river navig. commission	Some agreement
8/1981		U.S.S.R. proposes confidence building measures in Far East to China
9/1981		U.S.S.R. proposes resumption of border talks
12/1981		U.S.S.R. proposes nonpolitical exchanges
2–3/1982	river navig. commission	Some agreement
3/1982		Tashkent speech signaling U.S.S.R. willingness to improve relations

Table 8.1 Selected Sino-Soviet Interactions, 1960s–1990s *(continued)*

Dates	Venue	Outcome
4/1982		Agreement to resume border trade
6/1982		U.S.S.R. pledges no first use of nuclear weapons
7–8/1982		U.S.S.R. proposes resumption of U.S.S.R.-China negotiations without preconditions; China relaxes U.S.S.R. troop withdrawal precondition
10/1982	normalization talks in Beijing	Some agreement on border issues; China expresses Three Obstacles
11/1982		Death of Brezhnev
3/1983	normalization talks in Moscow	U.S.S.R. offers nonaggression pact; China invokes Three Obstacles
10/1983	normalization talks in Beijing	Agree to increase nonpolitical interactions
2/1984		Death of Andropov
3/1984	normalization talks in Moscow	Disagreement focuses on Sino-Vietnamese conflict
10/1984	normalization talks in Beijing	Agree on nonpolitical interactions
3/1985		Death of Chernenko; Gorbachev assumes power
3/1985	normalization talks in Moscow	Little progress
4/1985		China notes that if Three Obstacles too difficult to eliminate at once, U.S.S.R. could start with one (Vietnamese withdrawal from Cambodia)
10/1985	normalization talks in Beijing	Little progress
3/1986	river navig. commission	Some agreement
3–4/1986	normalization talks in Moscow	China reinvokes Three Obstacles but agrees to border talks resumption
7/1986		Vladivostok speech addressing Three Obstacles in conciliatory way; China responds by toning down verbal attacks
10/1986	normalization talks in Beijing	Both sides hint at compromise but deadlock on Cambodian issue
4/1987	normalization talks in Moscow	Agree on consular arrangement
10/1987	normalization talks in Beijing	No agreement on Cambodian issue
1/1988	normalization talks in Moscow	Begin discussion of troop withdrawals from border
8–9/1988	normalization talks in Beijing	Some agreement on Cambodian issue
9/1988		Kranoyarsk speech—U.S.S.R. states prepared to accept confidence building and other arrangements and discussions
2/1989		China compromises on Cambodian issue; Cessation of aid to Vietnam no longer demanded
4/1989		Vietnam announces intention to withdraw from Cambodia
5/1989	summit meeting in Beijing	Formalize end of Sino-Soviet dispute
4/1990	summit meeting in Moscow	Agree on border demilitarization
12/1992	summit meeting	Thirteen agreements signed
9/1994	summit meeting in Moscow	"Constructive Partnership" rhetoric; agree to not target nuclear weapons on each other
4/1996	summit meeting	"Strategic Partnership" rhetoric
4/1997		Agreement on demilitarization

Sources: based primarily on information found in Hart (1987) and Dittmer (1992) and supplemented by Pi-Ying-hsien (1989a, 1989b); Nelson (1989); Legvold (1993); Ellison (1993); Yahuda (1993); Chi Su (1993); Tow (1994); Anderson (1997); Harada (1997).

Table 8.2 Hypothesized Sources of Shocks to Existing Expectations

Significant changes in:

1. the perception of external threat(s)

2. adversary leadership and institutions that affect goal conflict

3. domestic preferences that alter the balance in the the attention given domestic and external problems

4. relative economic and other types of capabilities

5. decision-maker experiences with catalytic events

6. external patronage

7. military defeat

Finally, part of the ideological conflict between China and the Soviet Union had been over tactics and strategies concerning East-West relations and domestic economic policies. China under Mao had wanted a harder line to be taken with the West than Soviet ideas about coexistence encouraged. China under Deng sought substantial reform in domestic economic policies. Since the Chinese had worked out a working arrangement with the West on their own and since the Soviets were moving toward domestic reforms that were not unlike those being pursued in China, Sino-Soviet disputes over internal and external doctrine had been ameliorated considerably. Thus, in a very general sense, changes had occurred in "adversarial leadership and institutions that reduced goal conflict."

Four shocks may seem to be overdetermining the outcome. Interestingly, though, they were less than sufficient. Policy entrepreneurs on both sides were needed (Deng and Gorbachev)—a subject to which we will return shortly. More than just minimal reciprocity was also needed. The Soviet Union had begun to address the Three Obstacles raised by the Chinese as necessary for more cooperative relations. Soviet troops were being withdrawn from the border with China and disagreements about boundaries were being resolved. Nevertheless, some movement on the Kampuchean issue was needed and eventually forthcoming in 1989 more or less coterminously with the admission of Soviet failure in Afghanistan. Shortly after the Chinese learned that the Vietnamese would be withdrawing from Cambodia, the Sino-Soviet rift was declared dead in a Beijing summit meeting between the two former disputants.

One observation that comes across very clearly in scanning the interaction flow is that mere changes in policy entrepreneurs have not been sufficient in altering the Sino-Soviet relationship. Zhou, Mao, Deng, Brezhnev, Andropov, Cherneko, and Gorbachev had come and gone since the mid-1970s. The Soviets thought the death of Mao might facilitate the quick restoration of good relations between the two states (Ellison 1993: 96), but it did not. Andropov and Gorbachev were thought to be especially open to accommodating Chinese demands but neither were immediately successful. Deng also pursued some form of deescalation with the Soviets but success eluded him for a number of years.

On the contrary, leadership changes may have delayed a Sino-Soviet accommodation almost as much as they contributed to change. The Soviet Union experienced several consecutive changes in leadership between 1982 and 1985 that could not have been conducive to negotiating a higher level of cooperation or a change in the relationship. While state funerals offered opportunities for low-key negotiations, they also suggested high levels of uncertainty about the likely direction of future policies. One important reason is traceable to the lag between assuming and consolidating power. Deng assumed power in 1977 but was not in a position to make overtures to the Soviet Union until 1979. Similarly, Gorbachev came to power in 1985 but did not make his concessionary bid toward China until the following year. Both leaders first had to purge domestic sources of resistance to their proposed changes in policy (on Gorbachev's purges, see Chi Su 1993: 53). Both were ultimately successful in doing so but not to the point where people wedded to older ways of doing things could return to power in subsequent years. Such consolidation struggles tend to be ongoing processes—as opposed to a one-time suppression of domestic opposition. They can create windows of opportunity for dramatic changes, but not indefinitely. If the deescalation process stalls or other shocks occur, the windows can close as positions of influence are resumed by people associated with older ways of doing things.

The role of continued reinforcement is also underscored by the Sino-Soviet, now Russian case. The Soviet Union treated the Tianamen Square massacre very gingerly. Both the collapse of the Soviet Union and the subsequent failed attempt to restore it might have altered the strategic environment sufficiently to derail the deescalation of tensions between the two states. Table 8.1 suggests that this has not happened yet. While there appear to be reservations on both sides about how far to push their reconciliation (Goldstein 1994: 224; Anderson 1997), the summitry rhetoric indicates that the rift has not reemerged and that, verbally at least, the relationship between the two states has become more cooperative in the 1990s, rather than less.

There is more than mere reinforcement going on here. The other factors, especially the effects of earlier shocks and policy entrepreneurship, are still influencing the relationship. Neither side has seen any reason to upgrade the perceived threat emanating from their former opponent. Both sides have increased reason to cooperate and perhaps to collude in opposition to U.S. policy in Asia (Nelson 1989: 131; Legvold 1993: 77; Ellison 1993: 101). Moreover, the former asymmetry between the Soviet Union and China has not returned as might have been the case if Russia had been able to reconstruct a successful political-economic-military foundation for great power in foreign affairs. This has yet to happen. Both sides continue to value a relatively peaceful external environment so that attention can be focused on domestic problems. Both sides also benefit from their increased economic and military interactions—another side of the reinforcement coin.

In accordance with the expectancy theory, then, the confluence of multiple factors (shocks, expectation revision, policy entrepreneurship, reciprocity, and reinforcement) were necessary to tip the Sino-Soviet relationship from one of intense conflict to one of at least moderate cooperation. It follows that something on the same order will be required to tip Chinese and Russian expectations, strategies and behavior, back to the types associated with strategic rivalry.

THE EXPECTANCY THEORY AND AN EVOLUTIONARY PERSPECTIVE

Not much has been said explicitly about an evolutionary perspective so far. Where does the expectancy theory fit within an evolutionary perspective? Basically, it is an (and not the) interpretation of microevolutionary learning processes. A dyad at time t is characterized by a relationship described as rivalry that, in turn, is predicated on a mutual set of expectations about one side's rival and the ability to deal with the rival. The consequent rivalry behavior reflects a routine of strategies developed by both sides to deal with the problems posed by their adversary. Given the confluence of shocks, consolidated policy entrepreneurs, reciprocity, and reinforcement, expectational revision is possible and probable. Some change in strategies should follow, although not necessarily immediately. If enough expectational revision and strategic change occurs, the dyad at time t + 1 may either no longer be in a state of rivalry or their rivalry will have been deescalated significantly.

Figure 8.1 should help to clarify how microevolution fits into a macroevolutionary scheme. One begins at the top of the chart with a system encompassing multiple dyads and a population of strategies. For the sake of illustration, let us assume that all dyads are characterized by rivalry relationships and conflictual strategies. These strategies persist and are subject to considerable inertia, which is to say that they will remain conflictual in nature even if modified at the margins by successive decision-makers. The conflictual strategies also diffuse throughout the system. However, since we are assuming that all strategies are conflictual at the outset, diffusion in this context means that they reinforce one another and that new actors introduced into the system are likely to adopt similar strategies.

The second step in Figure 8.1's flow chart is the introduction of innovation to the population of strategies. Innovation can be introduced by random mutation or experimentation. From the vantage point of the expectancy theory discussed above, policy entrepreneurs given the right setting carry out policy experimentation or innovation in their respective dyads. As Young (1998) stresses, no one intends to change the macropopulation of strategies. Macrochange hinges on multiple microdecisions. Let us further assume that the innovations lead to more cooperative (as opposed to even more conflictual) strategies and behavior. If so, the population is now characterized by some variation in the types of strategies that are

Figure 8.1 Macroevolutionary Learning Process

Population of strategies subject to inertial persistence and diffusion

x

x

x

Innovation by chance mutation or experimentation

x

x

x

Variation in population

x

x

x

x

Sociopolitical-economic selection processes

x

x   x

x   x

x   x

Persistence	Substitution
of some	of some
strategies	strategies

x   x

x   x

x   x

x x

Evolving population of strategies
subject to inertial persistence and diffusion

Source: based on the discussion in Modelski (1996: 336) with some modification in wording.

prevailing. Variation then creates the opportunity for evolution in the population of strategies. Selection processes (that is, a combination of domestic and international politics in the case of strategic rivalries) will determine which strategies persist and which ones are substituted. Assuming some substitution, the strategy population (after innovation, variation, and selection) will have experienced change. It will have evolved in some respect. In terms of the conflict/cooperation dichotomy that we have been using as an example, the population will be more cooperative at time $t+1$ than it was at time t. The opportunity for genuine diffusion, given the creation of variation, is thus greater. Conflictual dyads "may choose," again given the appropriate theoretical setting, to emulate the newly cooperative dyads.

The real world, of course, is more complicated than the illustration provided. In a world of literally thousands of dyads, a change in one dyad might not make much difference to the overall population of strategies. Then again, it depends on which dyads change (evolve). The Sino-Soviet(Russian) case is a good example. All dyads are not of equal weight in shaping the landscape of international politics. Imagine a landscape characterized by a collection of mountains, hills, and bumps. Most interstate dyads can be compared to the bumps. A few are hills. A very select few constitute the mountains of international politics. By global standards, there may be some reason to question whether the Sino-Soviet case was a mountain. It certainly was not the tallest mountain in the post-World War II landscape. But the Sino-Soviet dyad was certainly more than a bump and probably more than a hill. By Asian standards (as opposed to global standards), it was clearly a mountain—just as the Russo-Chinese relationship remains one of several mountains in the Asian international political landscape.

Figure 8.2 shows some of the reasons why this is the case. The Sino-Soviet rivalry had importance because of the large populations and military capability of the two states involved. But the rivalry also had importance because it was interdependent with a wider set of rivalries and relationships. How the Soviet Union (Russia) related(s) to China and vice versa has implications for a number of other dyads. It certainly mattered to the most important major power triangle (the United States, the Soviet Union, and China). Just how it mattered, and whether it still matters, is the subject of debate. Yet Soviet-American detente first encouraged Chinese conflict with the Soviet Union and then encouraged Chinese rapprochement with the United States. Ironically, it may later have also encouraged the deescalation of Sino-Soviet rivalry.

However the major power triangle works (has worked), it is clear that Sino-Soviet(Russian) conflict influences the way in which Chinese-Vietnamese and Sino-Indian rivalries operate. Without Soviet/Russian support, Vietnam and India

Figure 8.2 Selected Rivalry Linkages

```
                              (N. KOREA-S. KOREA)
          AFGHANISTAN                  x
IRAN ---- PAKISTAN                     x
                                       x
               x          SOVIET UNION x
               x          (RUSSIA) xxxxxxxxxxxxxxxxxxxxxxx UNITED
               x                   x                      STATES
               x                   x
               x                   x
               x                   x
       INDIA xxxxxxxxxxxxxxxxxxxx CHINA xxxxxxxx TAIWAN
                                   x
                                   x
                                   x
                                   x
          THAILAND xxxxxxxxxxxxxxxxxxxxxxxxx VIETNAM
```

have demonstrated less overt hostility toward China. The collapse of the Soviet Union had to have been a shock for Vietnamese and Indian decision-makers. These altered relationships could also be expected to have consequences for rivalries "once removed," as in the cases of Vietnam-Thailand and India-Pakistan. Other East Asian rivalries, China-Taiwan and the two Koreas, and non-rivalries, China-Japan and Russia-Japan, should also be expected to feel the reverberations of the change in the landscape (the reduction of the Sino-Soviet(Russian) mountain). And since the collapse of the Soviet Union was closely related to Afghani turmoil, it is not too far fetched to relate the deescalation of Sino-Soviet rivalry, albeit indirectly, to the former rivalry between Pakistan and Afghanistan and perhaps the incipient one between Pakistan and Iran.

The Sino-Soviet rivalry was not your average run-of-the-mill protracted conflict. It had and continues to have implications for relationships in the Asian major power triangle, as well as for relationships in Northeast, Southeast (both the continental and the maritime subregions), and South Asia. No doubt one could make a case for extending the reach of the rivalry to the African continent as well. The deescalation of the Sino-Soviet rivalry had significant reverberations throughout the system not unlike if not quite on the same order as the deescalation of the Soviet-American rivalry.

Returning to the abstract population of strategies, some strategy substitutions have more weight than others in landscapes characterized by highly uneven topographies. In the case of strategic interstate rivalries, the course of the contemporary evolutionary pattern has substitution outgaining persistence. The population of strategies in world politics, as a consequence, is becoming more cooperative. However, from an evolutionary perspective, one must be cautious about projecting this trend into the future. As the case of the Sino-Soviet(Russian) dyad suggests, the rivalry mountains are eroding—but given the right (wrong) conditions, some rebuilding is not inconceivable. Perhaps a better analogy is the movement of glaciers forward and back depending on average temperatures. As temperatures rise, the glaciers recede and life becomes more pleasant in areas that were once frozen. We can easily equate warm and cold temperatures with cooperation and conflict, respectively. The analogy comes naturally because we are already in the habit of making this exact same analogy on an everyday basis. What we cannot predict with any certainty is whether the temperatures will continue to rise—nor whether they will continue to rise linearly or spasmodically.

Nonetheless, the population of strategies in world politics does appear to be evolving toward more cooperative strategies. A theoretical analysis of the Sino-Soviet rivalry deescalation suggests one way in which microevolution at the dyadic level contributes to macroevolution at the population (world) level. Still, a case study can only be suggestive. Many more cases and more rigorous examinations will be required to assess the utility of the expectancy theory in explaining the drift away from conflict and rivalry and toward variable degrees of cooperation.

NOTES

My thanks to Ned Lebow for comments on an earlier version of this chapter.
1. Modelski's (1996) treatment is dedicated exclusively to global politics, which requires some adjustments for more general applicability.
2. Less explicitly, one might include Jervis (1997) in this group as well. A more overt linkage can be made to Maoz and Mor (1998).
3. Other pertinent analyses on rivalry termination include, but are not limited to, Rock (1989); Goertz and Diehl (1995); Bennett (1996 1997 1998); Ganguly (1997); Sommer (1997); and Diehl and Goertz (2000). All of these studies also include some of the elements represented in the expectancy theory.

REFERENCES

Adler, Emanuel. 1991a. Cognitive Evolution: A Dynamic Approach for the Study of International Relations and Their Progress. In Emanuel Adler and Beverly Crawford, eds. *Progress in postwar international relations* (New York: Columbia University Press).
———. 1991b. Seasons of Peace: Progress in Postwar International Security. In Emanuel Adler and Beverly Crawford, eds. *Progress in postwar international relations* (New York: Columbia University Press).
Anderson, Jennifer. 1997. *The Limits of Sino-Russian strategic partnership.* Adelphi Paper 315. New York: Oxford University Press.
Armstrong, Tony. 1993. *Breaking the ice: Rapprochement between East and West Germany, the United States and China, and Israel and Egypt.* Washington, D.C.: U.S. Institute of Peace.
Bennett, Scott D.. 1996. Security, Bargaining and the End of Interstate Rivalry. *International Studies Quarterly* 40: 157–84.
———. 1997. Democracy, Regime Change and Rivalry Termination. *International Interactions* 22: 369–97.
———. 1998. Integrating and Testing Models of Rivalry Termination. *American Journal of Political Science* 42: 1200–32.
Chi Su. 1993. The Strategic Triangle and China's Soviet Policy. In Robert S. Ross, ed. *China, the United States, and the Soviet Union: Tripolarity and policy making in the cold war.* Armonk, N.Y.: M.E. Sharpe.
Diehl, Paul and Gary Goertz. 2000. *War and peace in international rivalry.* Ann Arbor, Mich.: University of Michigan Press.
Dittmer, Lowell. 1992. *Sino-Soviet normalization and its international implications 1945–1990.* Seattle: University of Washington Press.
Ellison, Herbert J.. 1993. Soviet-Chinese Relations: The Experience of Two Decades. In Robert S. Ross, ed. *China, the United States, and the Soviet Union: Tripolarity and policy making in the cold war.* Armonk, N.Y.: M.E. Sharpe.
Ganguly, Sumit. 1997. War and Conflict Between India and Pakistan: Revisiting the Pacifying Power of Democracy. In Miriam F. Elman, ed. *Paths to power: Is Democracy the answer?* Cambridge, Mass.: MIT Press.
Goertz, Gary and Paul Diehl. 1995. The Initiation and Termination of Enduring Rivalries: The Impact of Political Shocks. *American Journal of Political Science* 39: 30–52.
Goldstein, Steven M. 1994. Nationalism and Internationalism: Sino-Soviet Relations. In Thomas W. Robinson and David Shambaugh, eds. *Chinese foreign policy: Theory and practice.* Oxford: Clarendon Press.
Harada, Chikahito. 1997. *Russia and North-east Asia.* Adelphi Paper 310. Oxford: Oxford University Press.

Hart, Thomas G. 1987. *Sino-Soviet Relations: Re-examining the prospects for normalization*. Brookfield, Vt.: Gower.

Jervis, Robert. 1997. *System affects: Complexity in political and social life*. Princeton, NJ: Princeton University Press.

Lebow, Richard Ned. 1995. The Search for Accommodation: Gorbachev in Comparative Perspective. In Richard Ned Lebow and Thomas Risse-Kappen, eds. *International relations theory and the end of the cold war*. New York: Columbia University Press.

———. 1997. Transitions and Transformations: Building International Cooperation. *Security Studies* 6: 154–79.

Legvold, Robert. 1993. Sino-Soviet Relations: the American Factor. In Robert S. Ross, ed. *China, the United States, and the Soviet Union: Tripolarity and policy making in the cold war*. Armonk, N.Y.: M.E. Sharpe.

Maoz, Zeev and Ben D. Mor. 1998. Learning, Preference Change, and the Evolution of Enduring Rivalries. In Paul Diehl, ed. *The Dynamics of enduring rivalries*. Urbana: University of Illinois Press.

Modelski, George. 1996. Evolutionary Paradigm for Global Politics. *International Studies Quarterly* 40: 321–42.

Nelson, Harvey W. 1989. *Power and insecurity: Beijing, Moscow, and Washington 1949–1988*. Boulder, Colo.: Lynne Rienner.

Pi-Ying-hsien. 1989a. Normalization of Peking-Moscow Relations: The Process and Prospects. In David S. Chou, ed. *Peking's foreign policy in the 1980s*. Taipei, Taiwan: Institute of International Relations, National Chengchi University.

———. 1989b. Peking-Moscow Relations Since Gorbachev. In David S. Chou, ed. *Peking's foreign policy in the 1980s*. Taipei, Taiwan: Institute of International Relations, National Chengchi University.

Robinson, Thomas W. 1994. Chinese Foreign Policy from the 1940s to the 1990s. In Thomas W. Robinson and David Shambaugh, eds. *Chinese foreign policy: Theory and practice*. Oxford: Clarendon Press.

Rock, Stephen R. 1989. *Why peace breaks out: Great power rapprochement in historical perspective*. Chapel Hill: University of North Carolina Press.

Shambaugh, David. 1994. Patterns of Interaction in Sino-American Relations. In Thomas W. Robinson and David Shambaugh, eds. *Chinese foreign policy: Theory and practice*. Oxford: Clarendon Press.

Sommer, Henrik. 1997. Rivals at Risk?: Democratization and Interstate Rivalry. In Gerald Schneider and Patricia Weitsman, eds. *Enforcing cooperation: Risky states and the intergovernmental management of conflict*. London: Macmillan.

Stein, Janice Gross. 1995. Political Learning by Doing: Gorbachev as Uncommitted Thinker and Motivated Learner. In Richard Ned Lebow and Thomas Risse-Kappen, eds. *International relations theory and the end of the cold war*. New York: Columbia University Press.

Thompson, William R., ed. 1998. *Great power rivalries*. Columbia: University of South Carolina Press.

Tow, William T. 1994. China and the International Strategic System. In Thomas W. Robinson and David Shambaugh, eds. *Chinese foreign policy: Theory and practice*. Oxford: Clarendon Press.

Yahuda, Michael B. 1993. The Significance of Tripolarity in China's Policy Toward the United States Since 1972. In Robert S. Ross, ed. *China, the United States, and the Soviet Union: Tripolarity and policy making in the cold war*. Armonk, N.Y.: M.E. Sharpe.

Young, H. Peyton. 1998. *Individual strategy and social structure: An Evolutionary theory of institutions*. Princeton, N.J.: Princeton University Press.

chapter 9

Political Shocks and the Deescalation of Protracted Conflicts
The Israeli-Palestinian Case

Karen A. Rasler

INTRODUCTION

Students of conflict resolution maintain that the deescalation of protracted conflicts ultimately depends on conducive background conditions that encourage adversaries to believe in settlement. Shifts in these background conditions create moments of opportunities or "ripeness" when peace-making efforts are likely to have favorable outcomes. Table 9.1 provides a list of the many factors that scholars have linked to the deescalation process. It shows that deescalation may arise from domestic conditions, international affairs, and the relations between the adversaries (Kriesberg 1991).

Past research indicates, however, that there is no simple direct relationship between any of these factors and the termination of protracted conflict across many domains (Licklider 1993: 303). All of these variables have different sorts of impacts under different circumstances. Hence, we have no single pattern or theory of conflict resolution. Licklider (1993: 303–04) argues that conflict resolution more likely reflects a set of processes in which there are certain critical-choice points. Decisions at these points form alternative strategies of conflict termination. However, which situations (factors or combination of factors) present critical choice points and why is left unclear.

I propose that an evolutionary framework is best positioned to answer these questions. It offers a viable means of weaving together a wide range of seemingly disconnected variables into a coherent explanation of deescalation. I maintain that protracted conflicts are evolutionary processes that are subject to change in the context of environmental challenges. In other words, protracted conflicts are sustained by the strategies and policies of adversaries and their institutions. Over time, these strategies are reproduced in a routine fashion that produces inertia (Modelski 1996: 333–34).

Protracted conflicts deescalate when adversaries adopt new interpretations, understandings and expectations of their opponents (Adler 1991). When does such innovation occur? I argue that environmental crises are the critical factors in bringing about the realization of other conceivable expectations. Crises threaten

Table 9.1 Conditions that bring about Deescalation in Protracted Conflicts

Hurting stalemates	Zartman & Aurik 1991; Zartman 1993
Promise of requitement or reciprocity	Ward 1982; Touval & Zartman 1985; Goldstein & Freeman 1990; Zartman 1993; Lebow 1995; Rajmaira 1997; Goldstein, et al. 1998.
Extending peace initiatives	Kriesberg 1992
Leadership changes and shifts in the internal distribution of power	Evangelista 1991; Licklider 1993; Bennett 1997; Goertz & Diehl 2000; King 1997; Mendelson 1998
Leadership autonomy	Stein 1993a
Third-party mediation	Touval 1975; Pruitt 1981; Bercovitch, et al. 1991; Bercovitch & Langley 1998; Wall & Lynn 1993; Kriesberg 1998; Hartzell 1999; Regan & Stam 2000
Mutual trust and credible commitments	Kelman 1995; Walter 1999
Organizational failure and learning	Stein 1995
Shifts in the external distribution of power (e.g., military defeats, loss of patronage)	Mitchell 1995; Huth 1996; Kriesberg 1998
Internal economic crises	Stein 1993b; Waterman 1993
New perceived threats to security	Lebow 1995; Thompson 1998

the political survival of actors who, in an effort to secure their positions, question the viability of existing conflict patterns and repertoires of state action. As crises hasten the reevaluation process, actors move from one set of collective understandings to another. If the direction of the shift produces negotiations, these collective understandings will be diffused through diplomacy. That is, leaders will communicate their new understandings to their opponents which, hopefully, reinforces the process of negotiation and conciliation (Adler 1991). Cooperation and deescalation, therefore, are rooted in the strategies of political survival. How, why, and which environmental crises are likely to bring about deescalation is discussed in more detail in the following sections. Afterward, an application of the evolutionary framework is applied to the Israeli-Palestinian case.[1]

THE EVOLUTION OF EXPECTATIONS AND STRATEGIC POLICIES

Protracted conflicts reflect a partial equilibrium system. They exhibit stability over time but during certain periods the possibilities emerge for rapid, dramatic, and nonincremental change in the level and intensity of the conflict. The key property of protracted conflicts is their *inertia*—the point at which the adversaries' expectations and behavior are in equilibrium. In other words, the continuity (or stability) of protracted conflicts reflect the entrenched expectations that each side has of the other in terms of their tactics, strategies, and past actions. This period of stasis is eventually interrupted by shocks or incidents that tip the level and intensity of the protracted conflict into a new direction (for example, escalation or deescalation) (Young 1998: 12–15).[2]

Political shocks are necessary conditions for the initiation and consolidation of deescalation. They are transforming events that cause adversaries to adopt new ways of thinking. Adversaries realize that the strategy they had been pursuing cannot triumph or they cannot gain more by continuing it, and an accommodative strategy promises to offer a better alternative (Kriesberg 1998: 217). Therefore, shocks change the expectations and strategies of the critical participants who then undertake new policies that move intractable conflicts to seemingly less intractable ones.[3]

One last critical issue: shocks are "necessary but not sufficient" triggers for deescalation. They are not "sufficient," because shocks do not always result in initial accommodations, especially if they fail to elicit new ways of thinking in one or both of the adversaries. Moreover, shocks may have long-term impact as a result of their intermediary effects on other internal or external processes that more directly brings about changed expectations. What these shock-induced changes are likely to be are hard to predict given the variety of events and circumstances surrounding protracted conflicts. Hence, it is impossible to predict when and where shocks will lead to political breakthroughs.

CHARACTERISTICS OF POLITICAL SHOCKS

Shocks consists of an event or a short-term chain of events that are potentially major turning points in political behavior.[4] Shocks have both subjective and objective dimensions (Knight 1998). The objective dimensions are the event or series of events that occur abruptly and have the capacity to bring about a change in behavior. The subjective dimensions deal with the orientations, attitudes, or the perceptions of the adversaries involved. Adversaries are unlikely to change their policies unless shocks induce the realization that existing strategies (based on outmoded expectations) are infeasible or potentially disastrous if they continue. Only then does cooperation and compromise become possible.

What events qualify as potential shocks? Unfortunately, the list of possible candidates is long and diverse. However, recent empirical research by political scientists and sociologists on social movements, revolutions, regime transitions, and elite settlements point to the role of certain recurring events: defeat in warfare, economic crises, withdrawal of foreign support, and the loss of societal support for existing policies.

Military Defeats and/or the Withdrawal of Foreign Support

Although these events have typically been associated with revolutionary situtations, state breakdowns, and elite crises (Tilly 1978; Skocpol 1979; Goertz and Diehl

1997, 2000; Goldstone 1991; Oberschall, 1996; Dogan and Higley 1998), they also play a critical role in deescalating protracted conflicts. These events affect the capacity of adversaries to mobilize the necessary resources to sustain protracted conflict. Diminished resources (in terms of economic and/or political support) force parties to reevaluate the conditions under which they are willing to seek an initial agreement (Lichbach 1995: 167–209).

Economic Crises

A sharp deterioration in a country's aggregate economic performance (including the perception that economic conditions will continue to worsen) can threaten the political survival of ruling elites unless they can reverse the situation. Ruling elites, who face challenges from their opposition groups and mobilized publics, are likely to reverse policies that are construed as obstacles to economic recovery (Haggard and Kaufman 1995; Dogan and Higley 1998). Consequently, leaders will reevaluate their willingness to prolong conflicts that drain important societal resources or block needed reforms for long-term economic growth. Stein's (1993b) analysis of the bargaining environment in the 1979 Camp David Accords provides a good example. She argues that acute political and economic problems in both Israel and Egypt (although more intense in Egypt) changed the bargaining strategies of Sadat and Rabin who sought a political agreement that would reduce not just their security threats abroad but would pave the way for more foreign aid and economic liberalization at home.

Loss of Societal Support for Existing Policies

The reason why protracted conflicts last as long as they do is because they are sustained by policy monopolies within one or both of the adversaries (Baumgartner and Jones 1993). Policy monopolies reflect dominant political understandings about a policy issue—in this case the conditions surrounding negotiation with an adversary. They are reinforced by existing institutional structures (which limit access to the policy process) and powerful supporting ideologies that reside within these institutions. These buttressing ideologies are usually connected to core political values that are communicated directly through images and rhetoric to the public. Policy monopolies last until they are supplanted by new political/social movements that are predicted on new ideas that become popular and diffuse throughout the population (Baumgartner and Jones 1993: 6–16). Consequently, internal uprisings, civil strife, or protest cycles (Burton and Higley 1998; McAdam, Tarrow, and Tilly 1997) may reverse policy monopolies by either replacing old institutions and/or elites with new ones or encouraging old elites to reevaluate their modes of thinking. In either case, new expectations emerge that lead to policy changes vis-à-vis the adversary.

Policy Entrepreneurs

Shocks can induce indirect changes as well. Disasters and crises reinforce preexisting perceptions of a problem among elites and the public alike. If people perceive that existing policies are not meeting certain goals, that the costs of these policies are escalating or that they are generating unanticipated negative consequencs, public support for ruling elites and their policy monopolies will erode. Shifts in public opinion, for instance, will produce administrative or legislative turnovers from which policy entrepreneurs are likely to emerge. By their very definition, policy entrepreneurs (nonconformists) bring about the destruction of policy monopolies by hooking solutions to problems, new proposals to political/social movements, and political events to policy problems (Kingdon 1995: 182). They are strategic pioneers, willing to venture into new terrain by pursuing new solutions to old problems.

Yet, entrepreneurs are not just passive actors waiting in the wings for the appropriate constellation of factors to appear. They are proactive; they seize any opportunity to carve out more political space that makes policy changes possible. Shocks present these opportunities, especially if they have produced major structural breakdown, fragmentation, and dissension. Entrepreneurs are then in a position to restructure their political environments in ways that provide them with enough political power to overcome internal commitments to older, more entrenched policy strategies. In short, policy entrepreneurs have to have more than new ideas. They must have the sufficient political resources to support and sustain new strategic overtures toward peace with their adversaries.

AN EMPIRICAL ILLUSTRATION VIA THE ISRAELI-PALESTINIAN CONFLICT

Table 9.2 provides a chronology of the important events from 1974 to 1993 that brought about the 1993 Oslo Accords and the deescalation of the Israeli-Palestinian conflict. It should aid the following discussion.

Palestinian Shocks

The Israeli invasion of Lebanon (1982) and the rebellion within the PLO (1983)
The Palestinian Liberation Organization's (PLO) defeat in the Lebanon War with Israel and the subsequent civil war within the ranks of the PLO changed the PLO's institutions and factions in ways that concentrated more political power in both Arafat and the moderate elements of Fatah. Up until 1982, PLO decisions were made by consensus among a range of PLO factions (ranging from moderate to rejectionist) with autonomous institutional interests, power bases, and ideological affinities. No major concessions could be made that might jeopardize the political position of any faction (especially the rejectionist groups whose leaders had strong

Table 9.2 Israeli-Palestinian De-Escalation Chronology*

November 1974	Arab states at Rabat declare that PLO is the sole representative of the Palestinian people.
September 1978	Egypt and Israel agree on Camp David Accords.
June 1982	Israel invades Lebanon.
August 1982	The PLO evacuates Beirut, Lebanon.
May 1983	Fatah rebellion occurs in Lebanon.
December 1983	Arafat and 4,000 remaining PLO personnel evacuate Tripoli, Lebanon.
February 1985	Jordanian-PLO accord on negotiations with Israel.
December 1987	Intifada (Palestinian uprising) begins.
July 1988	King Hussein announces Jordan's disengagement from the West Bank.
November 1988	PLO declares independent state of Palestine; formally recognizes Israel's right to exist and condemns terrorism.
December 1988	U.S. opens a dialogue with the PLO.
March 1990	National Unity government in Israel falls; a new Likud, right-wing government follows.
January 1991	Persian Gulf War begins.
October 1991	Middle East Conference in Madrid takes place.
June 1992	Rabin and Labor Party defeat Likud in national election.
January 1993	Start of secret negotiations in Oslo, Norway between PLO and private Israeli representatives.
September 1993	PLO and Israel sign the Declaration of Principles in Washington, D.C.

*based partially on Kriesberg's (1998: 191) chronology of events.

ties to radical Arab states). Moreover, Arafat's decisions were influenced by his desire to preserve Palestinian unity and maintain the PLO as the sole representative organization (Sahliyeh 1986: 92).[5]

The Israeli invasion and the forced evacuation of the PLO from Lebanon resulted in the loss by the PLO of its political and military infrastructure that no other Arab country would have permitted to be built. Prior to 1982, the PLO had enormous freedom in Lebanon, operating as a state within a state. But, without Lebanon as a political and military base of operations, the PLO was unable to continue its long held strategy of engaging the Israelis militarily from a contiguous Arab country. It was too unlikely that guerrilla tactics could be used from remote territories in North and South Yemen, Algeria, and Sudan. Therefore, the potential of translating PLO military force into tangible political and bargaining power was remote if nonexistent.

Meanwhile, Arafat and other PLO moderates believed that the Lebanon War demonstrated the futility of armed struggle. They advocated a more aggressive diplomatic posture, intensifying contacts with the West (particularly the United States) while conveying a readiness to recognize Israel's right to exist. Their aim was to faciliate efforts by the West to exert pressure on Israel to make meaningful concessions to the Palestinians (Sahliyeh 1986: 93). These policies polarized political opinion within Fatah and eventually led to full-scale war among Fatah organizations in Lebanon.[6]

Actual fighting broke out between Arafat supporters and opponents in June 1983 with the explicit approval of the Syrians who wanted to eradicate Arafat's military presence in Lebanon altogether. As the fighting continued into the fall of 1983, Arafat's troops lost important strongholds in refugee camps in Syrian-controlled areas. Finally in November Saudi Arabia pressured the Syrians to end the fighting and to allow Arafat and his troops to leave Tripoli peacefully. In December 1983, more than four thousand Arafat supporters were transferred out of Lebanon (Sahliyeh 1986: 160–75).

After Arafat's exile in 1983, three major internal changes occurred within the PLO that produced significant changes in PLO strategy. First, the radical commando groups were removed from Fatah thereby increasing Arafat and Fatah's ability to pursue a diplomatic option while marginalizing Syria's hard-line influence in the process. Second, Arafat's power and influence were consolidated in the 1984 Seventeenth Palestinian National Council (PNC) when moderate elements beat back proposals from radical groups for organizational reforms that would have limited Arafat's authority.[7]

Last but not least, the wishes and interests of the Palestinians in the West Bank and the Gaza Strip were prioritized over Palestinian interests in the Diaspora. These "inside" Palestinians became Arafat's primary constituency. And, since the "inside" Palestinians endorsed territorial compromise with the Israelis, Arafat and the PLO began to adopt an even more flexible foreign policy. At this point, Arafat explicitly broke away from the principle of consensus building in favor of majority rule (Groth 1995; Hassassian 1997).

The Intifada

The Intifada was an internal uprising of Palestinians in the West Bank and the Gaza Strip against Israeli occupation. The campaign of civil disobedience—demonstrations, strikes, tax revolts, and boycotts—was conducted by a broad sector of Palestinian society that included students, teachers, labor unionists, construction workers, shopowners, and farmers as well as the poor and unemployed. The campaign started in December 1987 and was sustained by a highly mobilized public through 1989 (Hunter 1993).

The Intifada imposed on Arafat and the PLO the urgent need for new, decisive actions that reflected the interests of local Palestinians in the West Bank and Gaza who demanded more progress toward negotiations with the Israelis. The PLO leadership was aware that its lack of success could lead to a loss of influence over the territories; more than anything else it feared that Israel and the United States would strike a deal with the inside leaders at the expense of the outside Palestinians (Groth 1995; Muslih 1997).

In order to ensure their control over the territories, Arafat and the mainstream PLO leadership believed that a formal dialogue with the United States was necessary to bring about negotiations with the Israelis. The question was how to overcome U.S. opposition to PLO participation in the peace process. This question became more critical when Jordan announced its formal disengagement from the West Bank—opening up a real possibility that the Israelis might annex the territories unless the PLO took a strong stance quickly (Sayigh 1997: 622–24).

Therefore, at their November 1988 PNC not only did the PLO members announce their formal declation of independence but they approved U.N. Resolutions 242 and 338 and condemned the use of terrorism. This policy committed the PLO to support three major measures: an acceptance of Palestinian borders within Gaza and the West Bank (as opposed to the original pre-1967 borders) as a Palestinian state, the recognition of Israel's right to exist, and a preference for diplomacy, and a peaceful settlement with Israel (rather than an armed struggle) (Muslih 1997: 46–48). One month later and after a more explicit public statement by Arafat supporting these measures, the United States opened a formal dialogue with the PLO (Sayigh 1997: 624).[8]

Shift in Soviet strategic backing
The shift in Soviet support from 1985 to 1993 deprived the PLO of a global ally. Although the Soviets never really had much influence over Fatah or Arafat's policies, they supported the PLO largely because of its competition with the United States in the area (Golan 1997: 124). By the end of the 1980s, however, Gorbachev came to power advocating a new approach, the "de-ideologization of foreign policy," which led to a reduction of Soviet support for national liberation movements in the Third World, including armed struggle and terrorism. Gorbachev argued that it was time to end superpower competition in regional conflicts. In 1988, during Arafat's visit to Moscow, Gorbachev advised Arafat to accept Israel's right to recognition and security, along with the Palestinians' right to self-determination. Gorbachev sent the same message to several other visiting PLO delegations as well (Golan 1997: 126–27).

Nonetheless, the most serious development from the PLO point of view was the warming of relations between Israel and the Soviet Union, in particular the influx of new Jewish immigrants from the Soviet Union. Between 1989 and 1992, 375 thousand immigrants arrived in Israel from the former U.S.S.R. Republics and increased Israel's total population by 7 percent (Fein 1995: 162). The PLO was especially alarmed because the influx of immigrants would lead to massive expropriation of Palestinian lands and a wave of new Jewish settlements in the territories. These developments could only help to consolidate Israel's hold over the territories (Sayigh 1997: 639). The emigration issue dominated PLO-Soviet relations from

1990 to 1993 while PLO officials tried to convince the Soviets that Jewish emigration threatened the peace process and reinforced the hard-line policies of the
Israeli government (for example, Shamir's administration). As the growth of Jewish
settlements increased dramatically during this period, PLO leaders felt enormous
pressure to take decisive actions that would protect not only the "inside" Palestinians but their political legitimacy within the territories (Groth 1995: 25).

The 1990–93 financial crisis
The progress of secret talks between the PLO and Israel at Olso in the summer of
1993 was accompanied by severe financial strain within the PLO. Due to the
PLO's support for Saddam Hussein during the Persian Gulf War, the Gulf Cooperation Council (GCC) states cut aid to the PLO formally in March 1991 but it
began as early as 1990. The PLO budget declined 50 percent, from $320 million in
1990 to $140 million in 1992. The flow of funds to the occupied territories also
plummeted from $120 million in 1990 to $45 million in 1992 (Sayigh 1997: 656).
Meanwhile, the Gulf crisis and wartime curfews from 1990 to 1991 also aggravated
the economic conditions inside the territories: $600,000 million out of an annual
gross national product (GNP) of $1.6 billion was lost. In the spring of 1993, Israeli
border closures following Hamas bombings caused sharp drops in employment and
reduced Palestinian income by $2 million daily (Sayigh 1997: 656).

The deteriorating economic conditions lead to a disagreement between the
PLO and "inside" Palestinians over the next course of action. Local Palestinians
began to establish their own diplomatic connections with the United States and
Israel which were actively soliciting an alternative Palestinian leadership that would
prove to be more flexible. Meanwhile, the PLO faced still more challenges from
Hamas, who remained outside the Fateh framework and portrayed itself as an
alternative representative for a large portion of the Palestinian people. By the
summer of 1991, divisions between Fateh and Hamas were serious enough to provoke a series of clashes between their followers. Arafat feared that without any
progress toward negotiations, Hamas would accelerate its influence in the territories at the expense of the PLO (Abu-Amir 1993: 5–19).

Reluctantly, Arafat allowed PLO officials to accompany an "inside" Palestinian
delegation to the 1991 Madrid Conference and subsequent bilateral negotiations
with the Israelis in Washington, D.C. However, he obstructed and delayed any
agreement not signed directly by the PLO and himself between 1991 and 1993. As
dissension emerged between Arafat and the "inside" Palestinians over the terms of
a peace settlement, Arafat moved aggressively to seal a deal with the Israelis in
secret talks in Oslo (Sayigh 1997: 654–55).

Arafat preferred the talks in Oslo over the Washington, D.C. sessions for two
major reasons. First, the negotiations were purely between pro-Arafat officials and
the Israeli Labor party, ignoring their respective opposition groups and the input
from Arab states and the United States. Lastly, the Oslo negotiations gave the PLO

Israeli recognition as the sole legitimate representative of the Palestinian people (Groth 1995: 59).

The Oslo Accords were eventually signed by the PLO and Israel in a secret meeting on August 20, 1993.[9] Although the PLO was aware of the limitations of the Oslo Accords, it had little choice but to accept them. Its position in the post-Cold War and post-Gulf war era was very much weakened and thus it had consciously come to terms with Israel in order to secure a foothold on Palestinian soil before its regional and international standing eroded any further. The financial crisis, administrative and organizational breakdown, and political dissent during the last two years underscored the precariousness of the PLO environment (Sayigh 1997: 660).

For Arafat, the Declaration of Principles (signed in September 1993) offered two significant strategic advantages: Israeli recognition of the PLO and the guarantee that the PLO would emerge as the sole governing authority in the territories. Arafat was willing to make short-term territorial concessions to Israel and abandon the Palestinian diaspora in order to ensure the PLO's political survival (Sayigh 1997: 660). In the post-Oslo period, the extension of the PLO's influence into the new Palestinian Authority occurred very quickly while local Palestinian leaders and outside Palestinians were either co-opted or marginalized. The result was the consolidation of a neopatrimonial system with Arafat as sole leader (Sayigh 1997: 663).

Arafat as a Policy Entrepreneur

The shocks in 1982 (Israeli invasion), 1983 (Fatah rebellion), 1987 (Intifada) and 1990 to 1991 (changes in Soviet and Arab patronage) provided Arafat with opportunities to consolidate his personal power within the PLO while directing PLO policy toward a negotiated settlement in 1993. Before 1982, the major challenge facing Arafat was to maintain unity among disparate factions and to do so in the presence of constant intervention by one Arab state or another. This gave rise to the politics of consensus rather than majority rule, since the out-voted group could seek external support and threaten the PLO's claim to be the sole representative of all Palestinians (Sayigh 1997: 679).

Consensus politics granted disproportionate influence over decision-making to the smallest group so long as it had a seat on PLO bodies and by extension, to the Arab state backers of proxy groups such as Syrian-sponsored Sa'iqa and Iraqi-sponsored Arab Liberation Front. There was also very little incentive to deepen PLO unity by merging the different factions since each group could lay claim to a share of PLO funds and appointments according to an agreed quota (Sayigh 1997: 679).

The 1982 and 1983 shocks diluted the influence of radical Palestinian leaders who lost their power bases in Lebanon. At that point, Arafat began to weaken his remaining colleagues and potential rivals in order to consolidate his own political position within the PLO. For instance, he concentrated formal authority for a growing number of PLO departments and programs in his own hands, merging the military and finance sections of Fateh and the PLO on the one hand, and duplicating agencies that had not yet come under his control on the other. He also fragmented organizational structures and channels, relying instead on increased distribution of patronage to maintain his personal control (Sayigh 1997: 688). By 1991, all of the PLO instititions will include only those factions that did not participate in the rebellion against Arafat in 1983 (Groth 1995: 79).

During the Intifada in April 1989, Arafat secured the nomination from the PLO Executive Committee and Central Council as president of the recently declared State of Palestine. Although the post had little real political power at the time, later it would enable Arafat to stand above the PLO and Fateh when necessary (as in the case of the Oslo negotiations) and marginalize both structures (Sayigh 1997: 633). Four months later in August 1989 Arafat also consolidated his political control over Fatah by insisting on two new posts—Fatah commander-in-chief and chairperson of Fatah's central committee—to which he was selected. He then acted to dilute the influence of the core founding members of Fatah by expanding the institution's central committee and revolutionary council with a large number of second echelon leaders and middle-ranking cadres dependent on his personal patronage (Sayigh 1997: 633–34).

Meanwhile, Fatah's leadership within the PLO was eroding as Arafat's political influence was increasing. Deaths of key Fatah leaders in 1982, 1988, and 1992 increased the balance of power in Arafat's favor, particularly when they were not replaced by other senior leaders but rather with committees of several individuals who were much easier to manipulate. The remaining core members of Fatah, who had no constituencies of any significance in the territories, were no match for Arafat (Groth 1995: 21).

The financial crisis in 1990 to 1991 weakened the PLO as an organization but strengthened Arafat's personal leadership. In order to meet the exigencies of the crisis, Arafat reduced or slashed budgets for welfare, PLO institutions, armed forces, and diplomatic stations abroad. These policies revoked the social contract between the PLO and their traditional constituencies in Lebanon, Jordan, Algeria, Yemen, and other Arab countries—constituencies that were least likely to approve Arafat's post-1991 policies. Hence, the financial crisis enabled Arafat to complete a process that he had begun in 1982, namely, a restructuring of the PLO's institutions to suit an "occupied territories first" policy (Groth 1995: 75–76).

Israeli Shocks

Intifada and Likud's policy monopoly, 1977–1992
The Intifada did little to change the expectations and strategies of the Israeli government toward the PLO. From 1977 to 1992, the Likud Party had dominated Israel's foreign policy, including the two coalition governments with the Labor

Party from 1984 to 1990. Historically and ideologically, Likud was committed to permanent control over the territories. Although Likud leaders were willing to negotiate the terms of some form of Palestinian autonomy, they were unwilling to cede military control or give up their right to expand Jewish settlements in the area. Likud leaders were also adamant that if negotiations were to occur the discussions would be conducted exclusively with Palestinians from the "inside" territories, not with the PLO or any other delegations from the outside (Barzilai 1996; Telhami 1996).

The political impasse between the Israelis and Palestinians would end eventually but not until the 1992 national election when the Likud Party was defeated by a coalition of Labor and leftist/peace-oriented parties. The outcome in the 1992 national election was not only unanticipated but it was considered a major political turnover (Elazar and Sandler 1995). The Likud Party had dominated the Israeli government since its own upset victory over the Labor Party in the 1977 national elections and established a long policy monopoly over Israeli policy in the territories. Labor's return as the ruling party in the 1992 national elections paved the way for the 1993 Olso Accords. In fact, analysts argue that it was the "sufficient" condition for rapprochement between Israel and the PLO (Telhami 1996; Aronoff and Aronoff 1998).

Changes in Israeli public opinion and the end of Likud's monopoly
There is little doubt that the Intifada had a dovish impact on Israeli public opinion, a development that was carefully observed by the Labor Party but largely ignored by the Likud Party. Survey results (Goldberg, et al. 1991; Arian, et al. 1992; Arian 1996) showed that the Intifada heightened the public's sense of threat and increased popular support for a strong, harsh military response to the uprising. In the long run, however, the uprising had a steady moderating (or dovish) influence on the public's views about the future of the territories (Goldberg, et al. 1991: 5, 58; Arian 1996: 78). For instance, surveys showed that in 1984, only 35 percent of Israelis polled were willing to give up the territories in exchange for peace. By 1993, 54 percent of Israeli respondents were endorsing this position (Arian 1996: 99).

The gradual trend toward conciliation was also evident regarding the public's attitudes on the establishment of a Palestinian state. In 1987, a survey of Israeli citizens showed that 21 percent of the respondents supported a Palestinian state in comparison to 37 percent who favored it in 1994 (Arian 1996: 107). Meanwhile, negotiating with the PLO became a more acceptable option. In 1984, 21 percent of those surveyed supported negotiations, whereas 60 percent favored this option in 1994 (Arian 1996: 107).

Public opinion polls taken in early June 1992 (prior to the national election) showed that significant portions of the Israeli public indicated that the most important issue in choosing a party was its platform on the issues of security and the peace talks. Likud and Labor devoted their main efforts at capturing the votes in the center of the Israeli political spectrum. Unfortunately for Likud, voters evaluated Labor as the party that was most likely to end the Intifada and achieve peace with the Arabs (Arian and Shamir 1995; Shachar and Shamir 1995).[10]

The Labor Party was able to capitalize on the the changing trends in the Israeli electorate because it, too, had been moving in a moderate direction in the 1980s, particularly since the Israeli invasion of Lebanon. One obvious reason for this shift was Labor's attempt to highlight its differences with Likud (Inbar 1991). The dovish tilt in Labor's platform forced the hawkish elements of the party to leave, making room for dovish leaders to move into key leadership positions. Democratic reforms within the party also ensured the arrival of younger, more flexible leaders into important leadership roles (Aronoff and Aronoff 1998).

When the PLO in 1988 announced its formal recognition of Israel's right to exist and its renunciation of terrorism as a policy instrument, Labor leaders began to put greater pressure on Rabin (as Defense Minister) to make territorial concessions, recognize the Palestinian national movement, and be more open to a Palestinian state (Inbar 1991; Aronoff and Aronoff 1998). These policy positions correlated with the increasing trend of public support in 1992 for negotiations with the PLO, participation in an international peace conference, and territorial concessions that might lead to a Palestinian state (Arian 1996). Therefore, Labor was able to win over Likud in 1992 because it had carved out a policy position that was associated more closely with bringing about a peaceful agreement on the Palestinian problem that would ensure security and re-establish warmer relations with the United States

Rabin as a Policy Entrepreneur

Yitzhak Rabin and the Labor Party's electoral victory in June 1992 marked the first time in fifteen years that Likud was completely excluded from power. The public perception of Rabin as a security-minded centrist won him the support of crucial "swing" voters in the middle of the Israeli political spectrum. Rabin ran on a political platform that stressed the theme that Palestinian terrorism did not constitute a threat to the country, but rather was an issue of personal security, which would be enhanced not by fighting the Palestinians but by striking a deal with them (Makovsky 1996: 85).

In September 1993, Rabin negotiated a final deal with the PLO that opposed the basic principles outlined by Menachem Begin (Israeli Prime Minister) and the Likud Party in the 1979 Camp David Accords (for example, territorial withdrawal and recognition of the PLO). Moreover, from 1967 to 1987, Rabin consistently opposed any negotiations with the PLO and the establishment of an independent Palestinian state. He adhered to one particular solution: territorial compromise in the context of an Israeli-Jordanian confederation (Ben-Yehuda 1997: 207). What accounts for his change in thinking?

The Intifada played a significant role in bringing Rabin to the realization that the status quo was untenable (Aronoff 1999; Bar-Simon-Tov 1999). He became convinced that the uprising was being conducted by a politically-aware Palestinian population that was willing to carry out an uncompromising struggle over the long term. He also noticed a trend of increasing Palestinian radicalization and growing support for Islamic fundamentalist organizations. Persuaded that the Intifada was a "continuation of the Israeli-Arab conflict by other means," Rabin argued that a political agreement had to be sought through compromise (Ben-Yehuda 1997: 210).

After his national election victory in 1992, Rabin initially believed that the PLO's political and financial weakness would make it more malleable and enable him to achieve the agreement he had believed possible in 1989—a deal with the Palestinians in the territories rather than with the PLO leadership in Tunis.[11] By early 1993, Rabin concluded that the "inside" Palestinians could and would not act independently of the Tunis-based PLO leadership. He then turned to direct talks with the PLO in Oslo. By this time, Rabin believed that the international and regional changes offered Israel a short-term "window of opportunity" to resolve the core conflicts between Israel and its Arab neighbors. He argued that it was time for Israel to join the international movement toward cooperation and conciliation in order to enhance Israel's long-term security (Makovsky 1996: 112).

Meanwhile, Rabin perceived a new threat emerging in the territories—Hamas. He feared that the balance of power was shifting in favor of the radicals over the PLO, whose organization was bankrupt, financially and morally in comparison. Senior military and domestic intelligence officials repeatedly pointed out that the PLO's institutions were withering, especially in Gaza, while Hamas was stepping in to fill the void. Rabin decided to strike a deal with the PLO who then would have the primary responsiblity of containing the radicals. Any future Israeli withdrawals from the territories would depend on Arafat's ability to ensure Israel's security (Makovsky 1996: 112–13).

In the final analysis, Rabin reached the conclusion that there would neither be a solution to the conflict, and an end to terrorism, nor would security be enhanced without a long-term separation between Israel and a Palestinian entity side by side. Although he did not go so far as to endorse the concept of a Palestinian state explicitly, in private conversations after the accords were signed, Rabin appeared to have accepted such an outcome. Rabin's willingness to accept the risks associated with a Palestinian state that could prove to be destabilizing to both Israel and Jordan was the most significant change in his strategic thinking (Makovsky 1996: 124).

CONCLUSION

We have few studies that examine the transition of protracted conflicts from escalation to deescalation systematically. Of those that have, none have examined it more thoroughly than Kriesberg (1992, 1998). Not unlike the approach herein, Kriesberg (1998) argues that deescalation occurs as a result of changes in the conditions that underlay the emergence of a conflict in the first place and sustained its escalation. He goes on to say, however, that deescalating transformations are long, cumulative processes. They are not brief, clearly delineated events. The shift toward deescalation is produced by pressures building over time. If there are astounding moments of change, they usually follow from many less visible trends (Kriesberg 1998: 190). In short, the deescalation of intractable conflicts is not necessarily the result of immutable, large-scale forces or of the actions of a few brave individuals. Many circumstances need to converge and these must be interpreted in new ways in order for intractable conflicts to move toward deescalation (Kriesberg 1998: 216–17). Only in retrospection can we discern a long-term transformation toward deescalation (Kriesberg 1998: 24).

An evolutionary model would not disagree with many of the points made by Kriesberg (1998). While it would agree that changes in macroconditions must converge with new interpretations, it would not necessarily support the notion that transformations always entail long-term processes or that their effects have to be cumulative over time. On the contrary, change can occur quickly and be observable almost immediately. This is especially the case when environmental crises affect the political survival of policy-makers. In these instances, leaders have strong incentives to change their strategies and policies quickly. Although the shifts in their strategies or policies may not generate immediate outcomes of conflict termination, they can move protracted conflicts in new directions in relatively short periods of time. An evolutionary perspective leaves open the possibilities for short and long-term effects because the analytical effort is not to explain the precise moment at which conflicts end but rather the process by which protracted conflicts eventually end.

On the other hand, an evolutionary model does not have to be so imprecise that it cannot pinpoint moments of change. Political shocks tell us where the important turning points will be; they delineate the moment at which decision-makers are more likely than at any other time to reevaluate their expectations, strategies and policies. Without the environmental challenges that shocks pose, inertia overrides the inclination of decision-makers to pursue new, risky policies that could undermine their positions. Therefore, evolutionary models are indeed historically contingent but they are not so idiosyncratic that we cannot specify generalized patterns of behavior across many varied cases of protracted conflict. How far evolutionary models will take us in understanding the process of deescalation remains to be determined by future research in other cases of protracted conflict.

NOTES

Author's Note: This paper has been funded in part by NSF Grant No. 9511053: Regime-Social Movement Formation, Repression and Protest Waves in the Intifada.

1. A quantitative test of an abbreviated version of the evolutionary model in the Israeli-Palestinian case is conducted by Rasler (2000).

2. Shocks can escalate as well as deescalate protracted conflicts or rivalries. I do not assume, however, that the same variables that generate protracted conflicts will be the same ones that end them.

3. Once initial agreements are made, however, further deescalation is not guaranteed. New post-settlement shocks may either derail the process or reinforce the commitment by elites to abide by the initial accommodations (Burton and Higley, 1998). Consequently, conciliation and cooperation can take years, even generations, before the deescalation process is complete.

4. Shocks can be either exogenous or endogenous although neither is assumed to have a more important impact than the other. Exogenous shocks emerge from the environment that is external to the protracted conflict (for example, changes in the international or regional distribution of power; global war), while endogenous shocks occur within the domestic contexts of the adversaries (for example, leadership changes, polity alterations) See Goertz and Diehl, 1997, 2000).

5. Consequently, interfactional competition for power and influence on foreign policy tended to translate into free and lively debates, rather than real planning and implementation within both the PLO and Fatah (Groth 1995). Although urgent matters such as the PLO evacuation from Beirut in 1982 cut across factional lines and made the PLO able to respond quickly to short-term critical problems, these involved primarily tactical responses. Planning strategies for the long term were confined to the slower and more politicized bodies of the PLO that were unable to provide them (Groth 1995).

6. Fatah militants argued that Arafat's moves were illegitimate because they: occurred outside the routine PLO decision-making bodies; undermined the strategy of military struggle and abandoned the goals of an independent Palestinian state (Sahliyeh 1986: 142–53).

7. In fact, the PNC extended Arafat's authority by allowing Arafat and his colleagues within the PLO Executive Committee to decide on the issues of a political settlement in coordination with Jordan and Egypt. Arafat's freedom of maneuver was also enhanced by the appointment of leading moderate figures to key positions within the PLO (Sahliyeh 1986: 180–202).

8. Later, eighty-four countries extended full recognition of the new State of Palestine and some twenty others offered qualified recognition. In January 1989, the PLO gained the right to addres the Security Council on an equal footing with other member states (Sayigh 1997: 624).

9. The accords provided for the establishment of a self-governing authority by the PLO in Gaza and Jericho. Palestinian authority would extend eventually to the remaining Palestinian population centers of the West Bank in a second phase, which would coincide with general elections to form a governing council. After these interim arrangements, further negotiations would determine the final status of Jerusalem, Israeli settlements in the occupied territories, the fate of Palestinian refugees and other matters as part of a permanent settlement of the Israeil-Palestinian conflict (Farsoun and Zacharia 1997: 253–77).

10. Israeli analysts also argue that the large influx of new Soviet immigrants had a significant impact on the outcome of the 1992 election. Survey indicated that Soviet immigrants were less interested in ideology and foreign policy than the issues of

absorption, e.g., employment and housing. Labor and other left-wing parties were able to link foreign policy and absorption issues in a way that was more attractive than the Likud Party. Labor argued that if the government spent fewer resources on building projects in the territories, there would be more monies available for dealing with the problems of unemployment and inadequate housing. This issue increased the trend among the immigrant to support territorial concessions and the Labor Party in the 1992 election (Fein 1995: 168–73). It is acknowledged that the Soviet vote was not so much a vote in favor of Labor but a protest against the Likud government, which had failed to respond adequately to the needs of the new immigrants, and a demand for the next government to reorient its domestic spending priorities (Reich et al. 1995: 142).

11. Rabin initially rejected the PLO as a negotiating partner because of its insistence on a state encompassing all of the West Bank and Gaza and its claim to represent all of the Palestinians in the Diaspora whose dreams of return Israel could not accommodate. Rabin believed that a debilitated PLO would be forced to acquiesce to a deal made by local Palestinians to ease the occupation (Makovsky 1996: 110).

REFERENCES

Abu-Amr, Ziad. 1993. Hamas: A Historical and Political Background. *Journal of Palestine Studies* 22: 4 (summer): 5–19.

Adler, Emanuel. 1991. Cognitive Evolution: A Dynamic Approach for the Study of International Relations and Their Progress. In Emanuel Adler and Beverly Crawford, eds. *Progress in postwar international relations.* New York: Columbia University Press, pp. 43–88.

Arian, Asher and Michal Shamir. 1995. Two Reversals: Why 1992 Was Not 1977. In Asher Arian and Michal Shamir, eds. *The Elections in Israel 1992.* Albany, New York: State University of New York Press, 17–54.

———. 1996. *Security threatened: Surveying Israeli opinion on peace and war.* Cambridge, U.K.: Cambridge University Press.

Arian, Asher, Michal Shamir, and Raphael Ventura. 1992. Public Opinion and Political Change: Israel and the Intifada. *Comparative Politics* 24: 317–34.

Aronoff, Myron J. and Yael S. Aronoff. 1998. Domestic Determinants of Israeli Foreign Policy: The Peace Process from the Declaration of Principles to the Olso II Interim Agreement. In Robert O. Freedman, ed. *The Middle East and the peace process: The Impact of the Oslo Accords.* Gainesville, Fla.: University of Florida Press, pp. 11–34.

Bar-Simon-Tov, Yaacov. 1999. Israel and the Intifada. Adaptation and Learning. Paper presented at the Conference on Historical Roots of the Middle East Post 1945: Lessons for the Future? Stiftung Bruno Kreisky Archiv, Vienna, 10–11. October.

Barzilai Gad. 1996. *Wars, internal conflicts, and political order: A Jewish democracy in the middle east.* Albany, N.Y.: State University of New York Press.

Baumgartner, Frank R. and Bryan D. Jones. 1993. *Agendas and instability in American politics.* Chicago: University of Chicago Press.

Bennett, D. Scott, 1997. Democracy, Regime Change and Rivalry Termination. *International Interactions* 22(4): 369–97.

Ben-Yehuda, Hemda. 1997. Attitude Change and Policy Transformation: Yitzhak Rabin and the Palestinian Issue, 1967–95. In Efraim Karsh, ed., *From Rabin to Netanyahu: Israel's troubled agenda,* pp. 170–86. London: Frank Cass.

Bercovitch, Jacob and Jeffrey Langley. 1993. The Nature of the Dispute and the Effectiveness of International Mediation. *Journal of Conflict Resolution* 37: 670–91.

Bercovitch, Jacob and Theodore Anagnoson, and Donnette L. Wille. 1991. Some

Conceptual Issues and Empirical Trends in the Study of Successful Mediation in International Relations. *Journal of Peace Research* 28: 7–17.

Burton, Michael and John Higley. 1998. Political Crises and Elite Settlements. In Mattei Dogan and John Higley, eds. *Elites, crises, and the origins of regimes*. Lanham, Md.: Rowman & Littlefield, 47–70.

Dogan, Mattei and John Higley. 1998. Elite, Crises, and Regimes in Comparative Analysis. In Mattei Dogan and John Higley, eds. *Elites, crises, and the origins of regimes*. Lanham, Md.: Rowman & Littlefield, pp. 3–28

Elazar, Daniel J. and Shmuel Sandler. 1995. The 1992 Elections: Mahapach Or a Transfer of Power? In Daniel J. Elazar and Shmuel Sandler, eds. *Israel at the polls 1992*. Lanham, Md.: Rowman & Littlefield, pp.1–32.

Evangelista, Matthew, 1991. Sources of Moderation in Soviet Security Policy. In Philip E. Tetlock, Jo L. Husbands, Robert Jervis, Paul C. Stern, and Charles Tilly, eds. *Behavior society and nuclear war, vol. II*. New York: Oxford University Press, 254–354.

Farsoun, Samih K. with Christina E. Zacharia. 1997. *Palestine and the Palestinians*. Boulder, Colo.: Westview Press.

Fein, Aharon. 1995. Voting Trends of Recent Immigrants from the former Soviet Union. In Asher Arian and Michael Shamir, eds. The Elections in Israel 1992. Albany, N.Y.: State University of New York Press, pp. 161–72.

Goertz, Gary and Paul F. Diehl, 1997. The Initiation and Termination of Enduring Rivalaries: The Impact of Political Shocks. *American Journal of Political Science* 39(1): 30–52.

————, 2000. *War and peace in international rivalry*. Ann Arbor: University of Michigan Press.

Golan, Galia. 1997. Moscow and the PLO: The Ups and Downs of a Complex Relationship. In Avraham Sela and Moshe Ma'oz, eds. *The PLO and Israel: From armed revolution to political solution, 1964–1994*. New York: St. Martins Press, pp. 121–39.

Goldberg, Giora, Gad Barzilai, and Efraim Inbar. 1991. The Impact of Intercommunal Conflict: The Intifada and Israeli Public Opinion. *Policy Studies* No. 43. Leonard Davis Institute for International Relations, The Hebrew University of Jerusalem.

Goldstein, Joshua and John R, Freeman. 1990. *Three-way-street: Strategic reciprocity in world politics*. Chicago: University of Chicago Press.

Goldstein, Joshua and Jon C. Pevehouse, 1997. Reciprocity, Bullying and International Cooperation: Time-Series Analysis of the Bosnia Conflict. *American Political Science Review* 913(3): 515–30.

Goldstein, Joshua, Jon C. Pevehouse, Deborah J. Gerner, and Shibley Telhami, 1998. The Dynamics of Middle East Conflict, 1979–90: A Time-Series Analysis. Paper prepared for the 1998 Annual Meeting of the International Studies Association (March). Minneapolis, Minn.

Goldstone, Jack. A. . 1991. *Revolution and rebellion in the early modern world*. Berkeley: University of California Press.

Groth, Allon. 1995. *The PLO's road to peace: Processes of decison-making*. Royal United Services Institute for Defence Studies, Whitehall, London. In RUSI Whitehall Paper Series.

Haggard, Stephen and Robert R. Kaufman. 1995. *The political economy of democratic transitions*. Princeton, N.J.: Princeton University Press.

Hartzell, Caroline A. 1999. Explaining the Stability of Negotiated Settlements to Intrastate Wars. *Journal of Conflict Resolution* 43(1): 3–22.

Hassassian, Manuel S. 1997. Policy and Attitude Changes in the Palestine Liberation Organization, 1965–1994. In Avraham Sela and Moshe Ma'oz, eds. *The PLO and*

Israel: From Armed revolution to political solution, 1964–1994. New York: St. Martins Press, pp. 73–92.

Hunter, F. Robert. 1993. *The Palestinian uprising: A War by other means.* Berkeley: University of California Press.

Husbands, Jo L. 1991. Domestic Factors and De-escalation Initiatives: Boundaries, Process and Timing. In Louis Kriesberg and Stuart Thorson, eds. *Timing the deescalation of international conflicts.* Syracuse, N.Y.: Syracuse University Press, pp. 97–118.

Huth, Paul K., 1996. *Standing your ground: Territorial disputes and international conflict.* Ann Arbor: University of Michigan Press.

Inbar, Efraim. 1991. *War and peace in Israeli Politics: Labor party positions on national security.* Boulder, Colo.: Lynn Rienner Publishers.

———. 1998. Netanyahu Takes Over. In Daniel J. Elazar and Shmuel Sandler, eds. *Israel at the polls 1996.* London: Frank Cass, pp. 33–52.

Kelman, Herbert C. 1995. Contributions of an Unofficial Conflict Resolution Effort to the Israeli-Palestinian Breakthrough. *Negotiation Journal.* (January): 19–27.

King, Charles, 1997. *Ending civil wars.* Adelphi Paper 308. New York: Oxford University Press.

Kingdon, John W. 1995. *Agendas, alternatives and public policies.* 2nd edition. New York: Harper Collins.

Knight, Alan. 1998. Historical and Theoretical Considerations. In Mattei Dogan and John Higley, eds. *Elites, crises, and the origins of regimes.* Lanham, Md.: Rowman and Littlefield, pp. 71–94

Kriesberg, Louis. 1991. Introduction: Timing Conditions, Strategies, and Errors. In Louis Kriesberg and Stuart Thorson, eds. *Timing the deescalation of international conflicts.* Syracuse, N.Y.: Syracuse University Press, pp. 1–26.

———. 1992. *International conflict resolution: The U.S.–U.S.S.R. and Middle East cases.* New Haven, Conn.: Yale University Press.

———. 1998. *Constructive conflicts: From escalation to resolution.* Lanham, Md.: Rowman and Littlefield.

Lebow, Richard Ned. 1995. The Search for Accommodation: Gorbachev in Comparative Perspective. In Richard Ned Lebow and Thomas Risse-Kappen, eds. *International relations theory and the end of the cold war.* New York: Columbia University Press.

Lichbach, Mark I. 1995. *The Rebel's dilemma.* Ann Arbor: University of Michigan Press.

Licklider, Roy. 1993. What Have We Learned and Where Do We Go From Here? In Roy Licklider, ed. *Stopping the killing: How civil wars end.* New York, N.Y.: New York University Press.

Makovsky, David. 1996. *Making peace with the PLO: The Rabin government's road to the Oslo Accord.* Boulder, Colo.: Westview Press.

McAdam, Doug, Sidney Tarrow, and Charles Tilly. 1997. Toward an Integrated Perspective on Social Movements and Revolutions. In Mark I. Lichbach and Alan S. Zuckerman, eds. *Comparative politics: Rationality, culture and structure.* Cambridge, U.K.: Cambridge University Press.

Mendelson, Sarah E. 1998. *Changing course: Ideas, politics, and the Soviet withdrawal from Afghanistan.* Princeton, N.J.: Princeton University Press.

Modelski, George. 1996. Evolutionary Paradigm for Global Politics. *International Studies Quarterly* 40(3): 321–42.

Mitchell, Christopher R. 1995. Asymmetry and Strategies of Regional Conflict Reduction. In I. William Zartman and Victor A. Kremenyuk, eds. *Cooperative security: Reducing third world wars.* Syracuse, N.Y.: Syracuse University Press, pp. 25–57.

Muslih, Muhammed. 1997. A Study of PLO Peace Initiatives, 1974–1988. In Avraham

Sela and Moshe Ma'oz, eds. *The PLO and Israel: From armed revolution to political solution, 1964–1994.* New York: St. Martins Press, pp. 37–54.

Oberschall, Anthony. 1996. Opportunities and Framing in the Eastern European Revolts of 1989. In Doug McAdam, John D. McCarthy, and Mayer N. Zald, eds. *Comparative perspectives on social movements: Political opportunities, mobilizing structures and cultural framing.* Cambridge, U.K.: Cambridge University Press, pp. 3–121.

Pruitt, Dean C. 1981. Kissinger as a Traditional Mediator with Power. In Jeffrey Z. Rubin, ed. *Dynamics of third party intervention: Kissinger in the Middle East.* New York: Praeger, pp. 136–147.

Rajmaira, Sheen. 1997. Indo-Pakistani Relations: Reciprocity in Long-Term Perspective, *International Studies Quarterly* 41: 547–60.

Rasler, Karen. 2000. Shocks, Expectancy, Revision, and the De-escalationof Protracted Conglicts: The Israeli-Palestinian Case. *Journal of Peace Research.* 37: 699–720.

Regan, Patrick M. and Allan C. Stam, 2000. In the Nick of Time: Conflict Management, Mediation Timing, and the Duration of Interstate Disputes. *International Studies Quarterly* 44(2): 239–60.

Reich, Bernard, Meyran Wumser, and Noah Dropkin. 1995. Playing Politics in Moscow and Jerusalem: Soviet Jewish Immigrants and the 1992 Knesset Elections. In Daniel J. Elazar and Shmuel Sandler, eds. *Israel and the polls, 1992.* London: Rowman and Littlefield, pp. 127–56.

Reiter, Dan. 1994. Learning, Realism, and Alliances: The Weight of the Shadow of the Past. *World Politics* 46(2): 490–526.

Sahliyeh, Emile F. 1986. *The PLO after the Lebanon War.* Boulder, Colo.: Westview Press.

Sayigh, Yezid. 1997. *Armed struggle and the search for a state: ThePalestinians national movement, 1949–1993.* Oxford: Clarendon Press.

Shachar, Ron and Michal Shamir. 1995. Modelling Victory in the 1992 Election. In Asher Arian and Michal Shamir, eds. *The Elections in Israel 1992.* Albany, N.Y.: State University of New York Press, pp. 55–80.

Skocopol, Theda. 1979. *States and social revolutions: A Comparative analysis of France, Russia and China.* Cambridge, U.K.: Cambridge University Press.

Stein, Janice G. 1993a. International Co-operation and Loss Avoidance: Framing the Problem. In Janice Gross Stein and Louis W. Pauly, eds. *Choosing to co-operate: How states avoid loss.* Baltimore, Md: Johns Hopkins University Press, pp. 2–34.

———. 1993b. The Political Economy of Security Agreements: The Linked Costs of Failure at Camp David. In Peter B. Evans, Harold K. Jacobsen, and Robert D. Putnam, eds. *International bargaining and domestic politics: Double-edged diplomacy.* Berkley: University of California Press, pp. 77–103.

Stein, Janice G. 1995. "Political Learning by Doing: Gorbachev as Uncommitted Thinker and Motivational Learner. In Richard Ned Lebow and Thomas Risse-Kappen, eds. *International relations theory and the end of the cold war.* New York: Columbia University Press, pp. 223–58.

Telhami, Shibley. 1996. Israeli Foreign Policy: A Realist Ideal-Type or A Breed of Its Own? In Michael N. Barnett, ed. *Israel in comparative perspective: Challenging the conventional wisdom.* Albany, N.Y.: State University of New York Press, pp. 29–52.

Thompson, William R. 1998. An Expectancy Theory of Strategic Rivalry and Deescalation: The Sino-Soviet Case. Paper delivered at the Evolutionary Perspectives on IR Theory Conference, Indiana University, Dec. 4–6, 1998.

Tilly, Charles. 1978 *From mobilization to revolution.* Reading, Mass.: Addison-Wesley.

Touval, Saadia. 1975. Biased Intermediaries: Theoretical and Historical Considerations. *Jerusalem Journal of International Relations* 1: 51–69.

———, and I. William Zartman. 1985. Introduction: Mediation in Theory. In Saadia

Touval and I. William Zartman, eds. *International mediation in theory and practice.* Boulder, Colo.: Westview Press, pp. 7–20.

Wall, James A., Jr. and Ann Lynn. 1993. Mediation: A Current Review. *Journal of Conflict Resolution* 37(1): 160–94.

Walter, Barbara F. 1999. Designing Transitions from Civil War. In Barbara F. Walter and Jack Snyder, eds. *Civil Wars, insecurity, and intervention.* New York: Columbia University Press, pp. 38–72.

Ward, Michael D. 1982. Cooperation and Conflict in Foreign Policy Behavior: Reaction and Memory. *International Studies Quarterly* 28: 87–126.

Waterman, Harvey. 1993. Political Order and the "Settlement" of CivilWars. In Roy Licklider, ed. *Stop the killing: How civil wars end.* New York: New York University Press, pp.292–302.

Young, H. Peyton. 1998. *Individual strategy and social structure: An Evolutionary theory of institutions.* Princeton, N.J.: Princeton University Press.

Zartman, I. William and Johannes Aurik. 1991. Power Strategies in De-Escalation. In Louis Kriesberg and Stuart Thorson, eds. *Timing the de-escalation of international conflicts.* Syracuse, N.Y.: Syracuse University Press, pp. 152–81.

Zartman, I. William. 1993. The Unfinished Agenda: Negotiating Internal Conflicts. In Roy Licklider, ed. *Stopping the killing: How civil wars end.* New York: New York University Press, pp. 20–36.

part IV

Applications to the International Political Economy

chapter 10

Egalitarian Social Movements and New World Orders

Craig N. Murphy

Here is a puzzle: Over the past quarter-century, throughout most of the world, liberal democracy has flourished and the status of women has improved. The percentage of us who live within liberal democracies has doubled since 1975 (Ward et al. 1999). Gaps between men and women on a whole host of measures including income and access to jobs have decreased in almost all countries (UNDP 1995), and they have decreased the most rapidly in the places where once they were the greatest (Tzannatos 1998). Yet, during the same period income inequality among occupational classes and among different regions of the world has increased more rapidly than in any period about which we have reliable knowledge (Murphy 1999; UNDP 1995; World Bank 1995). Today, much more than ever before, "The rich get both richer and fewer" (Pritchett 1995; 12–13). In the North the most privileged classes in all societies have gotten relatively wealthier while the incomes of the South and those of the least-privileged social classes have stayed the same.

What accounts for the difference? Is it, at least in part, a matter of politics? Throughout the whole period there have been social movements pushing for political equity, gender equity, greater economic equality within societies, and the rapid development of poorer societies. Why have one set of movements been more successful than the other? Is it because the political opportunities open to democracy movements and to gender-equity movements have been greater? Is it because they have developed cleverer strategies to exploit those few opportunities that have been available? Is some combination of political opportunity and effective strategy involved? If so, why have differing political opportunities been available? And why have different social movements arrived at different strategies to exploit them?

One clue to this contemporary puzzle may be found in the recurrent roles that egalitarian social movements have played in each of the *globalizing transitions* between industrial eras that have taken place since the Industrial Revolution. This chapter proposes two hypotheses:

1. Egalitarian social movements have played a role in the emergence of each new industrial era by advancing and promoting the resocialization of some of the social relations that had been marketized in the later phases of the waning indus-

trial era. In doing so, the movements have helped powerful social forces temporarily resolve conflicts that are inherent to industrial capitalism. That conflict resolution, in turn, has encouraged the kinds of investment that are essential to the emergence of the new industrial era. Arguably, women's movements and democracy movements have played that role in the current transition from "the Automobile Age" to "the Information Age."

2. The political opportunities available to social movements during those periods that are conducive to some resocialization have been influenced by the nature of the conflicts in the later stages of the waning industrial era. Egalitarian movements involved at the center of conflicts in the waning industrial era rarely contribute to the resocialization that marks the beginning of the new industrial era. Thus, for example, the relative failure of third-world movements and of international labor movements in the 1980s and 1990s can be linked to their centrality to the conflicts of the 1970s.

To illustrate the plausibility of these hypotheses this chapter begins by outlining the larger evolutionary perspective on industrial history of which they are a part. It then considers the differing roles that egalitarian movements play in what I call the *clash* phase as distinct from the *build* phase of each industrial era, and makes the argument that the politics of one clash phase affects the political opportunities in the next build phase and the current period in light of this argument. The final section contrasts the perspective here to other traditions of evolutionary analysis in international relations (IR).

THE LESSONS OF LEADING INDUSTRIAL ECONOMIES

This chapter is part of a larger project aimed at understanding the relationship between persistent patterns of human *inequality* and the issues at the center of IR: *statecraft*, or the consolidation of power across people and territory, and institutionalized relations between different societies. The project follows from my 1994 book *International Organization and Industrial Change* in that industrialization has been the proximate cause of some the greatest inequalities that we know (Bairoch 1993) and international organization has often been conceived by liberals and socialists as an essentially egalitarian form of statecraft, although the actual impact of international institutions on human equality has not been as straightforward.

In the larger project I use the experience of egalitarian social movements, especially their many failed strategies, to help understand the connection between IR and inequality. While the failed strategies of the disadvantaged may be of little interest to many students of IR, this chapter begins with a topic of wider disciplinary interest: The successful political and economic strategies of the leading industrial economies, the economic models that Volker Bornschier (1995) argues have placed "substantial adaptive pressure upon other societal models," meaning that other societies have been, "forced to incorporate the [model's] economically and politically superior institutions if they did not want to risk being outdone by the competition for core position."

At least since the Industrial Revolution one key to successful great-power statecraft has been an economy that regularly generates new *lead industries*, sectors that are disproportionately responsible for economic growth. George Modelski and William R. Thompson (1995) demonstrate that the connection between the ability to generate lead sectors and successful leadership can be traced back much further within Western civilization and perhaps even across Eurasia. Thus, at the beginning of the industrial era, Great Britain's ability to generate cotton mills of the Industrial Revolution and the rail and steel industries of the Railway Age was central to its powers throughout the nineteenth century. The ability of Germany and the United States to catch up to Britain in the Railway Age was followed by their new electrical, chemical, and packaged-consumer-products industries of the second Industrial Revolution that occurred at the turn-of-the-century. This was then followed by the development of the mid-twentieth-century industries of the Automobile Age. These advancements enabled both Germany and the United States to challenge, and let the United States eventually surpass, Britain as the global power.

Even outside the realm of great-power rivalry, participation in the generation of new global lead industries has been central to the continuing power of those states that have entered the industrial *core* of the world economy. Finland, Spain, and South Korea all have generated parts of the new computer and telecommunications-based industries of the emerging Information Age, something that distinguishes them from Russia and other major powers of the semi-periphery (see Table 10.1).

Since Adam-Smith-liberals in the classical tradition have had at least a partial explanation for the relative success of the capitalist industrial powers and other core states in generating new lead industries. The core countries have all had *republican* governments. In Smithian terms, that means that political power has never been monopolized by one of the three fundamental classes: capitalists, agricultural landlords, or laborers. In particular, Smithian liberals fear giving capitalists complete control over the state. Capitalist interests assure that they would use their control of the state to create monopolies against the commonweal. This point, Smith argued, was proven by the experience of the colonial companies that controlled the state in India and North America. In contrast, the immediate interests of both the landed aristocracy and the working class were the same as those of society at large; both classes desired continuous improvements in the material wealth of the nation. Under republican constitutions (divided government) aristocratic and/or working-class interests in the commonweal would balance the economically dynamic, but asocial, interests of the capitalist class, leaving a state in which capitalist competition would assure ever-greater productivity (via the

Table 10.1: Characteristics of the Industrial Eras

Industrial Era	Lead Industries	Capitalist Industrial Powers	Other Industrialized Core Regions
Industrial Revolution circa 1780–1835	cotton mills	Great Britain	
Railway Age circa 1835–1890	railways steel	Great Britain	German Customs Union, United States, Benelux Countries, France
Second Industrial Revolution circa 1890–1945	chemicals electrical goods branded consumer products	British Empire German Empire United States	Benelux, Nordic, and Anglo-Pacific Rim (Canada, Australia, New Zealand) Countries, France, Italy
Automobile Age circa 1945–2000	automobiles aircraft electronics computers	United States	EC and EFTA, Anglo-Pacific Rim, Japan
Information Age circa 2000–	communication equipment and services software biotechnology	United States European Union Japan	Anglo-Pacific Rim, South Korea, Taiwan, Singapore, Hong Kong

increasing division of labor) and aristocratic and/or working-class power would assure capitalist competition (Smith (1981/1776: 265–66, 630–34; Murphy 1994: 14–16).

There are many flaws in this line of argument: It overlooks the world-systemic factors that have made it difficult for republican governments to survive in poor and exploited societies,[1] and it certainly also must overlook some other factors that explain why, despite their long-lived republican constitutions, India and Costa Rica have so far failed to let them enter the core. More troubling is the fundamentalist faith in economic *laissez faire* despite the evidence that the states that have entered the core after Great Britain—from the United States and Germany in the 1800s to the largest of the Asian tigers today—have all initially nurtured competitive industries in relatively closed national markets.[2] The argument also ignores the weak or nonexistent republicanism of some governments throughout the period in which they first made successful bids to enter the core (for example, Imperial Germany, Japan, Taiwan, and South Korea). Republican governments and openness to international competition may be essential to assure that a society can contribute to the *new* lead industries of the next industrial era, but republican governments may not be essential, and complete international openness may be detrimental, to the task of catching up with the lead industries of the day.

Nonetheless, there is a rational core to the Smithian argument connecting limitations on the ability of capitalists to control the state to the social conditions that are conducive to the emergence of a new set of lead industries. In order to specify that significant kernel, it is useful to consider two sets of problems inherent to industrial capitalism that must be overcome for new industrial eras to arise: (1) the political problem of *economic globalization,* and, (2) the current manifestations of the social *conflicts* inherent to industrial societies.

THE PROBLEM OF ECONOMIC GLOBALIZATION

By *economic globalization* I mean simply the tendency for successful industrial economies to outgrow their political boundaries. In Smithian terms a successful economy is one in which there is an ever-increasing division of labor, something inherently limited by "the extent of the market; market growth—not growth in the amount of money that is following through the market, but growth in the number of workers (or even more precisely the labor power) united within a single market—is a long-term requirement of a successful economy. Smith's insight ultimately is not one about markets, per se, it is one about the *technical* 'division of labor' "; as Karl Polanyi (1957: 49) recognized: To have continuous economic growth requires constantly increasing the number of people across whom the "division of labor" takes place.

When Marx and Engels (1932/1848: 13–14) translate the same insight into their own term, Smith's intuition becomes the basis for the Marxian image of the bourgeoisie progressively turning the entire world into a single productive machine. Marx's key idea, Kees van der Pijl (1998) writes, is that of the incremental, ultimately global, *socialization* of labor via the inherently asocial processes of the market. Capitalists need markets to expand beyond the social and political boundaries that once contained them and despite the support that any current set of bounded political entities might have given to industrial capitalism in the past.

Economic globalization, understood in this sense, has never been smooth or continuous. It has occurred in a step-wise fashion in response to political changes, the development of new, larger social orders. Political coalitions among capitalists are needed to support such "new orders" since no individual, capitalist industrial or financial sector reflects the general interest of capital *per se* and there are always more- or less-powerful sectors that benefit from the current, less-than-global, social order. Similarly, at any time there will be more- or less-powerful socially protected noncapitalist forces who will oppose the next phase of globalization.

The large steps in the step-wise process of globalization have occurred in conjunction with the periodic changes in lead industries because the beginning of each new period is initiated, in part, by large investments, which, in turn, have typically required market areas larger than those that typified the lead industries of the waning industrial era. The Industrial Revolution involved large, often public, investments in the power systems for mills. The Railway Age involved large investments in railway networks. The second Industrial Revolution required network investments in electrical power systems and phone systems. The waning Automobile Age involved even larger investments in roads, modern railway networks, airports, the modern mega-factories, and the marketing and research facilities typical of twentieth-century industry. The Information Age has required the even larger investments in the Internet and in the computerized design and factory systems, such as for the Boeing 777. As has been the case with the Internet (and as was the case with American railroads), these bulky investments can be made piecemeal, but, since the Industrial Revolution, those network-building investments at the beginning of an industrial era always have taken place over a larger geographic scale than the network investments of the previous era. Other large investments, such as those needed to build power plants or to fund the costly research operations of a modern chemical firm, actually require a large market in order to assure that enough of the product or service can be sold so that investors can be confident that their investment will be paid back (Murphy 1994: 123–27, 229–34; similarly, Sterman and Mosekilde 1994, compare Modelski and Thompson 1995).

In theory, the problem raised by the pressures toward economic globalization could be solved by means other than the geographic expansion of the fundamental political/economic units of industrial society. The size of the community over which the division of labor takes place could be achieved by natural growth in population, by imperialism, or by the progressive integration of industrial societies. So far, though, integration has been the essential solution. Human populations have not grown as rapidly as "potential productivity"—that is, human inventions that offer new ways of doing things that involve seemingly less labor input—will allow economies to growth; imperialism is a relatively costly endeavor. Moreover, to assure industrial grow via imperialism in less-industrialized societies (the British strategy of the late-nineteenth century and the strategy of Italy and France in the first half of the twentieth century) adds the cost of political control to the cost of the investments in infrastructure and human capital needed to make the strategy successful. Finally, to assure industrial growth via imperial control of other core societies (the Nazi strategy in Europe) requires fighting other industrial powers, powers that may be able to defeat you.

Figure 10.1 below illustrates this perspective on globalization by highlighting the growth and integration of the market areas of lead industries since the Industrial Revolution.

The Conflict Problem

Despite the fact that integration rather than imperialism is the characteristic mode of "globalization," the process does not occur without conflict. Students of IR immediately recognize that many of the blank time periods in figure 10.1 cover periods of

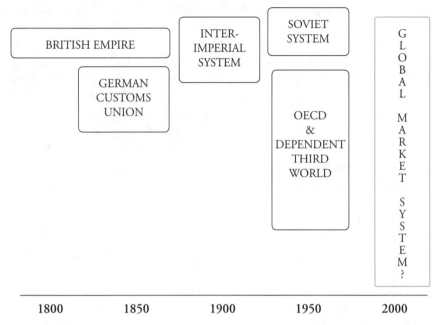

Figure 10.1 "Globalization": Market Areas of Lead Industries, 1800–present

great conflict: the American Civil War, the Franco-Prussian War, and the World Wars. In *International Organization and Industrial Change* and in subsequent papers on the histories of four core regions (the United Kingdom, Germany, the Northeastern United States, and Japan [Murphy 1995, 1998a]), I argue that even successful industrial societies have had to cope with four types of fundamental social conflicts that are either inherent to industrial society or else inherent to the less-than-global stages of globalization that we have experienced so far. These are conflicts between those who benefit most from the emergence of new industrial eras and

1. industrial *labor*, ultimately over democratic control of production;
2. all of those who have received political-economic advantage from their special connection to *older sectors* (that is, agriculture and older lead sectors);
3. citizens and local rulers of *"the third world,"* that is, those regions within the market area that will not experience all the benefits of the new lead industries, regions whose economic roles will be limited to providing low-wage labor and resources (natural and agricultural) for the industrial core; and
4. *rival industrial centers* (other core powers within the same system) or *other industrial systems* especially those based on alternative forms of industrialism or proto-industrialism, that is, the Southern slave system, German and Italian fascism, or Soviet socialism in contrast to what van der Pijl calls the "Lockean" systems of the industrial powers that have so far been the most successful.

While managing these four types of conflict is the central, fundamental new task of modern statecraft, the fundamental conflicts of preindustrial civilizations remain:

1. conflicts between humanity and the rest of the living world that are rooted in our incomplete transition to a settled form of life;
2. conflicts over gender inequality that are rooted in the gendered origin of the state; and
3. conflicts between "inner" and "outer" ethnic groups that are rooted in the characteristic response of settled societies to their vulnerability to raiding/warrior societies (Murphy 1999).

The intensity of all of these conflicts changes over time and is linked to the regular pattern of transition from one industrial era to the next in what can be summarized as a *build, thrive, clash-grab-hoard cycle* (Murphy 1994: 26–45, 261). This formula could be thought of as providing one way to summarize stages of the economic long wave.

The *build* phase is characterized by the temporary resolution of most of the conflicts. Scholars who base their analysis on the insights of Antonio Gramsci write about the formation of a new *historical bloc,* reflected in a mix of governance strategies of firms, states, international institutions, and popular social forces. The social calm thus established encourages and is reciprocally encouraged by relatively large fixed investments that fuel the take-off of new leading industries. This leads to a period of relative prosperity (*thrive*), also characterized by the mitigation of the social conflicts inherent to capitalist industrialism. This period, along with the build phase, may be characterized by a Gramscian form of hegemony.

The last years of this period are apt to be marked by a kind of high cosmopolitanism, a widespread willingness of governments to risk resources in new liberal internationalist projects. This is the phase in which the first of the new market-expanding international institutions that become relevant to the *next* phase of industrial growth have been established: the International Telegraph Union of 1865, which helped create the infrastructure of the extended national markets of the second Industrial Revolution take-off in the 1890s, the Radiotelegraph Union of 1906, which helped link the intercontinental markets of the Automobile and Jet Age, and Intelsat of 1965, a provider of the key infrastructure for today's Information Age.

However, almost simultaneously with this high cosmopolitanism, some of the inherent conflicts reemerge: conflicts with labor, conflicts with those on the periphery of the privileged capitalist core, conflicts among different industrial centers of the core, and especially conflicts with other social models governing parts of the world economy. These *clashes* mark the beginning of a long period of reduced prosperity, the next phase of which begins with the reassertion of capitalist power in a profit-*grabbing* mode that may include cost-cutting globalization. As Henk Overbeek (1990: 28) argues, this period is one in which productive capital is in crisis and the "concept of money capital," liberal fundamentalism, "'presents itself' as the obvious, rational solution." Governments adopt cost-cutting policies and begin to focus on issues of international competitiveness, and the institutions responsible for the stability of the international financial system begin to impose liberal fundamentalist policies on states that are increasingly desperate for such international or transnational support.

The scholars who borrow from Gramsci argue that while this phase of reassertion by capital, especially by financial capital, may be marked by significant economic activity, much of it is apt to be speculative, and of little lasting importance. Moreover, when speculative bubbles burst, the habit of under-investment in production is apt to continue, leading to the stagnation of the *hoard* phase of even more defensive strategies and greater political parochialism—the phase that many Gramscians, like many world-systems and long-wave analysts, fear the world economy has now entered.

In slightly different ways Robert W. Cox (1992), Kees van der Pijl (1998), and I have described the transitions that take place at this point as involving the second half of what Polanyi called the *double movement* against the extreme market logic of the liberal fundamentalism that becomes so predominant in the grab phase. That movement involves the intellectual leadership of "experts in government" or the *cadre class,* men and women who have often been *critical* liberals who partially accept the liberal logic, but who also see a larger roles for government. Van der Pijl sees them, in the twentieth century, as most typically found among the core supporters and officials of social democratic parties. These intellectual leaders have marshaled both political leaders and industrial leaders (most often, of the new potential leading sectors) in what Gramsci called *passive revolutions,* comprehensive reformist projects that, nonetheless, require no "fundamental reordering of social relations" (Forgacs 1988: 428).

One of the most distinctive aspects of the Gramscian accounts of both nineteenth- and twentieth-century transitions has been the argument that these passive revolutions have been supported by international institutions, something that makes sense when one considers the need for international integration suggested by the forces behind globalization. Transnational and intergovernmental bodies have not only played a role in the internationalization of the economically coercive aspects of state power (that is, the role of international financial institutions at the beginning of each transition). In the build part of the cycle international institutions have promoted new, less-defensive strategies for both firms and states; the kind of strategies that can contribute to an effective governance mix.

An earlier attempt to test this account of the role of conflicts in transitions between industrial eras (Murphy 1995, 1998a) suggests that it does successfully capture key elements of the political and economic history of Bornschier's regions that have exerted "substantial adaptive pressure." But that research did not give unambiguous support for the hypothesis that "New government strategy comes from critical liberals of the cadre class." The next section of this chapter proposes a slightly different version of this crucial element in this evolutionary account, linking innovation to the action of egalitarian social movements.

Before turning to that section, let me summarize the argument thus far: There have been a series of stepwise changes in the scale of industrial economies from the regional/national economies of the early Industrial Revolution to the intercontinental markets that linked the Organization of Economic Cooperation and Develoment (OECD) countries and the third world in the Automobile Age. As each transition to a more encompassing industrial order has initially been marked by a period of relatively slow economic growth in which rapid marketization takes place, the state seems to retreat, and uncompromising versions of *laissez-faire* liberalism triumph. Up to now, a second phase has always followed, marked by the increasing role of a more socially oriented liberalism. This second phase, or, in Polanyi's terms, the second part of this "double movement," has been associated with the consolidation of the whole range of governance institutions—from the interstate level down to the shop floor. Those institutions, for a time, help maintain a period of relative peace and relative prosperity over a larger industrial market area in which a new generation of lead industries become dominant. In time, however, various social conflicts, including those that arise from the restraints on liberal innovation imposed by each era's governance institutions, lead to crises, to which *laissez-faire* liberals provide the initial, successful social response. The two-stage pattern is consistent with core arguments of the liberal internationalist tradition that goes back to Adam Smith who expected that any putatively republican state that was captured by the interests of profit-takers would not be able to sustain a liberal, highly productive economy. Instead, an economy based on cartels, monopolization, and so forth would take hold—as it had in company-run colonies of Smith's day.

EGALITARIAN SOCIAL MOVEMENTS IN THE CLASH AND BUILD PHASES

An economy based on cartels and monopolization caused by the capture of the state by capitalist forces is also the way Susan Strange (1996) characterized the world economy in the 1980s and early 1990s. Within the logic of Smith's or Strange's arguments we can imagine powerful egalitarian social movements playing a role in the restoration of the "divided government"—the *substantively* liberal, republican polities—that allows a liberal economy to be a source of prosperity, human dignity, and peace. The recent decades of relatively slow economic growth, rapid marketization, and the relative retreat of the state may be a stage in the development of a wider liberal world order. If the earlier pattern holds, the prospects for the next phase may be linked to the relative success of the whole range of egalitarian social movements.

Egalitarian Movements from Periods of Prosperity to Periods of Conflict

When one thinks of the historical links between egalitarian social movements and industrial cycles what immediately comes to mind is not this hypothesized link to the construction of new industrial orders, but the clear connection between egalitarian politics and the social conflicts that mark periods of relatively slow economic growth. Labor movements, anticolonial movements, development movements, women's movements, movements for ethnic and racial equality, and more comprehensive movements for democracy and human rights all serve to identify and articulate the fundamental conflicts that emerge within industrial societies.

Much of the most persuasive literature on social movements has emphasized the modernity of social movements, their "modular" (replicable and replicated) character, and the way in which they are facilitated and limited by the political opportunities created by modern nation-states (see, for example, Tarrow 1998). Nonetheless, these findings should not serve to obscure the connection between economic and social conditions and the likelihood that egalitarian movements will form and act. Eighteenth-century settlers in Britain's American colonies organized their anticolonial republican movement in response to the increasingly harsh direct rule necessitated by the long (if successful) British hegemonic conflict with France as well as to the political opening created by an increasingly distracted imperial power. The British Chartist and factory hours movements responded both to the harshness of the labor regime in the early mills as well as to the political opportunities created by proximity and by the opportunity for alliances with embattled Tory interests. Turn-of-the-century labor and anticolonial movements tried to expand the limits of the possible in an era when unprecedented prosperity and relative peace promised a more fundamentally democratic future. Similar economic and social conditions influenced the civil rights movements, development movements, and new social movements of the 1950s and 1960s.

Standard arguments about the intensity of domestic conflict should lead us to expect that egalitarian social movements will become active during periods of relative peace and prosperity and that they will become intensely contentious if the high expectations that they have during those "good times" are frustrated by more powerful social forces bent on maintaining the inegalitarian status-quo. My earlier study of Britain, the United States, Germany, and Japan demonstrated the involvement of specific egalitarian movements in the early "clashes" that marked the ends of periods of relative prosperity (Murphy 1995).

Table 10.2 Egalitarian Movements and Conflicts at the End of Periods of Growth

Clash Period	Egalitarian Movements Involved
Pre-Industrial Revolution Britain	Settler colonists, poor people's
Pre-Railway Age Britain	democracy, labor
Pre-Railway Age United States	labor
Pre-Railway Age Germany	democracy
Pre-Second Industrial Revolution Britain	anticolonial, labor
Pre-Second Industrial Revolution United States	antislavery (Civil War)
Pre-Automobile Age Britain	labor, anticolonial
Pre-Automobile Age United States	labor
Pre-Automobile Age Germany	labor
Pre-Information Age Britain	labor, civil rights
Pre-Information Age United States	third world, labor

Egalitarian Movements from Periods of Conflict to Periods of Prosperity

If we look at a more inclusive level of analysis, that is, not at nation-states or subnational units, but at the level of the geographic units in which the leading industries of industrial economies have developed (as outlined in Figure 10.1), the dominant conflicts of each clash period have often been between alternative economic centers and alternative social orders: the conflict between industrial North and slave South in the United States; the series of brief wars between Prussia and Denmark, Austria, and France that helped unify the German Empire while securing its specific geographic class structure; and the World Wars that bracketed thirty years of this century. It is commonplace, and relatively accurate, to conclude that the political-economic models of the social forces that lost these "international" conflicts bridging the periods between industrial eras played no role in the historical blocs (the combination of ruling social forces, ideas, and institutions) that defined the new industrial era. The social model of the American slave Confederacy played little part in the social order of the Gilded Age and Progressive Era United States and its new empire in the Caribbean and Central American "near abroad" and in the Pacific. The Austro-Hungarian vision of Germany and Napoleon III's vision of Europe played little role in the new Prussian German Empire or in the European Inter-Imperial System that provided German firms with the market area needed to be part of the Second Industrial Revolution. The Fascist vision of Eurasia and Africa and the idea of an Asian Co-Prosperity Sphere played little role in the "Free World" order established under U.S. hegemony after the Second World War.

The hypothesis I want to advance is that something similar may be the case when the dominant conflict preceding an industrial era is "domestic," or, at least one contained within the older economic unit: The social forces that "lose" play little role in the next world order. When Chartists and early industrial labor movements challenged the early nineteenth-century social orders of Britain and New England, that may have helped assure that the Railway Age would, in both regions, remain a period of little concrete improvement for wage workers. When the Indian revolutionaries of 1857 failed, they nonetheless raised the perceived long-term costs of maintaining the economically crucial empire, and that may have contributed to Britain's commitment to an increasingly coercive imperialism throughout the rest of the century. And when Vietnamese Communists, OPEC oil barons, and other elements of the diverse third world reaction to American hegemony contributed mightily to the end of the post-World War II "Golden Years," but failed to create a New International Economic Order, they may have helped assure that the Information Age would be particularly harsh on the societies condemned to be providers of resources, low-wage products, and cheap labor.

These are, indeed, just hypotheses. To confirm them would require detailed historical analyses of the "build" phase of each of the industrial eras in each of the separate industrial regions. However, earlier research on the North-South politics of the 1970s to the present, in particular, on the way in which U.S. elite perceptions of third world states and peoples, and OECD policies toward the third world, have developed as a consequence of the Vietnam War. The oil crisis suggests too that a plausible case can be made about the most recent period (Augelli and Murphy 1988, 1993, 1995).

Some may find these hypotheses neither particularly interesting nor surprising. Why should we should we find it remarkable that social movements of those who suffer from persistent structures of inequality play no role in the development of new social orders? It is only surprising when we recognize that *some* movements of that sort have played such role as part of the double movements that have marked the transitions from one industrial era to the next (Murphy 1998a). For the most part, the relevant movements have been "domestic," labor and progressive parties, suffragists, antislavery movements in the United States and Britain, and anticolonial movements within empires. Yet, there has long been a transnational character to many of the most successful egalitarian movements. The antislavery movement in the United States originated in transnational (often Quaker or Jacobin, that is, French-Revolution-inspired) associations, was fostered and transformed by world associations of the African Diaspora who opposed the Anglo-American "progressive" solution of resettling all black slaves in Africa, and helped nurture and maintain the social movements that fought to end slavery in Latin America (Charnovitz 1997: 192–93; Keck and Sikkink 1998: 41–51; Goodman 1998). Anticolonial movements have relied upon strong transnational links that transcended the realms of individual colonial powers throughout this century (Ansprenger 1989; MacFarlane 1985; Nyerere 1980). The modern movements for women's suffrage and women's rights have always been transnational (Keck and Sikkink 1998: 51–72).

And, of course, in the beginning "internationalism" was simply "labor internationalism" (Lynch 1999; Waterman 1998: 14–44).

In the current period of transition, egalitarian social movements, now, almost always involving transnational links, have played demonstrably significant roles in the development of the social order connecting the industrialized OECD core to the dependent third world and to semi-peripheral societies in Latin America, Eastern Europe, the Middle East, and Southeast Asia. Democracy movements and human rights movements, transnationally linked and often supported by core governments (especially since the mid-1980s) have played a central role in the transformation of Latin American, African, and East European societies, and continue to play significant roles in the remaining few large states that have not made "irreversible" movements toward liberal democracy: China, Indonesia, and Nigeria (Ward et al. 1999; Chilton 1995; Gaer 1995; Robinson 1996). Similarly, transnationally linked women's movements have been instrumental in transforming the "development" agenda of intergovernmental agencies to one that emphasizes the empowerment of women. At the same time women's movements have linked national struggles for gender equity allowing lessons learned in one area to be applied in others and contributing to the rapid diminution of legal gender discrimination as well as to substantive gains in women's access to income, wealth, job opportunities, and political positions (Chen 1995; UNDP 1995; Higer 1997; O'Brien et al. 2000).

The influence of these social movements on the verbal commitments of governments and intergovernmental agencies, on the allocation of international aid funds, and on domestic legislation (whether enforced or not) is clear from a number of regional studies. Yet, it is equally clear that neither these movements, nor the "unsuccessful" movements promoting the interests of labor and the third world have been able to reverse trends toward widening income gaps within and across societies. Moreover, as the current global financial crisis demonstrates, outside the United States and the European Union conditions hardly encourage the pattern of bulky investments needed to build the Information Age global economy. In large parts of the semi-periphery and the periphery, the former Soviet Union, parts of Latin America and South Asia, and much of Sub-Saharan Africa, a kind of kleptocratic anarchy remains (Chin and Tiwon 2001; Dawson 2001; Robinson 2001; Steady 2001).

Nonetheless, even today the outlines of the social compromises at the center of the "next world order" may be visible. Temporary resolutions of the fundamental conflicts of industrial societies may emerge from the small victories of the egalitarian social movements that have found political opportunities in the 1980s and 1990s. Many of us who live in industrialized societies are, for example, aware of the way in which the massive entrance of women into the wage labor force has allowed household incomes for most families to remain stable or shrink less dramatically despite the fact that most of the economic growth of the past decades has gone to the top 5 percent of wage earners (Laurin and McNichol 1997). In this context the slightly rising incomes and protections for dual incomes of working families associated with the "third way" economic policies of Bill Clinton, Tony Blair, and Italy's post-1996 center-left governments have created a surprisingly strong and broad sense of social legitimacy; this has extended even to the business elites who are regularly interviewed by the International Institute of Management Development and the World Economic Forum (Murphy 1999). As a result we someday may look back on this period as one in which the "victories" of women's movements in the industrialized world help temporarily to resolve the fundamental labor conflicts that would otherwise have impeded the emergence of the Information Age.

Similarly, empirical studies of the massive impact of gender-based small-scale lending, primary education for girls, and other elements of the emerging "global consensus" on developments that have been fostered by transnationally connected women's movements suggest that some aspects of "the third world problem" may, without conscious strategic decision, end up being managed by seemingly marginal and "low-cost" gender-related changes in North-South relations (Evans 1998; Mayoux 1995). The recent wave of "democratization without development" in Latin America, Africa, and Eastern Europe has been more self-consciously supported by some Northern governments (especially the Reagan administration) as a strategy to manage the increasingly fraught North-South relationship, and we may someday also look back on it as part of the historical bloc that maintained the period of relative peace and prosperity associated with the Information Age (Augelli and Murphy 1993).

How to Have Impact on the Next World Order

I have argued that one important constraint on the influence of transnational egalitarian social movements may be their perceived role as a primary source of the conflicts that destabilized the earlier period of relative peace and prosperity. The relevant perception is, of course, that of the more powerful social forces—the "ruling classes" and "ruling states"—or, to be more operationally specific, the groups that serve as "political parties" (in Gramsci's sense) for the dominant economic interests and states, the groups that effectively articulate the worldviews and political programs followed by powerful nations, international institutions, and individuals. The relevant perception is that of the political movements of the powerful.

Table 10.3 below takes each of the industrial systems that are precursors to the emerging "global" market system of the Information Age and gives a shorthand reference to the political movements, or Gramscian "parties" of the powerful who provided the primary set of innovations for each era. The sources of the table are disparate, my own work on the major powers and on the international organiza-

Table 10.3 Innovators Associated with Industrial Orders

Industrial System ("World Order")	Primary Innovators
Late Industrial Revolution Britain	William Pitt the Younger's Conservatives
Railway Age British Empire	Disraeli's Conservatives
Railway Age German Customs Union	List's German Nationalists
Railway Age American "States Union"	"Hamiltonian" Jeffersonians (ala Tickner)
Second Industrial Revolution Inter-Imperial System	Large-enterprise German liberals, Rhodes's liberal imperialists
Second Industrial Revolution Pan-American System	American "Progressives," McKinley, Theodore Rooselvelt
Automobile Age "Free World" System (OECD and dependent third world)	New Deal Liberals, Ford, Keynes, Monet
Soviet Industrial System	Lenin, Stalin, Bolsheviks

tion system (Murphy 1994, 1998a), J. Ann Tickner (1987) and Daniel Duedney's (1996) analyses of the antebellum United States, and the Amsterdam School analysts Henk Overbeek (1990) and Kees van der Pijl's (1998) accounts of British, European, and trans-Atlantic social movements in relation to the emergence of industrial orders (Murphy 1994: 35–37).

In many of these cases the social movements of the powerful acted as political leaders promoting institutional innovations that had earlier been articulated by "cadre class" civil servants and their political parties or party factions of the democratic left. The forces that maintain this class "dedicated" to resolving social conflicts assure that there is at least one source of the innovations needed to resolve the periodic crises of a conflict ridden, globalizing industrial capitalism, just the ever-growing relative power of the capitalist class (partially as mediated through powerful states), provides the "selection mechanism" that determines which innovations will be institutionalized, thus providing the two necessary parts of any evolutionary explanation.

Yet the periodic need for social-conflict-resolving and globalizing institutional innovation also creates political opportunities for social movements that are more firmly connected to egalitarian goals than the left-sympathetic "experts in government" may be. To act effectively within this arena the history of successful egalitarian social movements suggest that they need to include at least five elements in their strategic mix.

First, a dedication to what John Braithwaite and Peter Drahos (2000) call "model mongering," meaning the constant experimental promotion of an evergrowing array of possible (egalitarian) solutions the conflict and globalization problems faced by governments and powerful social forces. For example, small-scale gender-based lending, reproductive freedom, primary education for women, and other elements of a quarter-century old women in development agenda have been well "mongered" across a host of institutions whose primary concerns are not gender equality, but who have become convinced that these programs will reduce poverty, minimize costs of development assistance, placate an increasingly powerful northern women's constituency, help clean up the environment, and so forth.

Second, to be able to both successfully innovate in the interests of less-advantaged groups and to sell those innovations to status quo–oriented institutions requires a division of labor within the social movement into more and less radical elements *that maintain active cooperation with one another.* Amy Higer (1997) notes the importance of this element in the success of the International Women's Health Movement and similar conclusions have been drawn about the antislavery movements of the nineteenth-century (Goodman 1998).

Third, a unified central cadre of activists operating across the regional lines separating the emerging, more global industrial system. Again Higer's account of the International Women's Health Movement, historical accounts of antislavery movements, and the experience of nineteenth-century labor internationalism and twentieth-century anticolonialism make this point. To go back even further to the very beginning of the social movement era, one might argue that any successful movement needs its Thomas Paines, that is, men and women who act in relation to a number of states and who can temporarily help protect the egalitarian activists of one society by offering sanctuary or marshaling diplomatic pressure from another.

Fourth, successful movements need a willingness and ability to learn of local movements in one part of the new "globalized" region to lean from the experience of local movements in other regions. Again, this seems to be a key element of the success of contemporary women's, democracy, and human rights movements, perhaps in sharp contrast to labor and third world movements that have been riven by regional differences and perceptions that fundamental differences in interests (say, between industrial workers in Bangladesh and industrial workers in the United States or between Africa and Latin America) make cooperative learning impossible.

One of the strongest pieces of evidence supporting both the third and fourth points comes from the response of status-quo powers to the international conference system and especially to the nongovernmental organization (NGO) forums that now regularly take place alongside the intergovernmental meetings on the rotating list of major topics (for example, human rights, the environment, women, population, social development). There is a widespread belief among NGO participants that the NGO forums serve as a major venue for interregional learning as well as the primary locus for the development of a transnational cadre linking various regional social movements. And, in fact, the belief in the efficacy of the NGO conferences for exactly that purpose has been a primary motivation for the work of conservative forces within the United States to end the global conference system (Fomerand 1996).

The fifth and final issue is related: Successful egalitarian social movements have been those willing to marshal the (albeit limited) powers of "international" organizations to promote and test the movements' proposed institutional reforms. Again, contemporary democracy and human rights movements, which have added forms of political conditionality to intergovernmental development assistance and have convinced the central organs of the UN to be service providers to almost every state involved in a democratic transition, illustrate the point (Sørensen 1993; Boutros-Ghali 1995; Joyner 1999).

IS THERE A "GRAMSCIAN" APPROACH TO EVOLUTIONARY THEORY IN IR?

What has been offered so far is a politically relevant evolutionary or "Darwinian" account of the formation of the development of successive cycles of international regulation of industrial economies. The account is one that sees institutions as developing, as Thorstein Veblen (1897) put it, through a process of "selective elimination." The account is evolutionary in that the institutions that survive are selected by powerful forces within their political and economic environments; the various institutional mechanisms that come to regulate a "new world order" do so, in the final instance, because the social order that they maintain serves the interests of powerful industrial firms and powerful states by expanding the effective markets of industrial goods and "solving" (temporarily) the problems that arise from conflicts that an unregulated market economy cannot solve. The account is also evolutionary in that the selection of the actual institutions that come to regulate the "world order" is done from among a host of potential institutional innovations offered (or "mongered") by a variety of people. For some of them (the "experts in government," van der Pijl's "cadre class") offering new institutional innovations is "their job." For others (the egalitarian social movements), it is their passion.

In a strictly "Darwinian" theory, the innovations offered at any moment of transition to a new world order may be thought of as relatively random, as an unbiased agenda from which powerful social forces choose. However, the account offered here suggests that the agenda offered *can* have a political bias, and, in fact, the politically relevant part of the account comes from that element; the "lessons" of the previous section may be read as just that—as lessons relevant to egalitarian social movements concerned with changing the world, with making history within the current material constraints.

The particular account offered is part of a research program in historical political economy that that is influenced by Antonio Gramsci. Some might argue that, because it is an evolutionary account, what is offered here contradicts the methodological premises that make Gramscian accounts distinctive and worthwhile (see Yanarella and Reid 1996; Robinson 1998; Germain 1999). Gramsci is often remembered as the Marxist who placed human agency at the center of his accounts of social action. His own accounts of Italian politics are deeply historicist and the most prominent of the Anglophone Gramscians in IR has often spoken of his doubts about the entire enterprise of social science, arguing that he has always told his colleagues that the only form of social analysis that he knows is the production of contextualized, unique, histories.[3] Moreover, Enrico Augelli and I (1997) have argued that Gramsci's concept of political myth describes the motivations that lead many institutions to be "selected" more accurately than the rational-choice selection mechanisms implicit or explicit in many evolutionary explanations, and we have followed Richard Falk (1997) in arguing that that is one reason IR "Gramscians" distinguish themselves from world-systems analysts and from more structuralist evolutionary analysts such as Modelski and Thompson (Murphy 1998b).

However, these differences with evolutionary theorists focus on only one side of the critical realist or historical political economy tradition of which Gramsci and Cox are both part. One of the most important intellectual influences on Gramsci was the Italian revisionist Antonio Labriola [1843–1904], who "joined Marx to Darwin and other evolutionary theory" (Ross 1991: 207; see Labriola 1897/1966). Gramsci accepted Labriola's view that material conditions affect humanity through the intermediation of our habits of thought and action. To explain social action meant, for both "materialists," describing the nested network of mechanisms of "selective elimination" from the material limits of the possible down through the daily habits of thought and action that replicate any institution. Gramsci, like most evolutionary theorists, assumed that, unless doomed by their own radical incompatibility with their natural and human environment, institutions (habits of thought and action at all levels) would remain, even if only as part of the layer upon layer of the cultural detritus he called "common sense." Certainly Gramsci expected, and wanted to be able to account for, those manifestations of human creativity that would not be explicable within the Darwinian/Marxist models of revisionist social scientists like Labriola, but the power of material reality—and the human ability to understand that power—made Gramsci search for historical accounts that fit the pattern of "selective elimination."

There is an interesting historical link between many contemporary forms of evolutionary social science analysis and the kind of analysis favored by historicist, critical realists like Cox. Historian of American social science Dorothy Ross points out that a great deal of today's evolutionary analysis in economics, sociology, and politics is rooted (directly, if sometimes at a great historical distance) to the older forms of institutionalist economics associated with Thorstein Veblen. Of course, contemporary evolutionary economists make their connections through Veblen's more politically mainstream students like John Commons and National Bureau of Economic Research founder Wesley Mitchell. It is relatively easy, for example, to link about half of the social scientists on Modelski's (1999) bibliography, Essentials of Evolutionary Thought in the Social Sciences, back to Veblen. The same, I hazard, would be true of the theoretical works cited in this volume.

Ross (1991: 207) writes of the American source of various strands of current evolutionary social science, "Veblen was the American Gramsci, drawn to the problem of false consciousness and training in idealist philosophy into a revision of Marx's theory of history." Given that both Gramsci and Veblen turned to a view of history involving the selective retention of the myriad institutions envisioned by creative minds, we should not be surprised to find similarities between the accounts of world politics given by Gramscian and by "Evolutionary" scholars.

NOTES

1. Core powers remain relatively willing to undermine democracies in weaker states in which democratic governments challenge powerful core economic interests and international financial institutions (IFIs) that are maintained by core liberal democracies. This assures that the stability of international financial markets have been willing to undermine third world democracies, if doing so seems essential to achieving the IFIs' central goals. Moreover, stable democracies have tended to arise as a consequence of the power of labor and/or mass-based nationalist movements in capitalist societies that do not have an entrenched sector of coerced agricultural labor. Many power countries have such a sector and many have no powerful labor movement. See Rueschemeyer, Stephens, and Stephens (1992). Finally, relatively inegalitarian societies—typical of much of the third world—also breed protracted social conflicts that tend to undermine liberal democracy (Muller and Seligson 1987).

2. Tickner (1987) illuminates the strategic issues that are often overlooked in purely economic explanations of why successful industrializing powers rely on illiberal strategies in order to catch up with older industrial states. The current version of the economic logic behind this phenomena—an update of the infant industry arguments of Hamilton and List—can be found in the so-called "new international economics," (Krugman1986).

3. One of the most interesting occasions on which he made such remarks was in March 1997 at the reception in which he and Jessie Cox received the *Festschrift* edited by Gill and Mittelman.

REFERENCES

Ansprenger, Franz. 1989. *The Dissolution of colonial empires.* London and New York: Routledge.

Augelli, Enrico and Craig N. Murphy. 1988. *America's quest for supremacy and the third world: A Gramscian analysis*. London: Pinter Publishers.

———. 1993. "International Institutions, Decolonization, and Development." *International Political Science Review,* 14(1): 71–86.

———. 1995. "La nuova teoria della pace delle Nazioni unite. In Gian Giacomo Migone and Olga Re, eds. *A cinquant'anni dalla nascita delle Nazioni unite,* a special issue of *Europa/Europe* 4(4): 97–121.

———. 1997. Consciousness, Myth, and Collective Action. In Stephen Gill and James Mittelman, eds. *Innovation and transformation in international studies.* Cambridge: Cambridge University Press.

Bairoch, Paul. 1993. *Economic and world history: Myths and paradoxes.* Chicago: University of Chicago Press, pp. 101–10.

Bornschier, Volker. 1995. West European Unification and the Future Structure of the Core. In Christopher K. Chase-Dunn and Volker Bornschier, eds. *The Future of hege-*

monic rivalry. Department of Sociology, The Johns Hopkins University. Baltimore, Md., February.

Boutros-Ghali, Boutros. 1995. Democracy: A Newly Recognized Imperative. *Global Governance* 1(1): 3–12.

Braithwaite, John and Peter Drahos. 2000. *Global business regulation.* Cambridge, U.K.: Cambridge University Press.

Charnovitz, Steve. 1997. Two Centuries of Participation: NGOs and International Governance. *Michigan Journal of International Law*, 18(2): entire issue.

Chen, Martha Alter. 1995. Engendering World Conferences: The International Women's Movement and the United Nations. *Third World Quarterly*, 16(3): 477–94.

Chilton, Patricia. 1995. Mechanics of Change: Social Movements, Transnational Coalitions, and the Transformation Processes in Eastern Europe. In Thomas Risse-Kappen, ed. *Bringing transnational relations back in.* Cambridge, U.K.: Cambridge University Press.

Chin, Christine B. N. and Sylvia C. Tiwon. 2001. Capital, Crisis, and Chaos: Indonesia and Malaysia. In Craig N. Murphy, ed. *Egalitarian politics in the age of globalization.* London: Palgrave.

Cox, Robert W. 1992. The United Nations, Globalization, and Democracy. The 1992 John W. Holmes Memorial Lecture. Providence, R.I.: The Academic Council on the United Nations System.

Dawson, Jane. 2001. Egalitarian Responses in Post-Communist Societies: Russia and the Former East Bloc. In Craig N. Murphy, ed. *Egalitarian politics in the age of globalization.* London: Palgrave.

Duedney, Daniel. 1996. Building Sovereigns: Authorities, Structures, and Conflicts in Philadelphian Systems. In Thomas J. Biersteker and Cynthia Weber, eds. *State sovereignty as a social construct.* Cambridge, U.K.: Cambridge University Press.

Evans, Tim. 1998. Bangladesh Country Report. Global Health Equity Initiative, Social Determinants Project. Santa Fe, N.M., October.

Falk, Richard. 1997. The Critical Realist Tradition and the Demystification of Interstate Power: E. H. Carr, Hedley Bull, and Robert W. Cox. In Stephen Gill and James Mittelman. *Innovation and transformation in international studies.* Cambridge, U.K.: Cambridge University Press.

Fomerand, Jacques. 1996. U.N. Conferences: Media Events or Genuine Diplomacy? *Global Governance* 2(3): 361–77.

Forgacs, David, ed. 1988. *An Antonio Gramsci reader.* New York: Schocken Books.

Gaer, Felice D. . 1995. Reality Check: Human Rights Nongovernmental Organizations Confront Governments at the United Nations. *Third World Quarterly*, 16(3): 389–404.

Gill, Stephen and James Mittelman, eds. 1997. *Innovation and transformation in international studies.* Cambridge, U.K.: Cambridge University Press.

Goodman, Paul. 1998. *Of one blood: Abolitionism and the origin of racial equality.* Berkeley: University of California Press.

Germain, Randall D. 1999. Globalization in Historical Perspective. In *Globalization and its critics: Perspectives from political economy.* London: Macmillan.

Higer, Amy. 1997. Transnational Movements and World Politics: The International Women's Health Movement and Population Policy. Doctoral dissertation in the Department of Politics, Brandeis University, Waltham, Mass., May.

Keck, Margaret E. and Kathryn Sikkink. 1998. *Activists beyond borders: Advocacy networks in international politics.* Ithaca, N.Y.: Cornell University Press.

Joyner, Christopher. 1999. The United Nations and Democracy. *Global Governance* 5(3): 333–59.

Krugman, Paul R. 1986. *Strategic trade policy and the new international economics.* Cambridge, Mass.: MIT Press.

Labriola, Antonio. 1897/1966. *Essays on the materialistic conception of history.* Charles H. Kerr, trans. New York: Monthly Review Press .

Laurin, Kathryn and Elizabeth McNichol. 1997. *Pulling apart: A State-by-State analysis of income trends.* Washington, D.C.: Center on Budget and Policy Priorities.

Lynch, Cecelia. 1999. The Promise and Problems of Internationalism. *Global Governance,* 5(1): 83–102.

MacFarlane, S. Neil. 1985. *Superpower rivalry and third world radicalism: The Idea of national liberation.* Baltimore, Md.: The Johns Hopkins University Press.

Marx, Karl and Frederick Engels. 1932/1848. *Manifesto of the communist party.* New York: International Publishers.

Mayoux, Linda. 1995. From Vicious To Virtuous Circles? Gender and Micro-Enterprise Development. UNRISD UN Fourth World Conference On Women Occasional Paper No. 3, Geneva, May.

Modelski, George. 1999. Essentials of Evolutionary in the Social Sciences, An Annotated Bibliography, 2nd ed. Found on the internet at <http://faculty.washington.edu/modelski/biblio1.html>

Modelski, George and William R. Thompson. 1995. *Leading sectors and world powers: The Coevolution of global economics and politics.* Columbia: University of South Carolina Press.

Muller, Edward N. and Mitchell A. Seligson. 1987. Inequality and Insurgency. *American Political Science Review* 81(2): 425–50.

Murphy, Craig N. 1994. *International organization and industrial change: Global governance since 1850.* Cambridge and New York: Polity Press and Oxford University Press.

———. 1995. Globalization and Governance: "Passive Revolution" and the Earlier Transitions to Larger Scale Industrial Economies in the United Kingdom, Germany, the Northeastern United States, and Northeastern Japan. Prepared for the Annual Meeting of the American Political Science Association, Chicago, September.

———. 1998a. Globalization and Governance: A Historical Perspective. In Roland Axtmann, ed. *Globalization in europe.* London: Pinter Publishers.

———. 1998b. Understanding IR, Understanding Gramsci. *Review of International Studies* 24(3): 417–26.

———. 1999. Inequality, Turmoil, and Democracy: Global Political-Economic Visions at the End of the Century. *New Political Economy.* 4(2): 289–304.

———. (2001. Gender Inequality and the Realpolitik of Settled Agricultural Societies. In Mary Ann Tétreault and Robin L. Teske, eds. *Feminist Approaches to Social Movements, Community, and Power.* Columbia: University of South Carolina Press.

Nyerere, Julius. 1980. *Introduction to Mason Sears, years of high purpose, from trusteeship to nationhood.* Washington, D.C.: University Press of America.

O'Brien, Robert, Anne Marie Goetz, Jan Aart Scholte, and Marc Williams. 2000. The World Bank and Women's Movements. In *Contesting global governance: Multilateral institutions and global social movements.* Cambridge, U.K.: Cambridge University Press.

Overbeek, Henk. 1990. *Global capitalism and national decline: The Thatcher decade in perspective.* London: Unwin Hyman.

Polanyi, Karl. 1957. *The Great transformation: The Political and economic origins of our times.* Boston: Beacon Press.

Pritchett, Lant. 1995. Divergence, Big Time. World Bank Policy Research Working Paper 1522.

Robinson, William I. 1996. *Promoting polyarchy: Globalization, U.S. intervention, and hegemony*. Cambridge, U.K.: Cambridge University Press.

———. 1998. Beyond Nation-State Paradigms: Globalization, Sociology, and the Challenge of Transnational Studies. *Sociological Forum* 13(4): 561–94.

———. 2001. Latin America in an Age of Inequality Confronting a New "Utopia." In Craig N. Murphy, ed. *Egalitarian politics in the age of globalization*. London: Palgrave.

Ross, Dorothy. 1991. *The Origins of American social science*. Cambridge, U.K.: Cambridge University Press.

Rueschemeyer, Dietrich, Evelyne Huber Stephens, and John D. Stephens. 1992. *Capitalist development and democracy*. Chicago: University of Chicago Press.

Smith, Adam. 1981/1776. *An Inquiry into the nature and causes of the wealth of nations*. Oxford: Oxford University Press.

Sørensen, Georg, ed. 1993. *Political conditionality*. London: Frank Cass.

Sterman, John D. and Erik Mosekilde. 1994. Business Cycles and Long Waves: A Behavioral Disequilibrium Perspective. In Willi Semmler, ed. *Business cycles: Theory and empirical methods*. Boston: Kluwer Academic Publishers.

Strange, Susan. 1996. *The Retreat of the state*. Cambridge, U.K.: Cambridge University Press.

Steady, Filomena. 2001. Engendering Change Through Egalitarian Movements: The African Experience. In Craig N. Murphy, ed. *Egalitarian politics in the age of globalization*. London: Palgrave.

Tarrow, Sidney. 1998. *Power in movement: Social movements and contentious politics*, 2nd ed. Cambridge, U.K.: Cambridge University Press.

Tickner, J. Ann. 1987. *Self-reliance versus power politics: The American and Indian experience in building nation states*. New York: Columbia University Press.

Tzannatos, Zafiris. 1998. Women and Labor Market Change in the Global Economy: Growth Helps, Inequalities Hurt and Public Policy Matters. World Bank Social Protection Discussion Paper 9808.

van der Pijl, Kees. 1998. *Transnational classes and International Relations*. New York: Routledge.

Veblen, Thorstein. 1897. Review of Antonio Labriola, *Essais sur la conception materialiste de l'histoire*. *Journal of Political Economy*. 5(3): 390–91.

UNDP. 1995. *Human development report*. New York: Oxford University Press.

Ward, Michael D., John O'Loughlin, Jordin S. Cohen, Kristian S. Gleditsch, David S. Brown, David A. Reilly, Corey L. Lofdahl, and Michael E. Shin. 1999. The Diffusion of Democracy, 1946–1994. *Annals of the association of American geographers*.

Waterman, Peter. 1998. *Globalization, social movements, and the new internationalism*. London: Mansell.

World Bank. 1995. *World development report*. New York: Oxford University Press.

Yanarella, Ernest J. and Herbert G. Reid. 1996. From 'Trained Gorilla' to 'Humanware': Repoliticizing the Body-Machine Complex Between Fordism and Post-Fordism. In Theodore R. Schatzki and Wolfgang Natter, eds. *The Social and political body*. New York: The Guilford Press.

chapter 11

Technological Capacity as Fitness
An Evolutionary Model of Change in the International Political Economy

Sangbae Kim and Jeffrey A. Hart

INTRODUCTION

The resurgence of U.S. international competitiveness on the basis of its relative strength in the new leading sectors—computers and other information industries—has brought about a debate on adopting the U.S. model of business and industrial institutions among firms and governments in other countries. The United States is currently the most successful country in the world in adjusting to the so-called Information Revolution. The existence (or creation) of appropriate governance structures—industrial structures, government policies and institutions, and other institutional environments—explains the U.S. success in the computer and other information industries (Hart and Kim, 2000).

This is in a sharp contrast with the 1980s when the relative decline of U.S. international competitiveness was a major topic of debate. Then, American firms and governments were trying to learn from Japanese business practices and industrial institutions, especially the Toyota-style production system (also called "lean production"). Japanese international competitiveness in automobiles, consumer electronics, and computer hardware components could be explained by its unique form of industrial governance, which they created during the catch-up period of economic growth.

In this chapter, building on Borrus and Zysman's (1997) work, we attempt to understand the impact of governance structures in the United States on the computer industry by using the concept of *Wintelism*, a term derived from combining the *W* from Windows—Microsoft's popular operating system—and *Intel*, the world's leading producer of PC microprocessors. *Wintelism writ small* refers to the structural dominance of Microsoft and Intel in their respective parts of the global personal computer industry. *Wintelism writ large* signifies the transformation of the whole computer industry toward horizontal value-chain specialization, which gives rise to new governance structures (Kim and Hart, forthcoming).

In particular, we understand the rise of Wintelism both as a new mode of technological competition in the global computer industry and as a new *industrial paradigm* that we believe is of profound importance beyond the boundaries of the computer industry. Wintelism as a new industrial paradigm is potentially comparable to the British industrial model in the nineteenth century, Fordism in the early and mid twentieth century, and Japan's so-called Toyota production system of more recent vintage.

The idea of an industrial paradigm implies not only a set of new technological changes but also a set of practices and institutional arrangements that become increasingly important if not dominant in the global political economy. Much of the earlier literature on industrial paradigms contains debates about the ability of various social systems and political regions to adjust themselves to technological changes and the subsequent global impact of a shift in industrial paradigms. In this sense, the rise of Wintelism as a new industrial paradigm will present similar challenges of adjustment to firms and governments as did the rise of previous industrial paradigms.

In this chapter, we will focus on the question of the transition from earlier industrial paradigms to the Wintelist paradigm. What factors will influence the decision of firms and governments to switch over to the practices that are consistent with the new paradigm? What factors will permit some firms, regions, or countries to insulate themselves from the necessity of adjusting to the new global paradigm? Finally, what are the opportunity costs of not adjusting? By answering these questions, we aim to clarify the evolutionary and interactive dynamics of technological change and institutional adjustment in the International Political Economy (IPE), and to explain changes in international competitiveness in an industry as the consequence of technological versus institutional changes.

In particular, we offer a *theory of technological fitness*. In our theory, success or failure in industrial sectors depends not only on a *fit* between the properties of technology in individual sectors and types of governance structures in national institutions, but also on the abilities of nations to adjust their institutional capabilities to the given technological conditions. In other words, selection of industrial practices depends on the *fitness* of those practices with respect to a given economic environment. Fitness also depends on the degree to which a particular economic environment is insulated from global competition, whether by natural or manmade factors, and on the practices of both firms and governments that are appropriate in a given industry.

In subsequent sections of this chapter, after critically reviewing existing approaches to technology and institutions, we ask whether each technological system requires a particular governance structure. In particular, we will modify Herbert Kitschelt's (1991) framework on the fit between technological properties and governance structures to develop an evolutionary model of industrial paradigm change in the global political economy. We further examine the issue of technological fitness and institutional adjustment in an evolutionary context. Finally, we explain how nations can succeed or fail in adjusting to the rise of new technological systems, and how they may decide to specialize on particular industrial sectors through different industrial learning paths.

EXISTING APPROACHES TO TECHNOLOGY AND INSTITUTION

The prevailing neoinstitutional approaches to industrial innovation and competitiveness in the IPE are not adequate for conceptualizing the interactive dynamics of technological change and institutional adjustment. They mainly concern national variations of institutional capabilities for creating and diffusing technological innovations that influence the competitiveness of specific industries. These approaches describe national patterns of industrial performance in terms of the relationships among domestic institutions that specify the rules of interaction among actors— business, government, labor, and so forth. They then evaluate the extent to which each set of domestic arrangements helps or hinders nation-states in their attempts to achieve national economic performance goals (Katzenstein 1978, 1985; Zysman 1983; Zysman and Tyson, eds. 1983; Hall 1986; Hart 1992).

These national-level analyses can provide us with useful concepts to understand the impact of a nation's institutional inheritance on policy outcomes and national variations in innovative performance, but they do not provide the sector-specific understandings of industrial change that are often critical to capture the dynamics of policy responses. Scholars who rely on *sectoral analyses* criticize those using nation-wide approaches for conducting their analysis at too high a level of aggregation. Indeed, the description of sweeping aggregate national patterns may hide considerable policy variance across industrial sectors within each country (Kitschelt 1991). A national-level institutional framework that is hospitable to one set of technologies may not be to another. Many national-level analysts, however, provide categories of institutional conditions that they expect to be similar across sectors without closely examining the sectoral variations (Shafer 1994).

Sectoral approaches in contrast rely upon sector-specific properties and endowments—variously defined—to explain actor's behavior, and, in turn, political-economic outcomes (Kurth 1979; Rogowski 1989; Gourevitch 1986; Frieden 1991; Shafer 1994; Gilmore 1997). They use aspects of technology, markets, or other inputs—ownership or liquidity of capital, source of income, labor markets, and so forth—either alone or in combination as independent variables to determine the preferences of economic actors in a specific sector. Their research questions are primarily on how to explain cross-national and intra- national variations in the capacity of states to implement policies to promote industrial competitiveness, to help firms adjust to technological change, and to seize opportunities in international markets, under the assumption that there will be sectoral variation.[1]

These studies have made major contributions to our thinking about the relevance of sector-specific policies and institutions. However, they tend to overlook the continued divergence in *national systems of innovation* across nations engaged in the same industry, and thus a major source of divergence in state capacities for restructuring and sustained innovation. In this sense, sectoral and national approaches are antithetical, as Gilmore (1997) points out. In particular, the two disagree over the primary determinants of individual action and collective outcomes, and how institutions originate and change. However, what we want to do here is not to decide which approach is best, sectoral or national, but rather to explore the ways in which sectoral and national structures interact in shaping industrial adjustment and restructuring.

Both sectoral and national analyses generally overlook the coevolving processes of technological and institutional change—the adjusting of existing institutions to new technologies that goes on at the same time that technological choices are made with an idea to their fit with existing institutions. Instead, they view the two types of change as relatively independent of one another. A coevolutionary perspective may help us better to explain both changes in both sectoral and national governance structure over time. There are at least three approaches that qualify as essentially coevolutionary: (1) the neo-Schumpeterian approach, (2) the flexible specialization approach, and (3) the regulation approach.

Evolutionary economics, based on the Schumpeterian intellectual tradition, is the first of these approaches. It experienced a particularly notable rise in popularity in recent years with the publication of Richard Nelson's and Sydney Winter's (1982) pioneering study, *An Evolutionary Theory of Economic Change*. That work challenged the static framework of neoclassical economics and set forth an evolutionary theory of the economy. It treated "technical advance as an evolutionary process, in which new technological alternatives compete with each other and with prevailing practice, with *ex post* selection determining the winners and losers, usually with considerable *ex ante* uncertainty regarding which the winner will be" (Nelson 1998: 322).

In the same Schumpeterian tradition, Giovanni Dosi's concept of *technological paradigm* and Christopher Freeman's and Carlota Perez's concept of *techno-economic paradigm* provide useful frameworks for understanding the coevolution of technologies and institutions (Dosi 1982; Dosi et al. 1988; Freeman and Perez 1988). According to Freeman and Perez, for example, changes in technological paradigms

> have such widespread consequences for all sectors of the economy that their diffusion is accompanied by a major structural crisis of adjustment, in which social and institutional changes are necessary to bring about a better *match* between the new technology and the system of social management of the economy. (1988: 38)

Therefore, the definition of innovation should not be confined narrowly to a range of new products or industrial processes. Innovation includes new forms of work organization and management, new high growth sectors, new transport and communications technologies, new geographies of location, and so on. It is in this context that the computer revolution, which was accelerated by the microprocessor in the 1970s, has been followed by a growing recognition of the importance of organizational and managerial changes (*multi-skilling, lean production systems, downsizing, just-in-time*, stock control, worker participation in technical change, quality circles, continuous learning). The diffusion of a new techno-economic paradigm is a trial and error process involving great institutional variety. (Freeman and Soete 1997: 312).

Despite this apparent sensitivity to the contextual environment, in this view, the history of capitalism remains one in which new techno-economic forces always do the initial acting and old socioinstitutional frameworks the eventual reacting. The socioinstitutional context is clearly subordinate to the technoeconomical and its autonomy is strictly bounded.

The flexible specialization approach predicated on the neo-Smithian perspective is also useful for analyzing technological and institutional changes. (Sabel 1982; Piore and Sabel 1984; Sabel and Zeitlin 1985; Hirst and Zeitlin 1989, 1991) Michael Piore and Charles Sabel (1984) base their argument on a simple conceptual distinction between two ideal types of industrial production: mass production and flexible specialization. The type of industrial production affects the nature of institutions and governance structures. Piore and Sabel argue that craft production involves the use of general-purpose machinery and skilled labor, has low-fixed capital costs, and therefore promotes small firms in associative networks of exchange and reciprocity. In contrast, mass production utilizes dedicated (specialized) machinery and unskilled labor, has high-fixed costs, and fosters large integrated corporations in imperfectly competitive or oligopolistic markets.

However, Piore and Sabel argue further that technological choice must be endogenized within a sociocultural process. The emphasis is very much on social innovation and only secondarily on embodied technology. Central to this choice are the policy decisions taken by different actors that influence the diffusion of one or the other paradigm. Institutions are created in a context of conflict and rivalry. At rare historical turning points, or *industrial divides*, active choices taken in one direction or the other tend to consolidate into an epoch-making standard favoring either mass production or flexible specialization. "Thus one paradigm suffers because of the absence of supporting structures, while the other, it seems, gains in strength, because it comes to be seen as 'best practice' by industry, government and other institutions" (Amin 1994: 13–15).

As Herbert Kitschelt points out, Piore and Sabel's model places less emphasis on technological versus socioinstitutional factors as compared with that of the neo-Schumpeterians. Their model stands on two implicit premises: "The first is that technological systems, taken by themselves, do not determine which governance structures are efficient, and the second is that institutions are not adopted in a process of rational choice or evolutionary selection on the basis of their efficiency in delivering desired services" (Kitschelt 1991: 459). Indeed, Piore and Sable understand that a sociocultural process is relatively autonomous, and sociocultural models alone, not technology and efficiency, shape governance structure. In their view, governance structures are politically created and do not simply unfold according to an interior technological logic.

The third approach, the so-called *regulation school*, is consistent with the neo-Marxist tradition (Aglietta 1979; Lipietz 1987; Boyer 1988, 1990). In order to articulate and explain the systemic coherence of individual phases of capitalist development, regulation theory draws on two key concepts. One is the *regime of accumulation,* a "set of regularities at the level of the whole economy, enabling a more or less coherent process of capital accumulation." The other is the *mode of regulation,* "the institutional ensemble (laws, agreements, and so forth) and the complex of cultural habits and norms, which secures capitalist reproduction as such" (Nielsen 1991: 22). According to the regulation school, these two basic dynamics emerge out of the bedrock of capitalist social relations.

The regulation school's idea of a post-Fordist era of capitalism is a case in point. For them, Post-Fordism emerges from an interaction between technological trans-formations (a new regime of accumulation) and institutional transformations (a new mode of regulation). In their view, each particular mode of regulation is designed to control and stabilize a particular phase of capitalist growth, differing in important respects from the preceding phase. Institutional forms differ consider-ably between the regimes of early and mature *competition regulation* in the nine-teenth century and the *monopolistic* (or Fordist) mode of regulation in the period since the Second World War.

According to Elam (1994), the regulation approach sharply contrasts against the other two approaches. In contrast to the neo-Schumpeterian perspective that subjugates a diffuse and unspecified *socioinstitutional* framework to an irresistible and relatively articulate *techno-economic paradigm*, the regulation perspective pays more attention to autonomous institutional forms that fill the gap between tech-nological and institutional spheres. In contrast to the neo-Smithian perspective that subjugates politics and institutional arrangements to the invisible hand of the market, the regulation perspective sees markets as institutions usually encompassed by other institutions, which guarantee social cohesion through the coordination of private activities (Elam 1994: 57).

These evolutionary approaches may be more useful for explaining dynamics of technological and institutional changes than the sectoral and neoinstitutional approaches discussed earlier. However, all of them still lack an analytic method for describing the range of technologies and associated governance structures and for predicting the relationship between successful innovations and supporting institu-tional conditions. In particular, they have done little to develop theoretical tools that would enable us to understand the *selection mechanism* for determining the fitness of governance structures in relation to underlying technological conditions. Without such an analytic scheme, success or failure in adapting to coevolving technological and institutional changes cannot be explained.[2]

THEORETICAL FRAMEWORKS FOR EXPLAINING INSTITUTIONAL FITNESS

To develop a theoretical framework of institutional fitness for technological systems, we need to outline analytic types of technological systems and to distinguish types of governance structures to which they are expected to relate. Thus, we first rely on Herbert Kitschelt's (1991) theoretical framework for dealing with technological systems because, unlike the approaches discussed above, it makes predictions about the fitness of associated governance structures for various types of technological systems. We also draw upon neoinstitutional approaches to industrial change and international competitiveness in order to distinguish types of governance structures in national institutions that match each technological system. These theoretical resources help us to identify the mechanisms that establish the correspondence between technological systems and governance structures, and the interplay between sectoral and national conditions.

Kitschelt's Frameworks for Technological System

A definition of industrial sectors should be based on technological systems in order to develop a theory of the technological determinants of industrial governance structures. In this research, we adopt Herbert Kitschelt's definition of an industrial sector. He puts it this way:

> [An] industrial sector is often defined exclusively in terms of market conditions. But similar products and services may be delivered with different techniques and factors inputs. For this reason, I conceptualize a sector as a technological system within a particular market segment (1991: 460)

To distinguish analytic types of technological systems as industrial sectors, Kitschelt draws on recent contributions to organizational theory in sociology, economics, and business history. In particular, he relies on two main theoretical sources: Charles Perrow (1984) on technology and organization and Oliver Williamson (1985) on technological systems and governance structures. Kitschelt argues that any technology has two important dimensions that influence the choice of governance structures: One is the *degree of coupling* in the elements of a technological system, and the other is the *complexity of causal interactions* among production stages.

First, the tightness of coupling refers to the requirement for spatial or temporal links between different production steps. In tightly coupled systems, there are close spatial and temporal links between production steps. Thus, the production steps must be done at the same location or at the same time. In loosely coupled systems, however, each step or component of production is separated from every other step in space and time. Thus the production steps can be done in any sequence at any location. Tight coupling requires close supervision in order to contain problems that might otherwise spread quickly to other processes, but loose coupling permits less-centralized control because errors in system components do not easily affect the entire system. In short, the tighter technological elements are coupled, the more control needs to be centralized.[3]

This concept of coupling is closely related to the scale of the economy: the amount of capital investment required, the size of firms and individual production facilities, and so forth. If a technological system is tightly coupled, it generally requires a large economy with high levels of capital investment for local firms to be successful. However, if the technological system is loosely coupled, just the opposite holds. Kitschelt also relates the tightness of coupling to the organizational pattern of research and development research and development (R&D): "Tightly coupled systems require 'global' learning in which innovation addresses the mutual fit of all system components. Loosely coupled systems, in contrast, can afford more 'local' learning through improvement of individual system components" (Kitschelt 1991: 462).

Second, the complexity of causal interaction refers to the importance of feedback among production stages that is required to keep the whole process on track. In systems with complex interaction, elements influence each other mutually and engage in circular causal interaction. Thus, complex systems have large information requirements to manage the intricate flow of connections across processes. In systems with linear interaction that proceed from one stage to the next without feedback, the causality between elements is not complex. Thus, linear systems have fewer information requirements. In complex interactive systems, the monitoring, analysis, and correction of production processes take place in decentralized organizational units, because a centralized control would be quickly overloaded. In contrast, less complex systems with linear causality among the components are more amenable to centralized control because the straightforward intelligibility of systemic interactions reduces the probability that centralized control units will be overloaded with information processing.[4]

This concept of causal complexity is closely related to types of problem solving in R&D. If a technological process is in complex causal interaction, then its trajectories involve greater uncertainty in the interplay of system components, and are not readily predictable. Thus technological innovations have to be explored by trial and error, yielding fast-paced technological change with major breakthroughs followed by small incremental improvements. However, if the technological process is in causally linear systems, then its trajectories are predictable and production advances in continuous, incremental steps. These trajectories are associated with low levels of uncertainty and risk, thus facilitating programmed, incremental strategies of problem solving.

Based on his two criteria of technological systems—coupling and complexity, Kitschelt distinguishes five technological clusters from Mark I to Mark V technology, and matches them to possible efficient governance structures or favored institutional arrangements. In this research, we modify his categorization by reinterpreting Kitschelt's Mark III and Mark V categories. We divide his Mark III into two distinct technological clusters, Type 3 and Type 5a, and rename his Mark V as Type 5b.[5] Thus we create six types of distinct technological systems in all. (See Figure 11.1) These six types of technologies correspond to the empirical presence of *the leading sectors*—or the cyclical development of technological innovations—in the history of industrialization as described below.[6]

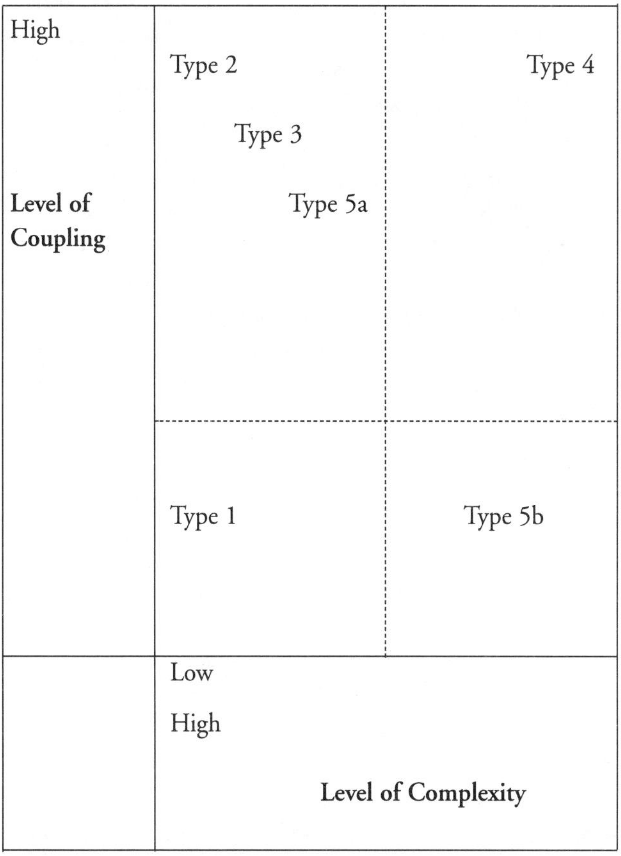

Figure 11.1 Analytic Types of Technological Systems

Sources: Modified from Kitschelt (1991) pp. 468–75, and Golden (1994) p. 129.

- *Type 1 technology* is a loosely coupled technological system with linear interaction among its components. Concentrated ownership is not necessary, nor are there important economies of scale. Because knowledge intensity is quite low, technological trajectories in this case are readily predictable. Therefore, new technologies are incrementally innovated. Consumer goods, light machine tools, and textiles belong to this type.
- *Type 2 technology* is a tightly coupled technological system with linear causal complexity. Because knowledge intensity remains fairly low, advances in product technologies are made incrementally along predictable trajectories. But, this type of technology requires large capital investments, and economies of scale increase rapidly over time. The heavy industries, such as iron, steel, and railroads, belong to this type.
- *Type 3 technology* is a considerably tight-coupled technological system with moderately low causal complexity. This type of technological system involves moderate knowledge intensity, and technological trajectories are readily predictable. Thus, product advances are made incrementally, but capital requirements are considerably high, and economies of scale are considerable. Chemical production, electrical engineering, consumer-durable goods, and automobiles belong to this type.
- *Type 4 technology* is a tightly coupled technological system with high causal complexity. Because this type of technology requires intensive knowledge, its trajectory is quite unpredictable. Advances in product technologies are made by leaps, not incrementally. Economies of scale are very large, and investment risks are very high. Representatives of this type of industry include nuclear power, aerospace, and large-scale computer and telecommunication systems.
- *Type 5a technology* is a relatively tight-coupled technological system with moderately low causal complexity. Because this type of technological system involves moderate knowledge intensity, the technological trajectories are generally predictable, and product advances are usually made in incremental steps with some breakthroughs. These are capital-intensive and high-volume industries that operate in commodity-like markets. Economies of scale are initially high, but decrease over time. Examples include consumer electronics and computer hardware components such as dynamic random access memories (DRAMs) and flat panel displays (FPDs).
- *Type 5b technology* is a loosely coupled technological system with high causal complexity. Because this type of technological system involves high intensity of knowledge, the technological trajectories are highly unpredictable. Problem solving for this type of technology is not readily predictable in time, cost, or in final results. Thus, innovations occur in these technological systems as a process of localized trial-end-error learning, often in interaction with customers. The economies of scale are initially moderate, but increase over time. Examples of this type of technology are computer software, microprocessors, and biotechnology.

Kitschelt's idea of analyzing the degree of coupling and the complexity of causal interactions is very useful in distinguishing types of technological systems and in predicting how well each type of technological system will fit a particular governance structure. Kitschelt hypothesizes that each technological system requires a distinct governance structure for maximum performance. Although the combination of coupling and complexity of a technological system do not determine a uniquely optimal governance structure, they do at least constrain the efficient possibilities. What types of governance structures match each technological system?

Neoinstitutional Frameworks of Governance Structure

To understand the potential *match* between technological systems and governance structures, it is necessary first to distinguish analytic types of governance structures. Although Kitschelt presents a framework for distinguishing types of appropriate governance structures, his framework is somewhat inadequate. Relying on Perrow's approach, Kitschelt's framework is mainly based on the distinction between *centralized* and *decentralized* governance structures. He relies on Williamson's work in order to add two more types—*market-oriented* governance structures, and *mixed* private and public networks—somewhere in between the centralized and decentralized extremes.

Kitschelt's typology of governance structures, therefore, is too one-dimensional—centralized and decentralized governance structures mark the endpoints on a continuum, whereas his typology of technological systems is obviously two-dimensional: with coupling and complexity forming the two dimensions. We thought it might be useful to match the two-dimensional categorization of technological systems with a two-dimensional categorization of governance structures.

As discussed earlier, some neoinstitutional approaches try to explain why and how particular types of domestic institutional arrangements—national-level governance structures—have succeeded in creating innovations, and in diffusing new technologies, while other types have had difficulties.[7] They attempt to show that variations in national institutions explain why similar sectors in different countries are associated with varying governance structures, and why different sectors in the same country develop similar governance structures. Among the institutional elements that account for sectoral variations, two key variables have gained special attention by neoinstitutional scholars on industrial innovations and competitiveness: (1) the organizing principle (or the pattern of integration) of corporate and industrial structure and (2) the industrial role of the state in relation to the societal sector (Fong 1990).

Analytic types of *industrial governance* can be distinguished by observing the characteristics of the industries and their firms that affect their economic behavior and impact upon government policy (Chandler 1977 1990; Aoki 1986; Utterback and Suarez 1990; Lazonick 1991; Grove 1996; Fransman 1999). Such industry characteristics include the size of the industry, the organizational structure of firms, the degree of concentration of ownership, the level of interfirm coordination, the degree to which user-producer (or manufacturer-supplier) links are utilized by firms in the industry, the presence of national or cross-national production and distribution networks, and the corporate and managerial cultures of firms and industries.

For the purpose of this research, we will categorize industrial governance into three main types of integration: *vertical, networked,* and *horizontal.* The more vertically integrated corporate or industry structure is, the more centralized industrial governance is expected to be; the more horizontally integrated it is, the less centralized industrial governance is expected to be.

- *Vertical Integration:* The industry's organizing principle is based on hierarchical control, and the degree of integration among industrial units is tight or closed. For example, inputs, assembly, and distribution are vertically integrated. The firms rely far less on outside suppliers than other types, tending to be far more self-sufficient in producing or procuring parts. Corporate and industry structure among the minicomputer firms along Route 128 near Boston and large American computer and communication companies, such as IBM and AT&T, are considered to belong to this type of industrial governance.
- *Horizontal Integration:* The industry's organizing principle is based on horizontal coordination, and the degree of integration among industrial units is loose or fragmented. For example, inputs, assembly, and distribution are horizontally integrated. The firms rely far more on outside suppliers than other types, tending to be far more interdependent in procuring parts. The semiconductor industry in Silicon Valley in California is a prime example of this type of industrial governance.
- *Networked Integration:* This type is located somewhere between vertical and horizontal integration. Japanese industrial organizations, as typified by interlocking business ties within *keiretsu* industrial groups, are examples.

Analytic types of *state governance* can be distinguished by observing the industrial role of the state or the patterns of industrial policy (Evans, Reuschemeyer and Skocpol 1985; Krasner 1984; Nordlinger 1981). The so-called *strength of the state*—the capabilities of government agencies and other national political institutions in relation to the business sector, including mechanisms of state penetration into society—or *state-societal arrangements*—defined in terms of the distribution of power among the state, the private business sector, and organized labor—is often considered to be a critical factor for understanding the nature of state governance (Hart 1992). More specifically, the industrial role of the state is embodied as industrial policy, which refers to the deliberate attempt by the government through a range of specific policies such as financial subsidies, trade protectionism, promotion of research and development, and procurement to determine the structure of the economy. Although we are mostly interested in these *micro* aspects of industrial policy popularly known as *industrial targeting*, we also take into account the effects of more generic, *macro* policies that differentially affect specific industries or create capabilities relevant to specific industries, such as antitrust policies, intellectual property protection policy, and educational policies.

For the purpose of this research, we will categorize state governance into three types: *interventionist, developmental,* and *regulatory.* The more interventionist the state is, the more centralized state governance is expected to be; the more regulatory the state is, the less centralized state governance is expected to be.[8]

- *The Interventionist State:* The role of the state is intrusive and interventionist in the economy. The *strong* state is largely autonomous from society and can direct economic activities in directions it considers socially or politically desirable. This type of governance involves a vertically coordinated and tightly controlled bureaucracy. The communist or fascist ideal of the state belongs to this type.
- *The Regulatory State:* The role of the state tends to be a minimal one. The predominant responsibility of the state is to correct market failures and provide public goods. That is to say, the state has principally a regulatory and facilitating role. These *weak* states frequently become the captives of interest groups. This type of governance is horizontally coordinated and loosely controlled. The so-called *liberal state* belongs to this type.
- *The Developmental State:* This type is located somewhere between the interventionist and the regulatory. The contemporary Japanese state, with its close cooperation between the state and business, is an example.

The neoinstitutional framework of industrial and state governance provides us with a useful guideline to distinguish types of governance structures at both the national and sectoral levels. In particular, Kitschelt's one-dimensional typology of governance structures—from centralized to decentralized structures—is obviously enriched by our two dimensional modification. Indeed, these principal components of national governance most directly affect industrial innovations and an economy's international competitiveness, and differentiate their systems of political economy in the contemporary world.

Institutional Fits for Technological Systems

How are these types of governance structures expected to relate to analytic types of technological systems identified above according to properties of technology? How do we relate each sector to a predicted governance structure? Efficient national governance structures shaped by properties of associated technological systems—from Type 1 to Type 5b technology—can ideally be described as follows (See Figure 11.2).

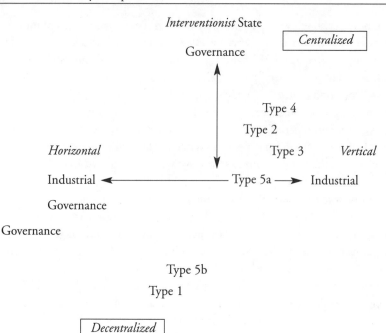

Figure 11.2 Institutionalized Fits for Technological Systems

- Governance structures for *Type 1 technology* (loose coupling and linear causal complexity) match a combination of *horizontal* industrial governance and *regulatory* state governance. This is *highly decentralized* market-oriented governance with a *weak* state and *strong* business. As Kitschelt (1991: 466) argues, "innovation in these systems stems from the disjointed, local, and incremental process of *learning by doing*, rather than from systematic research organization." Therefore, centralized involvement in technology development is often inefficient.

- Governance structures for *Type 2 technology* (tight coupling and linear causal complexity) generally match a combination of *vertical* industrial governance and *interventionist* state governance. This is basically a *centralized* government-guided governance model witnessed in the industrializing countries with *strong* state intervention during the early stages of industrial catching-up. As Kitschelt (1991: 466, 471) argues, "the domestic structures that gained advantage were those which facilitate industrial centralization, state involvement in industrial development, or a combination of both."

- Governance structures for *Type 3 technology* (considerably tight-coupling and moderately low-causal complexity) primarily match a combination of *networked* or *vertical* industrial governance and *developmental* or *interventionist* state governance. However, the increasing tightness and scale of the economy require this governance structure to bring about a *relatively centralized* mass-production model: high-volume production of mass-produced standardized goods or intermediate products using standardized machinery. The markets of Type 3 technologies shift from initially competitive to imperfectly competitive markets, and firm governance becomes increasingly vertical.

- Governance structures for *Type 4 technology* (tight coupling and high causal complexity) match a combination of and *vertical* industrial governance and *interventionist* state governance. This is *highly centralized* governance requiring *strong* state involvement, which often puts the burden of investment risks on public agencies, even in cases where the technologies could be developed or produced in privately owned facilities. According to Kitschelt (1991: 467–68), "because an efficient form of governance appears to be difficult to establish, (technologies of Type 4 develop) only under the tutelage of national governments, with private investors relieved from all or most of the investment risks through cost-plus contracts, favorable regulation, or outright public entrepreneurship."

- Governance structures for *Type 5a technology* (relatively tight-coupling and moderately low-causal complexity) primarily match a combination of *networked* or *vertical* industrial governance and *developmental* or *interventionist* state governance. In contrast to governance structures appropriate for Type 3 technologies, the role of state here is more limited and the pattern of industrial governance less vertical. This is a *cooperative* governance model between the state and other societal actors, infusing an element of flexibility into production systems and reducing the risks for individual firms of investing in new technologies. According to Kitschelt (1991: 472), this kind of governance structure "fostered networks of medium-sized companies with close linkages between customers and suppliers and close interaction with a nonprofit research infrastructure of universities and laboratories."

- Governance structures for *Type 5b technology* (loose coupling and high causal complexity) match a combination of a *horizontal* industrial governance and *regulatory* state governance. This is basically *decentralized* market-oriented governance. However, in contrast to the similar governance structure for Type 1 technology, this type requires more *sophisticated* institutional arrangements. The rise of clan-like and collegial groups, such as start-up firms with an entrepreneurship, are primarily expected; and small venture capitalists invest in the nodes of the network in which causal relations are sufficiently well understood. However, in cases where R&D uncertainties are substantial and markets for venture capital remain underdeveloped, a governance structure with mixed private and public R&D supports is required. Large corporations with decentralized structures or intercorporate alliances of various sorts are needed in order to provide necessary R&D costs. Moreover, a comprehensive public and semipublic infrastructure of technological development through universities, professional associations, and research centers can further R&D efforts. The regulatory role of the state to promote start-up firms and private investment like venture capital is also considered to be important.

The framework of technological and institutional fit, as outlined above, tells us that *industrial learning* about the technological fit of governance structures likely occurs in a particular sector, and the fit determines the outcomes. That framework, however, does not specify *how* industrial learning occurs. To account for the process of industrial learning, we must therefore further explore how sectoral (or technological) and national (or institutional) conditions interact to produce successful or unsuccessful outcomes of institutional adjustment, to what degree industrial learning occurs, and in what feedback process the adjustment strategy corrects itself. Moreover, we must answer what factors—incentives or obstacles—should be considered for the successful adjustment This must be related to the question that is probably the most interesting one from the national policy perspective: What strategies are needed for the countries to create—or emulate—efficient governance structures for a new technological system?

AN EVOLUTIONARY MODEL OF INSTITUTIONAL ADJUSTMENT

Now we apply the theoretical framework discussed above to explain the rise of technological systems and responses of the form of institutional adjustments as parts of an evolutionary model of technological fitness. This evolutionary model will help us understand the rise and fall of industrial paradigms in *leading sectors* of the global political economy, and further provide an explanatory framework for understanding the persistence of national institutional diversity.

Technological Fitness in the Evolutionary Context

As in any evolutionary analysis, we need to examine four basic mechanisms: variation, selection, amplification, and cooperation. Because our subject is the evolution of a set of social institutions and practices possibly modified by institutional adjustment strategies, the causes of variation, selection, amplification, and cooperation will be social rather than natural. Large changes, therefore, can be expected to occur over shorter time periods than they do in nature (Modelski and Poznanski 1996). Figure 11.3 provides a brief analytic summary of the hypothesized interactions between technological systems, national governance structures, and institutional adjustment in contributing to success or failure in industrial sectors.

The ultimate source of *variation* in industrial practices is technological change—that is, technological innovation in products and processes at the level of the firms or research laboratories. Occasionally technological innovations give rise

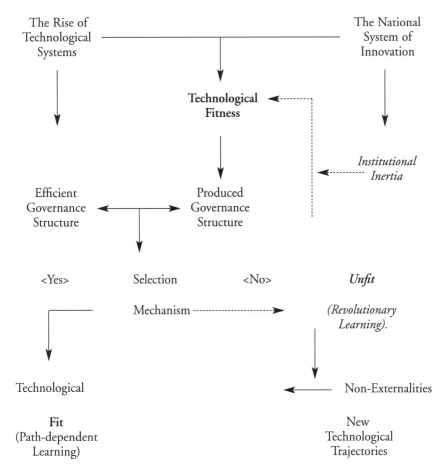

Figure 11.3 **An Evolutionary Model of Institutional Adjustment**

to a new technological system, or, as evolutionary economists call it, a *technological paradigm shift* (Dosi 1982; Freeman and Perez 1988). Since industrial sectors are defined by their underlying technological conditions, the rise of a technological system alters fundamental conditions within specific industrial sectors.

Technological innovations very often transform the economic characteristics of industries, the basic direction (and structure) of markets, the nature of opportunities and risks in those markets, the mode of competition, and the range of competitive strategies available to firms. The rise of new technological systems also transforms the institutional characteristics of industries. Because a new technological system often requires new governance structures for best performance, when a new technological system arises, institutional requirements for successful innovation and productive efficiency in those sectors also change. In the face of technological change, therefore, established firms have to make adjustments to handle new competitive conditions and states have to create new policy tools and adjust national institutional arrangements in order to be able to assist firms in dealing with technological change.

In the theory presented above, the outcomes of these adjustments depend on whether they can produce new governance structures that fit the new technological system. Kitschelt (1991: 480) amplifies on this point by saying that,

> ... success or failure depends not only on a match between the properties of technology in individual sectors and the national institutional capabilities but also on the abilities to translate these properties and capabilities into efficient sectoral governance structures.

We will refer to the closeness of the match between governance structures and technological systems as *technological fitness*. We will distinguish between short-term technological fitness that arises almost accidentally from a close fit between national governance structures and a new technological system and the long-term fitness that arises out of conscious efforts on the part of the state and other institutions to adjust to the new technological system.

Institutional adjustment is a critical factor in the success of firms in new industrial sectors over the long term. We focus here on adjustments in two key types of national governance structures—industry structures and the industrial role of the state. In this sense, we distinguish institutional adjustment from related terms in IPE such as *structural adjustment, industrial adjustment,* and *economic adjustment,* which define various forms of policy coordination for coping with structural changes in macroeconomic conditions or overall comparative advantage, but which do not necessarily focus on the fit between governance structures and technological systems.

To summarize, technological fitness works as a *selection mechanism* in the coevolution of technological change and institutional adjustment. The more a nation can develop technological fitness, the more it will succeed in an industrial sector. Over time, *selection* should yield nearly identical (or at least similar) governance structures in identical sectors, regardless of national differences in other areas. If the governance structures of a particular nation diverge from the structure needed to foster growth in a given technology, industries associated with that technology will not grow as rapidly in that country.

Path-Dependent Learning and Industrial Paradigms

Every nation has different institutions. All, without exception, have strengths and weaknesses for the development of particular industrial sectors. Thus, major technological changes tend to benefit some nations more than others. As Kitschelt (1991: 468–69) argues,

. . . countries will successfully innovate in those new sectors in which their prior institutional endowments are conducive to the emergence of governance structures optimal in those sectors. Under these circumstances, the cost of learning to master a new technological trajectory is quite modest and sectors will seize new opportunities quickly.

If a nation adopts a new technological system that fits an already existing pattern of governance, that nation can achieve success within a framework of *path-dependent learning* (following the **bold** line in Figure 11.3). Usually one or two nations—mostly through path-dependent learning—survive and prosper from the initial transition to a new industrial paradigm. Subsequent moves toward fitness in other countries/regions are primarily the result of conscious sociocultural change. Only through the process of adjusting national institutions to technological change, can they adapt to a new industrial paradigm. Occasionally, however, a new industrial paradigm emerges from an attempt on the part of a given nation (or region) to partially adapt its institutions to earlier technological changes. The new institutions still do not fit the dominant technological system but they are well suited to still newer technological systems that have the potential to create a new industrial paradigm of their own.[9]

Now, we present brief descriptions of six distinct industrial paradigms that have been created (or is being created) in leading sectors. (See Table 11.1) Each industrial paradigm emerges from a particular moment in industrial history and from a specific nation that benefits from an initial advantage in fitness and from cheaper path-dependent learning.

Table 11.1 Leading Sectors versus Industrial Paradigms

	Leading Sectors	Industrial Paradigms	The Fittest
Type 1	Consumer Goods, Light Machine, Textiles	The British Model	Britain
Type 2	Iron, Steel, Railroads	The Late-Industrializer Model	Germany
Type 3	Chemicals, Electrical Engineering, Consumer-Durables, Automobiles	Fordism	The United States
Type 4	Nuclear Power, Aerospace, Large-scale Computer, and Communication Systems	The Manhattan Project Model	The United States
Type 5a	Consumer Electronics, Computer Hardware Components	The Japanese Model	Japan
Type 5b	Computer Software, Microprocessor, Biotechnology	Wintelism	The United States

- *The British Model* in the late-eighteenth and early-nineteenth centuries: The *light industry-production* model supported free markets and the *liberal state*—noninterventionist and nonauthoritarian state governance combined with parliamentary supremacy and property suffrage—emerged during the textile industrialization in Britain. It matches *highly decentralized* governance in Type 1 technologies, such as consumer goods, light machine tools, and textiles (Kurth 1979).

- *The Late-industrializer Model* in the mid to late nineteenth century: The *heavy industry-production* model supported by oligopolistic markets and *authoritarian states*—along with large investment banks—which undertook large capital costs, emerged in the late industrializers, particularly Germany, Austria-Hungary, Italy, and Russia. It matches *centralized, government-guided* governance in Type 2 technologies, such as iron, steel, and railroads (Gerschenkron 1962).

- *Fordism* in the late-nineteenth and the twentieth centuries: The *mass production* model supported by large corporations and the *welfare state* emerged in the United States, and then became the model of industrial development in the years after World War II. It matches *relatively centralized* governance in Type 3 technologies, such as chemical production, electrical engineering, consumer-durable goods, and automobiles (Amin 1994; Bakker and Miller 1996).

- *The Manhattan Project Model* in the mid-twentieth century: The *megaproject* production model supported by the military like the *strong state*'s capabilities expending very large, highly engineered military R&D projects emerged in the United States century particularly during the Cold War period. It matches *highly centralized* governance in Type 4 technologies such as nuclear power, aerospace, and large-scale computer and telecommunication systems (Ferguson and Morris 1994: 172).

- *The Japanese Model* in the late-twentieth century century: The lean production model[10] supported by a cooperative, sometimes networked social structure of firms—the so-called *keiretsu* system—and the *developmental* state—a cooperative network between the state and other societal actors—emerged in postwar Japan. It matches *moderately centralized* governance in Type 5a technologies such as consumer electronics and computer hardware components (Kitschelt 1991).

- *Wintelism* in the latter part of the twentieth century (and possibly into the twenty-first century): The so-called Silicon Valley model supported by *horizontally segmented* industrial structures combined with a *regulatory* state is emerging as an industrial paradigm in the United States. It matches *sophisticated decentralized* governance in Type 5b technologies such as computer software, microprocessors, and biotechnology (Ferguson and Morris 1994; Borrus and Zysman 1997).

A new industrial paradigm created in a specific nation tends to become more general and diffuses to other nations over time. Once a nation succeeds in establishing an industrial paradigm in a leading sector, it is likely that other nations will try to copy it. In both cases of the British model and the American Fordism, for example, a single dominant style of production organization spread out from a single dominant core country—Britain in the former case, the United States in the latter. In the similar vein, since the early 1980s, Japanese management and production systems have attracted worldwide attention because they offer techniques and methods of production that outperformed existing U.S. and European systems. In this way, a successful model of industrial paradigm tends to diffuse across national boundaries.

Revolutionary Learning and Institutional Inertia

Those nations whose prevailing national governance structures do not match the institutional requirements of a new technological system—and whose weaknesses in institutional capabilities are critical obstacles for success—have fewer possibilities to be successful in the sector unless they deliberately attempt to create new governance structures. In this case, therefore, an alternative possibility is that nations will promote their technological fitness through *revolutionary learning*—involving a major break with past practices, as seen Figure 11.3, following the *dotted* line.

In the case of revolutionary learning, the task of institutional adjustment is more complicated because it requires adjusting not only industrial structures and industrial policies but also deeper aspects of the national system of innovation. Moreover, institutional adjustment through revolutionary learning may involve changing deeply rooted institutions such as educational systems or labor-management systems.

To conceptualize the deeper aspects of a social system relating to technological innovation, evolutionary economists adopt the concept of *national systems of innovation*—the "network of institutions in the public and private sectors whose activities and interactions initiate, import, modify and diffuse new technologies" (Freeman 1987: 1). In the very similar context, Margaret Sharp (1997) adopts the concept of *science and technology* (S&T) *infrastructure* to describe the deeper aspects of a national system of innovation. According to Sharp (1997: 101), S&T infrastructure involves high quality secondary education, a good vocational training system, a strong university sector, a well-found academic research base with a major postgraduate component, university-industry linkage, research associations that support technology dissemination to small and medium-sized business, and the encouragement of regional initiatives bringing together firms, universities, and research institutions.

S&T infrastructures differ markedly across nations. One major cleavage is between the S&T infrastructures of technological leaders and followers. S&T infrastructure in technological leaders tends to be *macroscopic,* providing a broadly based capacity for original thinkers to create new knowledge. General emphases are on enhancing human resources in basic research, creating and maintaining a strong university participation in R&D, and nourishing a *liberal* tradition in postgraduate educational institutions. In contrast, S&T infrastructure in catch-up or follower countries tends to be *microscopic,* implementing specific tasks necessary for catching up with the leaders. Thus, general emphases are on enhancing human resources in applied engineering, corporate initiatives in R&D, and nourishing a *developmental* tradition in both educational institutions and state bureaucracies.

When a nation has an already well-established national system of innovation or S&T infrastructure, it is much more difficult to achieve the goal of adjustment through revolutionary learning. This is because there is *institutional inertia.* Institutional inertia usually comes from an unwillingness to try new techniques when old ones have proven to be successful in the past. With regard to the institutional inertia, Robert Gilpin (1996: 413) convincingly holds,

> . . . past success itself can become an obstacle to further innovation and adaptation to a changed environment; a society can become locked into economic practices and institutions that in the past were congruent with successful innovation but which are no longer congruent in the changed circumstances. Powerful vested interests resist change, and it is very difficult to convince a society that what has worked so well in the past may not work in an unknown future. Thus, a national system of political economy that was most fit and efficient in one area of technology and market demand is very likely to be unfit in a succeeding age of new technologies and new demands.

Failures to adjust the system are caused mainly by assuming that the future will be like the past and that what was done in the past will work in the future. More importantly, however, failures are also caused by the continuing political strength of interests strongly associated with the methods and results of past successes. The system will not change as long as those established political forces successfully resist changes in the system and ignore the need for reforms.

Such institutional inertia often prevails when a nation attempts to adopt or emulate a new industrial paradigm of foreign origins. The new industrial paradigm is often embedded in a web of interrelated social institutions in the nation of origin that cannot easily be copied or adapted.

Much of the earlier literature on industrial paradigms contains debates about the ability and/or necessity of various social systems and political regions to insulate themselves from the global impact of a shift in industrial paradigms. For example, many countries in Western Europe had difficulties in adjusting to the American mass-production techniques typical of the Fordist industrial paradigm. Rather, they attempted to preserve the institutions that were compatible with traditional family-owned businesses with their smaller-scale and craft-related production.

Similarly, there is a more recent debate about the ability and/or necessity of both American and European firms and governments to adopt the practices associated with the Toyotaist industrial paradigm. Toyotaism requires a commitment by suppliers and assemblers to cooperate that is easier to obtain in national systems that encourage vertical integration of firms than in systems that discourage it. Countries with strong organized labor may have difficulties changing labor-management relationships to accommodate lean production practices like *just-in-time* delivery of components.[11] Without careful consideration of these cross-national differences in antitrust enforcement and labor-management relations, importing Toyotaist practices may not have the desired effects (Abo 1996).

Japan's difficulties in the computer software industry can be understood in the same context. Recently, Japan has been trying to adjust its system to adopt the so-called Silicon Valley model—or Wintelism—as an institutional solution for the computer industry. Wintelism is consistent with the existing cultural and institutional environment of the American system. However, the corporate cultures, educational system and other social institutions in Japan are not consistent with Wintelism even though they were supportive of past industrial success (Kim 2000).

In our theory, the inability or unwillingness to change out-dated systems due to institutional inertia lies at the heart of industrial failures. Unless they can find some other ways to compete in new industrial sectors—through revolutionary learning or path-dependent learning that encourages the rise of new industrial paradigms— then countries with such systems will suffer relative economic decline. If a nation cannot successfully establish appropriate governance structures in the industrial sector, technological leadership may pass to other countries better able to make the necessary institutional adjustments in new sectors, as seen in Table 11.1.

Before concluding, we call attention to the possibility of revolutionary learning by *non-technological externalities* as seen in Figure 11.3. This point is closely related to the argument contained in Modelski and Thompson's theories on long waves and the long cycle in global politics (Modelski and Thompson 1996; Thompson 1990). During international crises or wars, learning may sharply diverge from the path-dependent learning usually witnessed in governance structures. Victory or loss in a major war or a fundamental change in a country's position in the international system can serve as a motivating factor for revolutionary learning. The success of Type 4 technology and the emergence of the Manhattan Project model in the United States (and partially in France), for example, were obviously affected by the exigencies of World War II and the Cold War.

CONCLUSIONS: THE GLOBAL POLITICS OF INDUSTRIAL SPECIALIZATION

Even in an increasingly globalized world economy, nations tend to display very different institutional responses in adjusting to technological changes. Variations in national circumstances may often lead to diverse paths of institutional solutions, and result in diverse industrial outcomes. We cannot imagine the adoption of a single best solution for a technological system by every society. Likewise, we cannot posit that the adoption or emulation of a given industrial paradigm will always yield identical governance structures in identical sectors across national boundaries guaranteeing identical successes.

Given limited national resources and institutional capabilities, it is exceedingly unlikely that every country will succeed in creating or emulating all new industrial paradigms as they arise. Countries may choose (or may be forced to choose) to specialize (or *cooperate*) in particular sectors, in which they have advantages, rather than to invest in all industrial sectors. As a result, they may choose to continue to occupy sheltered *niche markets* within a larger economic environment. Usually, countries will choose those technologies and governance structures that *minimize* any possible adjustment costs. In other words, nations may choose only to emulate industrial paradigms that are located close to existing institutional arrangements (Kitschelt 1991: 470).

As a result, there will be always be some tendency toward specialization, even in the three major industrial regions—Western Europe, Japan and the United States. In Western Europe, for example, Germany specializes in engineering, chemicals, high-quality machinery, and intermediate equipment goods (Type 2 or Type 3); France in nuclear power and high-speed trains (Type 4); and the United Kingdom in finance and pharmaceutical (Type 1 or Type 5b). Japan continues to specialize in automobiles (Type 3), consumer electronics and electronic components (Type 5a). And, the United States specializes in aerospace (Type 4) and biotechnology, microprocessors and computer software (Type 5b).

In this process of industrial specialization, each country enters new industries under a different set of initial conditions affected by a different set of decisions and events; therefore, each nation followed its own path to its present position. Some pre-existing conditions worked well, while others did not. Countries succeed in one new industry, but not in others. Each country uses its national repertoire of strategies to take advantage of strengths built up in specific areas over decades of pursuing a specific institutional capability. For example, Germany takes advantage of the richness and quality of the skills of German workers, Japan takes advantage of its system of large firms and stable subcontractors, and the United States relies on the excellence of university research and the easy availability of venture capital (Boyer 1996: 52–53).

In fact, a new conceptualization of industrial specialization among nations is not based on different resource endowments, as understood in neoclassical theories of comparative advantage, but on varied institutional capabilities in relation to technological changes. In other words, specialization will be based on important differences among the countries in terms of *technological fitness* in a general context of institutional inertia. Nations will succeed in new industrial sectors when their existing industrial governance structures fit the institutional requirements of the new technological system. Also, nations will succeed in the new industries if they can successfully adjust their existing institutional capabilities to the requisite properties of the new sector.

Two further points about specialization can be made. The ability to support diverse industrial and state governance structures across industries will be a great advantage to any nation that aspires to be a major industrial power with competitive strengths in a broad range of industries. Second, a nation can partially compensate for its inability to adjust domestically by encouraging domestic firms to partner with foreign firms and by encouraging inward foreign investment on the part of foreign firms from countries with higher technological fitness. These options become less expensive as the world economy becomes more global.

When the firms of nations that have technological fitness in leading sectors dominate the most profitable businesses, the long-term consequences of global industrial specialization might be to increase the level of global economic inequality. Thus, there is a strong incentive for nations to develop institutional arrangements that permit multiple forms of industrial and state governance to coexist domestically. There is also some incentive for contemporary nations to support the continuation of trends toward economic globalization as a way of stemming increases in global economic inequality. There is much evidence from the past, that this is not an easy task. George Modelski and William Thompson (1996), for example, hold in their empirical research that rises and declines in leading sectors in the global economy—connected with the so-called Kondratieff waves—were linked to the rise and decline of world powers in what they call the long cycle of global politics. The world powers listed in Table 11.1 were countries that had technological fitness in leading sectors, and thus were able to define new industrial paradigms, but only for a limited time. The uncertainty about maintaining top-dog status in an environment of rapid technological change creates a new logic of international competition where the need to foster multiple forms of technological fitness simultaneously may overwhelm the tendency toward domestic institutional inertia.

NOTES

An earlier version of this paper was prepared for delivery at a conference on Evolutionary Perspective on International Relations, Indiana University, Bloomington, Indiana, December 4–6 1998

1. In his seminal work Michael Porter (1990) explores a similar question on nations' industrial performances not only across nations and across industries within the same nation, but even within the same nation and industry over time.
2. Presenting an advanced version of sectoral analysis, Gilmore tries to offer an explanation of the selection mechanism. He hypothesizes, "a state is more likely to facilitate innovation in those sectors in which institutional endowments and policy choices are conductive to both the pursuit of viable market strategies, and unfettered domestic rivalry." In his theory, "institutions and policies must *fit* the requisites of competition in global markets. Only then will policy makers enjoy the autonomy and relative capacity to effectively formulate and implement technology policy" (emphasis added) (Gilmore 1997: 41). However, his analytic framework of the *fit* between market condition and institutions is still inadequate to understand the dynamics of technological factors.

3. According to Kitschelt, Perrow's concept of coupling is in the same context as Williamson's concept of *asset specificity*. "Assets are considered highly specific if they are committed to a particular location, production process, or customer. In other words, high asset specificity establishes *tight linkages* (in Perrow's sense) between different elements and stages in the production process, whether it is based on purely technical or purely economic conditions, whereas low asset specificity established *loose linkage*" (emphasis added) (Kitschelt 1991: 464).

4. Kitschelt also places Williamson's concepts of *uncertainty* and *frequency of interaction between suppliers and customers* in the same context as Perrow's concept of *causal complexity*. "Uncertainty in contractual linkages has a technical and an economic face. High uncertainty often stems from the *complex causal interaction* among agents and techniques involved in the production process and requires, in Perrow's sense, decentralized intelligence and the autonomy of professionals. Conversely, low uncertainty is generally associated with *linear causal linkage*. In complex interactive production processes, it is difficult to specify contracts fully in advance and hence to enforce them. These circumstances also enable self-interested actors to take advantage of underspecified contracts by opportunistic behavior" (emphasis added) (Kitschelt 1991: 464).

5. There are two reasons we present type 5a and type 5b, instead of type 5 and type 6. On the one hand, it is still hard to distinguish clearly the two types of interrelated technological systems, which keep transforming; on the other hand, it is the critical part of our research design to contrast these two types of technologies, thus we use a set of paired labels: type 5a and type 5b.

6. Among various industrial sectors growing at different rates, *leading sectors* are expanding rapidly, and thus drive the rest of the economy. The leading sector is characterized by quantitative increases in output and qualitative improvements in the basic technology, and thus is a generator of high rates of profits, wages, and employment. From this leading sector, secondary and tertiary industries are spun off and radiate growth throughout the economy (Modelski and Thompson 1996).

7. In a similar vein, to explore these similarities and differences among nation-states, evolutionary economists adopt the concept of *national systems of innovation*—the "network of institutions in the public and private sectors whose activities and interactions initiate, import, modify and diffuse new technologies" (Freeman 1987; Freeman and Perez 1988; Lundvall 1992; Nelson 1993; Freeman and Soete 1997).

8. This categorization of state governance is usually based on the scale of technological systems—in Kitschelt's terms, the tightness of coupling. Some scholars have previously dealt with the relationship between governance structures and new technologies. For example, when Kurth (1979) argued that countries in which industrialization was driven by light consumer goods, rather than by heavy industry, were likely to end up as liberal democracies, one of his independent variables was the 'scale' of individual technological systems. See Kitschelt (1991: 457–58).

9. The concept of production systems—such as Fordism, Post-Fordism, or Toyotaism (the lean production model)—has been used primarily by the Regulation School to describe the range of particular methods of procuring and combining various inputs and managing the whole manufacturing process at the level of the workplace. An industrial paradigm is a broader concept that includes within it a production system—but goes beyond it to also include a set of institutional arrangements that fit that production system.

10. Origins of the Japanese lean production model are from the automobile industry such as Toyota and other Japanese auto companies. However, electronics producers

like Matsushita and Hitachi applied this lean production principles in order to innovate in traditional consumer electronics products with all solid-state televisions. As in autos, adoption of lean production techniques enabled Japanese electronics firms to create new and distinctive market segments by the late 1970s with the Walkman, VCR, and Camcorder, and by the early 1980s, to challenge U.S. leadership in semiconductors. In many respect, this model is the *Japanese-style Post Fordism.*

12. Scholars like Wolfgang Streeck argue that Toyotaism is inconsistent with the German model of labor-management relations, and that German auto firms will therefore have to find some other way to compete with Japanese auto firms in their main markets (Streeck 1996).

REFERENCES

Abo, Tetsuo. 1996. The Japanese Production System: The Process of Adaptation to National Settings. In Robert Boyer and Daniel Drache, eds. *States against markets: The Limits of globalization.* London and New York: Routledge.

Aglietta, M. 1979. *A Theory of capitalist regulation.* London: New Left Books.

Amin, Ash, ed. 1994. *Post-fordism: A Reader.* Cambridge, Mass.: Blackwell.

Aoki, Masahiko. 1986. Horizontal vs. Vertical Information Structure of the Firm. *The American Economic Review,* 76(5).

Bakker, Isabella and Riel Miller. 1996. Escape from Fordism: The Emergence of Alternative Forms of State Administration and Output. In Robert Boyer and Daniel Drache, eds. *States against markets: The Limits of globalization.* London and New York: Routledge.

Borrus, Michael and John Zysman. 1997. Globalization with Borders: The Rise of Wintelism as the Future of Global Competition. *Industry and Innovation,* 4(2).

Boyer, Robert. 1996. The Convergence Hypothesis Revisited: Globalization but Still the Century of Nations? In Suzanne Berger and Ronald Dore, eds. *National diversity and global capitalism.* Ithaca and London: Cornell University Press.

———. 1990. *The Regulation school: A critical introduction.* New York: Columbia University Press.

———. 1988. Technical Change and the Theory of "Regulation." In Giovanni Dosi, Christopher Freeman, Richard R. Nelson, Gerald Silverberg, and Luc Soete, eds. *Technical change and economic theory.* London and New York: Columbia University Press.

Chandler, Alfred D. 1977. *The Visible Hand: Managerial revolution in American Business.* Cambridge, Mass.: Harvard University Press.

———. 1990. *Strategy and structure: Chapters in the history of the industrial enterprise.* Cambridge, Mass.: MIT Press.

Dosi, Giovanni. 1982. Technological Paradigms and Technological Trajectories: A Suggested Interpretation of the Determinants and Directions of Technological Change. *Research Policy,* 11.

Dosi, Giovanni and Christopher Freeman, Richard R. Nelson, Gerald Silverberg, and Luc Soete, eds. 1988. *Technical change and economic theory.* London and New York: Columbia University Press.

Elam, Mark. 1994. Puzzling out the Post-Fordist Debate: Technology, Markets and Institutions. In Ash Amin, ed. *Post-fordism: A Reader.* Cambridge, Mass.: Blackwell.

Evans, Peter B., Dietrich Rueschemeyer, and Theda Skocpol, eds. 1985. *Bringing the state back in.* Cambridge, U.K.: Cambridge University Press.

Ferguson, Charles H. and Charles R. Morris. 1994. *Computer wars: The Fall of IBM and the future of global technology.* New York: Times Books, Random House.

Fong, Glenn R. 1990. State Strength, Industrial Structure and Industrial Policy: American and Japanese Experiences in Microelectronics. *Comparative Politics,* 22(3).

Fransman, Martin. 1999. *Vision of innovation: The Firm and Japan.* Oxford: Oxford University Press.

Freeman, Christopher. 1987. *Technology policy and economic performance: Lessons from Japan.* London and New York: Pinter Publishers.

Freeman, Christopher, and Carlota Perez. 1988. Structural Crises of Adjustment: Business Cycles and Investment Behavior. In Giovanni Dosi, Christopher Freeman, Richard R. Nelson, Gerald Silverberg, and Luc Soete, eds. *Technical change and economic theory.* London and New York: Columbia University Press.

Freeman, Christopher, and Luc Soete. 1997. *The Economics of industrial innovation,* 3rd ed. Cambridge, Mass: The MIT Press.

Frieden, Jeffrey A. 1991. *Development and democracy: Modern political economy and Latin America 1965–1985.* Princeton, N.J.: Princeton University Press.

Gerschenkron, Alexander. 1962. *Economic backwardness in historical perspective.* Cambridge, Mass.: Harvard University Press.

Gilmore, Kenneth E. 1997. *Politics in hard drives: Comparative responses to innovation in the computer industry.* Ph.D. Dissertation, the State University of New Jersey, Rutgers.

Gilpin, Robert. 1996. Economic Evolution of National Systems. *International Studies Quarterly,* 40(3), September.

Golden, James R. 1994. *Economic and national strategy in the information age: Global networks, technology policy, and cooperative competition.* Westport, Conn.: Praeger.

Gourevitch, Peter A. 1986. *Politics in hard times: comparative responses to international economic crises.* Ithaca, N.Y.: Cornell University Press.

Grove, Andrew S. 1996. *Only paranoid survive: How to exploit the crisis points that challenge every company and career.* New York: Doubleday.

Hall, Peter. 1986. *Governing the economy.* New York: Oxford University Press.

Hart, Jeffrey A. 1992. *Rival capitalists: International competitiveness in the United States, Japan, and Western Europe.* Ithaca, N.Y.: Cornell University Press.

Hart, Jeffrey A., and Sangbae Kim. 2000. Explaining the Resurgence of U.S. Competitiveness: The Rise of Wintelism. Paper submitted to *The Information Society.*

Hirst, Paul and Jonathan Zeitlin. 1989. Flexible Specialization and the Competitive Failure of UK Manufacturing. *Political Quarterly,* 60(3).

———. 1991. Flexible Specialization versus Post-Fordism; Theory, Evidence, and Policy Implications. *Economy and Society,* 20(1).

Katzenstein, Peter, ed. 1978. *Between power and plenty: Foreign economic policies of advanced industrial states.* Madison: University of Wisconsin Press.

———. 1985. *Small states in world markets: Industrial policy in Europe.* Ithaca, N.Y.: Cornell University Press.

Kim, Sangbae. 2000. *Wintelism vs. Japan: Standards competition and institutional adjustment in the global computer industry.* Ph.D. Dissertation, Indiana University.

Kim, Sangbae, and Jeffrey A. Hart (forthcoming in 2001. The Global Political Economy of Wintelism: A New Mode of Power and Governance in the Global Computer Industry. In James N. Rosenau and J. P. Singh, eds. *Information technologies and global politics: The Changing scope of power and governance.* Albany, N.Y.: SUNY Press.

Kitschelt, Herbert. 1991. Industrial Governance Structures, Innovation Strategies and the

Case of Japan: Sectoral or Cross-National Comparative Analysis. *International Organization,* 45(4).

Krasner, Stephen D. 1984. Approaches to the State: Alternative Conceptions and Historical Dynamics, *Comparative Politics* 16 (January).

Kurth, James R. 1979. Political Consequences of the Product Cycle: Industrial History and Political Outcomes. *International Organizations,* 33(1).

Lazonick, W. 1991. *Business organization and the myth of the market economy.* Cambridge, U.K: Cambridge University Press.

Lipietz, A. 1987. *Mirages and miracles: The crises of global fordism.* London: Verso.

Lundvall, Bengt-Ake. 1992. *National systems of innovation: Towards a theory of innovation and interactive learning.* London: Frances Pinter.

Modelski, George and Kazimierz Poznanski, eds. 1996. Special Issue: Evolutionary Paradigms in the Social Sciences, *International Studies Quarterly,* 40(3).

Modelski, George, and William R. Thompson. 1996. *Leading sectors and world powers: The coevolution of global politics and economics.* Columbia: University of South Carolina Press.

Nelson, Richard R. 1998. The Co-evolution of Technology, Industrial Structure, and Supporting Institutions. In Giovanni Dosi, David J. Teece, and Josef Chytry, eds. *Technology, organization, and competitiveness: Perspectives on industrial and corporate change.* Oxford: Oxford University Press.

———. ed. 1993. *National innovation systems: A comparative analysis.* New York: Oxford University Press.

———, and Sydney Winter. 1982. *An evolutionary theory of Economic Change.* Cambridge, Mass.: Harvard University Press.

Nielsen, K. 1991. Towards a Flexible Future: Theories and Politics. In B. Jessop, H. Kastendiek, K. Neilsen, and O. Pedersen, eds. *The Politics of Flexibility.* Aldershot: Edward Elgar.

Nordlinger, Eric A. 1981. *On the autonomy of the democratic state.* Cambridge, Mass.: Harvard University Press.

Perrow, Charles. 1984. *Normal catastrophes.* New York: Basic Books.

Piore, Michael J. and Charles F. Sable. 1984. *The Second industrial divide: Possibilities for prosperity.* New York: Basic Books.

Porter, Michael. 1990. *The Competitive advantages of nations.* New York: The Free Press.

Rogowski, Ronald. 1989. *Commerce and coalitions: How trade affects domestic political alignments.* Princeton, N.J.: Princeton University Press.

Sabel, Charles F. 1982. *Work and politics: The Division of labour in industry.* Cambridge, U.K: Cambridge University Press.

Sabel, Charles F., and Jonathan Zeitlin. 1985. Historical Alternatives to Mass Production: Politics, Markets and Technology in Nineteenth Century Industrialization. In *Past and Present,* 108.

Shafer, D. Michael. 1994. *Winners and losers: How sectors shape the developmental prospects of states.* Ithaca and London: Cornell University Press.

Sharp, Margaret. 1997. Technology, Globalization, and Industrial Policy. In Michael Talalay, Chris Farrands, and Roger Tooze, eds. *Technology, culture, and competitiveness: Change and the world political economy.* London and New York: Routledge.

Streeck, Wolfgang. 1996. Lean Production in the German Automobile Industry: A Test Case for Convergence Theory. In Suzanne Berger and Ronald Dore, eds. *National Diversity and Global Capitalism.* Ithaca, N.Y.: Cornell University Press.

Thompson, William R. 1990. Long Waves, Technological Innovation and Relative Decline. *International Organization,* 44(2).

Utterback, James M. and F. Suarez. 1991. Innovation, Competition, and Industry Structure, *Working Paper No.29–90,* Sloan School of Management, MIT.
Williamson, Oliver. 1985. *The Economic institutions of capitalism.* New York: Free Press.
Zysman, John. 1983. *Governments, markets, and growth: Financial systems and the politics of industrial change.* Ithaca, N.Y.: Cornell University Press.
Zysman, John, and Laura Tyson, eds. 1983. *American industry in international competition: Government politics and corporate strategies.* Ithaca, N.Y.: Cornell University Press.

chapter 12

Continuity versus Evolutionary Shift
Global Financial Expansion and the State

Brian M. Pollins

> The notion that something fundamental is happening, or indeed has happened, to the global economy is now increasingly accepted . . . we live in a period of major economic change; an era of turbulence and volatility in which economic life is being restructured and reorganized both rapidly and fundamentally.
>
> —Peter Dicken (1992)

> The economic changes that have occurred during the last quarter of a century . . . have unquestionably been more important and varied than during any former corresponding period of the world's history.
>
> —David A. Wells (1890)

Comments like Peter Dicken's cited above were found easily during the 1990s. Many aspects of global economic life are, indeed, changing, and several observers have succumbed already to the temptation to declare the arrival of the millennium. Not unlike early writers in the "interdependence" school thirty years ago, some major commentators today tell us the nation-state is obsolete, peace is at hand, and world politics is being transformed.[1] But this is hardly the first time that the world has experienced rapid change, as the above quotation from David Wells—made just over one hundred years ago—would suggest.[2] Recent developments must be considered in historical context if we are to assess their implications accurately. In my judgment, the current boom in international capital flows is the single most important feature among many changes in today's global economy. For this reason, I have chosen to focus on a study of capital flows in this chapter.

There is neither any doubt that capital flows are presently growing at breathtaking rates, nor is there any doubt that these flows are having important economic and political impacts as they expand. It is not yet clear, however, that the growth in volume is unprecedented in history, especially when compared to broad indicators of economic activity such as total investment or national product. The purpose of this chapter is to provide a longer historical view, and improve our understanding of recent developments by placing them in historical context.

International banking and finance have existed even longer than the state system itself. Feudal monarchs often financed public works, armies and navies, as well as lavish lifestyles with loans from wealthy merchant and banking families based in foreign lands. Cross-border capital transactions have ebbed and flowed—sometimes dramatically—ever since.[3] Over the span of centuries leading to the fateful year of 1914, one period stands out as particularly important to my present study. The years between 1870 and 1914 witnessed an unprecedented explosion in global capital markets. The volume of capital crossing borders grew annually, sometimes at dizzying rates. The banking business boomed in several countries. Economic activity and development in every corner of the earth were affected significantly by these new flows. Capital relations were even tied importantly to alliance patterns and geopolitics during this phase.[4]

If ever there was a time in global capital markets that mirrored our own (and I emphasize "if") then it was the period between 1870 and 1914. While I will offer some discussion of events and developments during other times, this study will focus strongly on a comparison between two periods: 1870 to 1914 and 1973 to 1991. Through this comparison, I hope to shed some light on several questions. These may be placed into two groups:

First, it is important to know *how the current expansion in capital flows is like or unlike earlier expansions.* Is the present increase truly "unprecedented," and if so, precisely how?

Second, when explaining the current explosion in international flows, published analyses of the current environment place great emphasis on changes in the regulatory regime governing international capital transactions. By comparing features of the monetary regime and national capital controls during these two periods, we should learn something about the *relationship between changes in institutional frameworks and international financial transactions.* To what extent can regime change serve as an explanatory factor in understanding global financial expansion?

Of these two groups of questions, this chapter addresses only the first systematically. The discussion I offer regarding the second will provide some insights, I hope. In the end, however, I will provoke more questions than I answer in the latter area. My objective in this discussion is to identify some specific questions regarding actors, institutions, and world politics in light of the following findings that I present below.

Before any of these questions can be addressed in detail, it is important to map the highly complex jumble of evolving financial relationships that come under the heading of "global capital." Capital relations cannot be pinned down exhaustively and definitively because of their evolving nature. Nevertheless, I will define terms in the next section to a degree that will allow comparison across periods and a reasonable yardstick for observing where the world has been and where it might be going. Following this, I will present descriptive data on global capital flows during the two focus periods of 1870 to 1914 and 1973 to 1991. The logic of this presentation will be driven by my interest in determining whether the present boom is sufficiently different in size or character from the pre-World War I boom to infer important consequences for global politics. I will then turn to an examination of the institutional framework within which these two financial booms occurred. Here, (as I will show) the differences between the two periods are as striking as the similarities. Insights into the relationship between rules, regimes, and international transactions are complicated accordingly. Next, I will discuss connections between financial interdependence and the study of world politics suggested by the story of the two financial booms. I conclude with thoughts regarding new directions for research in the field of "international" political economy.

TRACKING GLOBAL CAPITAL FLOWS OVER TIME

Tracking global capital flows is a daunting task for several reasons. First, unlike flows of merchandise trade, no comprehensive international reporting standard has ever been developed. Important advances have been made in very recent years, but reporting practices (especially in the area for foreign direct investment) still differ in some important ways country-by-country, and it took the Debt Crisis of the early 1980s to motivate the Bank for International Settlements (BIS) to strong-arm private banks into disclosing more information on their transactions.[5] Current BIS practices as well as ongoing international discussions to standardize recording will make life easier for future students of global financial relations, but those of us interested in long historical data series must make-do for now.

Second, the sources, form, and content of global capital relations evolve and innovate in ways that trade does not. New sources of capital can be invented, such as the novel creation by international agreement of one global and several regional banks after 1945, or the establishment of the increasingly important Eurobond market that operates largely outside the confines of any national borders. In addition, new financial instruments are conceived by government or private actors, and these can change the form and relative importance of various flows of capital. For example, currency options and futures, a key instrument in the present financial landscape, are one very recent invention which any comprehensive account of global capital must now consider.

Third, balance of payments statistics—a record I suspect many students of political economy would rely upon—miss completely much of the important action in global capital markets.[6] The chief reason is that capital account statistics in the balance of payments record *net* rather than *gross* flows. If a country both imports and exports capital, the flows may net out to a small number even though the gross flows could be enormous. This is a very important point, for, as I will show in the next section, that sizable two-way flows of capital are a central and unprecedented feature of the present boom. Another indicator of the inadequacy of balance of payments statistics is the often-discussed growth in the "Errors and Omissions" category of the accounts. Economists were already disturbed by the fact that total world "Errors and Omissions" averaged $72 billion per *year* throughout the 1980s. Then it was found that the discrepancy amounted to $122 billion in 1991. For these reasons I will not employ balance of payments data in this chapter.[7]

Despite these sobering limitations, we would be foolish to abandon all faith in recorded observations of capital flows. National statistics, though imperfect, have been compiled painstakingly. Many economic historians have labored to assemble this data in ways that afford a modicum of comparability across nations and time. Though remaining discrepancies are not trivial, these scholars have given us a good idea of the *caveats*. I will certainly apply these when appropriate. Finally, this study examines capital flows at a highly aggregated level, and existing numbers are very likely sufficient to provide us with a "low resolution" picture of the landscape. For this study, that is all I need.

To build a yardstick for cross-time comparisons, I begin by listing the major forms which international capital can take at present. These are displayed in Table 12.1. Very broadly, these forms are loans, bonds, and securities, direct investment, and trade in financial services and financial derivatives. Allow me to describe each very briefly:

Loans: These are simply obligations assumed by a borrower in exchange for currency or credits. Today, creditors may include private institutions (for example, banks), national governments, or international institutions such as the International Monetary Fund (IMF) or the Inter-American Development Bank. Hence we can speak of "private" as well as "official" debt. In recent decades, many banks have begun making loans in their "home" country denominated in *foreign* currency. This *is* a form of international capital, though it is a bit harder to trace, and it is missed completely by balance of payments records.

Bonds and Securities: The reader is certainly familiar with the form and function of stocks and bonds. I refer here to the same instruments whenever traded internationally. Note that governments as well as businesses may float bonds internationally (just as they do domestically). The International Bank for Reconstruction and Development (IBRD, or "World Bank") has funded much of its activity during the past forty years by offering bonds on private capital markets. An important innovation in recent decades in the private sector is the "offshore" bond market. This refers simply to any bond denominated in a currency foreign to its original country of issue. Daimler-Benz in Germany, for example, might issue a bond handled by Credit Lyonnais in Paris denominated in U.S. dollars. This "Eurobond" is considered "offshore" because the issuers created the security outside the United States, but are contracted to pay U.S. dollars to bond holders.

Foreign Direct Investment (FDI): Here, an investor in one country commits capital in another in order to gain some measure of direct control over the decision-making and operations of a foreign enterprise. Again, the reader is familiar with any number of examples such as Honda's construction of a large plant in Marysville, Ohio, or Coca Cola's operations in Brazil. FDI typically involves transactions among private enterprises, though governments—as part or whole owners of "national" firms—can be players here as well.

Trade in Financial Services. Prominent forms of capital in this category would include insurance (a company in one country underwrites risk for a firm based in another) and banking services (such as the fees and commissions a bank receives for managing transactions such as the Daimler-Benz—Credit Lyonnais example constructed above.)

Trade in Financial Derivatives. These instruments are recent creations. Concerns over the solvency of several banks arising from the threatened default of several developing nations in the early 1980s led to the creation of a secondary market for that debt. This allowed banks to limit their losses by selling the shaky paper at less than face value. Some governments also reduced their debt by buying back their own loans at reduced rates. More widely used derivatives include currency options and currency futures. These instruments allow traders (whether they trade in goods, securities, or currency itself) to hedge against fluctuations in exchange rates by operating today with one currency while holding an option to buy a second that they will want at some specified future date.

I will focus on long-term rather than short-term capital in this chapter because historical data regarding short-term flows remains highly scattered.[8] Long-term capital is usually classified as either "portfolio" investment or as "direct" investment. Direct investment is defined above, while portfolio investment refers to the forms classified as loans, bonds, and securities in the scheme presented in Table 12.1.

Table 12.1 Forms of Global Capital

International Bank Lending
    Cross-Border Lending (in any currency)
    Domestic Lending (in foreign currency)

Stocks and Bonds
    "Offshore" Bonds
    Securities Issued Domestically but Traded Internationally

Foreign Direct Investment (FDI)

Trade in Financial Services (such as Insurance)

Trade in Financial Derivatives
    Currency Options
    Currency Futures

Capital markets will continue to innovate. Future students of global capital flows will undoubtedly have new forms to place under the listed categories, and probably new categories altogether. In all likelihood, they will also have more comprehensive data, collected in more consistent and comparable formats. I will press on with information as it exists now.

A COMPARISON OF GLOBAL CAPITAL FLOWS DURING TWO BOOM PERIODS

Given the research questions delineated in the introduction, various descriptive measures for comparison of the two boom periods are relevant. These are:

1. volumes and rates of growth in global capital flows;
2. sources and recipients of global capital; and
3. volumes of capital in relation to measures of aggregate economic activity.

Volumes and Rates of Growth in Global Capital

Reports for figures during the pre-World War I boom (1870 to 1914) are highly aggregated. Data on specific categories listed in Table 12.1 are very scattered for this period, and some forms of capital listed in that table did not even exist.[9] Figures for "capital" during this earlier period, then, usually add together loans, bonds (government and private), and direct foreign investment in a single estimate. Following Cameron (1991: 13), I refer to this aggregation as Gross Foreign Investments (GFI).

For the current period, I have assembled data on private bank lending, bonds, and FDI because these three categories together most closely match GFI. I present the growth rate estimates in disaggregated form as there are interesting differences across categories.

The estimated growth rates are presented in Figure 12.1. In the pre-World War I era, international capital flows grew about 5 percent per year. The world was indeed becoming more financially interdependent during this time, regardless of measure. Maddison estimates that the major economies of this period (that also happen to be the capital exporters) grew at about 2.5 percent per year during these same years. Gross Fixed Capital Stock within these same economies grew at 3.4 percent, while international trade increased 3.9 percent per year (Maddison 1991: Table 4.9: 118). Whether we compare capital flows to general economic growth, to total fixed capital, or to trade, international capital was becoming a larger feature of economic life throughout the period.

The expansion of capital flows during the modern era has been more dramatic. This statement holds whether we look to FDI, bonds, or bank loans; growth has been truly striking. Contrary to the perceptions of some commentators, however,

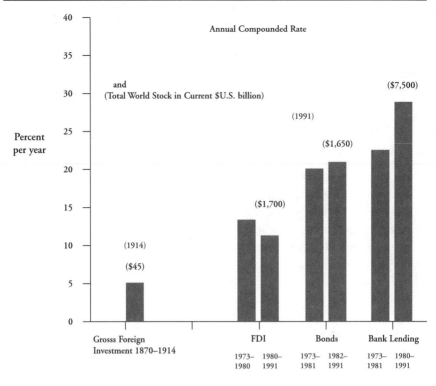

Figure 12.1 Global Growth Rates of Various Capital Flows
Sources: Cameron 1991, Dennis 1984, Crook 1992, Dicken 1992

high growth was not limited to the 1980s. Growth rates in all three categories between 1973 and 1981 were about as high as rates after 1981. If we also consider modern growth in forms of capital not included in Figure 12.1 (trade in financial services and financial derivatives, Eurocurrency accounts, stocks, loans from governments and international agencies) then we must conclude that capital is indeed becoming global at an astonishing pace.[10]

One difficulty in comparing the present era to the pre-World War I period is that the current expansion is ongoing. Might the present boom fade out? The great expansion of the late nineteenth and early twentieth century, after all, ended most abruptly. Moreover, it was followed by decades of slow growth and occasional contraction in global capital markets. Can we be sure that the present boom will not suffer a similar fate? Certainly, it is not possible for the recent expansion to continue at this pace indefinitely.

While it is difficult to be precise about future developments in an environment that is changing so dramatically, it is not premature to compare the two periods. Though it is still developing, estimates suggest the present expansion is genuinely historic. One additional calculation leads me this conclusion. Taking present stocks of bank loans, FDI, and bonds, I assumed *no further growth whatsoever* in these stocks to the year 2017 (to match the forty-four year span between 1870 and 1914). Counterfactually, if the expansion we have observed between 1973 and 1991 had instead taken forty-four years to develop (1973 to 2017) the annual compound growth rates would still be as large or larger than that observed for the pre-World War I era.[11]

Sources and Recipients

The most significant difference between the two financial booms is revealed when we look at ties between the sources and recipients of capital. Before World War I, this pattern was basically "North-South"; that is, advanced industrialized nations exported capital into developing areas. To be sure, those recipients tended to be countries with high growth potential (like the Newly Industrializing Countries [NICs] of today), but at that time they were in the process of industrialization. The top four "Lands of New Development" (in order of funds received) were the United States, Russia, Canada, and Argentina. France was the primary supplier of capital to Russia (fully 25 percent of all French foreign investment was placed there) while Great Britain was by far the dominant supplier for the rest. France, whose total GFI was about half that of Great Britain, also was a major supplier of capital to the Ottoman Empire and Egypt.[12] German investments made up the third largest total among capital exporters. The Germans tended to concentrate in southeastern Europe and in Austria-Hungary, though they had non-European holdings as well. In short, industrialized Europe supplied 89 percent of all world GFI by 1914, while "developing" Europe, the Lands of New Development, and the Near East received 67 percent of the world total.[13]

The period following the Second World War (1945 to 1973) brought a shift in this pattern. Advanced industrialized nations (conspicuously those devastated by the war) became major *recipients* of long-term finance for the first time. In addition, national governments, new international institutions such as the International Monetary Fund and the World Bank, as well as private banks and businesses were all increasing their participation in global capital markets in the two decades following the Second World War. The United States was the commanding source of this expansion, responsible for more than two-thirds of net long-term capital flows from the early 1950s to the mid-1960s. The second largest capital exporter, Great Britain, was the source for about 10 percent of these funds over the same period.

Developing nations (though a different set of countries than those described for the earlier era, of course) still received a significant portion of these flows, though their share was smaller than that of the earlier period. That share would become smaller still after the modern capital boom began in 1973, for despite the vast sums loaned to Brazil, Mexico and others during the late 1970s and early 1980s, most capital in the new boom is going to the very advanced industrialized nations. As many know, the United States became a major recipient of foreign capital (and a net debtor) during the 1980s.[14]

By 1981, capital market borrowing by Organization of Economic Cooperation and Development (OECD) member nations made up 69 percent of the world total, while countries classified as "developing" by that same organization received just over 25 percent.[15] In 1985, the proportions for FDI showed a similar concentration of activity within wealthier nations. Advanced industrialized nations hosted 76 percent of global FDI stock by that year. The United States alone hosted 29 percent of the world total (Grimwade 1989, Table 4.2: 149; Dicken 1992, Tables 3.2 and 3.3: 53–54). In the network of global capital, the United States has oddly come full circle: it holds the distinction of being the world's largest recipient in both eras examined in this study.

In sum, patterns of outward and inward capital flows shown in Figure 12.2 are quite different during the two boom periods. In the period before the First World

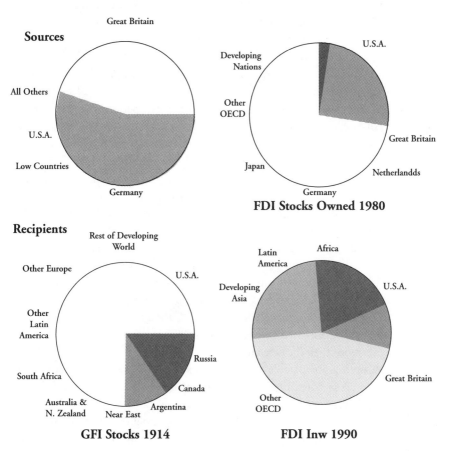

Figure 12.2 Global Capital: Sources and Recipients

Sources: Cameron 1991; Grimwade 1989; Crook 1992

War, investment poured from the most advanced nations into those who were developing most rapidly. Portfolio as well as direct investment fueled national economic transformations in several frontier nations (and was lost in certain cases as well). The modern boom has also limited its selection of recipients, but most importantly, capital has flooded from the most advanced nations into other nations within that group. The first boom prominently tied Britain to the Lands of New Development, the second is most noteworthy in integrating the richest nations with each other.

Volumes in Relation to General Size of the Economy

One striking feature of the pre-World War I era was the extent to which national capital markets were integrated. In 1983, economic historian James Foreman-Peck (1983: 127) observed "If ever a world capital market existed then it was in this period." In 1914, national stocks of GFI expressed in relation to Gross Domestic Product (GDP) was quite large for the top three capital exporters, amounting to more than 60 percent in the case of Germany, over 85 percent for France, and about 112 percent or more for Great Britain.[16] Foreman-Peck(1983: 130) notes that no less than 10 percent of British national income in 1914 came from returns on their foreign investments.

Constructing country comparisons between the two periods is made difficult by the transnational nature of the current era. It makes little sense, for example, to ascribe portions of the Euromarkets and other offshore sources to national ledgers of "France" since it is often not French capital that is exchanged there. This problem is more obvious if we consider major offshore financial centers like Panama or the Bahamas. It is possible, however, to get a sense of the size of capital markets during these two periods on a *global* basis. It is also possible with current data to calculate rough estimates of the ratio of FDI to GDP for the two period leaders, Great Britain and the United States. It is these results I present here.

First, we need a common yardstick to gauge the size of economies during the two periods. I have chosen to sum the GDPs for the G-5 (United States, Great Britain, Germany, France, and Japan). Measures of total world product are probably less accurate than the sum of these five, and, though Japan was not a major economy in 1914, these five together held some 89 percent of GFI in 1914 and are credited with more than 75 percent of FDI today (Julius 1990, Table 2.5: 39).[17]

Next, we need a comparable measure across time for world capital stocks. As before, I have taken contemporary estimates of bonds, bank loans, and FDI as most comparable to Cameron's measure of GFI for the pre-1914 period. Point estimates of these stocks for various years and the compound growth rates presented in Figure 12.1 were used to *approximate* their value in 1989, the most recent year that minimizes the amount of recalculation necessary to bring all figures onto common ground.[18] Again, a "low resolution" picture is sufficient for global comparisons.

The results of these calculations are presented in Table 12.2. The GFI estimates for 1914 are restated in 1985 U.S. dollars in order to employ Maddison's careful product calculations directly without any further manipulation.[19] Stated in 1985 dollars, total G-5 product in 1914 was just under $1 trillion, while world GFI in that year amounted to some $454 billion. Gross Foreign Investment, then, amounted to about 49 percent of G-5 product in 1914.

As shown in Table 12.2, world stocks in 1989 of FDI, bank loans, and bonds sum to just more than $5 trillion. The GDP of the G-5 nations in that same year amounted to some $10 trillion. The resulting estimated proportion is 50 percent, a figure surprisingly comparable to the relative size of the world capital market in

Table 12.2 Global Capital and National Product in Two Periods

World Gross Foreign Investment (GFI) Stock, **1914**
Recalculated to 1985 U.S. Prices

$454.37 billion

Gross Domestic Product of G-5 nations, **1914**
Recalculated to 1985 U.S. Prices

United States	$473.33 billion	
Great Britain	176.99	
France	113.74	
Germany	103.66	
Japan	57.56	
TOTAL	$925.28 billion	GFI/G-5 GDP (1914) = **49%**

Estimated World Gross Foreign Investment (GFI) Stocks 1989
Expressed in 1989 U.S. Prices

FDI	$ 969.65 billion
Bonds	1,050.30
Bank Loans	3,074.03
TOTAL	$ 5,093.98 billion

Gross Domestic Product of G-5 nations, **1989**
Expressed in 1989 U.S. Prices

United States	$ 5,250.03 billion	
Great Britain	887.63	
France	895.31	
Germany	999.13	
Japan	2,141.99	
TOTAL	$10,174.09 billion	GFI/G-5 GDP. (1989) = **50%**

Sources: Cameron 1991; Maddison 1991; Dicken 1992; Crook 1992

1914. Recalling additional new forms of capital that now circulate, I conclude that (in terms of volume) the present global capital market is at least as integrated as that of 1914, and probably more so.

Using the same data sources employed in Table 12.2, it is possible to compare the stock of FDI to GDP in Great Britain and the United States. A consensus of economic historians agree that these two countries defined opposite ends of the spectrum in 1914 in that the British held only 10 percent of their total investments in direct form, while Americans placed 75 percent of their total outward investment in FDI by that same year (Dunning 1970). For the present era, more solid estimates of outward FDI as a percentage of GNP are given by Julius for the year 1987, and I use her numbers directly. Table 12.3 shows that at present, the U.S. figure is slightly larger than it was in 1914, while the current British figure is substantially higher. Given that both nations are now significant recipients of FDI (as was the United States in 1914) I again conclude that the role of global capital in contemporary economic life is at least as significant as it was in 1914.

By several alternative measures, then, it appears that the present expansion of global capital markets is historic in scope. Rates of growth in this market are as high, and often higher than growth rates during the earlier era, a time recognized for the extent of its financial integration. The present period is distinguished from any time prior to World War II in that the bulk of capital flows remain within the most advanced market economies. The historical "North-South" pattern no longer predominates. Finally, the extent of capital integration—measured as a share of general economic activity—also appears to be as great or greater than the earlier heyday of global capital, 1870 to 1914.

We now have an interesting basis for historical comparison. Two periods since 1870 have witnessed rapid and substantial growth in cross-border flows of capital. By contrasting the national and international rules and institutions that governed

Table 12.3 Outward Foreign Direct Investment
and National Product Two Period Leaders

		Estimated Outward FDI Stock (Current $ U.S. billion)	Outward FDI/GDP
1914			
	Great Britain	26.51	11 or 12%
	United States	20.19	5 or 6%
1987–88			
	Great Britain	184.00	22%
	United States	324.00	7%

Sources: Cameron 1991; Maddison 1991; Julius 1990; Dunning 1970

these flows during the two periods, we could obtain insights into the relationship between rules and regimes on the one hand, and international capital transactions on the other.

MONETARY REGIMES, CAPITAL CONTROLS, AND GLOBAL FINANCIAL EXPANSION

Did the global monetary regimes and relaxation of national capital controls during these two periods help bring about these great expansions? The simple and obvious answer is a definite "yes." The problem is that this answer is *too* simple. First, the two respective monetary regimes—the classic Gold Standard of 1870 to 1914, and the (quasi) managed floating regime of the contemporary, post-Bretton Woods era could hardly be more different. Second, close examination of the process of expansion during these two eras leads me to question whether the recent liberalization of capital controls by so many governments is a *cause* of the expansion or an *effect* of processes beyond state control.

Monetary Regimes During the Two Financial Booms

The first investment boom of 1870 to 1914 coincides rather closely with the heyday of the Gold Standard.[20] Though most nations adhered to this regime only on a *de facto* basis, this was sufficient to provide the global economy with a unique period of exchange rate stability. John Dunning (1970: 16) is representative of most economic historians when he asserts that the pre-World War I Gold Standard helped create an environment "uniquely favorable to the free movement of capital." The argument for this connection is intuitively appealing. The stable regime of the Gold Standard reduced exchange rate risk, thus encouraging all forms of international economic exchange. Fixed exchange rates also reduced transaction costs, and returns on investment were more predictable (Foreman-Peck 1983: 160). As we know, this period did experience growth in trade and investment at rates never seen before that time. One could only be amazed had such a stable monetary regime failed to lead to a great expansion in trade in investment.

The puzzle, quite simply, is that we have now witnessed an even greater expansion in trade and investment under a monetary regime that, practically speaking, is the polar opposite of the Gold Standard. In fact, the very beginning of the present boom is best dated as 1973, coinciding with the final demise of Bretton Woods and the beginning of the most explicitly market-based (and probably the most unstable) monetary regime the world has ever known. Currency exchange rates fluctuate now on a daily basis, and government promises to support currencies at declared rates (even within bands) have proven devilishly difficult to fulfill. At least as far as the monetary regime is concerned, those involved in international trade and investment now operate in a highly uncertain environment. How could the present expansion have occurred? Possible answers to this question require an examination of national institutions and policies regarding the cross-border movement of capital.

National Banking Systems and Capital Controls

Another distinguishing feature of the pre-World War I era was the near-total absence of national regulations on the cross-border movement of capital. Dunning, Foreman-Peck, and others cite this explicitly as a reason for the first great global financial boom. Again, the connection is obvious. Without such controls, capital indeed faces a "borderless world" and moves wherever it sees the highest return with a speed as great as contemporary technologies will allow.

Cameron (1989: 204–16) emphasizes the importance of national bank practices and institutions during this era. Britain led the world, he argues, in part because the government allowed banks to proliferate in number and branches even as they grew in size. France and Germany followed this model generally, and all three nations saw their banking industry grow impressively in ways that supported global financial expansion. Solid central banks also lent stability to national banking systems in these countries. In contrast, the United States limited its banks most severely, proscribing branch banking altogether, and prohibiting joint-stock banks from engaging in outward capital transactions.[21] The U.S. central bank—the Federal Reserve—came into being only in 1910 to 1913. Interestingly, Meiji Japan initially adopted the U.S. model for its banking system, but switched to the western European scheme before the First World War. Clearly, the three giant capital surplus nations of this era—Britain, France, and Germany—enjoyed a liberal regulatory environment, and banking systems grew rapidly, strengthening global financial expansion.

By contrast, Bretton Woods supported strict and explicit national capital controls from its inception (Meerschwam 1989: 289–307). John Maynard Keynes himself saw such controls as essential to national macroeconomic management, and helped ensure their inclusion at the time of the regime's design. Banking industries in all major countries—even formerly liberal Britain—were highly regulated for most of the Bretton Woods period in ways that inhibited foreign capital transactions.

The Euromarkets, begun modestly in the mid-1950s, sprang the first leak in this system. Banks found higher returns in this market-without-a-nation than they could in their own, tight national environments. They responded as we would expect, and the Eurocurrency and Eurobond markets grew. Efforts to quash this market—primarily by the U.S. government—were frustrated by a lament from bankers that would be used over the years with increasing frequency and force: Regulate us further and we will be at a competitive disadvantage against banks in other countries. Ultimately, acquiescence by governments to this complaint brought the entire regulatory framework in several countries crashing down. Our contemporary era, therefore, *parallels* the pre-World War I period in that both were times of exceptionally relaxed capital controls and deregulated banking.

In fact, the demise of Bretton Woods and contemporary financial deregulation are closely related. Though few realized the full implications at the time, the end of the Bretton Woods exchange rate system created strong incentives to remove remaining national controls on the cross-border movement of capital. The reason for this is fairly simple: All international commerce carries greater risk than domestic commerce, and the demise of Bretton Woods *shifted the burden of carrying that risk* from governments to private entrepreneurs and banks. If governments would no longer manage exchange-rate risk, then the private sector would have to do so if it was to be managed at all.

I reason thus: Under Bretton Woods, international traders (whether they dealt in goods or securities) had confidence that currency exchange rates would remain stable because major national governments stood behind those rates. In this respect, Bretton Woods approximated the Gold Standard of 1870 to 1914. Under both regimes, governments lifted exchange-rate risk from the shoulders of business. The end of Bretton Woods by 1973, in this sense, "privatized" exchange-rate risk. Suddenly, business—and more specifically, private banks—found themselves with the added responsibility of managing this risk if trade and investment were to continue to grow.[22] Privatized management of exchange-rate risk required the creation of new financial instruments (such as new markets for forward contracts in currencies,) and these required relaxation of existing capital controls. In short, to give private banks the ability to discharge their important new responsibility, governments had little choice but to allow capital to flow more freely across international boundaries. In the long run, to paraphrase Keynes, regulation was dead.

In January 1974, only months after the floating exchange rate regime had established itself, the United States government eliminated all capital controls. Other governments (for example, Germany) had preceded the United States in this decision, still more would follow in the years to come. General sentiment for the liberalization of international finance grew, and in the twenty years that followed, capital became ever freer to flow where it wished. But the important point is this: The abolishment of capital controls certainly facilitated global capital expansion, but the decision to surrender those controls was as much an effect of prior expansion in that market as it was a cause of later growth. Governments "chose" to liberalize only in the sense that a chess player "chooses" a move under *zugzwang*: there is but one place to go if you wish to continue the game.

Students of international regimes thus have a fascinating puzzle to unravel: One great global financial boom was undoubtedly undergirded by an exceptionally stable monetary system. A second, still larger boom was catalyzed by the demise of a stable world monetary system. How can this be? Are regimes irrelevant?

DISCUSSION: FINANCIAL INTERDEPENDENCE AND WORLD POLITICS

At this writing, my answer to this puzzle is preliminary and admittedly *ad hoc.* I offer it to provoke further thinking and research by others, and to provide an *entre* to a discussion of the implications I see in this story for the study of world politics.

A Possible Explanation for the Two Financial Booms

My explanation of both financial booms rests on the institutional environment within which capital is exchanged.[23] Specifically, I speak of (a) barriers to its movement and (b) risks associated with its movement. Quite simply, the movement of international capital is negatively associated with both barriers and risks. This will surprise no one; the interesting question is how national policy and international regimes create or remove barriers, and raise or reduce risks (even, as is often the case, unintentionally).

Within this simple framework, it is clear that the absence of capital controls during the first boom (1870 to 1914) and their removal during the second (1973 to 1991) enabled an expansion of cross-border flows generated by economic forces, by and large. The role of monetary regimes in these cases is connected directly to risk management. The Gold Standard, really a network of government promises to fix currencies, was a means whereby political authorities freed business and finance from exchange risk by assuming its management. From this perspective, rules within the Bretton Woods regime operated at cross-purposes. The stability of the Dollar Standard encouraged international trade and capital transactions, but the explicit inclusion and strict operation of capital controls slowed global financial growth. To be sure, financial markets grew impressively under Bretton Woods (indeed, I would expect to find that this period marked the third largest expansion ever in global finance.) But growth rates were almost certainly slower than they otherwise would have been, and we must keep in mind that some growth which did occur during the Bretton Woods period resulted from deliberate actions by banks to circumvent the regime.

By itself, the collapse of Bretton Woods by 1973 would have moved the world one step closer to the kind of environment hostile to international economic exchange that was suffered during the inter-war years 1920 to 1939. Fortunately, there are *two* instruments to encourage international economic exchange: risk-management *and* removal of barriers. Finding themselves no longer able to bear the first beyond 1973, governments switched to the second. The rest of the story of the great boom of the late-twentieth century concerns the success with which risk-management was "privatized." Trade in financial derivatives, an invention of this era, has allowed traders and investors alike to hedge their positions when they deal in multiple currencies. The environment is anything but risk-free, but it would appear that the reduction in risk afforded by these new financial instruments has contributed mightily to the greatest expansion in global markets the world has ever seen.

Implications for the Study of World Politics

For students of politics, I find that the most interesting aspects of this story involve the interaction and mutual adaptation of systems. First, we have the global financial system, a network of private and public borrowers and creditors, exchanging money and promises in a growing variety of forms. Different national banking systems, each with their own participants, rules and resources also played a part. And of course, the system of rules that make up the international monetary regime defines an environment of constraints and opportunities, shaping flows of global capital. Each of these systems operated in ways that alternatively reinforced and undermined each other. Over time, the changing shape of each one is in some important part an adaptation to new demands or prospects created by developments in another of these interdependent systems. In fact, this study of the two great financial booms suggests that the very rhythm and tempo of market expansion is determined by this interaction and coevolution between systems.

If this is so, then it is clear that international regimes as well as government policy will continue to make a great difference in this arena. It is also clear that the impact of negotiated regimes and government policy will not likely be a positive one unless decision-makers improve current understanding of the interdependence of these systems. Discussions regarding deregulation and reregulation currently abroad in many lands will have to consider the extraordinary capacity for financial capital to evolve. The inventions hatched by this market may elude or frustrate regime control, as the Euromarkets did, or work to support the existing order as they did in recycling petro-dollars with surprising ease after 1973, or in managing exchange risk after the collapse of Bretton Woods. Decision-makers and international negotiators must learn to work *with* a very large and powerful system.

We purport to be students of the global political economy. Is there anything we can tell decision-makers? At present, my assessment is not optimistic. The story of the two great financial booms is, as I have said, a story of interdependence. Interdependence, of course, was a topic of tremendous scholarly interest between twenty and twenty-five years ago, and a great deal of work on this subject was published. Unfortunately, research within this program rapidly devolved in a few short years into one basic question: How do *states* create and maintain regimes? Bridgework to Waltz's structural realism was quickly built, and the resulting "neo-realism" has spanned our disciplinary horizon ever since. The concepts, data, and theoretical frameworks—the tools—we need to study global interdependence were left undeveloped.

Few of us reading *Transnational Relations and World Politics* on its publication in 1972 would have guessed this outcome.[24] The volume was offered as a direct challenge to the reigning paradigm of realism, a challenge Keohane and Nye (1989) would repeat explicitly in their 1977 book *Power and Interdependence*.[25] But ideas that confronted realism most directly—ideas important to the development of an understanding of the political economy of global capital—were dropped. Most prominent among these are:

The loss of macroeconomic control by nation-states (Keohane and Nye 1972: xi).

The transmission of disturbances (such as inflation or unemployment) from one unit to another; the "sensitivity" of one unit to developments or changes in another (Keohane and Nye 1989: 11).

The importance of intergovernmental and transnational actors in world politics; the general inadequacy of state-centric paradigms (Keohane and Nye 1972: x–xv).

In fact, this last point was declared initially to be the defining feature of the new approach. "The difference between our world politics paradigm and the state-centric paradigm can be clarified most easily by focusing on the nature of the actors," wrote Keohane and Nye in 1972. The importance of non-state actors was underscored in their definition of "Complex Interdependence" offered by the same two authors in 1977 (1972: 24–29).[26]

But in practice, the new paradigm remained completely state-centric. The conceptual discussion contained in the first three chapters of *Power and Interdependence* illustrates all points therein only by reference to interactions among governments or between governments and intergovernmental organizations. "Transnational" actors are only mentioned infrequently, and always in the abstract. The authors' four chosen case studies that make up the body of that book also fit this pattern. Finally, the second edition of *Power and Interdependence*, published twelve years after the first, contains an afterword discussion of more than two dozen published works by various authors said to have been shaped or influenced by the "Interdependence" program. *None* of these cited works is motivated centrally by any of the program's three challenges listed above, while *all* focus on interactions among nation-states, or between nation-states and intergovernmental organizations.[27] Keohane and Nye set out explicitly to free us from the bonds of state-centrism, yet fell victim to it immediately. Interdependence, as a field of study, has lain all but completely fallow since the first seeds were sown more than twenty years ago.

The development of the current global financial boom illustrates several of the key insights found in the original work on Interdependence twenty years ago. The effects of financial deregulation in one country have indeed been felt quickly in others, and via channels not controlled by nation-states. Growth in *private* global capital markets has eroded the capacity of states to control their own economic destiny (a point seen most clearly in the diminished capacity of central banks to affect exchange rates). Finally, transnational actors and institutions, such as international banks and the Euromarkets, are central to this story.

The origin, development, and political consequences of the current financial boom cannot be understood within a state-centric framework. *Non*-state actors, reacting to constraints and opportunities created by national policies and the global monetary regime, established patterns of exchange that circumvented national regulation as well as international regimes. Moreover, their actions and the resulting patterns of exchange *forced national policy and the monetary regime to change radically.* The story of both booms is not only one of non-state versus state actors, it is a story of interacting systems. Global finance, national and international politics, as well as the monetary regime can be seen to have distinct elements and different functions in this story. But it is only by understanding interdependencies between these systems that we can comprehend the result. We do indeed need a research program on interdependence, but we must employ a framework that pays genuine heed to non-state actors, and we need a framework that examines connections not only among those actors, but among *coevolving systems.* World politics is *not* merely a "game of nations."

CONCLUSION

The increase in global capital flows during recent decades is larger than any previous expansion in that market. Rates of growth have been impressive, and will mark this era as historic even if unforeseen events drastically curtail future growth. Expressed as a share of all economic activity, global capital relations have become at least as important (and very probably more important) to the organization of production and exchange as they were in the era before World War I. An important qualitative shift has also occurred, in that advanced market economies have displaced developing economies as the dominant recipients of these flows. These shifts have already had significant consequences for the global political economy, and their effects will continue to be felt. Given these developments, it is clear that any adequate understanding of the global economy in the present or future must include a description of the agents, rules, institutions, and regimes that allocate and regulate flows of capital across national boundaries. At present, our discipline is not well-equipped to develop this understanding.

The comparison offered in this study of two great financial booms revealed interesting similarities and differences in the institutional settings and international regimes within which they occurred. The absence or relaxation of capital controls was a feature shared by both periods; a feature that distinguishes them from times of slower growth or contraction in capital markets. Clearly, the reduction of barriers to cross-border capital transactions is a potent stimulant to growth in these markets. At the same time, the role played by international monetary regimes appears to be connected to the management of risk. Under both the Gold Standard and Bretton Woods, governments took the burden of exchange-rate risk management onto their shoulders, and capital transactions grew as a result. Capital controls were strongly encouraged under Bretton Woods, and thus the regime worked at cross purposes from the perspective of international capital markets. When governments were forced to abandon the dollar standard between 1971 and 1973 (due in part to growing capital transactions outside the regime's management) they were left with little choice but to liberalize capital controls. Capital markets responded creatively to this "privatization" of exchange-rate risk through a dramatic expansion of trade in financial derivatives. Thus it was the *coevolution of three interdependent systems*—private global finance, national regulatory systems, and the international monetary regime—that produced a new environment of unprecedented freedom for the cross-border movement of capital.

It is time for our discipline to revive the concept of interdependence. Ideas contained in the work published under that banner twenty years ago provide a small, but important starting point. However, we cannot afford again to ignore non-state and transnational actors in our reformulations as our predecessors did after paying them lip-service initially. We must develop understandings of interdependencies not only among a variety of global actors, but between transnational public and private systems as well. Systems as well as actors adapt to each other. The discipline of "international" political economy will never understand developments like the global financial expansion now shaping economic life. Instead, we must develop a richer appreciation for the interdependencies of transnational actors and systems that comprise the *global* political economy.

NOTES

Author's Note: The support of the Mershon Center at The Ohio State University is most gratefully acknowledged, as is the research assistance of Gul Sosay. An earlier version of this chapter appeared under the title "Global Capital: Two Financial Booms Compared."
1. Prominent heralds of this new global economic order include former Citibank chairman Walter B. Wriston (1992), McKinsey Associates' Chairman Kenichi Ohmae (1990), and economists Richard B. McKenzie and Dwight R. Lee (1991).
2. Wells served as Special Commissioner of Revenue in the United States government, as well as president of the American Social Science Association. He conducted one of the first detailed studies of global capital flows, and his work still serves as an important source for economic historians.
3. A good introduction to this history is found in Cameron (1989).
4. For example, when Japan sought loans from Parisian capital markets in 1901, Russia, an ally of France fearing Japanese expansion, requested denial of this access. France complied with the Russian request, and this helped motivate the signing of the Anglo-Japanese treaty in 1902. Access to London capital markets was granted to Japan immediately upon the signing of the treaty (Foreman-Peck 1983: 130–32).
5. A very good description of the current differences in FDI reporting among G-5 nations can be found in Julius (1990).
6. I confess that until recently I have told my own students to do just that.

7. This implies that the world is running an enormous capital account surplus with itself. As this is patently impossible, we must conclude either that workers in statistical offices are becoming increasingly incompetent at an alarming rate, or that innovations in capital relations are escaping the notice of established recording practices. I prefer the latter explanation. The quoted figures are taken from Crook (1992: 6).

8. Most studies conducted on capital relaitons prior to 1914 discuss long-term capital exclusively; exceptions to this rule are limited in their time frame and seldom make cross-country comparisons. See, for example, Cameron and Bovykin (1991). The importance of short-term flows to international economic interdependence, however, is not to be underestimated. For example, currency exchange rates (and all they entail for macroeconomic performance and policy) are very sensitive to short-term flows. But I am not able to compare present times with any earlier era, and for this reason alone I focus on long-term capital.

9. "Offshore" bonds, trade in financial derivatives, and domestic bank lending denominated in foreign currencies are the three forms listed above that were not invented until much later. Trading in securities other than bonds was not a prominent feature of this market either.

10. Rough and ready calculations I have made regarding Eurocurrency deposits, trading in stocks across national boundaries and trade in financial derivatives shows them to be growing at rates even greater than any shown in Figure 12.1.

11. Assuming zero growth in global financial markets to 2017, future scholars would learn that FDI and international bonds grew roughly 5 percent per year over the forty-four year span (about equal to the pre-World War I expansion) while international bank lending rose in excess of 8 percent each year (compounded!). They would also take account of lending by international institutions and exchange in financial instruments not included in my analysis. They would all but certainly conclude that this period witnessed the greatest expansion of global capital in history.

12. Given this portfolio, it is easy to see how French investors lost a full 50 percent of all their foreign holdings as a result of the First World War and the Bolshevik Revolution.

13. Australia and New Zealand are included among the Lands of New Development. Brazil, Mexico, South Africa, India, and China (in that order) were the largest recipients not included in groups discussed in the text above. Japan was a smaller recipient. The sources for this information are those used in Figure 12.2.

14. America's position as a net debtor assumes book value, not asset value for FDI. Asset value is more difficult to estimate, but using that criterion, the United States may still be a net creditor. Nevertheless, the swing in the U.S. position since 1980 has been enormous.

15. International organizations and Eastern Europe borrowed the rest (Dennis 1984: Table 8.2: 140–41).

16. These numbers are my calculations based on figures used in tables presented further on in this chapter. However, Foreman-Peck (1983) and others have also noted that the stock of British investments were substantially larger than their national product in 1914. See Cottrell (1991: 25).

17. It is safe to say that an even higher proportion of portfolio and short-term capital originates in these five countries.

18. The point estimates for various capital stocks were taken from Cameron (1991, Table 1: 13); Dicken (1992: Figure 3.3: 53); Julius (1990: Table 2.1: 21); and Crook (1992: 6–10). Product figures and U.S. price series were taken from Maddison (1991: Table A.2: 198–99 and Tables E.3-E.4: 300–07).

19. Maddison presents all product figures over long spans of history in terms of 1985

U.S. prices. As U.S. prices in Maddison's series inflated by a factor of 10 between 1914 and 1985 (10.097 to be exact) I used this figure as a multiplier on the 1914 GFI data. The result restates all 1914 GFI estimates (quoted originally in current dollars) in terms of 1985 U.S. dollars.

20. After World War I, the Gold Standard was partially revived in 1925 and endured until 1931. But it never again functioned as well as during the pre-war period examined in this study.

21. The United States permitted joint stock banks to handle inward foreign investment, and "private" or family banks could engage in all forms. Curiously, though Britain permitted all banks to engage in foreign investment, joint-stock banks largely eschewed this activity. I also find it interesting that the private banks that so strongly dominated global finance in this age were so often led by patriarchs who were transnational in their personal background. Very many were born and raised in one country, but made their fortunes only after emigrating to another. Some of the names fitting this description are De Geer, hope, Baring, Stern, Kleinwort, and Morgan (the elder) as well as that most peripatetic clan, the Rothschilds.

22. This segment of my argument has been influenced by David Meerschwam (1989) and Crook (1992) who himself builds on Meerschwam. The connection between the dissolution of Bretton Woods and pressures for financial deregulation are also discussed by Eatwell (1993: 121).

23. Other factors are important, of course. For example, surpluses for investment must be generated in one place while opportunities for growth and profit arise in another. Technologies from the telegraph and cable to the fax machine and fiber optics have also made major contributions to capital market growth. My discussion here focuses on factors most relevant to politics.

24. This work appeared originally in *International Organization* as a special issue in summer 1971. I cite this volume as probably the most representative collection within the body of work on interdependence, though ideas I will mention here appear in various works of the period.

25. The concept of "Complex Interdependence," introduced in chapter 2 of Keohane and Nye's volume is presented as an opposed and competing alternative to realism.

26. "Multiple channels" is listed as the first of three "main characteristics" of Complex Interdependence, and emphasizes the importance of transnational actors.

27. Well over half the subsequent work cited by Keohane and Nye in that afterword concerns itself with the negotiation, creation, and maintenance of international regimes by states. I suggest that the reader compare Figures 1 and 2 (pp. xiii-xiv) in Keohane and Nye (1972). The two diagrams distinguish the "state-centric" approach from Keohane and Nye's preferred "transnational" approach. I find it a disappointing but telling fact that almost all subsequent work by Nye, Keohane, their students, and their cited followers examine relations that fit most comfortably not within the "transnational" scheme portrayed in Figure 2 of that volume, but within the cramped "state-centric" framework they were asking us then to reject. Timothy McKeown's (McKeown and Lynn 1988) work on trade associations is one of the very few exceptions of which I am aware.

REFERENCES

Cameron, Rondo. 1989. The Growth in International Banking to 1914. In Carl-Ludwig Holtfrerich, eds. *Interactions in the world economy.* New York: Harvester Wheatsheaf.
———. 1991. Introduction." In Rondo Cameron and V.I. Bovykin, eds. *International Banking, 1870–1914.* New York: Oxford University Press.

————, and V. I. Bovykin, eds. *International banking, 1870–1914.* New York: Oxford University Press.

Cottrell, P.L. 1991. Great Britain. In Rondo Cameron and V. I. Bovykin, eds. *International banking, 1870–1914.* New York: Oxford University Press.

Crook, Clive. 1992. Fear of Finance: A Survey of the World Economy. *The Economist,* September 19.

Dennis, Geoffrey E.J. 1984. *International financial flows.* London: Graham and Trotman.

Dicken, Peter. 1992. *Global Shift,* 2nd ed. New York: The Guilford Press.

Dunning, John. 1970. *Studies in international investment.* London: George Allen and Unwin.

Eatwell, John. 1993. The Global Money Trap: Can Clinton Master the Markets? *The American Prospect* 12 (winter).

Foreman-Peck, James. 1983. *History of the World Economy.* Sussex, U.K.: Wheatsheaf Books.

Grimwade, Nigel. 1989. *International trade: New patterns of trade, production and investment.* New York and London: Routledge.

Julius, DeAnne. 1990. *Global companies and public policy.* New York: Council on Foreign Relations Press.

Keohane, Robert O. and Joseph S. Nye, Jr., eds. 1972. *Transnational relations and world politics.* Cambridge: Harvard University Press.

————. 1989. *Power and Interdependence,* 2nd ed. Glenview, Ill.: Scott, Foresman and Co.

Maddison, Angus. 1991. *Dynamic forces in capitalist development.* New York: Oxford University Press.

McKenzie, Richard B. and Dwight R. Lee. 1991. *Quicksilver capital: How the rapid movement of wealth has changed the world.* New York: The Free Press.

McKeown, Timothy and Leonard H. Lynn. 1988. *Organizing business: Trade associations in America and Japan.* Washington, D.C.: American Enterprise Institute.

Meerschwam, David. 1989. International Capital Imbalances: The Demise of Local Financial Boundaries. In Richard O'Brien, eds. *International economics and financial markets.* Oxford: Oxford University Press.

Ohmae, Kenichi. 1990. *The Borderless world.* New York: Harper Collins.

Wriston, Walter B. 1992. *The Twilight of sovereignty.* New York: Charles Scribner's Sons.

Wells, David A. 1890. *Recent Economic Changes and Their Effect on the Production and Distribution of Wealth and the Well-Being of Society.* New York: D. Appleton.

About the Contributors

Vincent S. E. Falger is Professor of International Relations at the University of Utrecht.

Jeffrey A. Hart is Professor of Political Science at Indiana University, Bloomington.

Paul R. Hensel is Assistant Professor in Political Science at Florida State University.

Sangbae Kim is a Research Assistant in the Department of Political Science at Indiana University, Bloomington.

George Modelski is Professor of Political Science Emeritus at the University of Washington, Seattle.

Craig N. Murphy is M. Margaret Ball Professor of International Relations at Wellesley College.

Stewart Patrick is a Research Associate in the Center on International Cooperation, New York University.

Brian M. Pollins is Associate Professor in Political Science at Ohio State University.

Karen A. Rasler is Professor of Political Science at Indiana University, Bloomington.

David P. Rapkin is Associate Professor of Political Science at the University of Nebraska, Lincoln.

Hendrik Spruyt is Associate Professor of Political Science at Arizona State University, Tempe.

Jennifer Sterling-Folker is Associate Professor of Political Science at the University of Connecticut.

William R. Thompson is Professor of Political Science at Indiana University, Bloomington.

Index